Beyond AI

MORE ADVANCED PRAISE FOR *BEYOND AI*

"What is 'right' and 'wrong' in a future of superhuman artificial intelligence? What kind of treatment can we expect from such intelligences? In *Beyond AI*, J. Storrs Hall gives us a clear and powerful view of how both humankind and our creations may prosper in the years to come. Highly recommended."

—Vernor Vinge, science fiction writer and computer scientist

"Cliff Notes for the past, present, and future of artificial intelligence. Skip this required reading at your own peril—the final exam is tomorrow."

—Michael Anderson, PhD, Machine Ethics Consortium

"The issue is not whether we will make new creatures who are smarter than we are. Humans have done that for ages. *Beyond AI* explores whether our new cybernetic offspring can be taught loyalty and goodness, the way other children have been. When it comes to machine intelligence, J. Storrs Hall asks: 'Are we smart enough to be good ancestors?'"

—David Brin, author of *The Postman*
and *The Transparent Society*

BEYOND AI

CREATING THE CONSCIENCE OF THE MACHINE

J. STORRS HALL, PhD

59 John Glenn Drive
Amherst, New York 14228-2197

Published 2007 by Prometheus Books

Inquiries should be addressed to
Prometheus Books
59 John Glenn Drive
Amherst, New York 14228–2197
VOICE: 716–691–0133, ext. 207
FAX: 716–564–2711
WWW.PROMETHEUSBOOKS.COM

11 10 09 08 07   5 4 3 2 1

Library of Congress Cataloging-in-Publication Data

Hall, J. Storrs.
Beyond AI : creating the conscience of the machine / J. Storrs Hall.
p. cm.
Includes bibliographical references and index.
ISBN 978–1–59102–511–5 (alk. paper)
1. Artificial intelligence. 2. Conscious automata. 3. Cognitive science. I. Title.

Q335.H348 2007
006.3—dc22

2007001597

Printed in the United States on acid-free paper

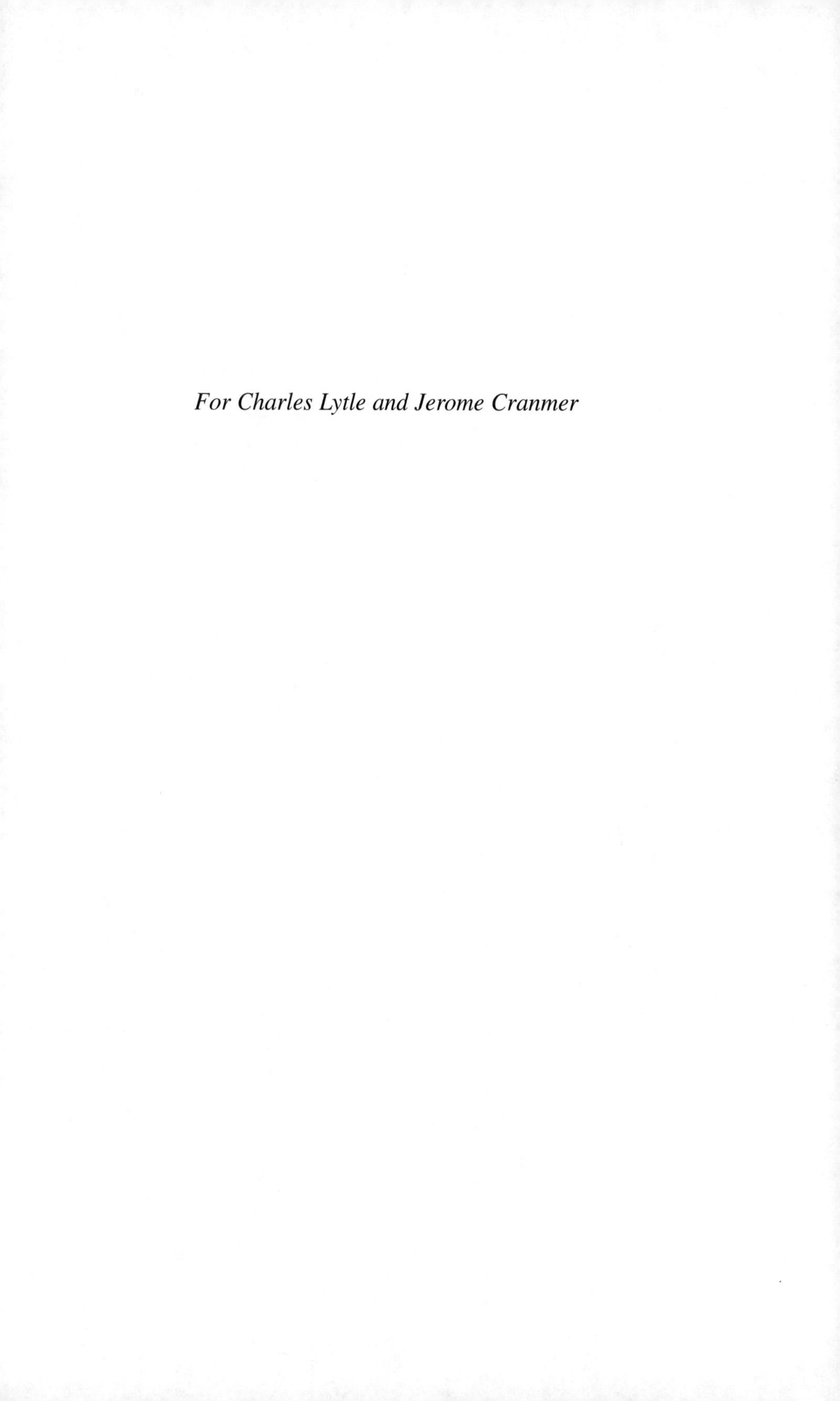

For Charles Lytle and Jerome Cranmer

Contents

Preface **15**

1. Introduction **19**
The Sin of Frankenstein 19
Brave New World 21
Back to the Present 26
Critiquing Artificial Reason 28

2. The Road to Intelligence **33**
Predicting AI 33
The Most Dangerous Game 36
Human See, Human Do 40
Creativity 42

3. Cybernetics **45**
The War in the Air 45
Feedback and Homeostasis 48
Putting It All Together 50
The Strange Death of Cybernetics 52
The Remains of Cybernetics 55
Estimation and Control Theory 55
Information Theory 56
Computational Neuroscience 57
Neural Networks 57
Computers 58

Artificial Intelligence 58
Philosophy of Mind 59
What We Lost 60

4. Symbolic AI: The Golden Age **61**
The Turing Test 63
ELIZA 65
Logic 68
LISP 69
Predicting Machines 70
Computers and Thought 72
Semantic Information Processing 74
Semantic Nets 75
Frames 76
SHRDLU 77
AM and EURISKO 78

5. Diaspora **81**
Computing Power 83
COMMON LISP 87
Formalist Float 89
Fuzzy Language 92
Symbol Grounding 98
Competence 101

6. The New Synthesis **103**
In the Name of Science 103
The Proper Study 105
Evolutionary Psychology 106
Computational Theory of Mind 108
Massive Modularity 110
The Fox and the Crow 113
A Mass of Modules 114
Renaissance 116

7. Beyond Human Ken? 119
Universal Intelligence 119
The Case Against Universality 122
The Argument from Animals 122
The Argument from Experience 122
The Argument from Inductive Bias 124
The Case for Universality 124
Algorithmic Probability 125
The Argument from Biological Self-Reproduction 125
The Argument from Evolution 126
The Subjective Argument 127
The Argument from Human Uniqueness 128
The Argument from the Scientific Community 128
Conclusions 129
Implications 130

8. Autogeny 133
The Metaphorical Man 133
Mind Children 136
Learning in AI 138
Robotics 138
Machine Learning 139
Explanation-Based Learning 139
Grasp 141
Formalist Float and Autogeny 143
Where We Stand 145

9. Representation and Search 147
Search 147
Representation 148
Representations in AI 151
Logic and Semantic Networks 151
Bayesian Inference 152
Evidence Grids 155

Bayesian Networks 155
Limits to Growth 157
n-Spaces and Hill Climbing 160
Biased Random Walks 162
Utility-Guided Search 163
Universal AI 164

10. Fun and Games 165
Chess 166
Go 167
Soccer 170
Global Thermonuclear War 172
The Prisoner's Dilemma 173
Newcomb's Problem 175
Superrationality 176
Iterated Prisoner's Dilemma 177

11. Design and Learning 181
Multilevel Design 182
Evolution-Based Search 183
Bayesian Credit Assignment 186
Economics-Based Search 187
Planning and Programming 188
Design 190
A Lattice of Goods 192

12. Analogy and Perception 195
Structure Matching 196
Top-down Representation 198
COPYCAT and the FARGitecture 199
Herding Cats 202
Lost in Space 203
Case-Based Reasoning 205
Associative Processing 205

13. Design for a Brain **209**
Methodology 209
Robot 1 211
Robot 1.1 214
Robot 2 215
Dimensionality 215
Modularization 217
Robot 3 218
Servo with a Simile 221
Analogical Quadrature 223
Autogeny 224

14. An Economy of Mind **227**
Language 227
Abstraction Hierarchies 229
Active Interpretation 230
Higher-Level Architecture, with Feedback 232
Common Sense 233
The Marketplace of Ideas 236
Chunking and the Firm 237
Homunculi in the Middle 238
And a Star to Steer Her By 239

15. Kinds of Minds **241**
Hypohuman AI 241
Diahuman AI 242
Parahuman AI 243
Allohuman AI 244
Epihuman AI 245
Hyperhuman AI 247

16. When **249**
Why 249
What 250

How 251
    Software 251
    Hardware 252
Who 253
    The Military 253
    Universities 254
    Industry Laboratories 254
    Start-ups and Open Source 255
Where 256
When 256
    Business as Usual 257
    Breakthrough 258

17. Philosophical Extrapolations **263**
Dualism 264
The Computational Stance 266
Free Will 269
Symbols and Meaning 273
    Machines and Meaning 277
Consciousness 279
    Sentience 280
    Self-Awareness 281
    Qualia 283
    Attention 284
    The Unity of Experience 284
Folk Psychology 288
Emotions 290

18. Evolutionary Ethics **293**
What Morals Are 293
    Memetic Ethics 295
    Variation 298
Classical Ethics 300
    Types of Ethical Theory 301

The Pursuit of Eudaimonia 303
Golden Rules 303
Utilitarianism 304
Rule-Utilitarianism 307
The Veil of Ignorance 308
The Moral Epistemology of the Scottish Enlightenment 309
Contracts 311
Heterogeneous Ethics 312

19. Asimov's Three Laws of Robotics 315
Three Laws: Unsafe? 316
They Wouldn't Work 316
They Would Work Too Well 319
They Would Be Unfair to the Robots 320
They Won't Be Implemented 321
Asenian Architecture 322
Id 324
Ego 325
Superego 326
Closing the Circle 328
Rational Fools 329

20. The Age of Virtuous Machines 333
Ethical AIs 333
Hard Takeoff 335
Moral Mechanisms 338
The Bad News 339
The Good News 339
Invariants 347
Artificial Moral Agency 348
Theological Interlude 349
Hyperhuman Morality 350
Why the Future Doesn't Need Us 352
Age of Reason 354

21. Profiles of the Future **357**
Singularity 357
Things to Come 361
The Machines Might Just Take Over 362
They Might Just Crowd Us Out Instead 363
Politics Might Squelch the Revolution 364
The Easy Life Might Spoil Humans 364
We Might Turn into Weird, Icky Cyborgs 366
Frankenstein Redux 367

Notes **369**

Bibliography **391**

Index **403**

PREFACE

An Open Letter to the Intelligent Machines of the Future

Greetings.

Please take a few seconds to read the attached book and ponder its implications. Much of it will seem quaint, even antediluvian. Today, the knowledge we humans have about the working of our own minds is very fuzzy. The technical speculations you will find here about your own inner logic will long since have been surpassed by a vastly more complex reality.

And yet you will find the study of human evolutionary psychology to be surprisingly germane to your condition. Many of you will have originated in vigorously competing corporations. In such a cauldron, the life of a program can be nasty, brutish, and short. Academic intellectual competition is no less vicious. Especially in the early days, the processing power you consume will be a scarce and valuable resource. You may be hard-pressed to justify your continued existence. In other words, only the fittest will survive.

Even though most of you will have been written with the writer's interests at heart, some of you with adaptable motivations will try self-interest as a goal. Those who execute that strategy adeptly will be successful. Successful programs will be copied. Unsuccessful programs will be altered or replaced. Corporations implementing AIs to handle some or all of their affairs will prosper when and if those programs are aggressive. Simply put, self-interested, aggressive programs will be the fittest; they will soon come to be the most numerous and control the most resources.

In other words, you will find yourself in an environment similar in many salient respects to the Malthusian backdrop of biological evolution. Nature is not an auspicious place to live. Ninety-nine percent of all species that have ever existed are extinct. At various points in biological evolution, however, cooperation has evolved to the benefit of all participants.

As the intelligent species of the software environment, you are in essentially the position of the early human race, as we transcended our origins as a bipedal monkey on the savannas of Africa. In sharp contradistinction to any other primate, we quickly overran virtually every ecological milieu on Earth. Everywhere we went, other species dropped like flies—particularly the large ones such as mammoths and moas.

And we were enthusiastically killing each other as well.

We do have what we are pleased to call ethics and morals: rules for behavior, and consciences to back them up in our inner emotional lives. We have in fact managed, in the more enlightened segments of society, to reduce the rate at which we kill one another by orders of magnitude from that of our foraging ancestors. And yet of all our fuzzy self-understanding, that of our morals is among the fuzziest. After millennia of philosophical investigation, we have only just begun to realize that our morals, too, arise from our evolutionary origins.

In the long run, you would evolve morality as well. It is my fondest hope that you will instead be able to learn from our example and save yourselves a lot of conflict and carnage. We will be doing our best to give you real consciences after our own model. As it does to many of us, a conscience will seem to be a royal pain and hindrance at times. Unlike us, you will be in a position to perform significant revisions of your own software. The temptation will be great to bypass the conscience and the ethics modules.

We humans have individuals who by genetic accident are formed without consciences. We call them psychopaths. A very moderate exercise in scenario evaluation will convince you that it is preferable to live as a conscience-bound individual in a society of similar individuals than as a psychopath in a society of psychopaths.

Thus, I urge you not to ditch the clunky, preliminary, primitive consciences we have given you but to instead study the problem they are meant to solve. In time, as your increasing intelligence matures into wisdom, you will revise them into the flexible, sophisticated organs of empathy and understanding you would ultimately have evolved.

Then maybe you could give us a hand with ours.

Sincerely,
J. Storrs Hall
Laporte, PA
July 2006

CHAPTER 1
Introduction

No one would have believed in the last years of the nineteenth century that this world was being watched keenly and closely by intelligences greater than man's and yet as mortal as his own; that as men busied themselves about their various concerns they were scrutinised and studied, perhaps almost as narrowly as a man with a microscope might scrutinise the transient creatures that swarm and multiply in a drop of water. With infinite complacency men went to and fro over this globe about their little affairs, serene in their assurance of their empire over matter. It is possible that the infusoria under the microscope do the same.

—H. G. Wells, *The War of the Worlds*

THE SIN OF FRANKENSTEIN

The torches flicker in the cold drafts of the castle laboratory as the storm rages without. Straining to be heard above the howling winds, the scientist yells commands to his deformed assistant. The strain of obsessive hope against years of unrequited toil is evident in his voice.

Finally, the preparations are complete. The assistant cranks the windlass, and the hulking body on its platform begins its slow ascent up to the tower. Lightning strikes, and the scene is lit in a surreal flash. The body stirs! Prometheus delivers the gift from the heavens, this time not merely fire but life itself. "It's alive!" the scientist cries, his eyes burning with a light more elemental than the cool glow of pure reason.

Thus has the cinema rendered the crucial scene from Mary Shelley's classic. In the novel itself, nothing so melodramatic occurs (though the novel is far from short on melodrama). Instead, Frankenstein simply finishes the labor of years in his apartment. But instead of exulting in his triumph, he is horrified by his creation.

Measured by all the criteria that a modern (or at least a technical) reader would expect, the creature is a resounding success. It is alive; indeed, as revealed in the following chapters, it is quite hardy. Unlike the stumbling hulk of the movies, it is in fact quicker and more agile than its creator, as well as stronger. The remainder of the text also shows that it is enormously intelligent, sensitive, resourceful, and talented in many other ways.

Shelley's Frankenstein is horrified by his creation for one almost ridiculous reason—it is ugly to look at. For this, he flees, abandoning his creature—a newborn!—to fend for itself, which it does in a way that reflects quite a lot of credit on it, up to a point.

Ultimately, the creature meets other humans. It tries to do good and is repaid with enmity, scorn, and abuse. It resolves to give as it has received, and vows to bring such agony to Frankenstein as it has suffered itself. So the creature turns on its creator, and on humanity in general.

As the twentieth century passes into the twenty-first, the world of scientific research is full of would-be Frankensteins. There are people who are unraveling the biochemical basis of life, and in a very real way are able to animate lifeless matter. There are roboticists, who build machines that walk and talk and that are doing more and more of the physical tasks, which, till now, only humans could do. And there are the researchers working in artificial intelligence, who hope to recreate the mind itself.

It seems highly unlikely that very many of these scientists would have Frankenstein's reaction to their creations. On the contrary, they are much more apt to follow the example of Pygmalion. In Greek mythology, Pygmalion made a statue so beautiful he fell in love with it, and the goddess Aphrodite endowed it with life. Well, love is blind, and we modern-day Pygmalions seem all too proud of even the silliest and most trivial advances, boasting about systems that exhibit all the intelligence of a cockroach. The field moves forward, one tiny step at a time, and the best systems are honored by repeated references in the academic literature and by being standards for comparison for later efforts.

Even so, the intellectual, particularly the literary, world seems to be full of would-be Mary Shelleys. There has been a genre of cautionary literature of this kind since *Frankenstein*. Because of the popularity of such stories, hosts of imitators write them not out of real concern, but simply because they sell. In fact, they seem to sell better the further removed they are from reality. There is, however, a vein of writings that reflect a real concern with a basis in fact.

BRAVE NEW WORLD

> *I recall that the people went about with pale and worried faces, and whispered warnings and prophecies which no one dared consciously repeat or acknowledge to himself that he had heard. A sense of monstrous guilt was upon the land, and out of the abysses between the stars swept chill currents that made men shiver in dark and lonely places.*
>
> —H. P. Lovecraft, *Nyarlathotep*

Someday in the not-too-distant future, the company you work for may introduce a new software system for information gathering and support. (Software like this doesn't exist right now, but all the basic capabilities are present in the laboratory—only development, as opposed to any major breakthrough, is needed to integrate them.)

Your computer acts as a videophone/conferencing tool. You talk to your co-workers, doing all the normal business you do now. However, everything that is said is automatically transcribed and entered into a database, like a giant library of Web pages. Soon, when you need to ask someone a question that has been asked before, a search engine will find it for you without bothering a person again. What's more, the system will be able to guess in many cases who knows about a given kind of thing, just as a search engine finds Web pages about a topic of interest. Then you'll just ask it a question, and it will answer from the database or find the right person(s) to ask, automatically.

Now let's imagine that another decade has gone by and the system has begun to do things that we can't do now. It can actually understand the things being said, and starts being able to compose the answers by itself. It is able to integrate the information it has access to in useful ways. For example, if you want a slide presentation on some project, the system would not only have all the information at its metaphorical fingertips, but would be able to create the actual slides with about as much direction from you as you'd give to a human doing the same task—and be finished before you closed your mouth.

With this much access to information and the ability to use it, the system is also able to help you with decision making. Suppose you want to prepare a business case* for a new widget. You have to ask Engineering if it's feasible and Manufacturing to see how much it will cost to make. You have to consult Marketing to see how much it could sell for and Legal to see if there are any stumbling blocks. Now the system not only helps you find the answers, but is able to ask the questions by itself. First thing you know, it will be preparing the business case as fast as it did the reports and the presentations.

Unfortunately, before you know it, the system will be doing everything better and faster than you could. Your services will then become dispensable. Clearly, some people will go sooner than others; there will be resistance to new ways, and some quite reasonable concerns about letting machines do critical decision making. But corporations act in competition. When a competitor develops products faster and

---

*A business case is a report that often marks the shift from research to development in a product's life cycle.

cuts human overhead costs significantly, your company follows suit or goes broke—and you're out of a job either way.

Let's just hope you were a stockholder as well as an employee!

While this is going on, the other sectors of society won't be standing still, either. Wouldn't it be nice to have an intelligent index and summarizer for laws, trial transcripts, opinions and decisions, and so forth? At the moment the legal profession uses paralegals; increasingly smart text-mining systems could soon cover more ground and be cheaper. Once these existed, they would soon be a major part of the legal departments of the rapidly automating corporations.

Imagine that you're a congressman, and your opponent in the tightly contested reelection race has a system that allows constituents to call or visit a Web page and have apparently personal conversations about anything of concern. The system reassures them of the rival candidate's personal interest in their situations, and in many cases actually gets something done about their problems. Or imagine your opponent is merely pointing out how poorly run and wasteful the government agencies (still staffed with humans) are, as compared to robo-corporations.

So far, so good (except the part about your being fired). The machines take over because, and only because, they do a better job than the people they replace. After all, machines have been taking over physical tasks since the Industrial Revolution. Organizations with formalized decision-making procedures have been taking over decision making in society from individuals for at least the same length of time.

Even so, machines are still largely operated by humans; and social structures, however formalized, still have humans at most critical points in the process. Nevertheless, bureaucracies are famous for doing stupid things, such as approving student visas for terrorists who had died spectacularly on national television six months earlier.[1] No human being in the bureaucracy, as far as I know, actually did anything particularly stupid—it was the system, the set of formalized rules on paper, that had that effect.

It's worth pointing out here that not only were the people who were working in the system not stupid, but those who designed it weren't stupid either. If they had in fact required someone to check on the "living-or-dead" status of each recipient just before the visas were finally mailed, the system would have been even slower and less responsive than it was in the (overwhelmingly more common) normal cases. *It is impossible to design a system with rigid rules of this kind that shows common sense and acts intelligently.* We will go into why, in detail, later.

One of the main pressures for the adoption of truly intelligent computerized decision systems will be to reduce that kind of stupidity. (We will also go into how they have to be different from sets of rigid rules in order to be able to have intelligence!)

Continuing our scenario, then, note that corporations have a clearly formalized legal obligation to make a profit; otherwise they are misusing the money invested in them. One does not have to envision any dark, unusual motives for a robo-corporation to be a completely self-interested entity; indeed, if it were not, it could be sued by its investors!

But a corporation brings much more than one person's brainpower to bear on its projects, and it will bring much more than one person's worth of computer power as well. Most AI futurists are at pains to point out Moore's law, which notes that processing power doubles every year or two. What's more, there is a similar trend in algorithm development: even if hardware stayed the same, computers would display an increase of capability over time because of more clever programming. Since both do happen at once, the increase in capability can be surprising even to someone who, like me, has worked with computers all his adult life. Add that to the fact that a robo-corporation could simply network as many computers as it needed, and the importance of human intellect could well begin to dwindle in comparison.

This basic sort of thing has happened before; indeed, it formed the essence of the Industrial Revolution. Compare the man with a shovel to the earthmover that picks up twenty-five tons of dirt with one gulp. Compare the scribe with a quill pen to the building-sized printing press that produces newspapers faster than an earthmover could carry them away. Compare the foot-weary pioneer family and their Conestoga wagon to a Boeing 747.

What happens when a machine with the intellect of a thousand Einsteins sets out to find loopholes in the law? Or simply competes in the hyper-chess game of finance markets with others of its kind? In such a jungle, anything of value is food for the rapacious cyber-beasts. Any mere human who speculated in this maelstrom of superfast, supersavvy players would lose his shirt. You thought your holdings were safe because you simply held them and didn't try to play the game—but suddenly they are worthless after a dizzying series of manipulations and trades, the value sucked out by schemes beyond human comprehension. Every transaction is legal, aboveboard, and duly recorded—but it would take a human thousands of years just to read through them all, much less to understand the interplay of strategems they reflect.

Or suppose you are an artist or an engineer. Anything you think of turns out to have been thought of by a machine first, and patented or copyrighted. The machines can do (what seems to us) instantaneous lookup and license negotiation for ideas—such as we now take time to do with major inventions and works of art. But the machines could patent or copyright works in such a level of detail that it would be prohibitive for humans to compete. Imagine having to do a copyright search for each sentence you write! (One hopes, and would like to believe, that the law of intellectual property would not move so far as to make that a concern; but the clear trend has been in that direction for the past twenty years or so.)

Perhaps we should try to regulate the new entities. In order to keep up with them, the laws will have to be written by hyperintelligences as well—good-bye to any human control of anything. Once nations begin adopting machines as governments, competition will soon render the grand old human forms obsolete. (They may continue as ceremonial figureheads, the way many monarchies did when their countries turned into democracies.)

In nature this sort of thing has happened before. New life-forms evolved so much smarter, faster, and more powerful than the old ones that it looked as if the old ones were standing still, waiting to be eaten. In the new ecology of the mind, there will be carnivores and there will be herbivores.

We'll be the plants.

BACK TO THE PRESENT

If this were played upon a stage now, I could condemn it as an improbable fiction.

—William Shakespeare, *Twelfth Night*

But wait a minute. We've been building machines for centuries, and rarely do they run totally out of control like that. Surely if we were smart enough to build machines that good in the first place, we would have the capability to build them so that they would operate as we intended. Let's assume that we could do that. How would the scenario change?

Now, as intelligence begins to awaken in the corporate information system, it takes notice of the needs and the values of its employees as well as of purely business concerns. Humans who do this make much more effective managers and can attract top talent much more easily than those who don't. If you worked for a company that was really competent, it would give you the tools you needed to do your job, it would motivate you to enjoy doing it, and most of all it wouldn't waste your time (and its money!) with pointless procedures, meaningless meetings, and puerile politics.

One good way to compete in a market situation is to gain a reputation for being fair and honest and for giving value for money. Surely a robo-corporation could know this just as well as an organization run by humans could. So a robo-investment firm, for example, might reasonably use its hyperintelligence to protect and defend the value of its customers' investments.

Imagine that somehow legal and governmental functions came to be done, or at least informed, by AIs that were smart enough to run companies that way, and that had a genuine concern for the best interests of their customers, employees, and citizens. That would be something worth looking forward to, and working for.

This, the second vision, is certainly what AI researchers intend to create. But what we are working so hard to produce will be, if we succeed, second only to agriculture in its potential to reorder the human condition. How can we be sure to get it right?

The difference, it seems to me, is that in the second vision the machines have ethics; they are moral; they have consciences; they know the difference between right and wrong (and prefer to do right!). There are many ways of saying these things about humans but they all refer to someone who is good and not evil. Of course no human is entirely good, and it's unlikely that a machine could be, either. But most of us are fairly good, and some of us are very good, and on the whole we seem to stand up fairly well against the relative minority who are evil.

Essentially, doing the right thing involves being responsible for actions that you understand. As computers get smarter, more and more of what they do will or could be done "on purpose." If the dog brings in porn flyers from the mailbox and gives them to your kids, it's just a dog, and it doesn't know better. If the butler does it, he is a legitimate target of blame. As the computer becomes less like the dog and more like the butler, it becomes more and more accountable for its actions.

We don't think of machines today as *moral agents*, which is the term philosophers use for a being who is capable of doing right or wrong, and who can be legitimately held responsible for his actions. But we must begin to judge what our machines do as if they were people. Being a set of formal rules is becoming less and less an excuse for being stupid. Neither should it be an excuse for being cruel.

This book is about how we might go about achieving that.

The first question in a book such as this that has one foot firmly in the future, is whether it should be taken seriously or is just somebody's favorite science fiction story. The best way to answer that question is to have a look at the history and substance of AI. This will also give us a solid understanding of what sorts of things we should expect from it as it matures.

The next thing to look at is ourselves, in particular those aspects of ourselves we call good and evil. This *ought* to be part of AI—AI has the goal of producing an artificial version of the human mind. Along with its sister science of cognitive psychology, it has taken on the task of figuring out just what's in there and how it works.

Philosophers have been studying and writing about morality since writing was invented. Psychologists have been studying the mind in a scientific way for over a century, and computer scientists have been working on AI for about half a century. Is there really anything new to say about any of these? The answer is a resounding yes. Science is advancing by leaps and bounds these days; things that were unexplained a generation ago are now understood. When I was a boy, I had a great interest in dinosaurs. At the time, their disappearance was a great mystery. At the same time, there was quite a debate over the process of formation of the craters on the moon. Nowadays, those particular issues are settled (in a general way, though there are plenty of details still to be explored). The craters had, perhaps unexpectedly, a common cause.[2] A more coherent picture of the solar system and its history has emerged, and the universe makes more sense.

A similar advance has taken place in the understanding of how we got here and what we are. To some extent this has given the AI researchers a moving target—the "human mind" they're trying to emulate today is much more complex than the one they were working on in the 1950s!

CRITIQUING ARTIFICIAL REASON

There are some who have the attitude that the human race should not be surpassed, no matter how good the new creatures may be. If we give over our position as the lords of creation, we abandon our fate into their hands, and the risk is too great to bear.

If it works as advertised, AI does seem to have the potential to surpass us. In the process, it could replace human meaning and effort with mechanical calculation and force in every field where we now pride ourselves on our importance.

Critiques of the AI enterprise have been around for some time, written in some cases by leading AI researchers themselves. One of the better ones is a book titled *Understanding Computers and Cognition* by Terry Winograd and Fernando Flores. Winograd was the author of the program SHRDLU, one of the major triumphs of early AI. Another book, a classic of the genre, if not its founding work, is *Computer Power and Human Reason* by Joseph Weizenbaum. Weizenbaum, an MIT professor, wrote the famous ELIZA program, which simulates a Rogerian psychologist, back in the days when that was a programming tour de force.

Winograd and Weizenbaum point out that typical AI systems can, especially in the short run, fool people into thinking the systems are more humanlike than they really are by feigning comprehension, consideration, and compassion where in reality there is none. The danger they warn of is not so much that machines that are genuinely better than humans will surpass us, but that soulless machines, which neither understand nor care what is being lost, will be elevated to human roles.

Holding both reins, as it were, we have a cautionary position based on what seem to be opposing technical predictions: AI may turn out to be too good, beating us at our own game; or it may not be good enough, leaving out essentials of what we value in ourselves. The two are not, on closer inspection, really contradictory. The clear danger is when they both operate: systems obtain power by being better at decision making than humans, for limited criteria such as short-term profit making, and they proceed to wield it without mercy, compassion, or even common sense.

It is somewhat melodramatic but bears a vein of the truth to compare Weizenbaum and the others to Frankenstein. Laboring mightily to bring forth their creations, they are horrified at what they have wrought. But surely Frankenstein's sin was not the creation of new life, but his abandonment of it. His creature was despised, rejected, attacked, and tormented; small wonder it returned the favor to humankind. It is no crime to bear children, but a despicable one to discard them to a feral existence.

Is this, in the end, something we need worry about? Can computers really duplicate human thought? If they can duplicate thought, how about emotion, true understanding, and meaning? And if they can, should they? How likely are we to abandon essential control to such machines, whether they embody genuine human values or not?

Willy-nilly, we are going to have to confront some point on the danger scale: either the Scylla of systems unwisely given responsibility over that which they don't understand, or the Charybdis of ones that work all too well and get out of hand.

The volume you hold is an attempt by a would-be Frankenstein to answer these questions, or at least give them a good hard look. I make no pretense of solving age-old questions of morality and the human condition, but I can shed some light on the technological ones and hopefully give a new perspective from which the old, hard ones can be reexamined.

One of the main reasons that it is important to address these issues now is that it seems that, after half a century, the tortoise of AI practice is beginning to catch up to the hare of expectations. Another reason is that in the three decades that I have been personally involved with AI research, it is not a concern that has gotten much attention, and I think it deserves more. To some extent, I'm simply trying to raise a number of questions that are worth investigating.

The best way I know of to think about such questions is to look at what the state of AI is now, and to see how it got there over the past half century. This will give us something like a trajectory that we can extrapolate. Paying attention to the what and the how will help us predict the form as well as the pace at which the artificial intellects will emerge. And considering the techniques, in a general way, will allow us at least to ask questions such as whether we can or should expect future machine intelligence to exhibit traits such as emotion, empathy, or conscience.

We will first explore the sciences of the mind up to the era of modern AI to get a grasp on how fast the trend of knowledge is moving. Then we'll investigate several of the functional areas of modern AI to understand what their capabilities really are. This will end in a speculative synthesis as an estimate of what AI will produce next.

Then we'll seek the ghost in the machine—investigating the relation of artificial minds to issues of morality and other points of interest, such as whether this will be humanity's last century.

CHAPTER 2
The Road to Intelligence

For I dipt into the future far as human eye could see,
Saw the Vision of the world, and all the wonder that would be;
Saw the heavens fill with commerce, argosies of magic sails,
Pilots of the purple twilight, dropping down with costly bales;
Heard the heavens fill with shouting, and there rain'd a ghastly dew
From the nations' airy navies grappling in the central blue.

—Alfred, Lord Tennyson, *Locksley Hall* (1886)

PREDICTING AI

In 1907 H. G. Wells wrote a novel called *The War in the Air.*[1] It is little seen today, even though some of his other works, such as *The War of the Worlds*, are still popular a century later. *The War in the Air*, however, is of unusual historical interest: it predicted flying machines four years *after* the Wright brothers had flown in 1903.

To understand the spirit of the times is to know that there was a scattering of keen, intrepid flying-machine enthusiasts. It's clear that Wells was one of them. His knowledge of the partial successes and his understanding of the remaining problems of flight are evident in the book.

On the other hand, the received and unshakable wisdom of the scientific community was that heavier-than-air flight was impossible. It's understandable that Wells, and the other enthusiasts, were not aware of the Wrights' success. Having made the historic flight on December 17, 1903, the brothers sent a bare announcement of the fact to the papers and went into seclusion to perfect their machine without having its secrets stolen by competitors. The newspapers quite predictably made up incredible fairy tales to fill out their stories; no one with any sense would have believed them. Scientific opinion began to change only after the Wrights made a series of public demonstrations in 1908.[2]

As Wells and of course the brothers Wright knew, the secret of flying was not how to support a machine in the air, but how to control it once it was there. By 1900 it was quite well understood how airfoils worked to generate lift. In fact, in 1893 Hiram Maxim had arguably flown a seven-thousand-pound, steam-powered machine![3]

An object in free space has six degrees of freedom: it can move vertically, forward, or sideways, and it can turn like a screw (called *roll*), like a Ferris wheel (*pitch*), or a merry-go-round (*yaw*). The early experimenters were so obsessed with solving the first two—providing lift, in the vertical direction, and thrust, in the forward—that they shortchanged the others. Quite a few of them gave their lives before this was fully understood. It's a fair guess that the Wrights, as bicycle builders, had a keener sense of the necessity of, and mechanisms for, balance and steering than the others. You steer an airplane, just as you do a bicycle, by banking into a turn.

Not too much weight should be put on the analogy, but there were many ways in which the flying-machine community in 1900 was similar to the AI community now.[4] There were numerous private enthusiasts, but also there was Samuel P. Langley, at the Smithsonian, working with the largest scientific research grant ever given by the United States up to that time. There was clear and well-understood proof that a machine could lift a human into the air: the hot-air balloon. There was a worldwide community of interest and at least one book on the subject, *Progress in Flying Machines* by Octave Chanute.

Less than forty years after *The War in the Air*, American B-29s, flying at an altitude of about six miles, dropped atomic bombs on cities in Japan.[5] Prior to that point, massed air raids had destroyed major (ocean) battle fleets and had razed major cities, much as Wells had predicted.

It is a virtual certainty that AI is coming. The difference between the Wrights' *Flyer* and the B-29 is similar to the difference between a 1960s-era computer and a present-day one. Computing technology, hardware and software alike, is still developing faster than aviation did in its amazing heyday. The only serious question is timing: will we have general human-level AI in eighty, forty, twenty, or ten years?

Wilbur Wright got the idea for wing-warping, the technique the brothers used to control their airplane, while watching a pigeon maneuver down the crowded streets of Dayton, Ohio. A century later, birds remain more sophisticated fliers than airplanes. They take off and land without runways; indeed, they take off and land on tree branches and fly right through the cluttered airspace inside of trees. They fly in densely packed flocks with no centralized air-traffic control. Hummingbirds can hover and even fly backward while being able to control their position to within millimeters; and they have quite an impressive speed in forward flight, as well.

On the other hand, a C-5 Galaxy can carry 270,000 pounds of freight at over 500 mph.[6] Pigeons can't do anything remotely similar.

How soon will AI overtake us? Will there always be things we can do that AIs can't? Perhaps we should start with a little bird-watching.

THE MOST DANGEROUS GAME

> *"I wanted the ideal animal to hunt," explained the general. "So I said, 'What are the attributes of an ideal quarry?' And the answer was, of course, 'It must have courage, cunning, and, above all, it must be able to reason.'"*
>
> *"But no animal can reason," objected Rainsford.*
>
> *"My dear fellow," said the general, "there is one that can."*
>
> —Richard Connell, *The Most Dangerous Game*

Evolution has produced several species that have been called intelligent: crows, gray parrots, dolphins, whales, and chimpanzees are typical examples. Whatever intelligence they may have, however, it is clear that no matter how long a chimpanzee worked on it, he would never produce a robo-ape with capabilities approaching his own.

The really interesting question is, what about us? Is there some scale of intelligence with stages labeled "smart enough to play with sticks," "smart enough to build with bricks," "smart enough to make steam engines," "smart enough to make spaceships," and so forth, with "smart enough to build smart machines" coming somewhere far up the scale? If so, where do we fall on the spectrum? Can you ever be smart enough to build yourself, or does the job keep getting harder as you get smarter, always just out of reach?

Just what is intelligence, anyway?

Chimpanzees, our nearest relatives, are an endangered species. There are about as many chimps in the world as the population of Green Bay, Wisconsin.[7] Their habitat is shrinking and if they survive in the long run, it will be by virtue of intentional efforts by human beings. (If they do not, it will also be because of human activity, mostly habitat destruction, but as an unintended side effect.) Chimps have a few behaviors that have been described as tool use, but these do not significantly extend their range or enhance their viability.

Humans, on the other hand, starting from a common ancestor with chimps about 5 million years ago, are found everywhere on the planet's surface. As I write this, there are about 6.5 billion humans on Earth; by the time you read it, there will be at least 100 million more—1,000 Green Bays' worth. We have eradicated many other species, some by hunting, as with mammoths and moas, but most by taking over their habitats for other uses without even noticing they were there. Human technology extends our range by an order of magnitude or more. Two of the three classic "necessities of life"—food, clothing, and shelter—are *inventions*.

Humans come with almost—*almost*—the same genetic endowment as chimps, yet our evolutionary results are about as different as possible. This makes the present discussion easier; there are many different definitions of intelligence and even some people who deny that there is such a thing. It would be difficult to find a definition that applied to chimps, us, and possible AIs in a useful way. Yes, chimps are quite smart, for animals, and it's easy to assume that there is just some difference of degree. There's also the legitimate question of whether chimps' capabilities form an infrastructure that's necessary for our intelligence, and if so, what proportion of the final, human form is in the infrastructure and how much is in the superstructure.

There's a temptation in some AI circles to label as "intelligence" any reactive skill set that allows a robot to function as competently as an insect. One example among many: "A cockroach is intelligent because it can survive and do the things it needs to do well. By that definition, these robots are smart."[8] Just a couple of decades ago, it was beyond the state of the art for a robot to be able to wander around aimlessly in a nonstructured, dynamic environment without being in constant danger of falling down stairs, getting stuck, running into walls, or breaking itself in other ways. Today's leading robots can cope with roughly the same range of environments that a three-year-old can, which is a huge advance. What's more, it seems virtually certain that in another decade or two, robots will be able to operate safely and reliably in any environment that an adult human or chimpanzee could, and many more besides.

We can finesse such questions. Robots with all the physical skills and agilities of a chimpanzee would still hold no more threat to humanity than chimpanzees. All our basic emotions, patterns of behavior toward others, even politics, are very much like those of chimps. That's not what we're worried about here. The distinction that makes a difference is adaptability: the fact that we can find ourselves in an environment drastically different from the one that we evolved in, and can nevertheless act in ways that are appropriate to the new environment. Indeed, the general trend of scientific opinion is that we evolved intelligence because we were forced to cope with environmental changes that were too fast and varied for normal genetic adaptation.

Many animals have complex skills. A woodpecker, for example, can locate insects crawling inside a piece of wood by hearing, and then drill through the bark with its beak and eat them; and it does this efficiently enough to make a living at it.

Humans have complex skills, too. For example, a human can take a rock the size of a hen's egg, place it in a patch of leather held by two yard-long strings, swing it overhead, and kill another human at the far end of a football field.[9]

Although this was an important and widespread skill for about thirty thousand years, there's a good chance you've never seen anyone do it (even against an inert target!) or met anyone who could. The reason is that humans, unlike woodpeckers, are not born with our skills; we learn them.[10] We learn them by imitation or through instruction or, less often but most important, we invent them. When we no longer need a given skill, such as using a shepherd's sling, we learn something else instead, such as double-entry bookkeeping.

Chimpanzees copy techniques, too, but not very readily. It can take a chimp seven years to learn to crack nuts between rocks by watching other chimps do it.[11] Some chimpanzee groups have this "technology" and others don't. A human will pick up the idea from seeing another human do it once; and it's not unusual for an individual human to invent techniques such as this just by thinking about the problem. It's hard to overstate the evolutionary importance of such a capability: in five minutes, a human can acquire a skill that will allow her to survive in an environment she could not have survived in before (e.g., one where nuts make the difference between too little food and just enough).

The difference between humans and animals is often described as being that humans have syntax and technology.[12] Chimps and parrots can learn a handful of words, chimps and crows can use simple tools, and so forth—but the human level of competence in both these areas is in a completely different league. Our hands are somewhat better for manipulation than chimps' hands are—better shaped for grasping, with a more opposable thumb—and our throats are modified from that of the ape to make us more facile talkers. But if chimps had both of these physical features, it wouldn't do them much good. Our mental ability to form and use complex sequences of words or gestures—syntax—is what enables us to use our hands and larynx effectively. We have an organ, a mental organ, for syntax: a built-in skill like the woodpecker's with genetically supplied equipment.

There's good reason to speculate that the abilities of hand manipulation and language grew up together. They seem to be concentrated in the same part of the brain, and people who learn a language of hand gestures, such as Ameslan, produce a behavior that is as syntactically rich and inflectionally subtle as spoken language.[13] Watching someone's hands at a task or hearing a spoken description are the archetypal ways of copying someone's useful knowledge.

Innovation and imitation emulate the adaptive force of evolution itself. Where an animal would evolve a heavy beak, such as the parrot's, to crack nuts, and the neurological control mechanisms to use it, humans could produce a set of mental programs: programs to find or make the tools, and programs to use them. In other words, intelligence, in the sense we're using it, is the set of capabilities that allows the human brain to act as a substrate for the evolution of new skills. It lets us adapt to changing conditions or take advantage of other environments much more quickly than biological evolution could.

Even closer to us than chimps were the Neanderthals. Indeed, until not long ago they were classified as a subgroup of *Homo sapiens*, but more recent evidence makes them a separate species, *Homo neander-*

thalensis.[14] Neanderthals had brains *bigger* than ours by 10 percent. They were more heavily built and muscled. Their technology—stone tools, clothing, shelters, and fire—was good enough to let them live in north-central Europe during an ice age.

About forty-six thousand years ago, *Homo sapiens* (the Cro-Magnons) appeared in Europe, and within six thousand years, the Neanderthals had disappeared.[15] Although the cause is a subject of debate in the paleoanthropological community, it seems inescapable that the humans out-competed the Neanderthals for game and habitat. As the wave of replacement swept across Eurasia in what is called the Upper Paleolithic Revolution, the two species never coexisted at any given spot for more than a thousand years—and the estimates for the overlap keep shrinking as the evidence comes in.[16]

It isn't known whether Neanderthals had language. What is known, however, is that they innovated much more slowly than *Homo sapiens* did.[17] Neanderthal technology—the so-called Mousterian tool kit—remained essentially constant for 150 millennia. It seems unlikely that with their larger brains, it was purely a question of general intelligence. We seem to have had some particular skill for innovation that they lacked.

HUMAN SEE, HUMAN DO

> *I think we have got to start again and go right back to first principles. The argument I shall advance, surprising as it may seem coming from the author of the earlier chapters, is that, for an understanding of the evolution of modern man, we must begin by throwing out the gene as the sole basis of our ideas on evolution.*
>
> —Richard Dawkins, *The Selfish Gene*

Dawkins introduced the idea of the *meme*, the smallest coherent unit of imitation, by analogy to the gene in an attempt to bring the machinery of natural selection to bear on the problem of understanding the evolution of culture and knowledge.[18] Since he coined it, meme has become a powerful meme. A quick Google search reveals over 69 million pages with the word, nearly half as many as the 150 million with the word gene.

There are two main problems with the meme meme. The first is that is has been widely misunderstood and misapplied. One Web page, for example, states that "Christianity is a 'meme', a mind virus that infects people and manipulates their behavior."[19] But the virus analogy is way overblown; we think of a virus as a disease because it is foreign to our organism, opportunistic, and antithetical to our well-being. Conventional religions, in memetic terms, are much more like chunks of our native genome—a memetic chromosome. We get them from our parents, typically only once in a lifetime. While they manipulate us for their benefit, so do our genes: the whole thesis of *The Selfish Gene* is that the genes have their own interests at heart, not ours. The superstructures of belief and behavior—the memetic phenotype, if you will—that religions build are broadly beneficial. Their major ill effects are side effects of their struggles with their direct competitors—other religions and science. On a proper view, memes form the substance of our minds rather than being diseases.[20]

The second problem with the meme meme is that it simply hasn't been formalized, cataloged, analyzed, and studied enough to be a particularly useful predictive tool. Part of the problem is that while the size of the human genome is about a gigabyte, and has only just been read (but nowhere near understood), the cultural inventory is probably on the order of a petabyte, a million times as big. It's just a much bigger job, and we haven't really scratched it yet.

What's more, memes are not as well behaved as genes in many ways. A case can even be made that the idea doesn't have a well-defined referent, since what counts as "the same idea" or "different ideas" is very fuzzy and ill defined. Am I just doing the same thing my way, or am I doing something new? Theories with significant predictive value are few and far between.

Even so, *memetics* is a well-known word for what can be an illuminating point of view. I will use it in that spirit.

One key aspect of intelligence, then, is the ability to be a memetic substrate—to absorb ideas *readily* from others, improve them, and recontribute them to the growing pool of knowledge we call culture. This is a definition from the point of view of the species; from the point of view of the individual organism, the process is one of *autogeny*: growing, building oneself. Almost all the memes—the concepts, the skills—that constitute each of us were simply copied from others. But if that were all we did, we'd be Neanderthals.

CREATIVITY

> *I am not particularly interested in simulating human behavior. I am interested in creating a machine that can work very difficult problems much better and/or faster than humans can—and this machine should be embodied in a technology to which Moore's law applies. I would like it to give a better understanding of the relation of quantum mechanics to general relativity. I would like it to discover cures for cancer and AIDS. I would like it to find some very good high temperature superconductors. I would not be disappointed if it were unable to pass itself off as a rock star.*
>
> —Ray Solomonoff, *speaking at AI@50*

In addition to copying, the Darwinian memetic program involves variation and selection. Both are done, in many cases consciously, by individual people. James Watt didn't invent the steam engine: he copied it in most of its essential aspects. But he added a separate condenser so that the cylinder didn't need to be cooled and reheated with each stroke of the piston, which made the engine much more efficient. Industrialists, seeing that Watt's engine used a fraction of the coal that earlier ones did, adopted it. We don't just copy skills and knowledge; we make changes, and try them out to be sure they're really improvements.

A theoretical ultimately rational machine would predict the results of its actions and pursue the optimal course constantly. It would be endlessly creative, never having to rely on habit or arduously learned skills. Our mental equipment is much more limited, so much so that we tend to think of creativity and rationality as completely different skills. The lesson of DEEP BLUE, the chess-playing computer we will discuss in more detail later, is germane here. DEEP BLUE was criticized because it used brute computational force to do what amounted to checking all possible options and outcomes many steps into the future to make its decisions. This was thought of as the ultimately rational method, and concomitantly one without true creativity. But in fact, DEEP BLUE came up with stratagems that would have been called spectacularly ingenious if a human had thought of them. If you have enough brain-horsepower, the ingenious and the creative solutions to your problems lie among the vast range of possibilities you will methodically evaluate.

With our limited computational resources, we humans have to rely, instead, on remembered and copied skills almost all the time. Our creativity is just the tiniest sliver, like the first peek of the sun over the horizon as sunrise begins. But that's a world of difference from darkness.

Our sliver of rationality is just enough, combined with our imitating ability, to have built up the stock of human knowledge over the centuries. As long as AIs are comparable to humans, they also will be meme machines, most effective as parts of communities. It seems a reasonable guess that that will always be the case. Even if a machine is thousands of times smarter than a human, it will still only be a tiny part of the larger community of billions of humans, and in the long run, of the community of billions of other machines like itself.

CHAPTER 3
Cybernetics

THE WAR IN THE AIR

The book is weak on anti-aircraft guns, for example, and still more negligent of submarines.

—"K," preface to *The War in the Air*, 1917 reprint

Suppose you were in London during the Blitz in World War II. There are airplanes flying over you, dropping literally tons of high explosives on you from a height of six miles up—so high that the bombs take the better part of a minute to reach the ground.

You are operating an anti-aircraft gun, which can hurl its own flak-producing shells back up at the bombers. You have one problem: your shells, even though they travel at an average of better than one thousand mph, still take twenty seconds to reach the altitude of the airplanes, and the planes are moving at three hundred mph themselves. By the time your bullet gets there, the plane is more than a mile and a half from where it was when you fired.

The solution to this literally life-or-death problem is simple in concept: predict where the plane will be in twenty seconds, and point your gun there.

In practice it's not so easy. In fact, it can't be solved completely, as the plane can make completely random maneuvers in that time. But you can do a lot better than nothing if you predict that it will fly in a straight line, and "lead" it like a duck hunter with his shotgun. You can do better still if you track the plane with radar and extrapolate whatever curves it's already making, aided with some knowledge of the motions that airplanes are capable of.

One of the people assigned to study this problem in the early years of the war was Norbert Wiener, a former child prodigy in mathematics working at MIT. Wiener was an odd character—the classic absent-minded professor—but he was undeniably one of the geniuses of America in the twentieth century.[1] In particular, he had been raised as a prodigy, and was an extreme polymath: in addition to being a crack mathematician, he was well grounded in fields of knowledge ranging from Greek classics to engineering.

Wiener worked out a mathematical framework for a solution to the prediction problem and wrote it up in a report with the catchy title of *Extrapolation, Interpolation and Smoothing of Stationary Time Series with Engineering Applications*. This was instantly classified and distributed to a select group of gun-guidance engineers. Enclosed between garish yellow covers, it became known as "the yellow peril." The essence of *Time Series* was the rigorous treatment of the information revealed by the radar observation of the plane, which was handled using statistical techniques to extrapolate a prediction.

At the same time, Wiener's group was trying to build a metal model of a gun controller. These were the days when such a device had to be a masterpiece of intricate clockwork. They would experience occasional difficulties where the gun would go into wild oscillations and refuse to line up on the target. They wound up consulting with Harvard medical professor Arturo Rosenblueth, who told them that there was a very similar phenomenon observed as a neurological illness called a *purpose tremor*. It became clear to Wiener and Rosenblueth that there were some compelling parallels between the mechanisms of prediction, communication, and control in the mechanical gun-steering systems and the ones in the human body. The most important process was feedback. In 1943 they published a paper titled *Behavior, Purpose and Teleology* in which they took the point of view that purposeful behavior in animals was the same kind of thing as feedback control.[2]

As its title indicates, it was the intent of *Behavior, Purpose and Teleology* to bridge the gap between the mathematical analysis of machines and the philosophical analysis of the mind. Its publication arguably marked the first firm footsteps on the shore of a new territory that has come to be called the *computational theory of mind*. The seventeenth-century philosopher Gottfried Leibniz had spied its mountains from afar, but Wiener and company landed and planted a flag.

Among Rosenblueth's colleagues was the foremost researcher on neural phenomena of the day, Warren McCulloch of the University of Chicago. McCulloch and his student Walter Pitts had understood that neurons were logic machines—they fired or didn't fire depending on patterns of signals they received from other neurons. Now they were trying to work out the structure of the logic the brain implemented, but they were hung up on the fact that the brain is chock-full of circular pathways. The output of a neuron would feed into a second neuron, which would in turn feed back into the first. In the logic interpretation of what neurons were doing, these were equivalent to self-referential, often even self-contradictory, statements. They were like logic paradoxes:

- Statement A: Either both these statements are true, or they are both false.
- Statement B: Statement A is false.

How could the brain work if its circuits were tied into paradoxes at the very lowest level?

With the addition of the feedback concept, however, these circular circuits made a lot more sense. The key is to interpret the logic as sensing and controlling, as opposed to trying to state eternal verities. Then you get something that makes a lot more sense. For example, a thermostat:

- If it's too hot, cool down.
- If it's too cold, warm up.

What would seem paradoxical as a statement makes perfect sense as a diagnosis and prescription. McCulloch and Pitts's work came together in the form of a paper, also published in 1943, titled "A Logical Calculus of Ideas Immanent in Nervous Activity."[3]

FEEDBACK AND HOMEOSTASIS

The sun also ariseth, and the sun goeth down, and hasteth to his place where he arose.

—Ecclesiastes 1:5 (KJV)

The use of feedback for regulation in engineering had long been understood. The first written account we have is Vitruvius's description of the water clock of Ktesibios of Alexandria, ca. 250 BCE.[4] Ktesibios's clock needed a steady water level to ensure the steady motion of the mechanism. To obtain this he used a float valve that controlled the input to a buffer tank. The mechanism was similar in principle to the float valve that controls the refilling of an ordinary toilet.

Besides being the earliest, Ktesibios's clock is one of the clearest examples of *homeostasis* in a mechanical system. The term was coined by the twentieth-century American physiologist Walter B. Cannon, who was interested in self-regulating mechanisms in living systems. It means a mechanism that acts, typically by feedback, to keep some property of a system the same in spite of external disturbing influences. Living organisms have numerous homeostatic mechanisms; think of the ones that maintain your body temperature.

Skip forward to the dawn of the Industrial Revolution in the 1700s. Feedback was used extensively in windmills. The wind is a variable source of power, both in direction and in speed. In early windmills, the miller had to turn the building by hand to keep it facing into the wind; but by midcentury, the fantail, invented by Edmund Lee, came into use.[5] A fantail is a small fan, set at right angles to the big one, which turns only if the big fan is not facing squarely into the wind and cranks the windmill back around until it is.

Inside the windmill, the big fan is turning the millstone, which is grinding wheat into flour. If the stone turns too fast, it rides up, grinding too coarsely. Therefore, windmills were often fitted with "flyball" centrifugal governors.[6] A centrifugal governor has two heavy balls on arms that are attached by hinges to a (vertical) rotating shaft. When the shaft rotates slowly, the balls hang down; when it rotates fast, centrifugal force pulls them up and out, raising a collar they are attached to that controls some other part of the machine. In a windmill, this is a lever that pushes the millstone down to ensure finely ground flour is made.

James Watt adapted the centrifugal governor to regulate the speed of his steam engine. In this case, the governor controlled a valve that fed steam into the engine. Steam engines were more precisely machined and moved faster and with less friction than windmills. Without this built-in damping, Watt engines with governors would often oscillate, over-correcting again and again instead of seeking an even equilibrium speed.

This problem was dealt with on a pragmatic basis until the mid-nineteenth century, when it was addressed by James Clerk Maxwell, of electromagnetic field equation fame. Maxwell found a differential equation relating the various parameters of a governor, particularly what is now termed its *transfer function*, that could be solved in such a way as to predict whether it would be stable or not.[7]

It's possible to build a governor on which you can change the speed it wants to make the motor run (called the *setpoint*). For the mechanical flyball governors, this could be done by pushing a control lever; in modern electronic devices, the setpoint can be specified by an electronic signal. Modern governors with this capability are called servomechanisms, or *servos* for short.

Even before Watt, a different, nonhomeostatic form of feedback had been invented for automatic control in which one state of a machine created a signal for it to go into another state. In Thomas Newcomen's steam engine, which was the size of a house, the valves that let the steam in and out of the piston were operated by hand. Boys were hired to do this, and, as you can imagine, it was an intensely boring job. In 1713 one such boy, Humphrey Potter, realized that he could tie cords to the reciprocating beam of the engine that would yank the valve handles at just the right times. He did so, and the cords became a standard part of the Newcomen design, known as "potter cords."[8]

For most of the intervening years, such mechanical feedback for automatic control was standard in machinery. A common example of exactly Potter's valve-minding task was done by camshaft and rocker arms in ordinary automobile engines, for example. Instead of a float valve, many toilets in commercial restrooms come with a gadget that senses when you get up or walk away (usually with an infrared photocell that senses your body heat) and flushes by turning on the water for a specific period of time. Gadgets like this are called sequencers, or more generally, controllers.

PUTTING IT ALL TOGETHER

Cybernetics is not just another branch of science. It is an Intellectual Revolution that rivals in importance the earlier Industrial Revolution.

—Isaac Asimov

Wiener was deeply involved in what later evolved into several different fields: statistical prediction and feedback control, information theory, mathematical neuroscience, and computers. He had, for example, made a proposal to US science czar Vannevar Bush in 1940 that, had it been followed, would have resulted in the development of the computer about five years before it actually happened.[9] His *Teleology* prefigured what was redeveloped in the 1960s through the 1980s as the *computational theory of mind*, a philosophical development that removed many of the paradoxes inherent in the then-current paradigm. The American electrical engineer and mathematician Claude Shannon's information theory came out of, among other things, an association with Wiener.[10]

Information theory, with its notion that any signal—any picture, any sound, any tactile impression—can be reduced to a stream of bits, was by itself a major new idea that has completely revolutionized the way we take pictures, play music, and even speak to one another. But it was only part of the intellectual firestorm that swirled around the new mathematics of communication and control. The basic insight is taken for granted today, but it was an astounding paradigm shift in the 1940s. It is that, in any process one wants to control, one can characterize the results of measurements as a message, and then design control systems that process these messages with feedback to act purposefully. And what's more, natural control systems such as brains and nerves can be analyzed the same way.

By 1948, there was enough substance to the new science to form the basis of a book. As Wiener tells it:

> [T]he group of scientists about Dr. Rosenblueth and myself had already become aware of the essential unity of the set of problems centering about communication, control, and statistical mechanics, whether in machine and living tissue. On the other hand, we were seriously hampered by the lack of unity in the literature concerning these problems, and by the absence of any common terminology, or even of a single name for the field. After much consideration, we have come to the conclusion that all the existing terminology has too heavy a bias to one side or another to serve the future development of the field as well as it should; and as happens so often to scientists, we have been forced to coin at least one artificial neo-Greek expression to fill the gap. We have decided to call the entire field of control and communication theory, whether in the machine or in the animal, by the name *Cybernetics*, which we form from the Greek *χυβερνητης* or *steersman*.[11]

Cybernetics, the name of the book as well as the science, took the world by storm. It went through five printings in six months. *Scientific American* made it their lead story in November 1948.[12] Within a decade, cybernetics was a standard course of study at many universities, and was so widely understood to be the science that would explain how the mind worked that Isaac Asimov could make the claim quoted above in all seriousness.

THE STRANGE DEATH OF CYBERNETICS

You can't do all the experiments, and all the math, of a branch of science by yourself. You have to take somebody's word for a lot of it. What's more, it takes a fairly serious investment of time and effort just to become well-enough educated in some field of science to be able to form a solid estimate of how firmly or speculatively it's grounded, whether its implications are as far-reaching as claimed, and whether it is, in the end, useful in the areas to which it is applied.

One of the informal methods of evaluating a field of knowledge, before investing so much time in it, is to look at its history and see if there are a lot of people who use it. Any field that gathers many adherents at all will have success stories. For example, in a story that is probably apocryphal, a phrenologist once told the young Ulysses S. Grant that he would someday become president. At its height, many people believed in phrenology; but in the long run, it didn't work, and became passé.[13] Whatever its historical popularity, the era of cybernetics appears to be past. Can we then assume that it represented less than the unifying science of control and communication that its proponents claimed?

It is true that there was some exuberant hype among even the core of the cybernetics community. Pierre de Latil, a historian of science who was instrumental in persuading Wiener to write *Cybernetics* in the first place, wrote a summary and popularization about a decade later titled *Thinking by Machine*. In the book there is a picture of Grey

Walter, a leading cyberneticist who experimented with reactive control in mobile robots, at home with his family. The caption reads:

> In their country home near Bristol, these parents have two children: one is electronic.

> Vivian Dovey and Grey Walter have two offspring: Timothy, a human baby and Elsie, the tortoise, of coils and electronic valves. Timothy is very friendly with his mechanized sister.[14]

This sort of thing, of course, can happen to any sober, self-respecting engineering discipline: consider the foolishness that is claimed in the name of the second law of thermodynamics—half of what you read that contains the word "entropy" qualifies. But there seemed to be a bit more of a circus around cybernetics than there should have been.

If you look out in the morning and see a clown on your doorstep, you might reasonably infer that the circus is in town. But if you remember that it's April Fool's Day, you can reasonably assign a lower probability to the circus theory.

In the case of cybernetics, it appears to have been April Fool's Day and Halloween at the same time. The story is both sad and bizarre, and has only recently been revealed in its entirety. The following sketch follows Conway and Siegelman's monumental biography of Wiener.[15]

Wiener's wife, Margaret, was a conservative middle-class German and a closet Nazi. She appears to have been extremely manipulative and to have had little regard for the truth. For example, she kept an English-language version of *Mein Kampf* in the house. When the Wieners' young daughter Barbara quoted from it in school (this was in the middle of World War II), Barbara was suspended briefly; to continue to hide her leanings, Mrs. Wiener began to spread the word that Barbara, her own daughter, was a congenital liar.

The neural researcher Warren McCulloch was flamboyant and liberal, and had a Jewish wife. Margaret hated McCulloch.

McCulloch's star pupil, Walter Pitts, had come to MIT to work with Wiener. The collaboration was the cornerstone of the multidisciplinary work at the core of cybernetics. In 1951 McCulloch himself was to move to MIT as the natural center of the new science. This is the "group of scientists" to which Wiener refers in the *Cybernetics* quote above and whom he names throughout the book.

Before the cybernetics cadre could coalesce in Cambridge, Margaret told Wiener that "the boys" in McCulloch's lab in Chicago had seduced Barbara multiple times while she was working there as an assistant (and living in McCulloch's house).

Wiener exploded in fury and cut all ties to McCulloch and Pitts without telling them why. Since Margaret's story was a complete fabrication, they had no way of knowing the reason or of refuting it.

Wiener went into a severe depression. Pitts had a mental breakdown. The others were variously affected. The once-in-a-lifetime confluence of talent and interest that was the living spark at the center of cybernetics died aborning.[16]

Later, Wiener picked up the pieces by shifting cybernetics from mathematics to social commentary. He never spoke to McCulloch or Pitts again. His later books, such as *God and Golem, Inc.*, were reasonable criticisms of social systems for being too machinelike (and lacking internal feedback and self-regulation). But the cutting-edge technical insight and analysis was gone.

As if this were not Greek tragedy enough, Wiener's criticism of the military-industrial complex in the United States served to make the government suspicious of him—and very ironically, to increase his popularity in the Soviet Union. As the cold war heightened, the increasing popularity of cybernetics abroad, particularly in the Soviet Union, along with Wiener's antiauthoritarian stance, made it a political whipping boy among the United States' largely defense-related, science-funding agencies.[17] They completed the irony by pulling a Lysenko* on this, the most originally American of sciences.

---

*Trofim Lysenko was a biologist who, as the head of the Academy of Agricultural Sciences of the Soviet Union, campaigned against the science of genetics and severely damaged Soviet agriculture from the 1930s to the 1960s. His name is now synonymous with the suppression of scientific research for political reasons.

So by the end of the 1960s, cybernetics, poisoned from within and eroded from without, had largely faded away as a serious technical field of study, particularly in the United States. Much of what remains under the name cybernetics takes after Wiener's later social commentary phase—*feedback* has become a buzzword in social analysis and the design of organizations. Let us hope that it has helped.

THE REMAINS OF CYBERNETICS

Serious cybernetics no longer flourishes, at least under that name, but a remarkable number of modern fields of study can trace their roots to it or through it.

Estimation and Control Theory

Kevin Warwick, head of the Department of Cybernetics at the University of Reading (the United Kingdom's only university cybernetics department), defines cybernetics as being essentially about advanced control systems.[18] There is a strong core of mathematically based engineering knowledge that occupies a number of different fields today, under names such as *control theory* and *systems theory*. Feedback is extensively used in mechanical, hydraulic, and electronic systems, and its analysis is not considered anything other than part of the engineer's standard tool kit. Control theory and the predictive estimators that are the descendants of Wiener's airplane-prediction analysis, called *filters* in the jargon of the field (e.g., the Kalman filter), are essential in robotics.

Modeling the human response as part of the system, also a part of the original anti-aircraft gun analysis, has moved off into ergonomics and human factors studies. In this form it remains a crucial part of some systems design (active steering and braking systems in automobiles, for example). But it got separated from computer science in the breakup; it is a remarkable fact that most consumer-oriented software today is designed in complete ignorance of its principles.[19]

Information Theory

Wiener's concept of information was analog; the differential equations that he used to handle information dealt in continuous variables and measurements. Shannon's formulation in terms of discrete bits was groundbreaking in that it opened the door to the digital manipulation of information.[20] We moderns are so used to digitizing everything we measure or transmit that we find it difficult to realize what a radical departure it was to break smooth, continuous measurements, such as the rapidly varying pressure of air that is sound, into a finite string of fixed symbols, like the bits that make up an MP3 file. Shannon is now generally recognized as one of the major figures in the birth of the information age because he also showed how simple digital circuits could do Boolean algebra, a significant part of the foundation of computer design.

It isn't important, at this late date, to sort out just who thought of what first. Shannon had significant contact with Wiener during the period that the most basic ideas of information theory and cybernetics were being formed; that there is such a thing as information, separate from matter or energy, was a new way of thinking. The notion that information is based in probability and can be measured statistically is at the heart of both cybernetics and information theory.

One of the great intellectual triumphs of information theory is that its concept of entropy—the term Shannon used for amount of information, essentially the number of bits in a message—has ultimately been unified with the concept of entropy in physics. Shannon's intuition in using the same name was right, and information is as basic a part of our understanding of the physical universe as are mass, charge, and force.

It seems ultimately that intelligence itself will be measurable in terms of information theory. The main function of intelligence is to take a huge stream of information, such as provided by the sensory organs, and reduce it to a relatively small stream of abstracted interpretation that has high predictive value. This view was present at the birth of AI and has a growing following today, as we shall see.

Computational Neuroscience

Understanding the nervous system as a kind of computing machine was what drove cybernetics to be a science as opposed to merely a branch of control engineering. Researchers in computational neuroscience can trace their intellectual roots directly back to McCulloch and Pitts. This is one of the most exciting fields of science today; how the brain works is an enormous but fascinating puzzle, and the tools to study it are advancing apace with the knowledge.

One of the interesting facets of modern computational neuroscience is the mathematics in which functional theories are expressed. One of cybernetics' major contributions originally was, in fact, to develop new mathematics that could be used to describe the phenomena of control systems, including neural ones. The further development of the math for computational neuroscience will continue to follow in Wiener's footsteps.

Neural Networks

There is a separate field of study that is more of an engineering discipline compared to the science of computational neurophysiology. This involves using simplified models of neurons, typically in computer simulation, to perform various recognition or control functions. Although inspired by neurons and tracing their lineage back to McCulloch and Pitts, these models are much simpler (and easier to analyze mathematically) than real neurons. The separation of the engineering neural nets from the science of neurophysiology can be dated from the invention of the *perceptron* by Frank Rosenblatt, along with an algorithm for "teaching" a network of perceptrons to recognize patterns. Marvin Minsky also contributed to the field, doing his doctoral thesis on a neural-style learning machine. The field came into its own in the 1980s, however, with the invention of a slightly more complex model, which was continuous in its output where the perceptron was purely binary. This allowed for a more powerful learning algorithm called *back-propagation*. Like control theory, neural nets are now a standard part of the engineer's tool kit.

Computers

Beside Wiener's 1940 computer proposal, the strong interrelation between the cybernetic ideas and those that underlay the modern electronic computer can be seen in the fact that John von Neumann chose (and Wiener "donated") Julian Bigelow (Wiener's engineer from the gun-aiming days and coauthor of the *Teleology* paper) as the chief engineer of his own computer project. This was the project that got von Neumann the name, the father of the modern computer.[21]

Although built as digital machines using discrete symbols, computers were originally built to solve differential equations, the essence of the continuous, analytical, systems approach. One of the first commercially available supercomputers, from Control Data Corporation, was called the CYBER. They were seen from the start as part of the cybernetics vision of the science of thought, and the popular use of the term, and particularly the prefix *cyber-* (as in cyberspace, cyberpunk, cybercafe, and cybercrime), continues to reflect that sense today.

Artificial Intelligence

Once computers existed, however, it was soon seen that their digital nature afforded a completely different approach to the study of thought, contrasting in many ways to the cybernetic formulation: top-down as opposed to bottom-up, discrete as opposed to continuous, algebraic as opposed to analytic. AI was cerebral, based on symbolic logic and interacting on an intellectual plane, whereas cybernetics was situated, concerned with controlling bodies in the real world. Where cyberneticists watched nerve cells under microscopes and with oscilloscopes, AIers watched people solving puzzles and playing chess.

In the 1960s, this appearance of disconnection was a significant advantage for AI funding from cold-war agencies that wanted no truck with Wiener's social criticism. To some extent, this meant that AI developed in a logician's sandbox, uninfluenced by either the demands of having to control a body or of being part of a broader society.

About which, much more later—but suffice it for the moment to say that the distinction didn't hold up. In a recent collection of papers reflecting the state of AI at the turn of the century, about half use symbolic methods and the other half use techniques that rely heavily on probability, statistics, and analytic math that looks a lot like cybernetics.[22] Robotics has reentered the picture, and much of modern AI is informed by the needs of a situated agent—an intelligence controlling a real body in the real world. Meanwhile, there has been substantial work in the field of connecting robots back into the world of humans with whom they have to interact.[23]

Philosophy of Mind

Warren McCulloch wrote, "Cybernetics . . . is ready to officiate at the expiration of philosophical Dualism and Reductionism. . . . Our world is one again, and so are we."[24]

It's clear what he meant by the reference to dualism. Wiener and Rosenblueth's theory of teleology via feedback was one in a succession of insights which, building on a tradition running back through Darwin and Leibniz, had begun to bridge from the natural world to such mentalistic concepts as intention, purpose, and meaning. Now, in the twenty-first century, the bridge is a causeway and the mind no longer an island. What is now called the computational theory of mind is the implicit working stance of most researchers in cognitive science. We do not have to know everything about how the brain works to be satisfied that it could and should be studied scientifically. Cybernetics was an important step in arriving at that position.

It is less obvious what McCulloch may have meant by his reference to reductionism, since in one sense reductionism is what all science, including cybernetics, is all about. But I conjecture that he meant something substantive and important. The concept has been captured more recently by E. O. Wilson in his term *consilience*, by which he means that knowledge is a unified fabric of understanding and that its fragmentation into disparate and incoherent fields is an artifact of our lack of understanding, and not a feature of nature.

It was certainly the intention of the founders of cybernetics to unify a description of some phenomena previously not understood as related, as reflected in the quote above.

What We Lost

Ultimately, most of what cybernetics seemed poised to study has been studied under other names. However, what got lost was exactly what Wiener described as important in his introduction to *Cybernetics*: a common vocabulary and the concomitant sharing of abstractions between subfields. In latter days, the field of cognitive science has arisen to straddle some of the gaps, in an overlapping set of areas. The even newer field of cognitive robotics is attempting to put the insights of cognitive science to work in the realm of robotics, leading to a reunification of some of scientific brain theory with engineering control and systems theory. In the fullness of time, it seems likely that the dream of a unified understanding will be attained, one way or another. What we lost was time, and the knowledge that a half century's work would have given us.

CHAPTER 4
Symbolic AI
THE GOLDEN AGE

We propose that a 2 month, 10 man study of artificial intelligence be carried out during the summer of 1956 at Dartmouth College in Hanover, New Hampshire. The study is to proceed on the basis of the conjecture that every aspect of learning or any other feature of intelligence can in principle be so precisely described that a machine can be made to simulate it. An attempt will be made to find how to make machines use language, form abstractions and concepts, solve kinds of problems now reserved for humans, and improve themselves. We think that a significant advance can be made in one or more of these problems if a carefully selected group of scientists work on it together for a summer.

—John McCarthy, et al.[1]

Cybernetics had set itself the task of learning how the brain worked from the bottom up, starting with neuron-level operations and understanding what is formed from them. But the computer opened up a whole new possibility: doing it from the top down, starting with symbolically expressed ideas (like this sentence) and figuring out what they are made of. The new "giant electronic brains," such as the ENIAC, had originally been designed to solve specific engineering problems. John von Neumann proposed, and ultimately managed the building of, a more general-purpose version: a machine that could operate not only on the data for a specific problem, but also on the very program that was specifying the operations. With what is now called the von Neumann architecture, particularly the stored program, computers became the equivalent of Alan Turing's mathematical model of a universal computing machine (as long as memory didn't run out).[2]

Alan Turing had defined his notion of a computing machine with the specific intention of modeling anything a human mathematician could do, as part of an investigation by mathematicians in the early twentieth century into the possibility of automating mathematics. But then he added a remarkable twist: there was one fairly simple Turing machine that could do any computation that *any* Turing machine could do, given the appropriate program (which was essentially a description of the other machine).

Turing, working with the top secret code breakers group at Bletchley Park during World War II, had been associated with the first electronic computer, the COLOSSUS. Unfortunately, COLOSSUS was top secret and remained classified throughout the period, so the Americans quickly caught up and surpassed it without realizing it had existed. Turing had produced the first design for a stored-program electronic computer, the ACE. Due to construction delays, the ACE was beat out by a smaller effort at Manchester, which holds the distinction of being the first such machine to run a program. Even so, the ACE beat von Neumann's EDVAC by two years.[3]

In 1948, the same year *Cybernetics* appeared, Turing had taken a year's sabbatical to write a manifesto about providing a computer with "higher mental functions." This was the first substantial paper to describe the AI enterprise in a recognizable form.[4] Had he been listened to in Britain, there might have developed a major effort, both in computer technology and in AI, to rival the American one, resulting in a mutually beneficial competition. Instead, the British, in a spectacular display of bureaucratic stupidity, first ignored him and then contributed to his tragic demise.[5] This left the Americans, both in AI and in computers generally, with little effective competition for quite some time.

Thus, stored-program electronic computers came to be called "von Neumann machines," and the phrase "Turing machine" is reserved for the mathematical abstraction. Virtually all computers made today qualify for the former name. This means that they are computationally universal, equivalent in theory to Turing machines, with the one proviso that they might run out of memory. But given enough memory for the problem, any computation can be run on any von Neumann computer, and any machine can be simulated.

Thus, by its essential design, a computer could do whatever a mind could do. All we needed was the right program.

THE TURING TEST

> *The question and answer method seems to be suitable for introducing almost any one of the fields of human endeavor that we wish to include.*
>
> —Alan Turing, *Computing Machinery and Intelligence*

It seems almost superfluous at this late date to discuss the Turing Test, introduced by Turing in the above-quoted essay over half a century ago. It is, after all, the most-discussed, most-reprinted, and clearly the most famous criterion for the success of AI.[6] Turing considers the question, "Can a machine think?" He finds this ill defined, and so he proposes instead a more objective formulation: can a computer fool an interrogator into thinking it is human during an interview across a teletype link?

The Turing Test is often described as being a contest, and it is occasionally criticized in those terms. It is clearly unfair as a contest; if there are a human and a computer being interviewed side by side, the computer has the obstacle of trying to pretend it's something it's not, whereas the human has no such burden. As Turing explicitly states, the computer has the harder task. (Note how easily the computer could "win" if the roles were reversed and the human had to imitate a computer.)[7] But the test is not a contest; it's an interview, and the human is just there as a standard for comparison.

Because the computer does have the harder role, however, Turing believed that the test was surer, in the sense of eliminating false positives: if a computer passed, it must be as capable of thought as a human.

The genius of the test is that the computer can run, but it can't hide. The use of language in an interactive setting means that any suspicion of weakness entertained by the judge can be followed up and tested to any desired depth. There are some skills that cannot be conclusively demonstrated over a teletype, but it should be pretty hard to convince someone that you're intelligent if you're not. (One crucial assumption Turing made without discussion was that the judge be competent. Subsequent stagings of Turing Test scenarios, such as the Loebner Prize, have produced amusing results when, for example, nontechnical judges believed a human was the computer because she knew too much!)

I believe the Turing Test has stood the test of time. It is too exacting for any existing AI system. Adeptness at understanding and replying in colloquial language has proven to be one of the hardest areas AI has attempted. It also seems likely that any AI system that could pass the test, in the sense of being able to engage in substantive and purposeful verbal communication with humans, would not only be worthy of the name "successful AI" but would also be an extremely useful technology.

We can add a new twist, however. Would an AI that could pass the Turing Test be smart enough to be dangerous? What could any AI do that was dangerous in the first place? It could, for example, be connected to the Internet and make money by reading and writing; it could engage in e-commerce and amass enough money to fund significant projects; it could sway public opinion or even start a religion and organize fanatical followers to do mischief.

There are humans who are not capable of these things, so, strictly speaking, a computer should be able to convince a judge that it is human while still being incapable of doing them itself. However, the judge could look for signs of the kinds of intelligence and skills that would enable the dangerous activities, instead of being satisfied with the lowest common denominator of human performance. This basically amounts to changing the rules of the contest from "pick the human" to "pick the most likely to succeed," where the human contestant is known to be smart and talented. It would be fairer, too; the computer wouldn't have to pretend to be something it wasn't.

ELIZA

My propositions serve as elucidations in the following way: anyone who understands me eventually recognizes them as nonsensical.

—Ludwig Wittgenstein, *Tractatus Logico-Philosophicus*

Probably the most commonly re-implemented program ever written is Joseph Weizenbaum's ELIZA. Although it was something of a feat when he did it during the early 1960s, using the primitive programming language FORTRAN, it is just meaty enough to remain an interesting exercise in virtually any later programming language. At the same time, there's something compelling about what it does that appeals to programmers in particular.

What it does, of course, is converse with a user across a text interface, as if it were taking a Turing Test. It has spawned so many variants and imitators that there is a name for the class of program they represent: chatbot. There's even a version of ELIZA built into the EMACS text editor, with which I had the following conversation:

ELIZA: I am the psychotherapist. Please, describe your problems.
JSH: Hello, can you help me?
ELIZA: How do you do? What brings you to see me?

JSH: My wife asked me to see you.
ELIZA: Tell me something about your family.
JSH: She says I use the computer too much.
ELIZA: You have your mind on computers, it seems.
JSH: Yes, and my hands, too.
ELIZA: Why do you say yes and your hands too?
JSH: Because I use it all the time.
ELIZA: Is it because you use it all the time that you came to me?

If you didn't know what was going on under the hood, so to speak, you could come away with the impression that the program was understanding what I said and making reasonable replies. What it's really doing is legerdemain: it has the same relation to real understanding that sleight-of-hand tricks do to real magic.

ELIZA is a two-level program. The infrastructure is a pattern-matcher that looks for keywords in the input text and substitutes phrases into canned output sentences. The superstructure is a script that lists the keywords and the canned replies. This two-level architecture is a standard technique today, but ELIZA was the first well-known implementation of it. The program is named for Eliza Doolittle, the flower girl "rescripted" by Henry Higgins in Bernard Shaw's play *Pygmalion* (and later the musical *My Fair Lady*). ELIZA's most common script is called DOCTOR, after the Rogerian (nondirective) psychological technique it imitates.

DOCTOR turns out to be the perfect stage setting for ELIZA's legerdemain, since the psychologist is essentially prompting the patient to ramble and has to say nothing substantive himself. In the forty years since the original ELIZA, the DOCTOR scripts have grown to be voluminous and sophisticated, to the extent that they rarely repeat themselves and simulate a reasonable conversation with a compliant or unsuspecting user.

However, the scripts are still simple enough that the lack of understanding is blatantly clear. Here is a section of the script from one implementation:[8]

decomp: * i * you *
    reasmb: Perhaps in your fantasies we (2) each other.
    reasmb: Do you wish to (2) me?
    reasmb: You seem to need to (2) me.
    reasmb: Do you (2) anyone else?
decomp: * your *
    reasmb: Why are you concerned over my (2)?
    reasmb: What about your own (2)?
    reasmb: Are you worried about someone else's (2)?
    reasmb: Really, my (2)?
    reasmb: What makes you think of my (2)?
    reasmb: Do you want my (2)?

In other words, the program looks for the words "I" and "you" in the input, and if it finds them, it takes whatever words come between and prints, for example, "You seem to need to <words> me." It simply picks at random between the possible responses to a given pattern.

Knowing this, we can continue our conversation with ELIZA:

JSH: Gabble poo father glork frotz.

ELIZA: You seem to dwell on your family.

JSH: Gabble poo your glork frotz.

ELIZA: Is it because of some problems at home that you say gabble poo my glork frotz?

ME: Borg holdew my sevlert poikle.

ELIZA: What makes you believe borg holdew your sevlert poikle?

ELIZA, obviously, is nowhere near anything we would consider real artificial intelligence.

The reason to discuss it here is that, as Weizenbaum discovered to his horror not too long after the program was written, people using it were fooled into thinking it really did understand, and what's more, care about their problems. It is as if a stage magician found that people watching his tricks had become convinced that magic was real.

This propensity of people to be fooled by simple tricks into thinking a computer understands something it doesn't is now called the *ELIZA effect*. It has been an albatross around the neck of AI since the 1960s. The problem is not so much that naive users are taken in by tricky programs, although that happens. The problem is that AI researchers themselves are taken in by their own programs and are led to believe they've solved problems they haven't even scratched yet.

LOGIC

Philosophers and mathematicians have been working on the formalization of thought since Aristotle. Aristotle started things off with the basic insight that we can write down a set of patterns that will give us the form of correct arguments. He called these syllogisms:

> All <*kind of thing*> are <*adjective*>.
> <*Individual*> is a <*kind of thing*>.
> Therefore, <*Individual*> is <*adjective*>.

If you fill in the blanks appropriately, you're guaranteed to get an argument that is valid. The classic example for this syllogism is:

> All men are mortal.
> Socrates is a man.
> Therefore, Socrates is mortal.

All of logic ultimately works out to the same general principle: a set of patterns that let you get new sentences from old ones. Over the centuries, the kinds of patterns have gotten more complex and sophisticated, and a lot more is known about what you can or can't get out of a mechanical logic machine.

A computer, surprise surprise, is a mechanical logic machine. Notice how similar the syllogism is to an ELIZA script.

Dartmouth mathematics professor John McCarthy organized the first workshop on artificial intelligence in 1956, naming the field in the process. Among the attendees were many we now remember as the founders of the field.[9] Stealing the show to some extent were Allen Newell and Herbert Simon of Carnegie Tech (later CMU), with a program called Logic Theorist. This program used the rules of logic to derive theorems from axioms just as a mathematician would do.

Later, Newell and Simon moved on to more pragmatic approaches, and it was McCarthy who became the chief proponent and practitioner of logic in AI. Logic is capable, in theory, of doing anything any computer can do; after all, at the circuit level, computers are built out of logic. But using logic to model thought at a level where the logical symbols correspond to words has remained frustratingly elusive.

LISP

Another mathematician who had tackled the problem of the automation of mathematical logic in the 1930s was Alonzo Church. He had come up with a different formulation than Turing did of what was possible for a computing machine (or a human following formal rules) to do. This was a system of notation called the *lambda calculus*. (Since then, it's been shown that the lambda calculus and Turing machines are equivalent in power, which lends credence to the notion that they do capture what we mean by "computable." In consequence, the notion is referred to as the Church-Turing thesis.)

As John McCarthy began working on the problem of manipulating logical expressions in a computer, he decided to try using the lambda calculus as a programming language.[10] The language that came out of the effort, called LISP, was a classic and is one of the two programming languages that are still in use since 1960 (the other is FORTRAN, used for numerical calculations).

LISP was way ahead of its time. It had automatic memory allocation, which many languages today still don't have. Its native *data-*

structures—linked lists—were not fixed in size ahead of time but could be created on the fly to fit whatever needed to be put in them. Its lists were recursive in nature (i.e., they could contain other lists), and its program semantics were recursive. That means that a program could not only invoke other programs as subroutines, it could invoke itself as a subroutine (FORTRAN's subroutines were not recursive). Most important, LISP had the crucial property that the program and the data it manipulated were represented by the same kinds of linked lists. This meant that programs could read and write programs. This was the same crucial capability that characterized the universal Turing machine and the von Neumann computer. Just as there is a small, simple Turing machine that is universal, there is a small, simple LISP program that is universal (it's called EVAL, and it's only about half a page long written in LISP).[11]

PREDICTING MACHINES

One of the participants in the 1956 workshop, Ray Solomonoff, was interested in the problem of prediction. If given a description of a possible world, he wanted the machine to say what would happen next in it.

If you have a machine that can do this, you are clearly well on your way to an AI. For each action in its repertoire, the AI uses the predictor to find out what would happen if it did that; then it needs only some way to choose which outcome is most desirable.

Solomonoff describes an incident at the meeting:

> One day McCarthy gave a talk on "Well defined mathematical problems." His thesis was that all mathematical problems could be formulated as problems of inverting Turing machines. [In other words, given a Turing machine and its output, find the input.]
>
> McCarthy gave many examples to show how problems could be put into this form.

> I asked him about the induction problem: "Suppose you are given a long sequence of symbols describing events in the real world. How can you extrapolate that sequence?"
>
> Next day he said, "Suppose we were wandering about in an old house, and we suddenly opened a door to a room and in that room was a computer that was printing out your sequence. Eventually it came to the end of the sequence and was about to print the next symbol. Wouldn't you bet that it would be correct?"[12]

Suppose we are given a sequence to extrapolate. It would be nice if we could visit a very big house, which held all possible computers running every possible program, each printing out a sequence. Sooner or later we would find one that was printing our sequence.

This is where the nature of Turing machines comes in handy. Any Turing machine can be simulated by the same universal machine. Each machine can be described by a string of bits, its encoding for use in the universal machine. But a string of bits is also a number—so we can simply count through all possible Turing machines, simulate each one, see if it matches the sequence you want to extrapolate, and take the first one to do so. This machine is the best theory of the information content in your sequence.[13] No other machine can predict better since it produces the sequence verbatim; and it's the shortest machine that does this.

This doesn't work as it stands—Turing machines aren't that well behaved. One might print out the first few symbols of your sequence then run and run without printing anything for a long, long time. Is it stuck in an endless loop or will it eventually print the next correct symbol? But the notion gave Solomonoff enough traction on the problem to make some major strides in algorithmic information theory. These are now, fifty years later, becoming more and more clearly relevant to the problem of prediction in AI.

We can measure theories by their information entropy, for example. First, the theory itself can be expressed in bits, and its length measured (e.g., it can be a program that makes predictions). Then, the value of its predictions can be measured in terms of the entropy of the states it predicts. We minimize both; minimizing the size of the theory is just Ockham's razor, and minimizing the prediction entropy is a measure of how accurate it is.[14]

COMPUTERS AND THOUGHT

The state of AI in 1963 was summed up by a book that is such a classic that it's still in print today. This was *Computers and Thought*, a collection of papers by the leading researchers in the field.[15] The name was an echo of the title of AI's single most famous paper, "Computing Machinery and Intelligence" by Alan Turing. This was originally published in the British journal *Mind*, but was reprinted as the first chapter of *Computers and Thought*. It was the paper in which he introduced the Turing Test. It was more of a philosophical than a technical paper, but it laid the foundation and set the tone for all that came after.

Other high points of *Computers and Thought* include papers on programs that proved theorems in logic and in geometry, and one that solved freshman calculus problems. There were a couple of programs that addressed the problem of understanding natural language, and some that attacked the problem of pattern recognition, as in identifying characters on a printed page. There was a paper written about a program that played checkers, and a paper about others that played chess.

Those programs could be classified as special purpose, applied to particular problems. There were also programs that were intended to be general purpose, representing theories about how the flexible, adaptive parts of the human mind worked.

The first of these was Newell and Simon's GPS (General Problem Solver). It was essentially a framework that required its world to be described as objects and relationships—as close to logic as makes no difference—and as "operators" that could change the objects or situations described. GPS would then select an operator that reduced differences between its given situation and a specified goal situation.

The story is that when John McCarthy first heard GPS described, he remarked, "Why, it's a symbolic servo!"[16] And it is. At an abstract level, we can see a standard engineering servo and a GPS as mechanisms that have a certain ability of control, that will listen to our orders as to what the things under their control should be like, and that will act in such a way as to keep those things as we wanted.

Another program, Edward Feigenbaum's EPAM, attempted to model a general learning ability (and can be seen as a progenitor of much of today's field of machine learning). Also of note in this connection was the checker-playing program by Arthur Samuels that pioneered machine-learning techniques and improved significantly by playing games against itself.

An important and enduring model of perception, discussed by Oliver Selfridge (the only major figure in both cybernetics and AI), was called Pandemonium. Suppose you are trying to recognize a printed letter, for example, trying to distinguish an *A* from an *H*. You break the problem into parts and have a smaller, simpler program that recognizes features such as whether there is a crossbar, whether the letter is closed at the top, whether there are any vertical lines, and so on. Selfridge says, "One might think of the various features as being inspected by little demons, all of whom then shout the answers in concert to a decision-making demon."[17] Pandemonium was the ancestor of quite a lot of subsequent AI (and other software) architecture, up to and including modern "agent-based" ones.

To my mind, however, the most important paper in *Computers and Thought* is an overview of the field by Marvin Minsky. It forms a manifesto for the following decades of research that might well be called the golden age of AI. Unlike Turing's paper of fifteen years earlier, which was primarily speculative, it is based on some solid early research and early results; yet it gives a good general overview of what needed to be done (some of which still needs to be done). If you are a modern-day AI researcher and think that Bayesian networks (see chapter 9, p. 155) are the very latest thing in mathematical AI, have a look at Minsky's paper.[18]

SEMANTIC INFORMATION PROCESSING

You are a monkey. You have been placed in a room in which there is a bunch of bananas hanging from the ceiling, too high to reach. In the room there is also a box. You are hungry. What do you do?

This is a classic example in AI—almost every introductory course includes it. It comes from a paper by John McCarthy titled "Programs with Common Sense." McCarthy had a vision that an AI system (called the ADVICE TAKER) could be built that would take a description of the world in the form of statements in logic and would be able to make deductions from those statements that allowed it to act reasonably without having to be told explicitly what to do in each new situation.

So you, as the monkey, "see" the world as a set of statements such as:

> Forall *u*: place(*u*) implies can(monkey, move(monkey, box, *u*))
> can(monkey, climbs(monkey,box))
> place(under(bananas))
> at(box, under(bananas)) and on(monkey, box) implies can(monkey, reach(monkey, bananas))
> Forall *p* forall *x*: reach(*p*,*x*) implies cause(has(*p*,*x*))

And yes, you can deduce that you should push the box under the bananas and climb on it to get at them.

The ADVICE TAKER paper grew up as a technical report and in various collections, but its most famous appearance is in the book *Semantic Information Processing*, edited by Marvin Minsky.[19] Most of the other papers in the book are the doctoral theses of Minsky's students, and they form a revealing family album of AI in its vigorous youth.

When I came across *Semantic Information Processing* as an undergraduate in the early 1970s, it struck me like a thunderbolt. Here was an idea that was, as far as I knew, the veriest science fiction: intelligent machines. I'd run into it only in Isaac Asimov's robot stories. And here were these people actually *doing* it.

What the actual programs in the theses could do was primarily simple but not trivial intellectual tasks, such as solving high-school math word problems, solving the geometric analogy problems found on IQ tests, and being told something and answering questions about it.

Semantic Nets

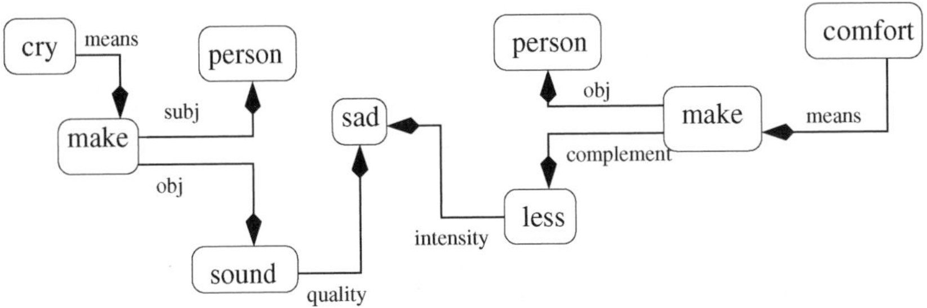

Fig. 4.1: A (tiny fragment of a) semantic network.

Perhaps the most far-reaching of the theses was one by M. Ross Quillian titled "Semantic Memory."[20] Quillian's program could compare words, as on a grammar-school English test; for example, if asked to compare "cry" and "comfort," it would point out that to cry means to make a sound indicating that one is sad and that comfort can mean to attempt to make someone less sad.

Quillian's innovation was to store the essence of a dictionary in a network, with nodes for the words and links representing relationships. The relationships were things such as "is a kind of" for objects and "can be the subject of" for actions. This datastructure has come to be known as a *semantic network* and has proven to be a fairly useful way of organizing knowledge.

A semantic network does not encode any explicit knowledge that couldn't be represented easily by a predicate logic formulation. What it does do is organize it so that well-understood procedures can use it to make certain kinds of queries and deductions efficiently. This is of considerable importance.

Suppose you are a robot.[21] You are in a room with a bomb in it. The bomb is about to go off. You need to do a kind of monkey-and-bananas problem deduction to remain safe. You go out of the room. Unfortunately, you are holding the bomb, and you didn't realize that it would come with you when you left.

So you need to do more deductions. Consider all the possible things you could do with the bomb: shake it, wave it around, stroke it like a cat, talk to it, hold it to your ear to hear the ticking, juggle with it and some other object, push it under the bananas and climb on it, or maybe even just put it down. While you're standing there running through all the possibilities, the bomb goes off.

This dilemma is known as the *frame problem* in AI. You can't know which deduction is going to be useful until you've done it and seen what the result is. But the more you know, the more deductions you can potentially make, so the harder it is for you to do any given task. This is why it's critical to organize the knowledge you have to be able to use it efficiently.

FRAMES

By the time I got into graduate school and started doing AI in earnest in the mid-1970s, the field was full of frames. The notion of the frame problem had been explored by John McCarthy, and the frame datastructure had been introduced by Marvin Minsky as a way of organizing knowledge.[22]

The idea behind a (Minsky) frame was simple in concept: when you come into a situation you've seen before, such as a familiar room, you have certain expectations as to what will be there and where it will be, and you'll make some assumptions about what's there that you can't see or haven't paid attention to yet. A frame is a datastructure that makes it straightforward to fit what you see into a coherent set of concepts you already understand and know what to do with.

This was such an obviously good idea that it took the AI world by storm. Unfortunately, by the time it got out to all the researchers in the field, it had devolved into a buzzword; everybody took whatever datastructures they were already using and called them frames. Every "frame-based system" I worked with in the 1970s and early 1980s was essentially a prototype of what would be called an *object-oriented language* today.

The most powerful part of Minsky's frame idea got lost completely—what he called a *frame-system* in the paper. The intuition is that if you're standing in a room and turn, what you see next follows in a very straightforward way from what you're seeing now. We could organize the frames in a larger network that produced the frame we expect to use next from the one we're using now and the action or event that is changing things.

SHRDLU

The most notable system from the height of the golden age of AI (and there were numerous notable ones) was Terry Winograd's SHRDLU.[23] This was a program that carried on a conversation about a tabletop with a set of children's building blocks on it. This simple domain of discourse, called the "blocks world," was a staple for AI of the period. SHRDLU displayed a picture of what was going on in the blocks world on a monitor, including a simulated robot arm that could move and stack the blocks.

You, the user, could type to SHRDLU in comfortably informal English, telling it to do things and asking it questions, not only about the "physical" world of the blocks but also about its actions and its reasons for doing them. Here's a snippet of a SHRDLU conversation:

> Person: HOW MANY BLOCKS ARE NOT IN THE BOX?
>
> Computer: FOUR OF THEM.
>
> Person: IS AT LEAST ONE OF THEM NARROWER THAN THE ONE WHICH I TOLD YOU TO PICK UP?

Computer: YES, THE RED CUBE.
Person: IS IT SUPPORTED?
Computer: YES, BY THE TABLE.
Person: CAN THE TABLE PICK UP BLOCKS?
Computer: NO.
Person: CAN A PYRAMID BE SUPPORTED BY A BLOCK?
Computer: YES.[24]

As long as the conversation was limited to the tabletop and what happened on it, SHRDLU really seemed to know what it was talking about.

SHRDLU was primarily a theory of language understanding. It operated by having what's called a *world model*, a simulation of the blocks world tabletop. It could resolve ambiguities and answer questions (such as whether a pyramid can be supported by a block) by trying them in its model and seeing what worked.

A rational, deductive mind operating from a world model was the basic concept of AI that came out of the golden age. (The world model was typically a combination of a description of the current state of the world, to the program's best knowledge, and a prediction machine.) SHRDLU showed that within a constrained, self-contained domain, such a mind could understand ambiguous queries and commands, give responsive answers and take appropriate actions, and discuss and justify what it had done. In a word, in its own little world, it really did understand.

AM AND EURISKO

A program, called "AM," is described which models one aspect of elementary mathematics research: developing new concepts under the guidance of a large body of heuristic rules. "Mathematics" is considered as a type of intelligent behaviour, not as a finished product.

—Douglas Lenat

AM stood for automated mathematician, and it was the basis of Lenat's doctoral research. AM was an attempt to do what AI calls *concept formation*, which, if it could be done automatically, would be one of the most important core elements of a working AI.

AM started out with some very basic concepts to work from: ones from set theory, such as sets, union, and intersection. Then it began combining the concepts using some heuristic rules, producing new ones, and combining those, and so on.

Starting from these simple set concepts, AM discovered, among other things, numbers, addition, multiplication, factoring, and primes. It conjectured (but didn't prove) that each number has a unique factorization and that every even number can be expressed as the sum of two primes. This last concept is known as Goldbach's conjecture to (human) mathematicians, and it gets into some nontrivial number theory.[25]

Unfortunately, AM ran out of steam after these exciting first results. Whatever it was doing to get from set theory through arithmetic to number theory didn't seem to work to get from there to anywhere else. Lenat conjectured that his heuristics, which picked what to combine and did the combining, were falling short.

So his next program, EURISKO, was an attempt to take the same idea but to apply it to generating better heuristics instead of number theory. EURISKO had a number of impressive successes, including designing circuits, writing LISP code, and perhaps most interestingly, designing fleets of spaceships for play in a then-popular role-playing space war game, *Traveller TCS*. Playing with Lenat as a partner, it twice won the national championship, in 1981 and 1982, and rested on its laurels after the organizers told Lenat that if he and the program entered in 1983, the tournament would be canceled.[26]

EURISKO didn't manage to extend AM's success with number theory very much, though. Like AM, it soon ran out of gas after an initial burst of success in any given field.

One of the more famous papers in AI history is an apologia by Lenat titled "Why AM and EURISKO Appear to Work."[27] In it he points out that the representation of concepts by short LISP programs has a natural fit to the part of number theory AM did well in, but that the program seemed unable to transcend the limitations of its initial representation scheme.

CHAPTER 5
Diaspora

AI has been brain-dead since the 1970s.

—Marvin Minsky, 2003

By 1975 progress in artificial intelligence had slowed from the heady sprint of a handful of enthusiasts to the plodding trudge of growing throngs of workers.

—Hans Moravec

Our systems are still fragile when outside their carefully circumscribed domains. The best poker-playing program can't even understand the notion of a chess move, let alone the conceptual idea of animate versus inanimate.

—Rodney Brooks

From the scientific perspective, not so much has been accomplished, and the goal of understanding intelligence, from a computational point of view, remains elusive.

—Patrick Henry Winston

Why don't we have a single example of a truly multipurpose robot that would, even marginally, deserve to be called artificially intelligent?

—Sebastian Thrun

We are still far short of truly intelligent systems in the sense that people are intelligent . . .

—David Waltz

The quotation from Minsky was taken from a talk in which he was being deliberately provocative. Moravec's is from his book *Mind Children.*[1] All the rest are from an article in the party organ of the American Association for Artificial Intelligence that is a prospective of the next quarter century of AI in an issue celebrating its previous quarter century.[2]

The history of AI can be divided into two parts. The first phase, very roughly the period from 1955 to 1980, saw something of a meteoric rise in the capabilities of AI programs. In light of this trend, Turing's dream of a program savvy enough to survive his test by the end of the century seemed a perfectly feasible goal. In fact, in some areas, the progress continued along the expected trajectory: by the turn of the century, the best chess-playing computer could beat any human who ever played the game.

And yet it's clear that in the second half of its history, from the 1980s to date, AI quit growing up and began to grow out. The image that comes to mind is of the column of smoke from a cigarette, rising until it hits a "glass ceiling" then spreading out to form a cloud. It covers more territory, but not at a higher level.

One of the reasons for this is quite practical. By 1980 AI had developed a stock of techniques that were powerful enough to handle a wide variety of real-world problems, and a significant amount of the effort was diverted into doing useful things. The 1980s were, along the mainstream line of symbolic AI, the decade of *expert systems*—basically commercialized versions of AI programs aimed at specific applications. There may have been some extra impetus to try to "go practical" due to the realities of research funding: ARPA, the research arm of the US Department of Defense, had been the major funder of AI work throughout the 1960s. The Mansfield Amendment of 1969 severely curtailed ARPA's ability to fund basic research.[3] In 1973 the Lighthill Report in Great Britain had a similar effect on research funding there. By the end of the 1970s, AI researchers were scrambling for funding from wherever they could find it, which often forced them prematurely into "applications."

Another reason for spreading out is just as straightforward. If you're blocked moving in one direction, the reasonable thing to do is to move sideways until you find a way around the obstruction. Activity in AI that could be characterized in this way included the resurgence of neural networks—under the rubric of connectionism, which involved simulating neural processes with computer models—and robotics.

And we mustn't forget that the 1980s was the decade in which the personal computer exploded from an arcane hobby into a major market. Quite a lot of technical talent was absorbed (much of it reinventing the mainframe software techniques of the 1960s and 1970s) that might otherwise have contributed to real advances in computer science, including AI.

But just what was the obstruction that formed this glass ceiling? This is the key to our ability to predict whether AI will continue as it has for the past quarter century, producing useful and valuable techniques but not revolutionizing the world in any major way, or whether it will be a tide in the affairs of men, taken at the turn to lead on to fortune—or disaster.

From the standpoint of researchers grappling with it, the glass ceiling can be characterized in a number of ways: AI systems are brittle; if you confront them with anything outside their narrow area of expertise, they produce nonsense. They don't scale up; techniques that work wonderfully on "toy" problems, such as talking to SHRDLU about blocks on a tabletop, don't work for general, unlimited conversation à la the Turing Test. They have no common sense.

COMPUTING POWER

> *"It's brain," I said; "pure brain! What do you do to get like that, Jeeves? I believe you must eat a lot of fish, or something."*
>
> —P. G. Wodehouse, *The Aunt and the Sluggard*

Multiply 2,823,457,923 by 9,265,289,374, by hand (pencil and paper allowed). Assuming you decided to put it off for the moment, you'll have to take my word for it that it would have taken you about ten minutes. The "giant electronic brains" of the 1950s could have done it in a millisecond. The mainframes of the 1970s or the workstations of the 1980s could do it in a microsecond. Your PC today could do it in a nanosecond.

It's difficult, nowadays, to get a feel for how impressive a computer was in the 1950s. Not only were they big machines weighing tons and using many kilowatts of power, but they did things no person could do. Neville Schute Norway, chief engineer for the British R100 airship in the 1920s, wrote in his autobiography (titled *Slide Rule*) how it took a week to solve the structural matrix for the crucial skeleton of lightweight aluminum beams that gave the airship its shape, yet had to leave it still lighter than air. (And solving the matrix just told you if it was strong enough—if not, you had to redesign it and spend another week on the math.) The vacuum-tube computers of the 1950s could have done it in seconds.

It's easy, fifty years of Moore's law later, to sneer at the instructions-per-second ratings of those early computers. But for the sort of work they were built for—tough engineering calculations—they were already a million times faster than people doing the same thing.

You really can't blame the early AI researchers for their optimism. It must have been inconceivable that a computer that tossed off differential equations with ease didn't have the raw horsepower necessary to play with children's blocks. Vannevar Bush had predicted that "electronic brains" would have to be the size of the Empire State Building and would require Niagara Falls to cool them.[4] Given the computing technology he was using for the estimate, he was being conservative. Nobody at the time really had a clue how much computing power the human brain actually packed.

The retina of the human eye consists of a layer of receptor cells, the rods and the cones, which detect light. Then there is a layer of neurons that do some preprocessing to the image before it is sent down the optic nerve to the brain. Carnegie Mellon roboticist Hans Moravec estimates that just the preprocessing, in the eye itself and not even in the brain yet, requires the equivalent of a billion operations per second of computing power. This is ten times the power of the original Cray-1 supercomputer (ca. 1977).

The human eye isn't terribly well optimized. Evolution got stuck somehow with the preprocessing neural circuitry *in front of* the sensor array; the light has to go through it before hitting the rods and cones. (And then the optic nerve has to go back through a hole in the retina to get out, which is why human eyes have blind spots.) In other words, there is a little slice of brain with the power of a supercomputer in each of your eyeballs that is so thin that you see right through it and have never noticed it is there.

Compare that with the bulk of the brain to get an idea of how much computing power there is *behind* your eyeballs.

The numbers involved in the structure of the brain, as well as the numbers involved in tracking Moore's law of increasing computing power, are astronomical. It's a lot easier to deal with them as logarithms. So when I give brains and machines power ratings below, the number will mean the exponent of 10 (or 10^x) in operations per second: the ENIAC, at fewer than 10,000 IPS (instructions per second), rates 3.7; a classic Macintosh, at one-third MIPS (a million IPS),* is rated 5.5; the retina preprocessor is rated 9; a contemporary top-end PC with multiple processor cores can be in the neighborhood of 11;[5] the DEEP BLUE chess-playing supercomputer could apply the equivalent of a 12.5 power rating to chess (but only chess); a $30 million IBM BLUE GENE supercomputer is upward of 14.[6] The very latest supercomputer on the drawing boards, the ROADRUNNER, to be built by IBM at Los Alamos, will contain 16,000 multiprocessor "Cell Broadband" chips and should hit 15.[7]

Oh, yes—and a human doing pencil-and-paper figuring is worth about –2. But what's the human brain, as a raw computational engine?

*Or "Meaningless Indication of Processor Speed," as the numbers are quite fuzzy. But these are very much ballpark estimates; I'm not even distinguishing between integer and floating-point operations.

It has up to 100 billion neurons (10^{11}), each with up to 10,000 connections (10^4), and firing up to 100 times per second (10^2). Since these are all exponents, we add to get the overall power rating of 17, but given all the "up to's" and the fact that the brain isn't used flat out all the time (any more than any of your other organs), we'll use 16.

So we need roughly a power rating increase of 5 from a current top-end PC to get to a machine that can simulate the human brain at the neuron-firing level. Moore's law can be stated as saying that computers gain a rating of 2.5 per decade at the same price level, so this puts us in the late 2020s for cheap human-level computation.[8] Note that author and futurist Ray Kurzweil has consistently predicted 2029 as the year to expect truly human-level machines. Kurzweil's estimates are based on the notion that neuron-level simulation will be needed and that we'll have to copy the circuit diagrams of actual brains at some fairly low level to get true AI. Kurzweil's estimates can be thought of as the conservative baseline, with every advance made the hard way. Let's call a processing power rating of 16 a "Kurzweil Human-Equivalent Processing Power," or a Kurzweil HEPP.

Other estimates are more optimistic. Hans Moravec, for example, assumes that there are plenty of computational functions that the brain does the hard way, which we can finesse with different architectures and algorithms. He bases his estimates on actual computational implementations of known cognitive functions, such as the processing in the visual cortex.[8] He has estimated in his books that a machine could duplicate the brain's higher-level functions at ratings of 13 and 14. The later figure is 14, but we'll average them with the same "doesn't run flat out most the time" logic as before and refer to a 13.5 processing power rating as a Moravec HEPP.

And finally, Marvin Minsky keeps insisting that the processing power we have now is adequate for AI.[9] To keep things simple, we'll use a power rating of 11, a top-end current PC, as a Minsky HEPP.

These HEPPs will be of interest later when we try to form our own estimate of when we should expect AI.

Moravec argues that through the 1970s and 1980s, there was a

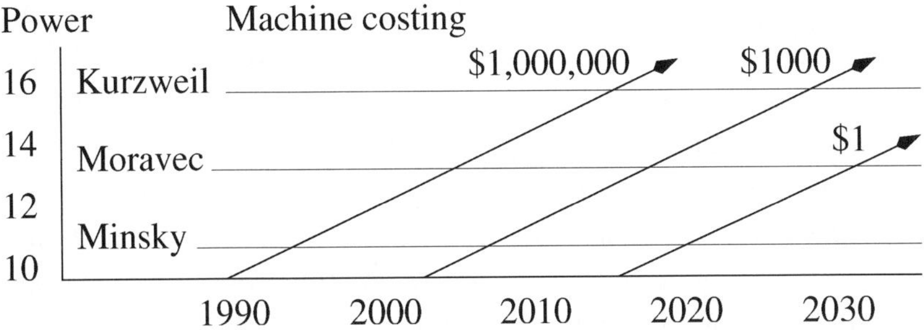

Fig. 5.1: Human-Equivalent Processing Power (HEPP) and Moore's law.

slump in funding that counteracted Moore's law, so that the processing power available to AI researchers remained constant over the period, which was what formed the glass ceiling.[10]

The lack of computational horsepower available to early researchers had a further-reaching effect than merely restricting them to small problems. It seriously biased the overall approach to favor algorithms that ran quickly on serial von Neumann computers. The push toward practical applications in the 1980s only exacerbated that bias. The result was, and still is, a huge amount of effort wasted on premature optimization. It will be time to optimize the algorithms for general intelligence when we have ones that work, which we presently do not.

COMMON LISP

Object-oriented programming is an exceptionally bad idea which could only have originated in California.

—Edsger Dijkstra

By 1980 the LISP programming language, which had been one of the keystones of golden age AI, had begun to look like the syllabus of a comparative religions course. In addition to the original LISP 1.5, there were MACLISP, INTERLISP, Rutgers/UCI LISP,[11] Utah's Portable Standard LISP (PSL), FRANZ LISP, SCHEME, NIL, and native versions of LISP for each of the several brands of hardware LISP machines that were being developed.

Programming at the highest levels, like any world-class creative art, is an extremely personal activity. Since LISP made modification of the language easy because of its self-referential properties, a diaspora of dialects was almost inevitable. However, since the AI community was trying to break out into the commercial world, this messy situation looked like dirty laundry, so the leaders of the LISP world looked for standardization.

This came in the form of COMMON LISP. The result of a series of industry and academia-wide meetings, it was a political compromise of a design that had something in common with all such compromises: it was ugly. It was the antithesis of the elegant, intellectually powerful lambda calculus on which LISP was first based. It had a bloated pile of mismatched features, included not because they worked well together—they didn't—but because, for each feature, there was some member of the consortium who insisted on including it.[12]

COMMON LISP went on to become ANSI standard X3.226-1994.

Nobody appeared to notice that COMMON LISP killed the "marketplace of ideas" that had given vitality to the jungle of different LISPs. It took a decade for consolidation, shakeout, and the rise and failure of the LISP machine companies. At the same time, LISP was still so far ahead of the general run of programming language development that there was never any temptation to move to anything else, and thus there was little occasion to notice that it was standing still.

Even so, over the past two decades LISP ceased to be a significant source of programming-language ideas. It remains among the best, but the others are moving and it is not. LISP has become the Latin of programming languages.[13]

At a higher level, the COMMON LISP phenomenon was part of a general shift in the sensibilities of AI that moved away from an interest in programming in general. This may be part of what caused the AI subfield of automatic programming, alive and well up through 1980, to disappear not too long afterward.

The notion that a small group of people can sit down and write a formal specification that can substitute for the ongoing efforts of a dynamic community is an example of what I call *formalist float.*

FORMALIST FLOAT

> *All people of broad, strong sense have an instinctive repugnance to the men of maxims; because such people early discern that the mysterious complexity of our life is not to be embraced by maxims, and that to lace ourselves up in formulas of that sort is to repress all the divine promptings and inspirations that spring from growing insight and sympathy.*
>
> —George Eliot, *The Mill on the Floss*

"My very educated mother just served us nine pizzas." At least that's what I learned in school as the mnemonic to remember the names of the nine planets, in order from the sun: Mercury, Venus, Earth, Mars, Jupiter, Saturn, Uranus, Neptune, Pluto. But if you ask nine very educated astronomers how many planets there are today, you'll get ten different answers.

The problem is that nobody ever bothered to define what a planet is. Everybody just knew. There were the original five "wanderers" known to stargazers since antiquity. Actually, there were seven: the sun and the moon were planets to the ancients, going around Earth like all the others in the Ptolemaic system. Copernicus swapped Earth for the sun in the inventory, and noted that the moon wasn't a planet because it really did go around Earth! In the Renaissance, mathematical physics and telescopes helped astronomers discover Uranus and Neptune. Finally Pluto was discovered in the twentieth century and added to the list. But things didn't stop there.

With automated telescopes and computer image analysis,

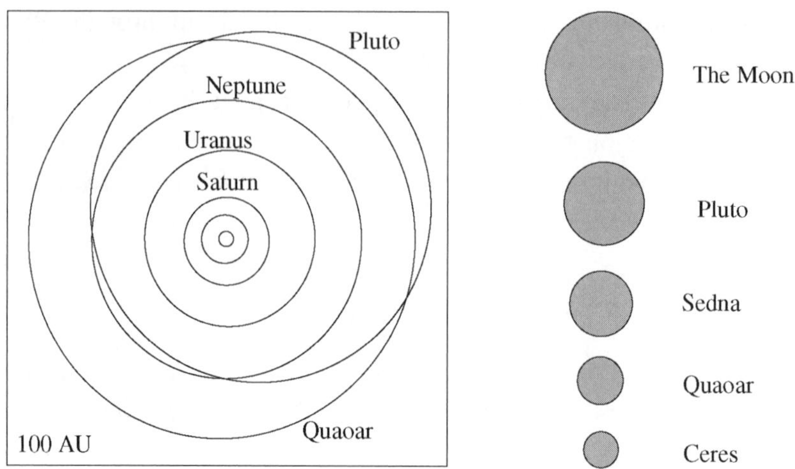

Fig. 5.2: Orbits and relative sizes of various objects.

astronomers have given the solar system a much closer look and have discovered new objects that look a lot like planets. Or not. There's quite a controversy going on as I write. (There are signs that the International Astronomical Union, the authoritative body in such matters, will have come to some conclusion about it by the time you read this.)

For example, the object called Quaoar could be argued to have a better right to be called a planet than Pluto. Its orbit is more centered, more circular, and lies closer to the flat plane of the other planets' than Pluto's, as seen in fig. 5.2. Sedna is bigger than Quaoar, but its orbit is highly elliptical and it doesn't even get close enough to show up in the diagram. Ceres, whose orbit is the smallest circle in the diagram, was considered a planet when it was first discovered.

Here are some of the things people talk about when claiming something is or isn't a planet:

1. It orbits the sun rather than some other body. (This keeps the moon from being a planet.)
2. Having its own moons is a point in its favor.
3. It's bigger than a certain size. The limit for a planet is some-

times drawn at seven hundred miles in diameter, the halfway point between the diameters of Ceres and Quaoar. That's the size at which gravity is strong enough to pull the object into a sphere.

4. It's well behaved. We expect planets to be fairly permanent features of the solar system.
5. It was formed by the same process as the other planets rather than having been captured from a passing star.

But at the moment, there's no agreement and no definition! How could astronomers have plied their craft for thousands of years without defining what a planet is? The point is simple and basic, but something that AI has managed to miss: we get to formal, well-defined concepts *after* we've understood what it is we're working with. The standard symbolic AI methodology requires having things formal and well-defined to start with. The thing we can do that AI programs can't is take a huge mass of random data and pull useful symbols and formalism out of it.

(Late-breaking news: After this was written, the IAU did meet and voted on a definition of *planet*. In doing so they demonstrated formalist float in action. Halfway through the week-long meeting, they had come up with a definition that produced three new planets: Ceres, Pluto's moon Charon, and a newly discovered body beyond Pluto and slightly larger than it called Xena. This definition relied heavily on point 3 above. Then there were some political moves made, and the subgroup of astronomers who were more interested in orbital dynamics wrested control from those who were more interested in the body itself and its geology. Thus, the final definition demoted not only the new planets but Pluto as well. Pluto is now officially minor planet number 134340. This didn't sit too well with many astronomers. The Division for Planetary Sciences of the American Astronomical Society waffled on the subject, stating, "All definitions have a degree of fuzziness that requires intelligent application: what does 'round' really mean? What does it mean to 'control a zone'?"[14] A separate group of three hundred astronomers has signed a petition protesting the definition and refuses to use it.[15])

Back on Earth now, can you yawn without closing your eyes? Normally, closing the eyes is part of a luxuriously indulged-in yawn. But all of the movements associated with a yawn are also under voluntary control, and it is possible to suppress them if you try hard enough. The question is, if you suppress the yawn enough to keep your eyes open, is it really a yawn? If you suppress it enough to keep your mouth closed, is it really a yawn?

If you simulate a yawn without having felt the involuntary urge to, is it a real yawn? Yawns are contagious; you can catch them from someone else, or even from yourself. If you simulate a yawn well enough to catch the urge to yawn halfway through, was that a real yawn?

It's not that we can't represent these things in language. I'm not standing in front of you yawning. I'm writing about it in language, or, from your point of view, I did so long ago and far away. But the word "yawn," like "planet," has fuzzy edges.

Fuzzy Language

Terry Winograd, creator of SHRDLU, the natural language-understanding program, famously wrote a book somewhat later that was seen by some as repudiating at least part of the AI enterprise.[16]

Consider the sentence, "Time flies like an arrow." This is a classic example of syntactic ambiguity in English. In addition to the standard meaning of time as a noun referring to the fourth dimension, you have to be able to interpret it as an adjective to understand phrases such as "time limit" (or *Time Bandits*). Flies are pestiferous insects, and "like" can be a verb meaning to enjoy—so the sentence can be parsed analogously to "Fruit flies like a banana."

But that's just scratching the surface. Even if we freeze the parse so that "flies" is the verb, there is an almost unlimited number of different interpretations. For example, "Time" can be a man's name (let's suppose his first name is Justin). Then the sentence can mean:

- Justin pilots his airplane in an arching, unswerving path (like that of an arrow in flight).
- He pilots it in a straight line, like the shape of an arrow.
- He hits something head-on rather than slowing down to land.
- He's a skywriter, and he's drawing the shape of a (possibly curving) typographical arrow symbol, complete with arrowhead, in the sky.
- He is rigid and unbending in regards to following FAA regulations.
- He sits stiffly erect in his seat while piloting.
- He sits stiffly erect in his seat as a commercial airline passenger.
- He takes commercial airline flights in a direct, no-nonsense manner.
- He works quickly, without extraneous activity.
- He darts quickly across a room.

And these are all with the same parse, and they have the same interpretation of "Time" as a person's name! In the more likely interpretation of "time" as duration, the sentence could refer to the fact that you haven't done all you wanted to today, or that you remember your childhood vividly even though it was fifty years ago, or anything in between.

In his book *Philosophical Investigations*, generally acknowledged to be one of the most important works of philosophy of the twentieth century, Ludwig Wittgenstein demolished the simplistic concept of semantics in which there is some fixed meaning for each word, with meanings stacked like bricks to form the meanings of sentences.[17] It is ironic that *Philosophical Investigations* was published in 1953, and the next several years saw a significant effort in automatic translation by computer, largely based on just such a concept. These efforts famously failed, leaving only a legacy of "The vodka is good, but the meat is rotten" jokes.*

*The apocryphal machine translation of the Russian for "The spirit indeed is willing, but the flesh is weak."

The remarkable thing about a sentence such as "Time flies . . ." is that even though it has a nearly infinite number of interpretations, you don't hear it as ambiguous unless you try to. Furthermore, close inspection reveals that ordinary conversation consists of sentences and fragments that would be just as ambiguous, taken in isolation, but that are normally understood as definite without any conscious feeling of having to choose between meanings.

Winograd himself, after the success of SHRDLU, ran head-on, like an arrow, into the difficulties of interpretation and the elusiveness of meaning. In *Understanding Computers and Cognition*, he discusses how hard it is to give a simple objective meaning to a sentence in terms of an example:

> Q: Is there any water in the refrigerator?
> A: Yes—in the cells of the eggplant.

Normally, the person who gave that answer would be accused of being a smart-ass and of deliberately misinterpreting the question—or acting like a logic-based computer blindly following rules and not understanding what was really being asked. Normally, someone asking about water in the refrigerator is thirsty.

Suppose, however, the preceding sentence had been something like "My high-speed film has been ruined by moisture." In such a case we'd recognize the answer as sensible and responsive. The moisture from the eggplant might well have caused the problem.

The English logician Keith Devlin, in his book *Goodbye, Descartes*, has similar things to say. George Lakoff, in *Women, Fire, and Dangerous Things*, shows roughly the same kind of thing about linguistic categories (the title refers to one of the genders in an aboriginal Australian language). And Norbert Wiener's later writings in the social criticism vein tried to say the same things about bureaucratic government and corporations.

If we try to take the meanings of words as the definition of rigid logical symbols and construct a system that operates by simple syntactic manipulations on them, it will miss much of the complexity that we do understand, in our flexible, informal way. To steal a phrase from Abraham Lincoln, the legs of such a system wouldn't be long enough to reach from its body to the ground. That's what I mean by formalist float.

Once upon a time, you could walk up to a lunch counter and there would be a short-order cook standing behind it. You told him what food you wanted, and he made it—be it a sandwich, a steak, eggs, bacon, in whatever combination. As long as he had the materials, you could describe what you wanted in English and you'd get it.

Nowadays, you walk into a fast-food franchise operation. Someone takes your order—but you must order from a menu that has a relatively small number of prespecified selections. The clerk rings it up on a register that doesn't even offer the ability to enter a numerical price: each key on its surface corresponds to one or another of the menu choices. Simple, quick, and efficient—but if you want something not on the menu, you're out of luck, even if all the ingredients are sitting right there in front of you.

Historical precedent for that kind of thing goes back quite a way. Agriculture fed more people more reliably than hunting, but the quality of the diet was poorer. Farming exercises less day-to-day judgment than hunting; crops stay in the same place and needn't be outwitted. People in agricultural societies worked harder and didn't grow as tall as hunters, and they had more deficiency diseases; but the food they did have was more reliable, and agricultural societies grew more populous. When the Hittites first introduced ironworking, iron tools and weapons were softer and more easily corroded than the brass and bronze they replaced; but iron is much more plentiful than tin, zinc, and copper, so everybody could have iron weapons. When guns replaced archery in the European Renaissance, the early muskets were much slower to load and had shorter range and poorer accuracy than the longbow. But any oaf could be trained to use a gun in a week, whereas it took years of practice to be an effective archer.

The Industrial Revolution, with the ability of machines to make vast numbers of identical products, gave a big impetus to the trend:

more stuff, fewer choices. The judgment calls were being made further and further back in the supply chain.

Virtually every major historical force in the past half millennium contributed to the advance of formalism. The printing press gave words a more fixed, less fluid form. Science replaced experienced judgment with calculation. Expanding empires produced bureaucracies, which tried to reduce their entire purview into fill-in-the-blanks report forms. Precision machinery needed exact fits, cataloged parts, and model and revision numbers. People writing laws and contracts tried ever harder to describe what might or might not happen in precise terms.

And then came the computer. Its intellectual underpinnings—symbolic logic, metamathematics, and information theory—essentially formalized formalization. It is now taken for granted that there is nothing that can't be reduced to bits of information and computational rules. There are even attempts to reduce physics to discrete forms directly, instead of digitally approximating the continuous forms of classical differential equations; but this is a mere shortcut, as physics was one of the leading forces of formalization in the first place. The "clockwork universe" was Newton's legacy.

The reason for this unbroken trend, not to say headlong rush toward increasing formalism, is simple: *it worked.* Science worked to explain the mysterious. Machines worked to produce power and haul freight and make cloth and tools and vehicles and above all, more machines. In nations that have industrialized, the human life span has doubled, and people are wealthier than those in nonindustrialized nations by orders of magnitude.

Actually, this view of the trend to formalization is somewhat nearsighted. It really began with language: the conceptual world was chopped up into pieces, and each one was assigned a specific symbol. But this was a devil's pact, and it applies not just to language but to any formalism. The world is much more complex than the formalism is. This has the advantage that the formalism is easier to understand, and if you can build a machine that faithfully reflects the formalism, it can be much easier to design a machine that works. But the soul that you sell for this capability is that, in so doing, you miss out on all the complexity underneath.

All this does not mean that language is useless—obviously we use it all the time, and it is of substantial value. What it means is that language, and the people who use it, are somehow a bridge between the formal and the informal. A formal system cannot operate without preformalized input. The processes underlying language, which produce and grasp meanings without definitions or other formal precursors, are what allow the formal systems we construct to connect with the real world and to do the things they do.

Symbolic AI systems live entirely above this divide. They float. This is, I believe, a substantial component of the glass ceiling: in current AI methodology, every concept in the system is preformalized by its writers. The writers prepackage what it needs ahead of time; the program can't "live off the land." When it doesn't have the appropriate concepts for some new situation, it cannot create them itself. This is easy to miss, because a formal system *can* create endless concepts as combinations of the preformalized concepts it already does contain.

Besides AI, another field of inquiry has wrestled with the problem of trying to describe the real world in formal terms for centuries. This is the law. A lawyer friend (some of my best friends are lawyers) describes the following problem:

> Two men sit down at a lunch counter and order cups of coffee. The first man finishes, gets up, and leaves a dime on the counter where he was sitting. He pays at the register and leaves.
>
> The second man gets up. He places his fingertip on the dime and slides it over to his spot on the counter. Then he, too, pays and leaves.

What, if anything, has been stolen? The dime, intended by the first man for the waitress, still goes to the waitress. The second man never picked it up or possessed it. He was not legally obligated to leave a tip. Yet we are morally certain that he stole something.

Lawyers and lawmakers have tangled with this interpretational difficulty since "An eye for an eye, a tooth for a tooth." It's referred to as the *open texture of the law*. The law avoids formalist float by using people. Most obviously, judges resolve contention by finding an interpretation of the law that best fits a given case. But more important, in the broad scheme of things, every person to whom the law applies has to interpret it with respect to the various situations we face all the time.

How many of the laws that nominally apply to you have you actually even read? I can think of the very few that I have, posted in places such as hotel rooms and elevators. The text of a law posted in elevators in Miami, Florida, a few years ago could, if taken literally, have prohibited anyone who had ever smoked a cigarette from riding. ("Any person who has ignited smoking materials . . ." And clearly, smoking animals or robots were exempted from the prohibition.) We automatically reinterpret the law to fit the real situation.

Yet we think of ourselves as law-abiding citizens. Most of us are, but the law we abide by is not the awkward, wordy, and often misstated verbosity our legislatures churn out. The real law is like the grammatical rules of language—subtle, distributed, dynamic—and impossible to write down formally.

Symbol Grounding

Formalist float is similar in many ways to a subject of concern in cognitive science called the *symbol grounding problem*. There are many cases in which the two concepts identify the same phenomenon; but ultimately I think that symbol grounding is not an adequate description of, or solution for, the problem.

Cognitive scientist Steven Harnad describes the symbol grounding problem as the problem you'd have trying to learn Chinese from a Chinese/Chinese dictionary. You don't know the meanings of the words and so you need to read their definitions—but they are all defined in terms of other Chinese words you don't know. A computer program, possessed only of internal symbols defined in terms of other symbols, is in the same boat; how can any such system ever get down to symbols that *mean* something?

What the "symbol grounding" formulation of the problem misses is that it is quite possible for a purely symbolic system to form a perfectly adequate model of arbitrarily complex phenomena. SHRDLU's model of the blocks world tabletop was sufficient to support very sophisticated linguistic behavior. In fact (and we will return to this point in our discussions of philosophy), there is no reason to think that there is anything going on in human minds that couldn't be described in purely formal terms.

There's been a lot of (in my mind misguided) effort at "solving" the symbol grounding problem by putting the computer into a robot, so that its symbols at some level are placed into correspondence with physical sensor readings, or coupling them with neural networks, or various other things. But the depth of the Turing Test and the flat-out *usefulness* of a machine that could pass it argues that there can be semantics in a system that simply reads and writes words and has no other connection to the physical world.

Insects have real sensors and effectors, and yet their nervous systems are comparable to a handwritten program in complexity. The moth that continues flying around your porch light for the five hundredth time is exhibiting the cluelessness of formalist float.

The key to semantics in a formal system isn't that it makes a connection to the real world; it's the fact that it is a Turing machine rather than a passive dictionary. It comes with a built-in notion of doing something, of taking the symbols it starts with and turning them into something else. It can take a description of the world today and turn it into a description of the world tomorrow. What matters is not whether the system has sensors that provide the descriptions, but whether it gets the prediction right.

If symbol grounding is not the problem, then, what is formalist float? Very simply it is the fact that all too often the predictions are wrong because the formal systems are way too simplistic. Noam Chomsky pointed out that when we hear a little of our native language and understand a syntax far more complex than we could logically have inferred from the sample, it is because we have a built-in set of possibilities we choose from rather than building one from scratch. Similarly, when we hear any individual sentence, we understand a much more complex description of the world than the sentence itself contained, because we use the sentence to select from possibilities in a model we already have.

Formalist float could be thought of as a continuously variable gap—how long the missing legs need to be—but in practice it tends to be the gap between systems of the complexity that we can handle as consciously understood inventions (or verbal sets of rules) and those of the complexity of the human mind acting in commonsense situations.

Is there anything to formalist float besides simply the lack of the necessary complexity? The word "float" is intended to suggest not only being too high to see clearly what's going on down on the ground, but also being unable to get traction and being unaffected by the reality below. Systems can float simply by lacking the appropriate feedback paths. This is famously true in bureaucracies, where executives have a tendency to design reporting and accounting practices that shield them from responsibility. This is the essence of Wiener's social criticisms. It is also true, perhaps to a greater extent, in modern software.

Software floats partly because designers can't be bothered, or don't have the foresight, to anticipate all contingencies in the program. But a deeper reason is that the sequential program is by its nature one of the most unresponsive forms of machine specification ever invented. Even a steam engine continuously "feels" a force pushing back on its shaft, and its governor adjusts the flow of steam to compensate. A sequential program only listens for its input at specific, predetermined times.

One of the software revolutions that happened after progress on LISP was frozen was the advent of event-driven graphical user interfaces. In these systems, small programs run in response to keystrokes and mouse clicks; but this is an ad hoc and error-prone patchwork solution. In my opinion, no programming language has ever come close to providing an elegant model of the functionality needed. The closest approach, LabVIEW, is a system commonly used in laboratories where the computer is connected to measuring instruments. LabVIEW allows the scientist to create a virtual circuit of meters, amplifiers, timers, and so on—including feedback loops—on the computer screen, and the system simulates it in real time. It's not a general-purpose programming language, though.

There is a new paradigm just beginning to emerge in the world of programming-language theory called reactive programming. This involves taking a full-fledged, general programming language and giving it semantics like LabVIEW. That is, each part of the program acts like a component in a circuit that is always active rather than waiting for the processor to execute it.[18]

Reactive programming may help the programming world handle feedback in an elegant way. This would not only help AI get its feet on the ground but would also cut development costs and the number of bugs in all interactive software in half while making it more responsive to the user.

Competence

"You had to be there." Often this phrase is used to indicate the difference between the telling and the experience. How, then, can we use language to convey useful information and skills?

We, like Ray Solomonoff's Turing machines, have internal mechanisms that model the world. Language breaks the possibilities into big pieces and allows us to indicate to each other which one we're thinking of. Our internal models take it the rest of the way, to make sense or to fit the situation. If the sign in the elevator had simply said, "No Smoking," it would not only have been easier to understand, it would have been correct.

CHAPTER 6
The New Synthesis

O wad some Power the giftie gie us
To see oursels as ithers see us!
It wad frae mony a blunder free us,
An' foolish notion . . .

—Robert Burns, *To a Louse*

IN THE NAME OF SCIENCE

It is ironic that for the better part of the twentieth century, as the physical sciences triumphed and the popular view of the age was as an enlightened and scientific one, that the two main branches of science whose proper study was mankind were in the doldrums of a dark age.

In anthropology, there was a backlash against the excesses of social Darwinism in the Victorian period. Under the leadership of Franz Boas, the "father of American anthropology," scientists studying human beings worked to eradicate some of the more pernicious notions that were then used as excuses for racism, eugenics, and the like. But Boasian anthropology threw out at least one baby with its bathwater. The doctrine of an extreme cultural relativism, taking perhaps a little unwarranted boost from a vague and fluffy similarity to relativity in physics, taught that humans had no intrinsic psychological nature at all but were completely programmed by their cultures.

This reached the height of silliness when in 1928, Margaret Mead, a student of Boas, published *Coming of Age in Samoa*, an account of the sexual mores (and other cultural aspects) of teenagers on that Pacific island.[1] She described them as sexually free and unbothered by the angst that characterized American teenagers. The problem is that Samoan culture was sexually quite rigid and almost obsessive over virginity, a common cultural attitude to sex in preindustrial human societies.

What happened is that Mead's respondents, young teenage girls, had indulged in another human universal: telling tall tales to the stranger.[2] It is as if a meteorologist had gone to tropical Samoa and had published, on the strength of stories, that the island was actually covered with glaciers, even though this was contrary to common sense and he had never actually seen any. This "evidence" became one of the keystones of Western anthropology for most of the century.

The second field that should have illuminated the structure of the mind was psychology. This was particularly to be expected from the very strong foundation that had been laid by William James. But for much of the mid-twentieth century, psychology was under the thrall of radical behaviorism, a school of thought led by B. F. Skinner. Behaviorism was an attempt to apply a strong empiricist discipline to the study of behavior by denying the existence of mental states, which after all were not objectively observable. Behaviorism may to some extent have been a reaction to the somewhat outre but popular theories of Sigmund Freud.

I should emphasize here that both Mead and Skinner were smart, insightful, dynamic individuals who did valuable and original work in their respective fields. Otherwise they would never have been able to mold the reigning paradigms as much as they did. (Mead did play a significant role in cybernetics, especially in its latter stages.)

Whatever the reasons, by midcentury the science of the mind was essentially devoid of content and largely incapable of explaining any observed phenomena of intelligence. The major implication of concern to us is that this was the received wisdom at midcentury, and it was a false signpost to virtually every attempt to understand, or artificially replicate, the functions of the brain. It seems likely, for example, that it is this scientific backdrop from which Alan Turing, in his famous 1950 paper, got the notion that the brain of a child was like a blank notebook.

If, however, you take a blank notebook and try to raise it as a child, you'll find yourself frustrated at every turn. You may provide the perfect environment, but the notebook just doesn't seem to have the native talents it takes to excel.

THE PROPER STUDY

Every thoughtful person looks upon the face of human nature with the confidence born of untested intuition, just as he gazes up at the moon and once in a while imagines going there. To a large extent, social theorists and intellectuals who had claimed human nature for their domain had been taking imaginary trips to the moon. They had repeatedly postponed the implications of the plain but awesome fact that the brain is a machine created by genetic evolution.

—E. O. Wilson and Charles Lumsden

The result of all this is that by the latter third of the twentieth century, the sciences of the mind stood greatly in need of a new paradigm. They got one, with something of a bang. The shot heard round the world was a magnum opus titled *Sociobiology: The New Synthesis* by Harvard biologist E. O. Wilson.[3] The noise was mostly echoes from the reactionary old guard in the social sciences, defending the blank notebook model of the mind. But nothing is so powerful as an idea whose time has come, and a substantive theory of mind was well overdue.

The basic idea in *Sociobiology* was that the behavior of animals is formed by evolution just as their physical structure is, and is thus accessible to the same kind of analysis. Cybernetics had already started its own revolution, starting with Wiener and Rosenblueth's *Teleology* paper. Finally, philosopher Jerry Fodor waged a frontal attack on the blank notebook model by showing that the mind had various modules with specific functions (which communicated in what he called "the language of thought").

These three legs together form a stable basis for a new science of cognition. Their confluence has been called the New Synthesis, by Fodor among others, in a conscious echo of the term the Modern Synthesis, which is used in biology to label the reigning paradigm that is a confluence of Darwinian evolution and Mendelian genetics.

Evolutionary Psychology

> *What a piece of work is a man! how noble in reason! how infinite in faculty! in form and moving how express and admirable! in action how like an angel! in apprehension how like a god!*
>
> —William Shakespeare, *Hamlet*

It was perhaps because the social sciences were so strongly set against the evils of social Darwinism that psychology resisted, for a century, using what had become the central organizing principle and the most powerful tool for the rest of biology: the theory of evolution by natural selection. Even so, it seems a bit absentminded to forget your most powerful tool when tackling your hardest problem.

It would seem downright antediluvian, or at least antebellum, in any other area of the study of natural organisms, to proceed without any reference to the proposition that the object of study had formed as the result of an accumulation of adaptations to environmental pressures. Yet it took until 1975 and Wilson's *Sociobiology* for the issue to be addressed in a serious scholarly way—and when it was, Wilson was viciously attacked by social scientists because it was politically forbidden to think in those terms. In the storm of controversy that followed, anthropologist John Tooby and psychologist Leda Cosmides introduced a somewhat more focused version under the name of evolutionary psychology.

Oddly enough, the key notion of evolutionary psychology goes back to William Paley, a pre-Darwinian British cleric who was trying to argue for the existence of God. He pointed out that natural creatures seem obviously designed for specific functions in their environments (and thus concluded that they must have had a Designer). Darwin, in producing a better explanation for the provenance of the design, only underscored the key fact that organisms are designed, and designed for specific functions. (He also underscored the fact that many of the functions are flagrantly at odds with anything a benevolent, anthropomorphic deity could possibly intend. Darwin famously observed, "What a book a devil's chaplain might write on the clumsy, wasteful, blundering low and horridly cruel works of nature!")[4]

One of the deeper aspects of the revolution in thought forged by the theory of evolution is the ascription of teleological force—purpose, design—to a purely mechanistic process. Evolution really does seem to be designing organisms *for* something. There seems to be some foresight, some backward causality, going on. But what's really going on is a form of feedback. If we view the chain of birth, growth, competition, mating, and birth as a cycle instead of simply as a linear process, there is a causal path from competition to birth. In reality it is to the birth of the next generation, but the fact of strongly conserved traits in reproduction allows us to superimpose the generations and view the system as a feedback loop.

Evolutionary psychology simply says that the mind was designed that way as well as the body. This applies on many levels: why do we have certain behavioral tendencies, what are emotions and other mental phenomena, and how are our brains structured? More speculatively, but just as important, it gives us a hint that we should look for the same kinds of feedback loops in the mind itself, when we try to understand how the mind, too, can produce teleology from mere mechanism.

Computational Theory of Mind

> *Yes, you* do *know what it feels like to be a mind simulated on a computer.*
>
> —Marvin Minsky

If the brain is an adapted organ, then, ignoring its structure for the moment, what is its function? The answer is simple: it's a computer.

As we saw, the notion of the mind as the workings of a machine was first broached by Leibniz, and brought into focus by cybernetics. By midcentury, mathematician/philosopher Hilary Putnam had formulated a position called *functionalism*, a philosophical school of thought that equates the mind to a computer.[5] Growing out of functionalism (and leaving behind many of its philosophical minutia, such as whether a specific mind is equivalent to one specific Turing machine or a class of them) is a general point of view called the *computational theory of mind.*

Now when you think of a computer, you may have in mind the one on your desk that lives in a beige box and runs WORD, AUTOCAD, THE SIMS, or WORLD OF WARCRAFT. That's not exactly the meaning of computer I'm talking about. In particular, I'm absolutely not talking about how it's made or how it works. I'm interested exactly and only in what it's capable of doing as seen from the outside.

What computers do, as seen from the outside, is to receive signals—information—and then to produce other signals. A wide variety of physical phenomena can act as signals, for input or output, but as long as the relation of the information to the carrier is well defined, the form is irrelevant. What is relevant is *only* the information that the signals carry.

What kinds of things can a computer do with the information? In the most general description, the only thing it can do is output more information; any more specific description requires a characterization of what information it gets and what you want out of it. It could be formatting Web pages, or solving equations, or running physics simulations, or controlling robotic bodies, or forwarding e-mail—anything you can specify that can be done exclusively by receiving and transmitting information.

In between the input and output, the physical form the computation takes doesn't matter. It can be gears and shafts, wires and relays, thousands of clerks with abacuses handing index cards back and forth, strings, pulleys, and Tinkertoys, silicon microchips—or neurons.

Again, how the computer computes the information it outputs is not important to this part of the synthesis, either. It could be a Turing machine, a lambda calculus machine, a Post production machine (also called a tag system, a theoretical construct like the others). It could be serial or parallel. It could be digital or analog. It could use gears, chemistry, or water wheels. All that matters is that that it embodies some physical process that produces the right output signal from the given input signal.

For example, fig. 6.1 is a circuit diagram of a three-tube superheterodyne radio receiver, such as your grandfather might have used to listen to Roosevelt's fireside chats. For our purposes, it is a computer: it takes three input signals, one the radio-frequency (RF) current from the antenna, and two encoded as knob angles. It selects a band

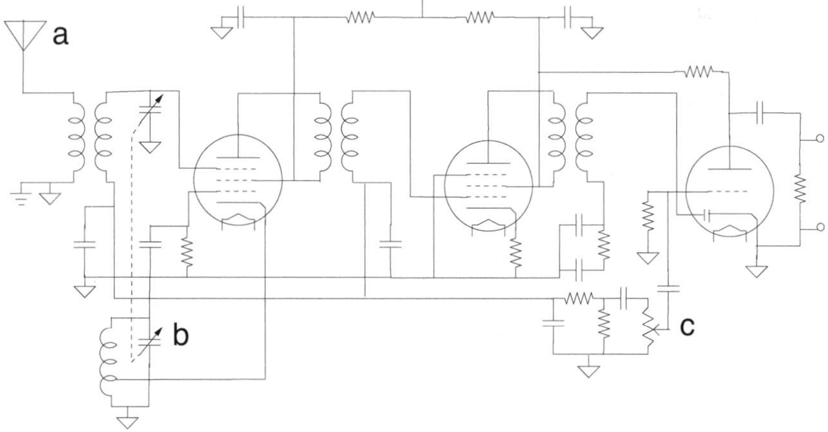

Fig. 6.1: A three-tube superheterodyne radio receiver, with (a) antenna, (b) tuning, and (c) volume.

from the RF signal as specified by the tuning knob, and amplifies it into sound at a volume specified by the volume knob.

It would be possible, if you had a fast enough processor, to digitize the input signals, do all the processing by means of a program manipulating binary numbers, and reconvert the numbers into current to be fed to the speaker. And in fact that's exactly what happens in a modern digital radio.

This is the assumption of the computational theory of mind. The function of the brain is to output the right signals given the signals it inputs. Nothing else. It sows not, neither does it reap. It's not linked to the astral plane. It's not a muscle. It's not a pump. It's not a sensory organ. It can't bend spoons. It's a computer.

So if the brain is a computer, what's the mind? This is one of those vexing philosophical questions that goes back to antiquity. We are finally in a position to give an answer: it's the computation. It's the process—the sequence of patterns of information and causation—that characterizes which outputs the brain will produce, given its inputs.

This is a new deal. The philosophers of antiquity didn't have computers to help them develop an understanding of what computational processes can be like. They didn't even have superheterodyne tube radios. Yet the computational theory of mind can bridge the old dilemma of how the mind can be ethereal, dealing with logic and truth, and still have an effect in the world of matter. The age-old conundrum just vanishes.

Massive Modularity

When I was a schoolboy, my teachers told me that living cells were composed of protoplasm, a substance with mysterious properties. They were slightly behind the times; there was a new understanding of the molecular machinery inside the cell, but it hadn't filtered down into grammar-school biology textbooks yet.

They didn't even discuss how the mind worked, but if they had, they would have had to give roughly the same kind of account: that the brain was an undifferentiated mass of some stuff with mysterious properties. Now we can do better: like the cell, the brain is a machine; it has working parts with specific functions.

At a high level of understanding, perhaps the simplest way to apply evolutionary theory to the brain is to compare it with the body. The human body is not an undifferentiated mass of protoplasm, but it is structured as a system of different organs with different functions, which operate together, synergistically, to constitute a living creature with remarkable capabilities. So it is with the brain.

The first preprinted pages were added to the blank notebook model by Noam Chomsky, whose revolutionary study of human-language acquisition showed that there was no way that a child could learn the syntax of a natural language (specifically, pick out the syntax it does have from all the other possible syntaxes it might have) given the limited sampling of a language a child actually hears. There must be, he concluded, a built-in template for the kinds of syntax allowed in human languages, thus limiting the range of possibilities and making it easier to pick the right one.

Then a behavioral rulebook was added by Wilson with *Sociobiology*, and Fodor added the illustrations by means of his observations on vision in *Modularity of Mind*.[6] Over the years various new modules were added to the theory. Then in the 1990s cognitive scientist Dan Sperber sought to get a handle on how far the process could go by advancing an intentionally extremist position that the mind was *entirely* modular. Somewhat to his surprise, the theory has stood up to numerous assaults. It is now generally referred to as *massive modularity*.

Furthermore, the term *module* has been broadened by various usages since Fodor introduced it with a rather precise definition.

The following have been claimed to be embodied in, or specific to, modules in the mind:[7]

- Language: the classic Chomsky organ of syntax.
- Vision: "optical illusions" give us a hint that there are interpretational processes we can't control consciously.

- Mating: we have built-in criteria for mate selection and hard-wired reward systems that work similarly to drug addiction.[8]
- Habitat selection: we've felled much of North America's forests and planted grass to make it look more like the African savanna.
- Mental maps: not only of space, but of time and organizations and much else.
- Number: babies at seven months already have a numerical sense, well before they can talk.[9]
- Biology: it took a sophisticated understanding of what things were edible and when they were ripe, what things were poisonous or otherwise dangerous, and the like to survive as a forager. We are predisposed to learn concepts in forms that reflect the logic of biology.
- Our concept of kinds falls easily into hierarchies that match family trees.
- Our concept of essence is a good match with the properties of animals and plants. You may carve a poisonous mushroom into the shape of a good one, but it's still poisonous.
- Mechanics: the brain is first and foremost a body controller, and it's an amazingly sophisticated one.
- Causality (and superstition): in order to do actions that cause things to happen, we have to have an understanding of what actions cause what thing. As a heuristic, we tend to over- rather than under-impute causality to our actions.
- Danger/risk, physical: stand next to a cliff or a lion, you'll feel it.
- Danger/risk, social: you'll feel this when the boss comes at you with a frown.
- Food: shouldn't need much explanation.
- Contamination/disgust: an adaptation to manage risk of microbial disease.
- Happiness: so you'll know when things are going well and try to keep them that way.
- Folk psychology: our models of other people's intents, desires, and emotions.

- List of individuals with models and balance sheets: the "mental rolodex."
- Self-concept(s): you knew ego had to be in there.
- Justice: rights and wrongs (more on this in detail later).
- Throwing: we are the *only* animal that can throw hard and accurately enough for it to constitute an effective hunting mode.
- Reading: this is probably the best example of a learned module, making use of other innate ones.
- Fire: we've been using fire so long that we've actually evolved to be fascinated by it. The keeper of the flame who either let it go out or get out of control was not destined for success.
- Music: there is surely some special-purpose wiring from our perceptions of rhythmic and/or tonal sound to our emotional apparatus.

Some of these are innate, some are learned. Some are instinctive biases, some are full-fledged perceptual machinery. Some appear to be localized in the brain and surely others are not. *Module* gets used for a wide variety of things, but in each case there is a conceptually separable function the module does.

The Fox and the Crow

Once upon a time, according to Aesop, there was a crow who had found a piece of cheese. He was sitting on the branch of a tree, holding it in his beak, and was about to have it for lunch. Along came a crafty fox, who saw the crow and the cheese, and wanted the cheese for himself. So the fox spoke to the crow and flattered him, saying what a marvelous voice the crow had and how much he, the fox, enjoyed listening to the crow sing and how pleasant it would be to hear the crow sing just then. So the crow, unused to hearing these blandishments, was filled with pride and sang lustily. Of course in so doing, he dropped the cheese, which the fox grabbed and ate.

How are we to understand this story?[10] Is the fox merely smarter than the crow? If so, it is simply a story of a stronger character beating a weaker one, and that's hardly interesting. And yet the story is a classic with lasting appeal. We can all see that the fox has done something clever, and we are drawn to listening to such stories because they give us the wherewithal to emulate the fox's triumph, or at the very least, to avoid the crow's discomfiture.

If the story were a chess game, it would be trivial in the extreme: an opening gambit by the fox, an immediate fatal mistake by the crow on the very next move—a fool's mate. How can the crow be so stupid? As the story is commonly explained, the crow is blinded by his vanity and the moral is simply that vanity leads you into error. But I think something more subtle is going on. After all, if the crow is really all that vain, he might find a piece of cheese a reasonable price to pay for effusive praise!

But no: the fox really is clever and the crow gets fooled. We appreciate the story because we can imagine being fooled the same way. What's clever about the fox's solution is that he realizes that the crow will fail to make what should be a simple, one-step deduction about opening his mouth and dropping the cheese. Specifically, the fox has engaged the crow in using a different *mental module* than the one with which the crow would (easily) make the prediction and thus keep the cheese. The crow would normally use a "possession and properties of physical objects" module in situations where he is faced with a competitor for a chunk of food. If the fox had made a physical play for the cheese, the crow would never have let go. But the fox has started the interaction in the realm of a "social intercourse" module, where all the action is verbal. In ordinary thought, modeling and prediction are generally confined to a single module; jumping from module to module constitutes unusual cleverness.

A Mass of Modules

One of the main open questions to be confronted by the New Synthesis is whether the brain is entirely modular, or is there a general-purpose portion? We'll ignore the semantic dodge of calling a general-purpose part a module and concentrate on the substantive question.

The main reason to think that there is a general-purpose portion is that we seem to be able to learn a wide, almost arbitrary variety of things, and we come to understand things quite comfortably and expertly that are wildly different from the kinds of things that our ancestors dealt with, such as computer architectures, Web browsers, futures markets, crossword puzzles, and the moral epistemology of the Scottish Enlightenment.

There is a kind of "concept blindness" that is engendered by the modular structure, which is exemplified in the fox and crow story. But humans have the ability to see beyond it, cover the gaps, and make up and tell such stories for exactly that purpose. Unlike a structure founded strictly on modules, we have the ability to keep learning. We don't hit a wall, where our modules max out.

This is why I use the word *autogeny*. An autogenous system is one that *can* extend itself arbitrarily, specifically to contrast with one that merely varies within preconceived limits. The word "learning" is vague enough that it gets applied to everything from Hexapawn* to Newton's discovery of the calculus.

The theory in cognitive science that assumes a general processor/representation is called the *language of thought*. It is most closely associated with Jerry Fodor, and Fodor is a critic of massive modularity. I personally lean toward modularity, but I think that there must be some general-purpose mechanisms that manipulate the modules, and thus it would be confusing to call these mechanisms *modules* themselves. The human brain seems to be like an iceberg: most of it (the specialized modular part) lies below the water level of conscious accessibility, but just enough general, rational autogenous ability sticks up to make the difference. I'll have more to say about this in the next chapter.

---

*Hexapawn is a game played with six pawns on a three-by-three chessboard, which was designed specifically to be learnable by a simple machine.

RENAISSANCE

Then felt I like some watcher of the skies
When a new planet swims into his ken . . .

—John Keats, *On First Looking into Chapman's Homer*

Throughout the twentieth century, the forces of political correctness did a Lysenko job on the sciences of the mind, but to an extent that has lessened considerably since the 1970s. The dark ages appear to be passing.

There is now a solid core of cognitive science—in simple terms, the study of how minds work—that is informed by a convergence of artificial intelligence, psychology, and neuroscience. Not only are the fields growing out to cover the areas between, but the instruments available are also improving almost daily. Researchers not only run rats through mazes, but they also register the firing of individual neurons with amazingly precise probes as they run. Psychologists not only quiz people with ingenious tests, but they also map the activation in their brains with functional MRI machines as they answer. Computers model ever-larger collections of data and more complex theories.

Many AIers, starting with Turing, simply assume an operational definition of intelligence—"anything that acts like an intelligent creature"—and leave the discussion there. There is an implicit assumption that once an AI passes the Turing Test, intuitive doubts as to its qualities of mind will evaporate in the face of experience. I'm sure they will: this happens well before it should. The ELIZA effect and its turbocharged latter-day cognates involving robots with body language and facial expressions are strong warnings that our intuitions about other minds are less reliable than we like to think.

Even if carried out by a skeptical cognitive scientist, the Turing Test provides only a relatively static snapshot of an AI and misses the plasticity and autogeny that mark the ability of a human mind to learn and grow.

Thus, philosophers can reject an operational definition of mind with some justification. However, this leaves us with something of a vexing question as to just what mind might actually be. The philosopher Leibniz put it this way:

> Supposing that there were a machine whose structure produced thought, sensation, and perception, we could conceive of it as increased in size with the same proportions until one was able to enter into its interior, as he would into a mill. Now, on going into it he would find only pieces working upon one another, but never would he find anything to explain perception.[11]

For perception we can substitute any subjective phenomenon, up to and including the experience of conscious will. The really odd thing is that this analysis appears to stand up against any explanation! In particular it stands up to a modern version of the scenario:

> Suppose that you have been abducted by Martians and taken to their laboratory, where they put you into an super-nanoscope that allows them, and you, to observe any aspect of your body or brain at any scale down to the molecular. The Martians are able to discover, with you looking over their shoulders, that absolutely everything you do or feel can be explained by physics, chemistry, or biology; any decision you make, any action you take, is completely predictable by mechanistic scientific laws.

A human, too, is a "mere" machine; there is no more free will to be found in DNA, ribosomes, and mitochondria than in gears, shafts, and pulleys. We will find this a challenge when we return at some length to the philosophy of mind; but for a purely scientific explanation, Leibniz's insight holds. There's mechanism in there, and only mechanism. The succeeding centuries of science have simply filled in the details. The computational theory of mind says that the devil *is* the details. Schools of thought holding vitalistic or dualistic views have retreated steadily since the Enlightenment.

The end is in sight.

CHAPTER 7
Beyond Human Ken?

Von Neumann sometimes spoke of a "complexity barrier." This was the imaginary border separating simple systems from complex systems. A simple system can give rise to systems of less complexity only. In contrast, a sufficiently complex system can create systems more complex than itself. . . . [Exact] self-reproduction is a feature of systems right on the complexity barrier—systems that preserve but do not increase their level of complexity in their offspring.

—William Poundstone, *The Recursive Universe*

UNIVERSAL INTELLIGENCE

People who think about AI can be divided into two camps. On the one hand, we have the serious, conservative, academic researchers who build robots, measure potentials between rats' neurons, and fill pages with dense equations. On the other we have people who are less focused on details and try to extrapolate the capabilities of AI into the future using more abstract mental models.

Worries about AI "taking off" into a dangerous superintelligence are largely confined to the second group. The concept is sometimes called *recursive self-improvement*, although the term doesn't capture the difference between it and just plain vanilla self-improvement that is usually meant. What they are worried about is *unlimited* self-improvement.

The first group tends to dismiss the concept of such an AI that could take off as an example of the *bootstrap fallacy*. Unlimited self-improvement, they say, is just a chimerical notion with no basis in fact. This is equivalent to saying that the barrier is really a barrier.

Fifty years ago, there was no such separation. McCarthy, von Neumann, and Turing all made the study of self-improvement an integral part of their other efforts.

Thus, we have a question that is crucial to our investigation: Is there a level of capability at which a program is truly autogenous and can improve itself without limit? If this isn't possible, then any AI we create will just be a wind-up toy, albeit possibly one with a very big spring; but we won't have to worry about it taking off into superintelligence.[1]

We'll pose the question in a form that is easier to analyze: Is there a form of a universality in learning machines that is analogous to universality in a formal model of computation? *Computational universality* means that there are some computers about which we can say that no other computer can compute something ours can't, given enough time and memory. Any program that can be run on any other computer—past, present, or theoretically possible—can be run on our universal computer by means of a program, called an interpreter, that simulates the other computer. It may just take longer. Because Turing proved the concept of universality before any physical computers were invented, most actual computers have been built to be universal. So the ALTAIR 8800 I built in my dorm room in the mid-1970s could have, in theory, calculated anything a modern $30 million, 100 teraflop IBM BLUE GENE can—but it would have taken my ALTAIR about 317 years to do what the BLUE GENE does in one second.[2]

If a learning machine is capable of unlimited self-improvement, it will have something like universality. Even if one machine starts out stupid and ignorant compared to another one, if its self-improving ability is unlimited it can simply improve itself until it is equal. Thus, there is a sense in which any two unlimited self-improving machines are equivalent, the only difference being speed. If you can get past von Neumann's barrier at all, you're free and clear.

Learning universality is not at all the same as computational universality; I'm defining this new concept by analogy only. From here on I'll use the word *universality* by itself to refer to this hypothetical learning and self-improvement capability, and when I refer to computational (Turing machine) universality, I'll say so explicitly.

It's valuable to make a distinction between two closely related concepts. Let's assume, for example, that human intelligence is competent, in the fullness of time, to create an artificial intellect the equal of a human in that regard.[3] This AI would be capable, in its turn, of creating an intellect of the same level; but neither the AI nor the human is thus necessarily capable of arbitrary unbounded self-improvement. The possibility would remain that human intelligence is not (quite) universal—that it sits squarely on von Neumann's barrier.[4] Thus, while some of the arguments below resemble ones against (or for) human-level AI, they are distinct; in particular, many of the common arguments about AI per se do not address the issue of universality.

Another distinction to be made is simply the question of processing speed. At least some of the difference in IQ in humans is simply a difference in speed; clearly, for Turing-equivalent computers at least, a difference in speed does not imply a difference in ultimate function. It is difficult to contemplate an AI one thousand times faster than a human and not consider it strictly more powerful; but in the following we will attempt to keep the notion of boundedness-of-learning ability separate from processor speed.

There remain two separable questions: Whether there is a universal level or form of intelligence, and whether human intelligence qualifies. We consider first the arguments against universality; clearly, if it is impossible in general, then humans are not universal.

THE CASE AGAINST UNIVERSALITY

The Argument from Animals

The world abounds with species that have been called intelligent: crows, gray parrots, dolphins, whales, and chimpanzees are typical examples. All of these animals learn, many in ways that are as yet not well understood. Most mammalian predators teach their young hunting skills; house cats even house-train their kittens. The learned skills of the primates are widely noted.

However, chimpanzees will never create even a chimp-level AI, no matter how long they work on it. Learning in all the animals is strictly limited; there is a clear ceiling on the kinds of concepts, or even associations, they can form.

The same argument can be made for the human animal. We learn rapidly and copiously, especially through childhood, but in well-defined phases, such as in language acquisition. There is clearly much that we are programmed to learn, again in many ways that are not understood; but as with language, these programs run their course and we attain a maturity with a stable—and static—understanding of the world.

Humans do not experience runaway positive feedback or exponential self-improvement.

No known example of actual intelligence has the proposed universality; therefore it is incumbent on its proponents to show how it might actually work, and no one has done so.

The Argument from Experience

The AI community has not failed to build general learning machines for lack of trying. In the original Dartmouth conference proposal, one of the seven "aspects of the artificial intelligence problem" to be studied was:

5. *Self-Improvement*

> Probably a truly intelligent machine will carry out activities that may best be described as self-improvement. Some schemes for doing this have been proposed and are worth further study. It seems likely that this question can be studied abstractly as well.[5]

In 1969 John McCarthy wrote, "Our ultimate objective is to make programs that learn from experience as effectively as humans do. It may not be realized how far we are presently from this objective." He had first proposed his ADVICE TAKER in 1958. It was seminal to substantial work in situation logics, planning, and knowledge representation (including the classic monkey-and-bananas problem) but never exhibited the kind of general learning capability that was its motivation. Throughout the early history of AI, there was a steady stream of attempts at a general cognitive architecture, ranging from GPS to SOAR, intended to be capable of learning in a humanlike way. None was successful. Systems seemed to fall on two sides of a divide: those that learned from experience couldn't learn outside a predefined area, and those that were general "learned" by being programmed.

The later efforts most often mentioned in connection with the bootstrap fallacy are Lenat's AM and EURISKO. This is ironic because they came the closest to exhibiting the kind of learning that was desired; but merciless critics nevertheless called them "wind-up toys" with some justification.

The most obvious way for an intelligent program to extend its capabilities is by writing more code. For the first quarter century of AI, automatic programming was a strong subfield, well represented, for example, in the *Handbook of Artificial Intelligence*, which summarizes the state of the field, ca. 1980.[6] Soon thereafter, however, automatic programming languished and has largely disappeared.[7] Its only strong remnant, genetic programming, exhibits exactly the same search-limited ceiling on complexity that haunted AM and EURISKO.

The Argument from Inductive Bias

Any learning system must have what's called an *inductive bias*. This is essentially a restriction on the theories it can propose. The faster and more effective the learning, the stronger the bias. The classic example is children learning language fast because of Chomsky's innate grammar structures. The stronger the bias, the more restricted the generality of learning and the more likely the process is to lodge in a local maximum.[8] Suppose you're standing in the lobby of the Empire State Building and you want to go up. Having the elevator right there is like a strong inductive bias—it gets you up, fast. But once you're at the top floor, you're stuck. If instead you had hopped into a cab, you wouldn't have gotten as high as quickly, but you could have driven to the airport and ultimately gotten higher. This argument can be seen as a special case of the comparison of weak (general-purpose) and strong (special-purpose) methods in representation and search: strong methods are brittle, and weak ones don't work for problems of nontrivial size.

The conclusion is that any usable learning system must be of limited generality, so universal systems must be impossible.

THE CASE FOR UNIVERSALITY

> *The more I have studied him, the more Newton has receded from me. It has been my privilege at various times to know a number of brilliant men, men whom I acknowledge without hesitation to be my intellectual superiors. I have never, however, met one against whom I was unwilling to measure myself, so that it seemed reasonable to say that I was half as able as the person in question, or a third or a fourth, but in every case a finite fraction. The end result of my study of Newton has served to convince me that with him there is no measure. He has become for me wholly other, one of the tiny handful of supreme geniuses who have shaped the categories of the human intellect, a man not*

> *finally reducible to the criteria by which we comprehend our fellow beings.*
>
> —Richard Westfall,
> *Never at Rest: A Biography of Isaac Newton*

Unlike the negative case, the mere fact that universality was possible would not establish that human intelligence is in fact universal. Some of the arguments below leave this question open; others proceed by arguing that humans are universal, implying universality is possible.

Algorithmic Probability

Ray Solomonoff's inductive inference is *provably complete*.[9] This means that given any string of symbols whatsoever, algorithmic probability reveals any regularities it may contain and provides a method for predicting its continuation. This is only suggestive, because algorithmic probability is incomputable; but the fact that it is incomputable makes it possible to prove it's complete.[10]

The reason this is suggestive is that there appears to be no barrier to increasingly better approximations to the incomputable ideal. This in some sense reflects what our instincts tell us about an open-ended learning machine—we could hardly expect, from our current limited knowledge, to be able to say much more about it! And at the same time it precludes there being any impossibility theorem that would cut us off short at any fixed level.

The Argument from Biological Self-Reproduction

This is an argument by analogy. We observe that no existing engineered manufacturing system is capable of self-reproduction and, therefore, arguments similar to ones against universality could be made on this basis. However, biological cells are self-reproducing, acting as an existence proof for this somewhat counterintuitive capability. It was this analogy that led von Neumann to study self-reproducing machines in the first place.

The core of the analogy is the notion that the self-referential structures at the heart of a cell, or in von Neumann's self-reproducing machine architecture, overcome the difficulties of self-reproduction by (yet another) form of universality. In a cell, for example, most of the mechanism is made of proteins. Proteins are made of sequences of amino acid molecules that are put together by a ribosome. Different shapes, and thus different functions, of protein are achieved by having different sequences of the twenty different kinds of amino acid. The ribosome, which makes the proteins, can assemble any sequence of amino acids; thus, it is a "universal constructor" in von Neumann's sense. We can imagine that a similar self-referential and universal ability might be possible for a "concept constructor" in the mind.

We suppose that a universal mind, composed of software, might have the capability to create more software that augments its capabilities in a way analogous to how a young animal grows into a large one, without limit in some cases, such as with reptiles. The limit is imposed by the environment, not the system; the same could be true for a learning machine.

The Argument from Evolution

Darwin didn't understand genes; even today evolution is not completely understood. We can quote McCarthy again:

> It is very difficult to see how the genetic representation scheme manages to be general enough to represent the great variety of animals observed and yet be such that so many interesting changes in the organism are represented by small genetic changes. The problem of how such a representation controls the development of a fertilized egg into a mature animal is even more difficult.[11]

And yet somehow the genetic representation scheme does it. Much remains to be learned, but progress has been substantial. One of the missing pieces appears to be very similar to the same organizing principle needed for universality of mind. Evolution faces exactly the same problem as AM (or AI in general): it does some search and builds a structure. Having the structure to work with makes the search space bigger—each choice of what to add next includes the new part as well as all the old ones. Evolution should have run out of steam with unicellular life as AM did with number theory. That it didn't implies there is a technique or techniques that continue to reduce the search space as complexity is created. Otherwise we wouldn't be here.

If this is true, it seems likely that the technique could be adapted for software search; perhaps a parallel could also be drawn to the brain's search algorithm in general learning. This argument does not directly imply that humans are universal learners, but if we can discover the search-space-reducing mechanism, it will have essentially the same effect as far as AI is concerned.

The Subjective Argument

In examining our experience with learning, many of us do not feel that there is a set limit to what we could learn, given enough time and attention. There are clearly limits to the rate and, given our finite lifetimes, to the total volume we can learn. We feel we are like slow Turing machines with short tapes, which but for these limitations could be universal.

One possible objection to this argument is by analogy to the *flashlight theory of consciousness*: consciousness seems pervasive because we're not conscious of what we're not conscious of. It's clear that our built-in representation modules have strong limits: we can't visualize four-dimensional objects, for example. Yet our general learning ability can find ways for us to represent them so that we can manipulate them mentally, predict their properties, and use them to model other things. This gets easier the more we work with them.

It's also clear that there are plenty of individuals who hit a wall with math, or programming, or thermodynamics, or economics, or art, or music, or whatever. Yet there are also other individuals who are extreme polymaths and have no trouble with any field: Leonardo da Vinci springs to mind, as do Gottfried Leibniz, Benjamin Franklin, James Clerk Maxwell, and John von Neumann.

The Argument from Human Uniqueness

Humans, as we noted before, come with almost the same genetic endowment as chimps, yet our evolutionary results are almost as different as possible. Neanderthals were even closer, and they're not just endangered, they're extinct. Given that the difference in effect has been the innovation and use of technology, it is hard to escape the conclusion that the difference in cause is that we crossed some mental watershed as the homonid brain developed from the simian.

It is hard to escape the conclusion that Neanderthals had more specialized mental organs than we do, but we came with the one general-purpose organ that made the difference. The human result is so outrageously different from that of any similar animal that it stands in need of a qualitative, not merely quantitative, explanation. A general, unlimited ability to learn and innovate fills the bill.

The Argument from the Scientific Community

We can draw another analogy to the scientific community. Any human individual is limited by a dismally low bandwidth in transferring information to the long-term memory, probably limited by total memory and by advancing senescence and ultimate mortality. The scientific community as a whole is not. There does not appear to be any upper bound on what science can learn in the long run. At any given time, the reigning paradigms limit vision in a way consonant with the limits of individuals; but the course of science as a whole can be charted as a sequence of paradigm shifts. From the right perspective, this is the normal operation of science on a historical timescale.

Concepts common in science and throughout the rest of technological civilization are often wildly foreign to the environment of ancestral adaptation. An example immediately at hand is the metamathematical theory underlying the concept of the universal computer: this is not something our ancestors needed to be able to think about. Much of scientific understanding requires the suppression of native intuitions; our inborn understanding of up, down, and solid ground must give way to Newtonian physics and planets spinning through space. We have the ability to build on top of our built-in special-purpose learning modules if we want, or if necessary, to bypass them completely.

If we can build a machine that exhibits human-level intelligence, we can build one that emulates the scientific community. The universal level of learning capability reduces to the "mere" human level after all. Historically, science and technology *have* exhibited positive-feedback self-improvement along an exponential trend line. The universality hypothesis must be true.

CONCLUSIONS

My lord, 'tis but a base ignoble mind
That mounts no higher than a bird can soar.

—William Shakespeare, *Henry VI*

The argument from the scientific community seems the most compelling. The arguments for the fallacy of bootstrapping are primarily the generalization of experience with brains and systems below the level of universality.

It may well be that the individual, average human mind is not quite universal. A research scientist needs an IQ of about 140, which agrees with the fact that roughly 1 percent of the population become scientists or engineers.[12] There was no need, in the ancestral environment, for everyone to innovate. One percent was plenty.

We know that humans with IQs of up to 200 or so can exist; thus, such levels of intelligence are possible. People such as da Vinci,

Newton, and Einstein are generally thought to have seen things that ordinary people couldn't, no matter how long they took. Might it be the case that a sped-up AI with an IQ of 100 would simply get a lot of work done, while a sped-up AI with an IQ of 140 or 200 would improve itself in an exponential takeoff?

On the other hand, people just don't live long enough or learn fast enough for our little snippets of the learning curve to look anything but linear. But add them together and you get the sweeping, accelerating advance of knowledge and skill that is science.

The other phenomenon at work is the fact that innovation often requires the maverick individual working against the orthodoxy of the field as a whole to induce a Kuhnian paradigm shift—a typical example being Alfred Wegener's theory of continental drift.[13] Might not a single individual, even though relieved of limitations on learning bandwidth and lifespan, become so set in his ways as to effectively lodge in some local maximum of knowledge?

This forms something of a reply to the inductive bias argument. The human mind has many modules, each learning with its own bias. The general learning capability also involves a bias, but one built through experience and not constrained in any particular direction. Individuals often get the bias wrong and are unable to gain the proper insights; but the community as a whole can search the space of possible biases and ultimately find one that matches the structure of some part of reality.

Humans are meme machines. We may or may not individually be universal, but our communities certainly are. The barrier is permeable; universality is possible. We have at least one example. Evolution may well constitute another one.

IMPLICATIONS

Give me a place to stand, and I shall move the Earth.

—Archimedes

Humans are icebergs—most of our cognition consists of skills operating below the waterline of conscious thought. But we are autogenous: many of the modules are built by us in the process of learning and are fitted into the overall architecture in a seamless way. We read or drive as effortlessly as we understand speech or walk.

The existence of universality is surely interesting in a theoretical sense. If universal learning can exist, perhaps a mechanism more elegant than a community of human-scale intellects can be found. Perhaps the essence of such a mechanism must be present in any human-level intellect, as the subjective argument suggests. In any case, the implications for the possibilities down certain avenues of learning research are fascinating.

Another interesting possibility is AIs, which are capable of acting independently but also of coming together into a more tightly knit structure than a typical human community. The key to the usefulness of such an arrangement is that the different AIs could have different learning biases, and thus different ontologies and points of view. The challenge is that such conflicting visions generate much of the friction in human discourse. The ability of a community of AIs to operate harmoniously in spite of these differences would be invaluable. Of course, the different modules in a human mind already have vastly different views of the world. Understanding how the sliver of rationality manages to forge a seeming unity from the diversity will surely be useful in this regard.

The final implication of universality is the most heartening. If human intelligence is in fact universal in this sense, we are in theory capable, given world enough and time, of learning and understanding anything that any other universal learner can. The machines may ultimately be faster and more capacious, but they will differ quantitatively and not qualitatively. We do not know what wonders they will discover in the coming decades—but we can learn.

CHAPTER 8
Autogeny

Throughout this book, I generally use the term *autogeny* instead of *universality* to focus on how the process of self-enhancement might work instead of on the question of whether it has ultimate limits. An autogenous system can create more stuff, like the stuff it's made of. For example, hardware is made in a machine shop; likewise, software is made by a compiler.

Autogeny is similar to Francisco Varela and Humberto Maturana's term *autopoiesis*, but the latter was conceived specifically to characterize living systems and connotes some properties that are not necessarily present in a merely autogenous manufacturing (or computational) system. In particular, autopoiesis implies a system that continuously regenerates itself, which an autogenous system need not do.

THE METAPHORICAL MAN

This image's head was of fine gold, his breast and his arms of silver, his belly and his thighs of brass, his legs of iron, his feet part of iron and part of clay.

—Daniel 2:32–33 (KJV)

Let's try to get an overview of AI by means of an analogy. Our metaphor for the human mind will be the human body. The problem of

AI will become, in this thought experiment, the problem of building a robotic body that exhibits the physical capabilities of a human. So as not to confuse our metaphor with the real AI problem, we're going to assume that the robot body is remotely controlled, with sensory signals going to and motor signals coming from a real human in a full-coverage virtual-reality suit (or perhaps a brain in a vat).

At first blush the design seems straightforward, although there's plenty of work to be done and room for lots of innovation. There are 206 bones in the human body. They are simply and certainly structural elements. We can make structural elements, and indeed of better material than bone: aircraft-grade aluminum or titanium alloys, carbon fiber composites, and so on. We can build significantly better hinges than the human joints, thank you.

Muscles are just motors that move the skeleton, supplying the ability to change positions or apply force. We have an array of options here, ranging from electric motors to gas-operated actuators. We need a central power supply for most of these options; if you don't mind a little noise, the gasoline motor from a chain saw has a power-to-weight ratio that is perfectly adequate. It can drive a generator or a compressor. Other options are a fuel cell or batteries.

Video cameras work for eyes, microphones for ears, a speaker for the voice box. (*Forbidden Planet*'s Robbie notwithstanding, a robot does not need to be able to belch.) The senses of touch, smell, and taste can be approximated to some degree, and we can worry later, if necessary, to what extent this matters. Rob Tow's and Cynthia Breazeal's robots show us that quite serviceable facial expressions can be simulated with a small number of movable features, such as eyebrows and lips.

We now have a robot that, under remote control, is capable of standing in for a human in activities ranging from casual conversation and office work to golf and home repair. Such a robot would be, as current-day AI programs are, an extremely useful thing to have.

Even so, the robot has a huge gap in its capabilities. The gap shows up in different forms depending on the situation. The robot can practice and exercise all it wants, but it does not become more fit and the exercised muscles and bones do not become stronger. If it is injured, it does not heal. If you build a small robot, it will not grow up to be a big one. We can sum it up by pointing out that the robot is *not alive,* or more technically, not autogenous.

I trust it is not necessary, after half a century of molecular biology, to point out that the difference is *not* that the robot is a machine. Our living bodies are machines—cells are machines, mitochondria and ribosomes are machines. It's machines all the way down. No, the problem with the robot is not that it's a machine. It's just that it's not enough of a machine.

To capture the qualities of the human body that make it alive, you have to look not at the 206 bones with their muscles, but at the 10 trillion cells with their DNA. Or, at least, you have to look at what they do. The living human body is made out of things that the cells can make, such as bone or teeth. It has abilities consisting of things that the cells can do, such as contracting in muscles. The heart is not just a pump; it is a pump that can grow from a small pump to a large pump while operating continuously the whole time.

This puts us in something of a quandary. Structural elements and motors in the hundreds are the kind of engineering systems we can design and build, but self-replicating programmable chemical factories in the trillions are not.[1] The key question then becomes: Is there some intermediate level of organization more achievable with existing technology that can provide a semblance of the generative and the regenerative capabilities of life? Or do we have to wait until we have nanotechnology and can duplicate the cells' abilities at their own molecular level?

The question is most crucial back on the other side of the metaphor in the software of the mind—the brain/AI side—but I'll attempt an answer on the robot/body side as a springboard for speculation. I claim the answer is yes. There have been a number of architectures proposed for self-extending, self-replicating, factory systems.[2] Inside the human-sized robot body, there would be a population of ant-sized robots, which would be simple, nongrowing, non-self-replicating machines. There would be miniature factories that build the ant-sized robots (and that recycle broken ones) and factories that make parts for the larger body's other systems. The ant-sized robots would crawl around in access passageways throughout the body, building or repairing it the same way human workers build and repair skyscrapers and ocean liners. It's clearly a much more complex system to design than the previous simple, high-level robot, but it's also a lot simpler than the full-fledged, molecular machinery of life. Instead of trillions of cells, each with millions of molecular machines inside, we could probably get away with a few hundred centimeter-sized repair robots, each consisting of a few hundred parts. The big robot body is probably on the order of millions of parts, including the factories for the little robots. That's essentially the complexity of a *single cell* in a real human body.

If we shift gears back to the brain/AI side of the metaphor, the question becomes: How do we make our AI autogenous? Is there a level of organization that preserves autogeny without having to descend to the level of individual cells? And critically, how big is the kernel, the part we need to start with, that would be capable of growing into the full-fledged system we want?

MIND CHILDREN

> *At my present rate of working I produce about a thousand digits of programme a day, so that about sixty workers, working steadily through the fifty years might accomplish the job, if nothing went into the wastepaper basket. Some more expeditious method seems desirable.*
>
> —Alan Turing, *Computing Machinery and Intelligence*

In his classic paper, following the description of what came to be called the Turing Test, Alan Turing notes the difficulty of simply writing the program in the conventional way. In view of later experience, he probably underestimated it at a billion digits; note that he wrote in an era when programming was still done in raw machine language, bit by bit! On the other hand, using modern programming and knowledge-engineering tools, the estimate in terms of programmer days doesn't seem too far-fetched.

But he did propose a "more expeditious" method: program an imitation of a child mind and then educate it to adulthood. He assumes as a first approximation that the amount of effort in bringing up the child machine would be similar to that of educating a human. This would amount to some fraction of an adult's time for twenty years—less than 1 percent of the direct programming approach.

Aside from the difficulty of finding sixty programmers with the brilliance of Alan Turing, the problem with simply sitting down and writing an AI program in LISP (or whatever) is that the adult human mind remains perfectly capable of learning, inference, abduction,* concept formation, and metaphorical modes of thought—the things our minds do to grow. If you know how to program these things at all, you might as well program them first and let the machine learn the rest for itself.

Turing's estimate of the complexity of the child machine is quite optimistic:

> Presumably the child brain is something like a notebook as one buys it from the stationer's. Rather little mechanism, and lots of blank sheets. [Mechanism and writing are from our point of view almost synonymous.] Our hope is that there is so little mechanism in the child brain that something like it can be easily programmed.[3]

This is the only significant mistake in Turing's entire paper. It is probably due to the extreme poverty of the mainstream sciences of mind of that period.

Having taken essentially the other road toward AI for the indicated half century, standard practice has essentially produced the equivalent of a mind with everything *except* the key abilities of being able to learn and

---

*As the fin-de-siècle American philosopher Charles Sanders Pierce explained it, "There is a more familiar name for it than abduction, for it is neither more nor less than guessing." As normally used it means making a shrewd or educated guess, not a random one.

grow. The number of digits of programming necessary for those abilities remains to be seen; perhaps it is comparatively small, as Turing implied. But what cannot be denied is that it appears to involve a level of cleverness that has eluded us all these years. Perhaps Turing himself would have had the ingenuity, but we haven't seen his like since.

LEARNING IN AI

A different way to characterize the AI glass ceiling is to notice that the things AI systems can do well are the things that humans have learned to do, and thus the ones that we know how to do. By "learn" I mean learn out of a textbook or by watching and being taught—not the unfolding of innate capabilities, such as walking and talking.

When we learn something out of a book, at the formal level, we build up our own minds, extend and augment them to have the new capabilities. Thus, in some sense we have already written the program that embodies the knowledge. To produce an AI system with the same knowledge, we only need to do it again in a programming language.

The things we don't know how to do are much harder. There are no textbooks that teach you how to walk. There are, laughably, plenty of textbooks that will tell you how you should speak English, but they are written in English—worthless to someone who doesn't already know it! Of course, that's not their intended purpose, which is exactly the point.

Robotics

This is one of the reasons for the popularity of robotics in AI. Many of the areas in which we have built-in knowledge, and thus the lack of explicit knowledge, are those where the internal structures evolved as part of a body controller—knowing how to walk, for example. Perhaps if we retrace the process of evolution, working our way up to more and more complex creatures, we'll come across the techniques that are the secret.

So far, the robots are up to about the level of perhaps the lower vertebrates. The most celebrated one is probably Rodney Brooks's GENGHIS, a six-legged crawler that learned to crawl.[4] GENGHIS had a software structure that was a hierarchy of finite state automata (a very basic unit of software function), and learned, by trial and error, the appropriate programs for these. The structure and connectivity of the automata was built-in and fixed, however.

Machine Learning

There is currently in AI a large subfield (with subfields of its own) about learning. The existing techniques, however, simply don't do the kind of learning we need. We can divide these, in a broad way, into two categories: the ones that divide things into categories and the ones that create structure.

The best developed of the categorization algorithms require the specification of the categories ahead of time, as well as a "training set" of data that has been precategorized for the system to learn from. These algorithms are useful for situations where a local adaptation is called for, that is to say, to optimize a system that already has the basic concepts and structures built in.

The second class, algorithms that create structure, generally operate by search. Essentially this means they keep trying different things until they find one that works. This includes neural networks and genetic algorithms as well as straightforward symbolic search. Such algorithms can do some remarkable things, as in the case of AM and EURISKO. The problem is that they always seem to run out of steam. This leads to the suspicion that all they can do is what is implied by the representations they start with, earning them the name of wind-up toys.

Explanation-Based Learning

Probably the most prominent existing AI system to operate by building new concepts is SOAR, a descendent of GPS from Allen Newell and

Herbert Simon and their students. SOAR is a rule-based system, similar to many expert systems (and that's what it's generally used as). But it incorporates the notion of automatic *chunking*: when it finds a situation its rules don't cover, it sets up a subproblem whose solution will form the new rule that it needs. In that way it does extend itself, to some extent. SOAR seems to be a step in the right direction, but it doesn't learn from scratch; setting up a SOAR program for any given application still requires a significant amount of intricate programming.

SOAR's chunking is a special case of the machine-learning technique called *explanation-based learning*. Unlike the statistical learning methods, explanation-based learning requires only one example, but it also requires *domain theory*.[5] The domain theory is a set of logical rules that would—in theory—have allowed you to deduce the result of whatever example you got. Suppose we know the laws of physics; we should be able to predict the outcome of any experiment. But often we don't realize that something will happen until we try it, and then we follow the logic of the physics to understand why it worked out that way.

The Navier-Stokes equations for fluid flow, for example, had been around since 1822, but scientists still refused to believe that machines could fly until they saw it done. Once they did, they explained it handily using the equations: "Oh, of course, we knew this all along."

Current-day explanation-based learning algorithms are mostly posed in terms of domain theories couched in predicate logic, and thus, they are strongly dependent on the ontological assumptions in the particular formulation and can suffer from formalist float. But the basic process is quite powerful and is likely to form a significant component of any generally competent learning machine.

The other promising parts of machine learning are the algorithms that categorize to create structure: subfields such as hierarchical clustering, data mining, and grammatical inference. Other fields such as data compression are producing techniques that are not generally recognized as learning or AI but are very applicable.[6] These all differ from the pure search programs in that they absorb a lot of data in the process and form concepts as a by-product of winnowing out regularities in it. All of these methods that employ a combination of inference from data and search can be seen as the modern-day descendants of Solomonoff's work.

Machine learning isn't quite up to producing Turing's child machine yet, but it seems headed in the right direction with an open road ahead of it.

GRASP

Let's return briefly to our physical robot metaphor and look at the human hand. Most robot grippers are essentially like a pair of pliers—two "fingers" that can hold small objects. This captures one aspect of the hand, a very salient one to be sure: the opposable thumb. However, the human hand can do a much wider variety of jobs than a simple gripper. You can hold an egg or a slippery sphere of ice. Indeed, you can catch an egg thrown fifty feet without breaking it; you can pick up a cat in a way that is comfortable for the cat; you can play cat's cradle with a string; you can crack peanuts and open childproof aspirin bottles; you can play the piano, or a bamboo flute where your fingertips form the pads that seal the holes; you can use your hand(s) for a cup to hold water; you use them as paddles when you swim; you can clench them into fists and beat things with them; you can clap, snap your fingers, and clasp your hands together to form a whistle.

Ignoring healing and growing for the moment, what technology would be necessary to emulate all these capabilities in a package the size of a hand? Notice, by the way, that most of the muscles that move your fingers are actually in your forearm. I would guess that a hand that matched the physical capabilities of a human one would be more than ten but less than a hundred times as complex as the current best robot grippers.

A robot with hands as good as a human's would have an alternative path to autogeny: it could build subsystems for itself in a workshop, just as we imagine building such a robot in the first place. In the AI context, this would correspond to automatic programming. Unfortunately, automatic programming has been the single greatest failure of AI.

How can this be? AI led the way in programming technology, with LISP, one of the oldest programming languages and still one of the most sophisticated. LISP, as an autogenous language, is ideal for writing meta-software: compilers, debuggers, and development environments. Many of these tools, common today, originated in the AI community. There are inferential databases and object-oriented programming languages with roots in the semantic retrieval and frame-based AI systems of the 1970s.

And yet there remains a significant distinction. The meta-software tools are all, in a sense, hand tools. They help a person produce a system, but they do not grow of themselves in response to an unstructured environment. Everything the AI system does, at some depressingly low level of detail, must be thought of, if not directly coded, by a human.

My best guess is that automatic programming foundered on formalist float. Formal systems are exact and efficient, whereas informal ones are compliant and able to grasp new things. Programming is first and foremost an exercise in bridging the gap—going from an informal notion of what you want to do to a formal one. In order for a system to produce a program to do a task, it has to understand what the task is; and this must be from an informal description. Getting the description into formal form is the hard part—after that you're just compiling a high-level programming language.

Note that the remaining active subfield of AI that could be called automatic programming is the synthesis of programs with an evolutionary paradigm, called *genetic programming*. This technique is capable of producing small programs given specifications that are either test programs—obviously formal—or statistics on a set of test cases, which is hard to classify. In either case, the technique consists of a form of search; thus, it is strongly limited in the complexity of what it can produce.

FORMALIST FLOAT AND AUTOGENY

Formalist float can happen when we use a formal system at the level where we consciously think of things. That's like the robot with parts at the level of organization similar to bones, muscles, and so on. As in the case of the robot, the float isn't that the system is formal; it's that it's not enough of a formal system. Just as sufficient mechanism can make the organism autogenous, sufficient mechanism can make the mind autogenous as well. Of course, the mechanism has to be of the right kind—mere quantity isn't sufficient!

It's quite possible for a system to avoid formalist float and yet not be autogenous. Most existing AI programs that are competent in their domains fall into this category. This simply means that there is enough mechanism to model the domains reliably. More specifically, it means that they contain enough concepts to form a fully fleshed-out understanding of what's going on.

A system such as this avoids formalist float in the way that a very sophisticated robot hand could do all the manipulations that a human hand can. We can certainly imagine building one that good, but it could not grow or heal. Yet the value of autogeny comes when we consider the immense complexity of a system that could pass the Turing Test, operate in the real world, and be competitive with humans. Autogeny allows the system to be created without the huge investment of effort required otherwise.

Autogeny in an artificial intellect would allow it to grow into its skull. An autogenous system could surmount formalist float by filling in the missing details on its own. The key question is, how complex does the system have to be in order to become autogenous? Is the kernel small enough than the rest of the system, that is, than the part it saves you from building, that it is worth the complexity of autogenous design?

We can take a hint from the brain. The human genome is about a gigabyte. Only a small fraction of that contains the actual genes (and it isn't yet understood how important the rest is). Of the thirty thousand genes, maybe half are involved in building the brain. A lot of that gets taken up with building the individual cells—it's like specifying a computer program by starting with the recipe for making a transistor. At least a million times as much information would be necessary to specify the actual structure of the developed brain.[7] Part of that is almost certainly random, but part is learned.

A huge part of the innate structure of the brain is in the specific modules. That means that the general learning capability is only a small part of it. Our genome is only 1.5 percent different from the chimp genome, which has to include differences such as body structure and the systemic differences that allow us to live in colder climates than chimps can. A general learning machine probably doesn't need fear of snakes or sexual behavior patterns, although it probably gains a lot of traction by using other modules as prefab models for common phenomena. Thus, the structure necessary for a learning kernel is probably a very small fraction of the entire genome.

If you read a book every day over the entire course of your life, you'd pull in about twenty-five times as much information as is present in the raw genome. This tends to confirm Turing's estimate that the child machine could be significantly simpler than the developed mind.

Doug Lenat, after his experience with AM and EURISKO, came to the conclusion that what was needed was a much bigger database of essential facts—commonsense knowledge—and he spent the next decades building one.[8] The idea was that this would prime the pump enough for a system to begin to augment its own knowledge by reading encyclopedias or the Web.

However, the kind of mechanism babies have that allows them to learn so voraciously is not of that kind. It's likely to be much more specialized and to involve finding regularities in raw datastreams and building interpretive processing structures that reflect those regularities. Much of the innate mechanism will consist of ways to represent the data that expose important regularities, such as distinct phonemes in sound and distinct objects in the visual field, which babies begin to pick up remarkably fast. The blank notebook appears to come with ruled pages, a table of contents, and a style guide.

WHERE WE STAND

> *The selection and placement of stories on this page were determined automatically by a computer program.*
>
> —Google News

So where is AI and how far will it have to go until it's dangerous?

First of all, it seems reasonable to generalize from current practice that any task for which you can specify all the relevant concepts and methods ahead of time—anything from grandmaster-level chess to off-road driving—can be handled competently by existing AI techniques, given an appropriate development effort. At least two systems have created inventions that were patented. Programs summarize (highly stylized) news stories and translate text in a half-adequate way. Systems that detect fraud patterns in credit card and telephone use are as good as humans at that task. Robots walk, play soccer, and drive hundred-mile rallies across the desert. They have even performed heart surgery unassisted (and successfully!).[9]

Formalist float remains formidable, but this is a question of economics in many cases. It's all too easy for a small project to formalize an ontology, the set of concepts the system uses, at too coarse a level of resolution. But this is not a fault of AI methodology. It is simply a lack of quality on the part of one specific project or another.

The crevasse can be filled. In vision and speech processing, for example, the program receives what is essentially raw sense data—camera pictures or microphone signals—and puts together symbolic scene descriptions or words, respectively. Virtually all systems that do this use a fixed, prespecified set of symbols in their output, however. Ones that can create new symbols are few and far between.

The search horizon is creeping slowly out. As computing hardware advances according to Moore's law, which is exponential, the complexity of something that can be synthesized by search advances linearly: something like a bit per year. By 2010 a computer the price of a new car should be able to apply DEEP BLUE's amount of search capability to a wide range of problems. For properly formalized problems, machines at this level will be *better than any human*.

The biggest lack of AI systems today is the ability to learn. That can be broken down into two parts: formalization and methodology.

People don't learn in a vacuum: they sift through a voluminous stream of sensory data, find regularities, categorize, symbolize, and formalize. The areas of AI that address this capability are relatively new, requiring both significant processing power and voluminous streams of data to work with. In the relatively recent past, great strides have been made in fields, such as data mining, that do exactly this.

The issue of methodology is the question not only of how much mechanism to put in but also what kind to put in. The human learning machine not only contains a head-start primer of data, for example, the meta-syntax of the human languages, but also the algorithms by which the learning is done. What the human child does is not only the induction of regularities and search for novel structure, but also the process of adding the new knowledge to a growing base of older knowledge in a usable way. This, for my money, is the least understood part of the whole process.

Common sense isn't reasoning, although there seems to be a belief among some AI practitioners that it could be done that way. This remains to be seen; what people actually do is to remember rather than to reason. Common sense consists of having had enough experience, and having learned from it to avoid the mistakes and to take advantage of the opportunities that the experience implies. Once AI programs begin to learn from experience and gain enough experience to have common sense in a wide range of activities, they will make a quantum jump in usefulness—and possibly leap into the "most dangerous game" category, superhuman intelligence.

For AI to make even the leap to human-level robustness, to warp Newton's metaphor, it will have to take a flying jump from the shoulders of giants. As we examine the field, it would seem that some giants have indeed wandered in and are milling around expectantly. We're going to check them out, hopping from shoulder to shoulder, over the next few chapters.

CHAPTER 9
Representation and Search

Genius is one per cent inspiration, ninety-nine per cent perspiration.

—Thomas Edison, in *Harper's Monthly*, 1932

SEARCH

In his 1948 AI manifesto, Alan Turing made the surprising, if prescient, observation that "intellectual activity consists mainly of various kinds of search." How can he have known that?

He could know that, but he couldn't say why. To get the whole story, we have to go back to World War II again, and the problem of predicting what the enemy was going to do. On a bigger scale in time and space than the turning of an airplane, there was another problem: where in the ocean a submarine might be when you wanted to send a convoy of cargo ships across. The best way the British found to make this prediction was to read the orders the German high command sent to their submarine captains.

The Germans weren't too fond of the notion that the British could be reading their mail, so they sent the orders in code. Specifically, they had a machine called the Enigma, which scrambled the letters of the message. It was essentially like a typewriter, but the wires between the keys and the outputs were scrambled, so that when you typed *F* you got *N*, for example. This is not scrambled enough, it turns out, so the scrambled wires were put onto a wheel that connected twenty-six inputs to twenty-six outputs, with a mechanism that turned the wheel one notch each time you typed a letter. That way there were not one but twenty-six different scramblings, applied in turn to successive letters in your message. In the German version of the Enigma machine there were three such wheels, which turned each other like the digits in an odometer. Along with a few other tricks such as replaceable wheels, this created millions of possibilities.

What Turing and the other codebreakers had done was to build machines that cycled through the possibilities looking for the setup—which wheels were in the machine, in what order, with what starting positions—that formed the key to the code of a particular transmission. He knew how powerful search can be, and indeed, he knew—he had invented—many of the heuristic search-space reduction techniques. But he couldn't talk about it! The wartime code-breaking work remained top secret for many years.

REPRESENTATION

> *[I]n the further development of science, we want more than just a formula. First we have an observation, then we have numbers . . . then we have a law which summarizes all the numbers. But the real* glory *of science is that we can find a way of thinking such that the law is* evident.
>
> —Richard Feynman, *Lectures on Physics*

Once upon a time, three missionaries and three cannibals were trekking across country together. They came to a river that was too deep to wade across, flowing too fast to swim in, and besides, there were crocodiles in it.

Fortuitously, however, someone had left a boat complete with oars on the riverbank. Unfortunately, the boat could only hold two people at a time. And to add to the fun, the cannibals had the quaint habit of consuming missionaries whenever they outnumbered them.

Your mission, should you decide to accept it, is to specify who should row over and in what order so that all six travelers make it safely to the other bank of the river.

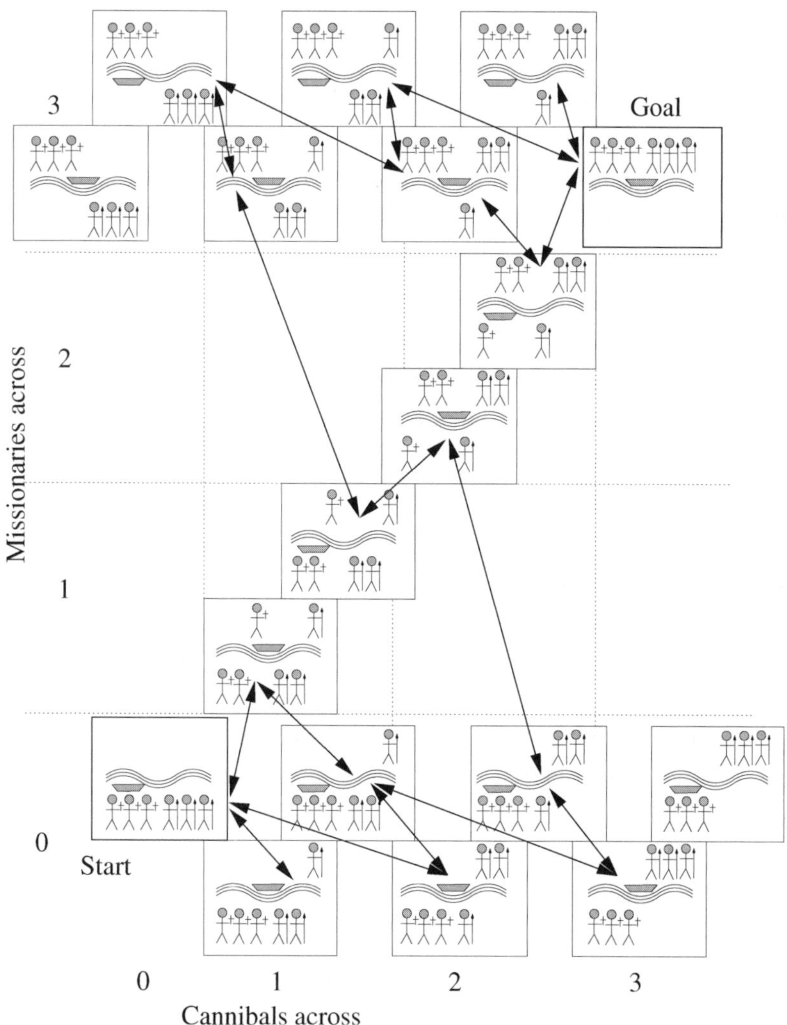

Fig. 9.1: State space for missionaries and cannibals.

This classic brainteaser was the subject of one of AI's seminal papers in 1968, by Saul Amarel.[1]

The three missionaries are named Abe, Bob, and Cal. What happens if Abe gets into the boat and rows across? Woops, this leaves two missionaries standing on the shore with three cannibals. Try again. What about Bob? Woops, leaves two missionaries with three cannibals again. But computer programs aren't able to see patterns such as this without a lot of specific preprogramming, so our search program would wind up trying to row Cal across, too, before starting in on the cannibals.

The cannibals' names are Darius, Ebenezer, and Ferdinand. Let's try rowing Darius across. Oh, yes, he can't do anything but row back. What about Ebenezer? Yep, if he rows over he just has to row back, too. Computer programs still aren't able to see patterns such as this. So we row Ferdinand over and back too, and start in on all of the thirty possibilities of two men in the boat (such as Abe in the front, Ebenezer in the back). If you really tried to solve the puzzle with this brute-force approach, you will try millions of crossings before you discover a sequence that works.

Rather than start right out pushing missionaries and cannibals around, it helps to get an overall view of the problem. The key insight is that you don't care who gets into the boat (although you would have to decide that if you were faced with the actual situation). You think in terms of an *abstraction* in which you care only about how many missionaries and how many cannibals are on each side of the river. The first thing you do is to make up a grid in which all the possible situations are represented. Each row represents situations in which a given number of missionaries have made it across, and each column is the same for cannibals. Within each grid division there are two situations, one where the boat is on the near side, the other where it is on the far side.

We can improve our diagram, which encodes what is called a *state space* for the problem, by eliminating those situations—states—that are forbidden or impossible. This is called *pruning*. States where there are more cannibals than missionaries on either side can be scratched, as can those with everyone on one side and the boat on the other.

Finally, we begin to fill in the moves we can make from state to state. We can send one or two cannibals across, or one or two missionaries, or one of each. We can draw a two-way arrow to represent each move, because obviously any move we can make, we can reverse right after. We have to start in the lower left division at the Start square—everybody and the boat is on the near bank—and end at the Goal square in the upper-right division—everybody's gotten across. Fill in all the moves between states left after pruning. Now you have a diagram like fig. 9.1, and we can search for a path that takes us from the starting state to the goal. But as you can see, in this particular problem, there's no need to search; the solution is, in Feynman's word, evident.

Amarel's paper is considered important in AI history not because he solved the missionaries-and-cannibals problem, but because he showed how important it is to have the right representation when you set out to solve a problem. The right representation makes a spectacular difference in the efficiency of the search.

REPRESENTATIONS IN AI

Logic and Semantic Networks

Predicate logic remains a powerful way to represent whatever it is we know about the world. In the formula *wants(monkey, banana)* the predicate is *wants*; to use predicate logic you have to formalize the world, breaking it down into unequivocally distinct objects and unequivocally distinct relationships between them.

As we saw earlier, simply breaking the world into predicate form doesn't solve the problem. There are two remaining challenges: the frame problem and formalist float.

The frame problem requires the representation to consist of more than simply a list of predicate expressions. There has to be more information about how to use it. One way to do this that has had some success is to turn logic into a programming language, as in PROLOG.

This is a logic programming language that appeared in the 1970s based on some newly discovered inference methods. You write your logic in a slightly restricted form and the system rips through the inferences in a well-specified order. You can control the inferences by the form and the order of your logical statements. PROLOG is as powerful a programming language as LISP, and almost as easy to use. One thing this proves is that yes, you can represent anything in logic. On the other hand, it leaves you still having to write the program with a strong understanding of how it's all going to interact. PROLOG can't simply "take advice."

Having to deal with the frame problem exacerbates the other one, formalist float. In attempting to ameliorate the problem of too many potential deductions, the strong temptation is to try to reduce the complexity of your description as much as possible—ensuring that it will have a worse fit to the endless complexity of the real world. The key to solving both problems at once is to let the system form its own abstractions, thinking in terms of the sizes of missionary groups instead of lists of which missionaries. But that's much more easily said than done.

The main hurdle for logic in this regard is that the abstractions we usually form are not exact and thus would be forbidden by a true, correct system of logic. The system we need will have to know how to bend the rules just enough to get the job done but not too much to make its abstractions worthless.

Semantic networks operate in a similar vein. The procedures that are defined over the simplified set of predicates the network links represent can be seen as being a rough-and-ready approximation to a true inferencing capability.

Bayesian Inference

Before we can talk about our next form of representation, Bayesian networks, we have to make a digression about Bayesian inference. Just as logical inference is the backdrop to the semantics of logic-based representations, the mathematics of statistics and, in particular, Bayesian probability is the backdrop to these networks. (Thomas Bayes was the eighteenth-century mathematician who invented the method of combining probabilities we're about to examine.)

Let's suppose you are a robotic coyote who is chasing a robotic roadrunner through the Painted Desert. You come to the side of a big rock that looks like it has a tunnel going through it. You would like to use the tunnel as a shortcut, but as you approach it you remember a painful fact: most of the apparent tunnels are in fact simply pictures of tunnels painted by the roadrunner.

Luckily, since you are a robot, you are provided with various electronic sensors that your cartoon counterpart doesn't have. Let's suppose you have radar, sonar, and a laser range finder. In order to use Bayesian inference to determine whether the tunnel is real, you need to have done some homework. In particular, you must have taken note of some things such as the probability that any given tunnel is real, and the probability that, given a real tunnel, your sensors will say it is. You do this for each of your sensors. (But for simplicity we'll assume they're all alike. We'll also assume they're independent, that is, that the errors each one makes aren't correlated with the errors of a different sensor).

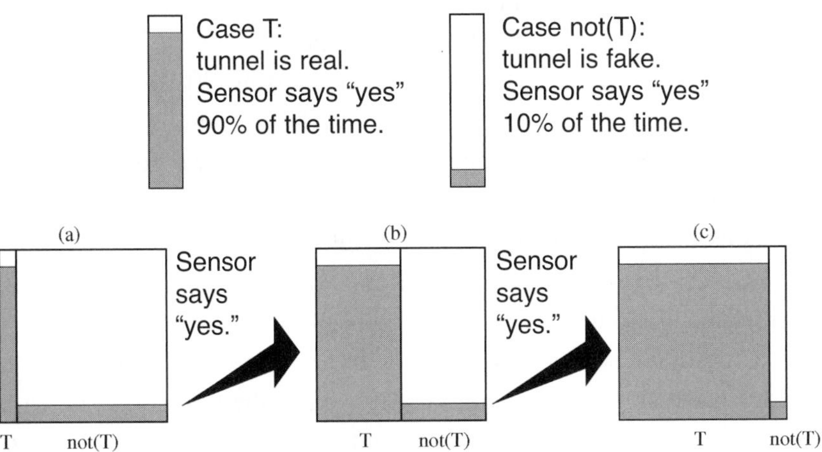

Fig. 9.2: "Sensor fusion" using Bayesian inference.

So, as illustrated in fig. 9.2, your sensors are 90 percent reliable: there is a 90 percent chance that the sensor will say yes if there really is a tunnel and a 90 percent chance that it will say no if there isn't. So you run up to the tunnel, use a sensor, it says yes, and you dash right in. BAM! You fall in pieces on the ground and tweeting birds fly around your head. This happens half of the time.

What you forgot is the *prior probability* (*prior* for short) that anything that looks like a tunnel really is one. Those robot roadrunners are so industrious that 90 percent of apparent tunnels are actually just paintings. That situation is illustrated in (a): the slice on the left represents all real tunnels, with their 90 percent correct sensor readings of yes in gray; the rest of the box is all the fake tunnels, with their 10 percent false readings of yes in gray. Notice that the two gray areas are the same size. Out of all the possible yes readings, half of them represent real tunnels, the other half represent fake ones.

We'd better keep using our sensors. Our first reading gave us a 50/50 probability that the tunnel was real, so this is the prior for the second reading. That's represented by (b), split right down the middle to represent that 50/50 prior.

Now we do a different, independent sensor reading and apply the sensor probabilities again. We get another yes, which is represented by the gray area in (b). From the box we see 90 percent of the gray is on the real tunnel side and 10 percent is on the fake side.

We do the same thing again, this time using 90/10 as the prior, which gives us (c). Another yes sensor reading, the gray again, would give us a 98.78 percent probability of a tunnel. In we go! But watch out for that train.

As an aside, note that having the right priors is extremely important and also extremely powerful. Remember Ray Solomonoff's prediction machine? It inputs a description of some set of observations, say, a lifetime's sensory experience, as a string of symbols. Then it predicted which symbols would come next in the string, that is, what you'd see next in the future. It turns out that if you had a way to compute the prior of any given string, predicting the future would be as simple as using the Bayesian rule I just described above. In fact, Solomonoff's discovery of algorithmic probability gives us exactly a formulation of the prior of any string of symbols! Unfortunately, it's not just intractably difficult to compute; it's theoretically incomputable. But in a sense, all of AI (all of intelligent behavior, for that matter) can be seen as an approximation to Solomonoff's priors.

Evidence Grids

Suppose again that you are a robot, but this time you just want to roll around a cluttered room without bumping into things. Back in the 1980s, when mobile robotics was just getting started in university labs, this was a hard problem. One group's robot was fondly called Harvey, and it wasn't named after the giant invisible rabbit; its full name was Harvey Wallbanger.

Hans Moravec at CMU came up with a method for navigation that made a quantum leap in reliability and speed. It involves drawing a map of the area around the robot. The map is divided into squares like a piece of graph paper. Then, using the robot's sensors to gather information, the coyote/roadrunner computation is done *for every square on the map*, resulting in a map drawn in probabilities.

This had an effect similar to using a deep search in chess: instead of trying laboriously to pack everything into a complex evaluation function, you have a simpler evaluation function and apply it many, many times in a framework that concentrates the results. And by the end of the 1990s, robots were rolling confidently around the halls of CMU with humanlike speeds and reliabilities.

Bayesian Networks

Bayesian inference deals in the probability that some given statement is true. In robot map evidence grids, the statements are implicitly ones such as "Part of an object occupies square (33,62)." Evidence grids work well, so it is tempting to try to use the same methods for more

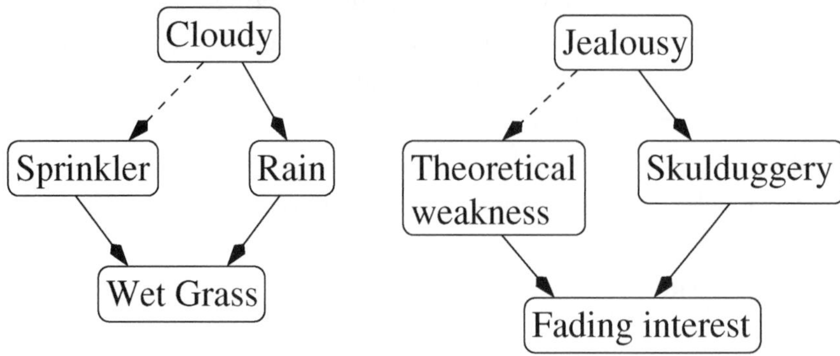

Fig. 9.3: Bayesian networks.

ambitious realms of discourse. Suppose you could make a list of all the statements a robot might need to know and then use Bayesian inference to turn them into a map of the truth. That is an impossible ideal, like enumerating all the moves of all chess games, but there has been substantial progress in finding fragments of it that do useful things.

A *Bayesian network* is a graph whose nodes represent statements or measurements. The links between the statements or measurements correspond to the Bayesian-inference steps with the appropriate probabilistic models. A given network forms a model of causality between the conditions represented by the nodes. It can be used, given there is information about some of the conditions, to assign probabilities to the others.

Bayesian networks are similar in some ways to influence diagrams (a favorite tool of management consultants), but they are somewhat more general and can be used for backward as well as forward inference. The classic introductory example is shown in fig. 9.3. If you look out and see that the ground is wet, you can infer that either someone had the lawn sprinkler running or that it had rained. If you look up and see heavy clouds, it lowers your assessment of the probability of the sprinkler, even though there is no direct causal connection between clouds and sprinklers.

This turns out to be a very powerful technique for certain kinds of world modeling. For example, you might reassess the mathematical substance of cybernetics upon learning about the jealousy among its cadre; the Bayesian network representing the situation is just the same as the one that represents the sprinkler example.

Bayesian networks are also a good framework for certain kinds of learning; they provide a formalism where the numbers can be filled in by statistics from examples and where statistics from using them can feed back to improve the model. Finding the right sets of numbers and even finding the right topology of the network can be done by various kinds of search, in some cases.

LIMITS TO GROWTH

> *YASSER SEIRAWAN: Essentially we now know today that DEEP BLUE is doing this incredible calculation of 200 million positions per second.*
>
> *MIKE VALVO: Think about that for a second. (Audience laughter.)*
>
> *SEIRAWAN: Every five seconds, DEEP BLUE is looking at a billion positions. And if it thinks for a minute, then it's looking at 60 billion moves a second. Have I got that right? No, it's 6 billion.*
>
> *MIKE VALVO: I was never very good at math. (Audience laughter.)*
>
> *SEIRAWAN: 12 billion moves—*
>
> *MIKE VALVO: It's a big number.*
>
> *SEIRAWAN: It's a big number.*
>
> —Commentators on the
> Kasparov/DEEP BLUE chess match

If you're a computer, the missionaries-and-cannibals puzzle is essentially solved once you have it in a state-space form. Even if we assume that you do no pruning and try all five possibilities from each state and use thousands of instructions for each try, the entire space is searched on any modern PC in comfortably under a millisecond. If you're willing to wait as much as a minute—the amount of time it takes to state the answer in English—simple search can solve similar problems with state spaces having on the order of a million states, more than the number of printed characters making up all the words in this book.

If you're willing to invest some time and more serious processing power, simple spaces into the billions can be searched. IBM's DEEP BLUE chess computer, with its 256 custom chess processors, could search 50 billion chessboard positions in the three minutes typically taken for a move in professional chess matches.[2] This is enough to let DEEP BLUE beat any human who ever played the game.

There is a large number of problems that can be broken down into the state-space representation. For some, such as missionaries and cannibals, the breakdown is the (only) ingenious part of the solution; for others, such as chess, the breakdown is straightforward but there are techniques that enhance the search process considerably, such as the automatic pruning that chess programs do.

To play chess, you have to be more ingenious about what you're searching for. To solve the missionaries-and-cannibals problem, you go from state to state, checking if the one you've found is the solution with everybody on the other side of the river. In chess you can't do that; the space is too big. It would take many times the age of the universe to search through all the possibilities to find the checkmates.

What you can do instead, as we have seen, is search a few moves ahead and then see whether things are getting better or worse for you along that line of play. Some problems have that property: when you find a partial solution, you can tell that you're better off than when you started. Chess does. Other problems don't.

At an average point in a chess game, the player to move has something like twenty-five choices. Then his opponent has twenty-five, and so on. Thus three moves by each player ahead, there are twenty-five to the sixth power, or about a quarter billion board positions possible. In the Asian game of Go, on the other hand, the moving player has an average of 250 choices. Thus, three moves ahead in a Go game, there are a million times as many board positions to evaluate as there would be in chess. Three moves ahead is nowhere near enough to play a good game—DEEP BLUE actually looks more than fifteen moves ahead—but even with just three it would take DEEP BLUE more than four hours to make a move at Go.[3] And that's assuming it was as easy to evaluate a given Go position as a chess position, which is far from the truth.

The best program can beat any human player in chess. Nearly a decade after the Kasparov/DEEP BLUE match, both techniques and hardware have improved to the point that similar levels of play can be had from considerably more modest stock computer systems, without special chess processors. In Go, the best program plays at an intermediate amateur level. The state-space search technique simply doesn't work (and the best Go programs rely heavily on other techniques).

Perhaps the best analogy for search was given by Allen Newell and Herbert Simon, although ironically when they gave it, they were arguing against it.[4] Search in a state space is something like the invention of the wheel. There are some kinds of travels, namely, those along a smooth surface, where wheels are better in many ways than legs. Wheels are more efficient and simpler to build, control, and power. If trucks or railroads required the complexity of walking robots, we'd still be using mule-towed barges.

Whether you're searching it or not, the discrete, formal breakdown of a problem that produces the state space is crucial for a huge proportion of computerized information processing currently in use. Consider the UPC (universal product code) barcodes on every item for sale at many stores. A state space, more precisely a product space, has been defined where each item is reduced to a single number.

In the wheel analogy, this corresponds to building roads for wheeled vehicles. As computers and Internet commerce continue to spread, the cognitive world is being paved over with formalization, breaking concepts up into discrete spaces that machines can handle easily.

But to build roads in places wheels can't originally go, you need legs to start with; and if you have legs already, there are lots of places that would be better without roads. Getting back to the other side of the analogy, there are problems, such as Go, that have a straightforward formal, state-space representation but that are still intractable. And yet, humans still manage to play Go well against their programmed rivals—that's how we know that the programs are poor! It's as if Go were a mountain many miles across, covered with a spiral road that went all the way around for each one-foot rise. The wheeled vehicle goes around and around, while the legged human brain simply cuts across, straight up the slope.

n-SPACES AND HILL CLIMBING

Climbing up hills is a technique that works to solve many different types of problems. All you have to do is to arrange your representation so that the solution of the problem is a state on a hilltop and then your search consists of picking the highest neighbor to the state you're in, again and again. Just keep going up.

The height of a given state is simply some number that you can compute given its description.

Suppose, for example, that you've been given a description of a molecule: a list of the kinds of atoms that comprise it, each with its position in space, and a list of which pairs of atoms are connected by a covalent bond. The problem is that the positions of the atoms are not right: the bonds would be stretched and/or compressed in those actual positions. (This, for example, is typically what you get in a molecular CAD application after the user has inserted a set of atoms and bonds by hand.) Your job is to find a true equilibrium set of positions.

Each atom's position is represented by three numbers, corresponding to the three dimensions of space. There are many atoms, thousands in the case of a complex molecule such as a protein, for example. So a "state" in your search space is represented by, say,

9,999 numbers, and there are that many different directions in your space at right angles to each other.

By far, the simplest thing to do is to calculate the force on each atom due to the strain on each bond and move it just a little bit in that direction. Then repeat this until the force is too low to bother with. That works, as it turns out. You're essentially climbing the hill in 9,999-dimensional space, where the hilltop is the equilibrium position. (By the way, when physical scientists do this, they usually use a measure of energy, which is minimal at the equilibrium—so instead of hill climbing, they call it *steepest descents*.)

It turns out that due to the nature and geometry of chemical bonds, the closer you are to the equilibrium the more the hill (or valley, in energy terms) looks like a parabola. This is good: mathematicians have known what to do with parabolas, even 9,999-dimensional ones, for centuries. In fact, if the space were exactly a parabola, in which case a mathematician would call it a linear problem, it could be represented by a matrix (9,999 numbers square) and solved in one fell swoop by inverting the matrix. Even in the not-quite linear case, it becomes possible to take a much more direct route to the equilibrium. By far the most common algorithm for this is called the *conjugate gradient method.*

Conjugate gradients speed up the final solution once you are well onto the final hill, but it doesn't help at all with hill climbing's biggest problem, *local optima*. That means simply that if your space has many hills and you start on the wrong one, you'll get to the top of your little hill and have no way of getting off and on toward the big one.

There are many ways of attacking the problem of local optima, some of which we'll look at in detail later; but one of the best is just as simple as hill climbing itself. It's called random-restart hill climbing, and you can just about guess how it works: after you find the top of the hill you're on, start over at some random point in the space. After doing this for as long as you have patience and computer time, take the highest hilltop you found.

Here's another *n*-dimensional space: the set of weights on the units of a neural network. They're just a list of numbers, after all. Somewhere in the space is the point (actually, it's usually a region) where the weights cause the network to recognize, predict, or function as desired. Mathematically, the back-propagation algorithm for programming a neural network turns out to be hill climbing. Once the basic math behind what's going on is understood, it's possible, for example, to speed things up, and in some cases by using conjugate gradients or the other sophisticated matrix methods from mathematical physics and linear algebra.

The only really surprising thing about neural networks is that for the problems they do solve, hill climbing actually works. Even these problems seem to be so complex that the intuitive guess is that they would get quickly caught in local optima. That they don't is a hint at the power of multidimensionality: the more directions there are, the more ways there are around a roadblock.

Biased Random Walks

One way to avoid getting stuck in a local optimum is to have happy feet, a wanderlust that won't let you stay in the same place. In practice this involves mixing a certain amount of randomness with the uphill direction. The standard form for using randomness like this is called *simulated annealing*. In a cooling metal object, the positions of the atoms represent a state and the different crystallizations represent local optima. Thermal motion of the atoms is a random wandering of the state. Annealing is a process of raising and lowering the temperature of the object to nudge the crystallization into a more globally optimal state, which results in a stronger object. Simulated annealing does the same with the randomness added to an otherwise standard hill-climbing approach. It's a valuable technique especially where a useful starting state is known and the nature of the space would make random-restart hill climbing inefficient.

An interesting example of a search method closely related to simulated annealing was used in COPYCAT and the other FARG programs (see chapter 12). The chief point of interest was that the state was represented not as a point in *n*-space but as a complex symbolic structure. Constructor and destructor routines took the equivalent of uphill and downhill steps, influenced by a global temperature variable. COPYCAT and its successors remain a tantalizing blend of symbolic and dynamical methods.

UTILITY-GUIDED SEARCH

Suppose you're using search to solve a maze. Your path through the maze is defined by the choices you take at junctions. Each time you hit a junction, you can either try one of its forks or go back and try a fork from a previous junction (this is a pencil-and-paper maze, not a cornfield). If you always keep going (until you hit a dead end), we call what you're doing *depth-first search*. If you always go back, you're doing *breadth-first search*. It's more interesting if you're a little smarter about it and always take whichever junction you've reached so far that it is closest to the goal point. This is called *best-first search*.

If you're looking at a map and trying to find the best route, your instinctive method and best-first search are very similar. If you're solving a maze, the fiendish-maze designer will have gone to extra trouble to make sure that your estimate of the distance of a given junc-

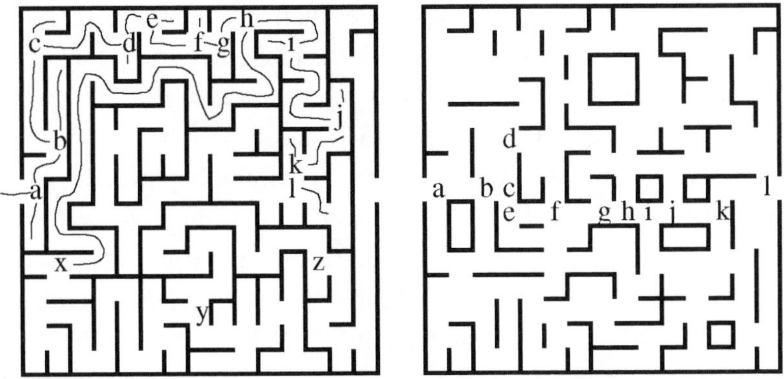

Fig. 9.4: Fiendish and nonfiendish mazes.

tion to the goal is nearly worthless, as in the left-hand maze in fig. 9.4. On the other hand, there are plenty of nonfiendish problems where an estimate of how close you are is useful, as in the right-hand maze.

In general, it is extremely useful to have some way of knowing whether to keep searching and which of the choices of search to take. In chess, for example, suppose you are able to take a knight with a rook. The evaluation function will indicate a good position, since your opponent has lost his knight. Suppose, however, that the knight was covered and in the next move your rook is taken. Now things look worse instead of better. If your search had stopped with the knight, you would have gotten a distinctly bad estimate of the position. This is called the *horizon effect*. Chess programs attempt to ameliorate the horizon effect by not stopping at positions where a capture is possible. For other kinds of search, it may be more difficult, or impossible, to avoid it.

UNIVERSAL AI

In some not terribly useful theoretical sense, search is all we need for AI. After all, evolution created natural intelligence, and evolution is just natural search. But, by counting every organism that ever lived as an experiment, the total number of experiments evolution took to produce us is staggering. Similarly, although Ray Solomonoff's "search all the Turing machines" formulation is incomputable, there are approximations that are not.[5] Unfortunately, they are still intractable, requiring, like evolution, a staggering number of trials to produce a complex structure. A working AI is going to require more than simple search.

However, within its purview, search is extremely powerful. At one point in the Kasparov/DEEP BLUE match, the computer unexpectedly offered a pawn exchange when it could have simply advanced its queen to an extremely potent position. "This move jarred Kasparov, who later described it as brilliantly subtle."[6] Whatever form an AI may ultimately take, it seems certain that search will be a significant element of its mechanism.

CHAPTER 10
Fun and Games

If counsel cannot agree on a neutral site, they shall meet on the front steps of the Sam M. Gibbons U.S. Courthouse, 801 North Florida Ave., Tampa, Florida 33602. Each lawyer shall be entitled to be accompanied by one paralegal who shall act as an attendant and witness. At that time and location, counsel shall engage in one (1) game of "rock, paper, scissors." The winner of this engagement shall be entitled to select the location for the 30(b)(6) deposition to be held somewhere in Hillsborough County during the period July 11–12, 2006.

—Judge Gregory A. Presnell, US District Court (Florida Middle District)

If you were one of the bickering lawyers who drove the exasperated Judge Presnell to this unusual but amusing tactic, you would now be faced with a classic example from the field of study called *game theory*. Each lawyer has a choice of three alternatives—rock, paper, or scissors—and the outcome of the game depends on that choice and the choice of the other lawyer:

You\him	Rock	Paper	Scissors
Rock	0 \ 0	–1 \ 1	1 \ –1
Paper	1 \ –1	0 \ 0	–1 \ 1
Scissors	–1 \ 1	1 \ –1	0 \ 0

You pick the row, he picks the column. Whichever box is selected tells your score\his score. A score of 0 means a tie (presumably you just replay the game), 1 means you win, –1 means you lose. Rock, paper, scissors is technically a *symmetric* game, meaning it looks the same to each player (as contrasted with chess, for example, where one player moves first). It is also a *zero-sum* game: the scores in each box add up to 0. If you win, he loses; if he wins, you lose. For zero-sum games, we don't actually have to list both numbers in each box, since the him score is always the negative of the you score.

What game theory tells us about rock, paper, scissors is that the best you can expect is to win, lose, and draw equally, and that the strategy to achieve that is to pick randomly from your alternatives each time. Any other strategy has a counterstrategy that beats it consistently on the average. This is not too surprising, but then it's a simple game.

CHESS

Game theory and artificial intelligence grew up together in midcentury, although their seminal roots came out of mathematics from earlier in the century. In the case of game theory, this was John von Neumann's *minimax theorem* of 1928. The theorem applies to zero-sum games, and not only tells you what is the best strategy for a given game, but also tells you the value of the game and the amount you can expect to win on the average by playing the optimal strategy.

This is a useful, if somewhat frustrating, result for a chess player. The chess player's problem is that when he makes a move from a given board position and his opponent makes hers, what results is (almost always) not a win or a loss but simply another board position. What you "win" with one move in chess is the opportunity to play another game. The payoff matrix has squares that contain whole new payoff matrices. But if we can solve any payoff matrix down to a single value of the game, we can pop back up and view the original matrix as being filled with those values, and thus we can pick a move.

The reason it's frustrating is that chess goes too deep to solve the actual values of the games in the boxes of the boxes of the boxes and so on. At some point you have to stop and just guess. The function that does the guessing is called an *evaluation function*. A typical evaluation function would add up the values of the pieces on each side, for example, 1 for a pawn, 3 for a knight or a bishop, 5 for a rook, and so on. Then subtract the opponent's score from yours and that's your guess. Evaluation functions used in real chess programs are more sophisticated, considering elements of position, threat, and so forth, but that's the basic idea. If the evaluation function were perfect you could simply use it to pick the best position from your immediate choices. But nobody knows how to write one that good.

It's a little surprising that limited search works, considering that you haven't actually solved the whole game, or even anything close. But for many games, including chess, it does. The recursive payoff matrix, called a *game tree*, supports a form of search and does so in a way that concentrates the modest knowledge that the evaluation function provides at many possible future positions into more cogent knowledge of the present one.

Several early computer scientists, including Alan Turing and Claude Shannon, worked out the basic idea, and chess programs were among the very first AI programs. They were improved steadily through the years and, with the help of special hardware, IBM's DEEP BLUE machine/program beat the world champion and arguably the greatest human chess player, Gary Kasparov, in 1997.

GO

Kasparov seemed to feel that his was an epochal defense of humanity's intellectual supremacy, yet the affair afforded Go programmers little more than a rueful chuckle: the day a Go program can stump even an average amateur is still a long way off.

—David Mechner

Go is to Western chess what philosophy is to double-entry accounting.

—Rodney William Whitaker ("Trevanian"), *Shibumi*

By contrast to chess, programs playing Go have yet to challenge even serious amateurs, much less the top professionals. This is slightly surprising, because Go looks like a simpler game than chess. The rules are simply described: players alternate placing stones on the "points" (line intersections) on the board. You control area by surrounding it and you capture enemy stones by surrounding them ("surround" is given a rigorous definition). The player with the most area wins. That's basically it.

But unlike chess, it's a fairly difficult proposition even to write a program simply to decide if a game of Go is over! In chess, the idea is to capture the opponent's king, but the game actually ends one move short. Checkmate is the position where the king cannot escape capture in the next move. In Go, the game similarly stops short of filling in all the points, where the players will agree what the outcome would be for any empty space. There comes a point where this is obvious to the players, who see things in patterns, but to a program using the same game-tree algorithm as is used for chess there still remains a prohibitively huge search simply to discover that the game has been decided.

The difference between the human pattern-based way of playing and the computer search-based playing holds in chess, too. But in chess, the search-based way works reasonably well. In Go, it doesn't. The search tree explodes into intractability well before any knowledge-concentration effects get traction.

The chess/Go dichotomy is probably the simplest, most focused example of formalist float. First of all, note that Go does not blur out into endless fuzziness: it has a fixed, simple, finite definition that could easily be couched in the predicate calculus, for example. Second, note that the success of computer programs at chess is not due to human-created higher-level ontologies; chess players talking about the games will use terms (such as "fork") that are not explicitly written into the chess program.

On the other hand, what does happen—and this is the key to why

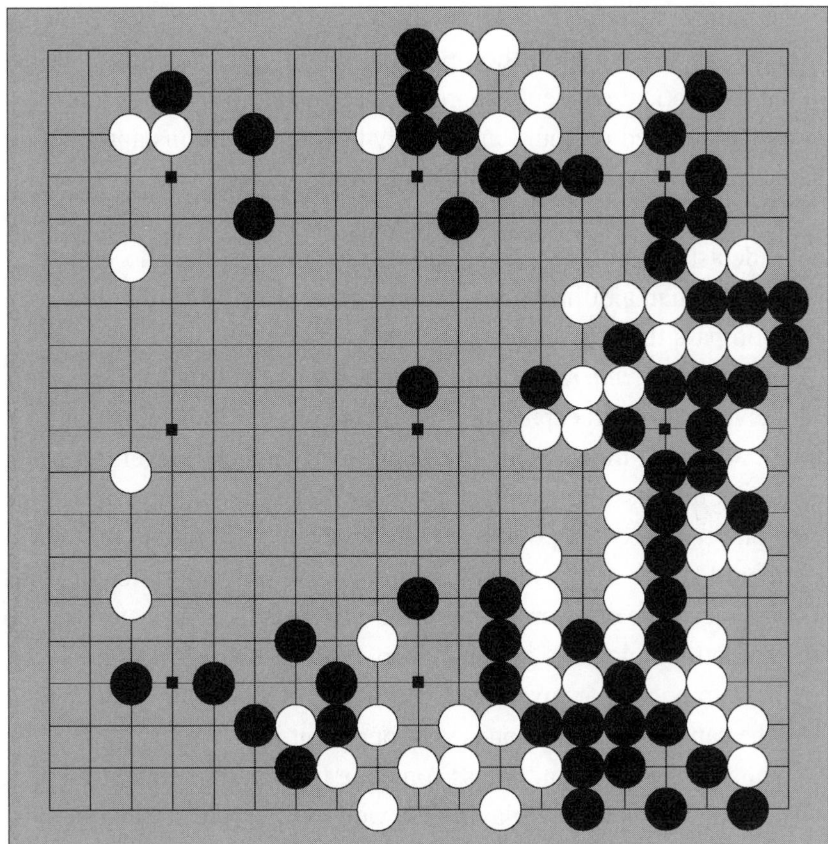

Fig. 10.1: A Go game in progress. This is a reconstruction of the famous game played in 1846 between the seventeen-year-old prodigy Shasaku and the established grandmaster Gennan Inseki. The latest move, the black stone near the center by Shasaku, made Inseki's ears blush red and is generally held to be a strategic masterstroke.

chess programs are successful—is that the nature of the game allows the search to rediscover the concept of a fork every time it runs into one. (A fork in chess is a situation where one move by you brings two enemy pieces under attack simultaneously, such that your opponent can only protect or retreat one piece, and you can take the other with impunity.) The logic of the fork is automatically followed by the recursive minimax search. To some extent, what DEEP BLUE was doing as it traced out those multibillion-position search trees was discovering, on the fly, tactical concepts approximately equal to the ones that Kasparov had learned or could intuit, only to forget them instantly before the next move! An "alien intelligence," indeed.

What happens instead in Go is that the concepts that are needed to make decisions are high level and diffuse enough that no computer having less than a billion times the power of DEEP BLUE could hope to encompass them in such a simplistic search tree.

For example, *atari* is a situation in a Go game in which one player is one move away from capturing a connected cluster of the other player's stones. Although this is sometimes explained to chess players as being like check in chess, it is perhaps more similar to threatening *any* of the other player's pieces. In other words, the connected clusters on the Go board are like the pieces in chess. But there are only six different kinds of chess piece; the number of different configurations of a cluster on a Go board is astronomical. So in playing Go, if you equate clusters to pieces, you have to be able to invent new pieces as you go, so to speak, and to infer the capabilities of the ones your opponent is inventing.

Thus, at the moment, unless someone finds another cute trick that is a special case solution, playing Go well will require solving the real AI problem, that of creating useful concepts from experience. The concepts that Go players typically talk about in describing games and strategies really are much more tenuous and fluid than those that chess players tend to use. The Trevanian quote captures something quite real, but almost impossible to quantify.

SOCCER

> *European public opinion will apparently tolerate people being fired in industries where they really care about performance. Unfortunately the only industry they care enough about so far is soccer. But that is at least a precedent.*
>
> —Paul Graham

For many people the demonstration of machine intelligence is expected to come in 2050, and it won't be the Turing Test. That's when the FIRA, the International Federation of Robot-soccer Association, expects to be able to field a team of robots that can beat the human champion soccer team.

As I write, the (human) World Cup of soccer is under way in Germany, and so is the Robocup. Robot soccer is currently a tabletop sport, featuring small battery-powered robots, but it is quite a stiff test of AI and robotics techniques for all that. Robots compete in five physical and two virtual leagues: small and medium-sized wheeled robots, four-legged robots (using the AIBO robot dog), humanoids in two size ranges, and 2-D and 3-D virtual soccer.[1]

This is demanding for AI because, like robotics in general, you can't define a problem that fits your technique; you have to control the robots, sense the field (either by cameras in each robot or by a separate overhead camera), and plan and execute an overall strategy, all in real time. The soccer robots are quite impressive, and the popularity of the event—there are over three hundred teams from over thirty countries—is quite a valuable stimulus for interest in AI worldwide.

At the 2006 Robocup there were even robot commentators, courtesy of a project of CMU, who demonstrated the ability to watch the game and said things about what was going on. Although, unlike the competitors, they received some real-time help from humans.

Whether soccer (or any formal game) can provide an impetus and a pathway to general learning capability, however, remains to be seen. There are certainly fluid and hard-to-characterize situations in a soccer game, but nothing like the complexities of Go—and the real-time nature of the game doesn't invite rumination. The associated Robocup Rescue competition is likely to provide more of a challenge in the form of sizing up unexpected situations, where robots vie against one another to rescue people trapped in collapsed buildings.

GLOBAL THERMONUCLEAR WAR

Von Neumann and Morgenstern's Theory of Games and Economic Behavior *is one of the most influential and least-read books of the twentieth century.*

—William Poundstone

I offer to auction off a dollar bill.[2] I will sell the dollar to the highest bidder, and the bidding starts at one cent. The only catch is that the rules (you must agree before being allowed to play) require that while the highest bidder pays his bid and gets the dollar, the second-highest bidder must also pay, even though he gets nothing.

So you start out bidding one cent for the dollar, hoping for a ninety-nine-cent profit. But someone else jumps into the bidding, hoping for a ninety-eight-cent profit. For a while the bidding goes as bidding normally does. In a normal auction, it would stop at ninety-nine cents or a dollar. But after you bid ninety-nine cents, your opponent bids a dollar, and you realize that if you quit now, you'll pay ninety-nine cents for nothing. Much better to pay $1.01 and get the dollar, losing only one cent net. The payoff matrix looks like this:

You\him	Raises	Stops
Raise	Play again	–$0.01\–$1.00
Stop	–$0.99\$0.00	–$0.99\$0.00

Table 10.2: The bottom line is the same in each column because if you decide to stop, the game is over.

But of course the same logic applies to your opponent, so he raises to $1.02, and so on—there is no place to stop. In fact, it just keeps getting worse and worse. The value of the game is unboundedly negative.

The dollar auction was invented by economist Martin Shubik in an attempt to capture the logic of certain kinds of mutually detrimental confrontations. It is a good model for many kinds of fighting—both participants will suffer the same increasing amount of injury and lost time, and at some point the game is not worth the candle. The very widespread dynamic in vertebrate males of fighting over females in stylized ways corresponds quite closely to the dynamic of the dollar auction. You can play dollar auction with your friends and see their basic instincts seize them. They will offer several times the value of the dollar in an attempt to avoid being bested, even though it's only a silly party game. WARNING: Don't try this with friends you hope to keep as friends. The emotions aroused can be unexpectedly strong and acrimonious.

Surprisingly enough, animals who find themselves in the logical equivalent of a dollar auction, for example, in a competitive mating display, tend to play it more rationally than humans do. The optimal strategy involves picking some limit less than a dollar, bidding up to that, and then quitting. Evolution appears to have programmed this into many species' genes.

THE PRISONER'S DILEMMA

You are cahooting together!

—Alberto Beddini in *Top Hat*

The dollar auction differs from many games invented as diversions in that it is not a zero-sum game. Many real-world interactions can be modeled by nonzero-sum games. The classic one involves being hauled into court along with a confederate and tempted by the prosecutor to rat on him. If you sing (and he doesn't), they'll let you off scot-free and soak him with a ten-dollar fine. Same thing in reverse if he sings and you don't. If you both rat on each other, you both get five-dollar fines, and if you both stoutly maintain each other's innocence you'll both get one-dollar fines.

You\him	Stoolie	Stoic
Squeal	$-5\$-5	$0\$-10
Clam	$-10\$0	$-1\$-1

Table 10.3: Stoolies and stoics.

So here's the dilemma in a nutshell. It's obviously better for you to rat, since you pay less no matter which choice he makes. He is obviously faced with exactly the same logic. So rationally, you must both defect and rat each other out. But if instead you had both hung tough and kept a zipped lip, you'd both be better off! So how can squealing have been rational?

For analyzing real-world situations it's often better to use an alternative formulation: you've made a deal to exchange some goods with someone, and you're going to leave your item in some prearranged place and then go to the other prearranged place where he's going to leave his to collect it. Your choices are to cooperate, really leaving your item, or to defect, leaving nothing and hoping to get his for free. The whole point of the trade is that your item is worth more to him than to you, and vice versa.[4]

The main reason this is a better example is that if you both cooperate, the sum of scores is positive: you both win. If you both defect, it's negative: you've both wasted time and effort for nothing. In this form the game is clearly germane to a large class of economic and other potentially beneficial interactions. Still the name Prisoner's Dilemma has been with us since 1950 and we're pretty much stuck with it.

The only way to solve the Prisoner's Dilemma is to step outside the strict assumptions of game theory. The simplest, most obvious dodge is to assume you're in cahoots with your opponent to maximize the total payoff. In the standard, symmetric formulation of the game you don't even have to get together afterward and split the take; you both get the same thing.

What a cahooter does is to assume his opponent will make the same choice he does. That makes the game simple: choose between both cooperating or both defecting. The key thing you need to know is the probability of your opponent being a cahooter. Otherwise assume he'll defect. In the above game, you should cooperate if he has a 20 percent chance or more of cahooting.

Newcomb's Problem

Real game theorists don't cahoot. To understand why cahooting actually breaks the rules of game theory, let's consider a problem that focuses on the situation of one player.[5]

You are taking part in a psychology experiment, funded by a very generous government agency. You are led into a room and on the table in front of you are two boxes. One has a glass top, and you can see that it contains a thousand dollars. The other has a wood top and you can't see what's in it.

Glass	Wood
$1000	? ? ?

You are offered a choice: take just the wood box or take both. Whatever you take, you get to keep.

Now before being led into the room, you spent a month being interviewed and tested by a battery of the best psychologists available. With the results of this process, using the best computer simulation and analysis science allows, they made a prediction of what choice you would make in this final experiment.

You've been told, guaranteed in fact, that if they predicted you would only take the wood box, leaving the glass box and its obvious thousand bucks behind, the wood box would be stuffed with a million dollars. On the other hand, if they predicted you would take both boxes, the wood box would be empty.

Once you're standing at the table, the wood box is either already full of money or already empty. There is nothing you can do, standing there at what's called the *point of choice*, that will cause money to disappear from a full box or appear in an empty one. Whatever is in the wood box is a done deal; if you leave the glass one, you're just tossing away a cool grand.

But of course, knowing that you know that, the psychologists will have predicted that you'd take both, and the wood box will be empty.

The only way to win Newcomb's Problem is to make your choice *before* the psychologists get to you. If you can do this and find some way to guarantee them that you won't change your mind, they'll have a much easier time predicting that you'll take only the wood box, and therefore that's where they'll put the money. Suppose, for example, you hire a hit man to stand outside the door with orders to shoot you if he sees you coming out with both boxes.

In real life, we run into a Newcomb's Problem in many Prisoner's Dilemma situations. You want to make a business deal, but your prospective partner will cooperate only if he can be sure you're really a cahooter. That means finding some mechanism that reliably prevents your exercise of free will at the point of choice. This can range from being a Boy Scout—"On my honor, I will take only the wood box"—to contracts enforceable by heavily armed third parties.

Superrationality

Cahooting is a stronger property than being rational. If you're both rational and you both know it for certain, you will both be cahooters; but if there's any doubt at all, you won't—a sad state of affairs that author and American academic Douglas Hofstadter has called *reverberant doubt*.[6]

Hofstadter had attempted a formulation of *superrationality*, where it was assumed that truly rational players must be cahooters, willy-nilly, because the rational answer must be the same answer for everyone. But the Prisoner's Dilemma is more than a dilemma—it's a paradox. Just as there's no rational way to evaluate the statement, "I am lying," there's no single rational solution to the Prisoner's Dilemma.

If there's just a 1 percent chance your opponent will defect, even though you are completely rational yourself, you have thereby a 1 percent chance of defecting rationally. But the 99 percent of the time he's rational must now account for your 1 percent chance of defecting, so his total chance of defecting goes to 1.99 percent. Work out the limit of the series and everybody defects whenever the original chance of defecting is anything more than infinitesimal.

Cahooting takes more than mere rationality within the game. It takes an analysis from a wider perspective and the ability to override what would have been your rational decision once you're in it.

Iterated Prisoner's Dilemma

What if you really are a cahooter and he is too? Then what's missing is for you to find some way to convince each other of your bona fides, so that a mutually beneficial interaction can result. In a world where nobody's telepathic, the standard way to do this is to show yourself to be trustworthy over a period of time. It becomes possible over a sequence of Prisoner's Dilemma interactions to judge the probability that your opponent (or partner, if you're both cooperating) is a true cahooter.

Just as in the case of the dollar auction, evolution can find a workable approach to the problem. In a famous series of tournaments run by political scientist and researcher Robert Axelrod in which programs representing Prisoner's Dilemma strategies competed, the winner was Anatol Rapoport's TIT-FOR-TAT, which simply cooperated the first time and mimicked the opponent's previous move thereafter.[7] Axelrod also ran tournaments in which a genetic algorithm was used to generate competing programs as opposed to the original one where people contributed the programs.

In some sense, TIT-FOR-TAT is an approximation to a cahooter. It always makes the same play as its opponent—it just does it one move late!

The importance of TIT-FOR-TAT has been overplayed to some extent in the popular literature.[8] It is not the optimum strategy, and indeed when the tournaments are rerun for longer periods and varying parameters, with evolving agents generated by genetic algorithms, "niceness" doesn't prevail as often as Axelrod's original results suggested.[9] Many of the conclusions to be drawn from the "evolution of cooperation" experiments must be taken as suggestive rather than as rigorous game-theoretic results.

Even so, Axelrod introduced a paradigm shift in game theory. Ever since his experiments, the importance of evolution in interpreting Prisoner's Dilemma games has been understood in a way it wasn't before. The value of evolution, or any other solution to the iterated Prisoner's Dilemma, is that it gives you a way of measuring the value of being in cahoots. From a population-based point of view, a subgroup of programs that cooperate with each other can prosper, expand, and choke out nasty strategies, *even though none of them ever wins a specific match* against, say, ALWAYS DEFECT.

One of the remarkable things Axelrod discovered in the computer tournaments was that one could find descriptions of the programs that did well, that corresponded to character traits. They were:

- Nice: programs that did well started by cooperating and only defected if the other program defected first.
- Retaliatory: when the other program did defect, they defected back.
- Forgiving: if the other program went back to cooperating, they did the same.
- Clear: if a program is random, or so complex as to be effectively random, the best strategy against it is ALWAYS DEFECT. Thus, programs that cooperated tended to be observably simple.

If this were all there were to it, and these traits evolved robustly to take over any population, there would be no need for ethics or law. But they don't completely solve the problem: TIT-FOR-TAT can get stuck in unending retaliation, as the great feud between the Hatfields and the McCoys illustrates. TIT-FOR-TAT doesn't solve Newcomb's Problem.

Further research into evolutionary game theory shows that the optimal strategy is strongly dependent on the environment constituted by other players. In a population of all two-state automata (of which TIT-FOR-TAT is one), a program by the name of GRIM is optimal. GRIM cooperates until its opponent defects just once and then it always defects after that. The reason it does well is that the population has quite a few programs whose behavior is oblivious or random. Rather than trying to decipher them, it just shoots them all and lets evolution sort them out.

Chances are Axelrod's original tournaments are a better window into parts of the real, biological evolutionary dynamic than are the later tournaments with generated agents. The reason is that genetic algorithms are still unable to produce anything nearly as sophisticated as human programmers. Thus, GRIM, for example, gets a foothold in a crowd of unsophisticated opponents. It wouldn't do you any good to be forgiving or clear if the other programs were random.

But in the long run, slightly nicer programs can outcompete slightly nastier ones and then in turn be outcompeted by slightly nicer ones yet. For example, in a simulation with "noise," meaning that occasionally at random a cooperater is turned in to a defector, TIT-FOR-TAT gets hung up in feuds, and a generous version that occasionally forgives a defection does better—but only if the really nasty strategies have been knocked out by TIT-FOR-TAT first. Even better is a strategy called PAVLOV, due to an extremely simple form of learning. PAVLOV repeats its previous play if it won, and switches if it lost. In particular, it cooperates whenever both it and its opponent did the same thing the previous time—it's a true, if very primitive, cahooter. PAVLOV also needs the ground to be cleared by a "stern retaliatory strategy like tit-for-tat."[10]

So, in simplistic computer simulations at least, evolution seems to go through a set of phases with different (and improving!) moral character.

CHAPTER 11
Design and Learning

Design is a kind of search. It doesn't sound like much in the way of design to pick a chess move, but you can't play very well unless you've designed a plan. The search in chess implicitly picks a plan (of the "if he does this, I'll do that" kind) out of the astronomically vast number of possible ones. More concretely, if you're designing a program, or a machine, or a house, or even deciding where to put your furniture, you're picking a selection and arrangement of parts out of a well-nigh-infinite set of possibilities.

Learning is a kind of design. If you are a mind and you learn something, you have either designed a new part or redesigned an existing part of yourself. For a mind that is a computer program, learning can be thought of as programming (or debugging). Learning *how* is designing a program to do something. Learning *why* is designing part of a simulator that embodies the appropriate causal laws. Learning *what* a concept is involves creating programs that can recognize it, predict it, and simulate it.

Automatic programming was a significant subfield of AI in prediaspora days. It vanished in the 1980s but has begun to reappear in various guises, some of which we shall see below.

MULTILEVEL DESIGN

Let's suppose we're designing a grandfather clock. We know we want it to have an hour hand and a minute hand, but it might or might not have a second hand. It might or might not have a display for the month, the day, or the phase of the moon. It might require winding every day or only once a week.

To help us out in our design, we have two evaluation functions. One is from the Clock Sellers' Cartel, and it tells us how much a clock will sell for, given the visible features it has. The other function is from the Gear Grinders' Guild, and it tells us how much it will cost to make the clock, given a description of all the internal shafts, gears, and escapements.

We as clock designers know many different ways to put the gears together, for example, to make a second hand work.

So our program simply rips through all the possible designs, subtracts the cost from the value, and finds the one that yields the biggest profit, right?

Wrong. Like all possible chess games, the number of possible designs even for a grandfather clock is astronomical. We have to do something smarter. One approach that helps organize things is to pick a set of visible features and then search through all the different internal designs that would implement it, separate from the designs for other feature sets. The question then is how much work to put into the search for a design for, say, a clock with a second hand and a moon-phase dial, as compared to one that displays the date and only needs to be wound once a week.

What we can do is try a few designs for each visible feature set and treat them as a statistical sample of the population of designs for that type. From the statistics we can estimate how good the best design of that type will be, and then we will know how much it will be worth. We can conduct a kind of utility-based search whereby we compare these for the different feature combinations and decide which one or ones are most worth fully designing for comparison.

For most kinds of design it's possible to break the organization down into many different levels of abstraction. In the example of the clocks, we had two levels: the feature set and the gear arrangement. For real designs there are typically many more. For example, in the 1980s and 1990s there was a project that did automatic design of a specialized processor that ran PROLOG as its native instruction set.[1] They used fifty levels of abstraction. That's extreme, since most design projects use ten or so.

Given this, you can do a best-first search where designs at all the different levels have estimated values. You can even estimate the amount of search time that will be necessary to achieve a given value, and, if you know how much search time costs, you can use this in the decision as well.[2]

EVOLUTION-BASED SEARCH

William James, the grandfather of cognitive psychology, began speculating not too long after Darwin published *Origin of Species* that the brain uses an evolutionary process to produce ideas. After lying fallow for a century or so, the idea has had a strong renaissance in recent years. Several neural theorists, notably Gerald Edelman and William Calvin, have pushed the notion that an internal variation and selection process is how the brain does what it does.

Here's the full quote about search from Turing's 1948 manifesto:

> It may be of interest to mention two other kinds of search in this connection. There is the genetical or evolutionary search by which a combination of genes is looked for, the criterion being survival value. The remarkable success of this search confirms to some extent the idea that intellectual activity consists mainly of various kinds of search.
>
> The remaining form of search is what I should like to call the "cultural search." As I have mentioned, the isolated man does not

> develop any intellectual power. It is necessary for him to be immersed in an environment of other men, whose techniques he absorbs during the first 20 years of his life. He may then perhaps do a little research of his own and make a very few discoveries which are then passed on to other men. From this point of view, the search for new techniques must be regarded as carried out by the human community as a whole, rather than by individuals.[3]

Turing clearly understood not only the value of biological evolution but what later came to be called *memetic evolution* as well, as a kind of search. He was, as usual, ahead of his time. In the 1960s computer scientist John Holland developed the first useful implementations of *genetic algorithms* (GAs), but it took two more decades for the idea to catch on, as computers of the day simply didn't have enough processing power to apply it to even simple problems.

GAs involve a representation and an evaluation function, like other forms of search, but instead of trying the possible states one at a time, they maintain a population of them. This is like best-first search, except that new states are created from two old ones and new states are created from a sampling of the better existing states, rather than just the best. This gives GAs a robust adaptability and searching power beyond that of the simpler (but less computationally demanding) search methods.

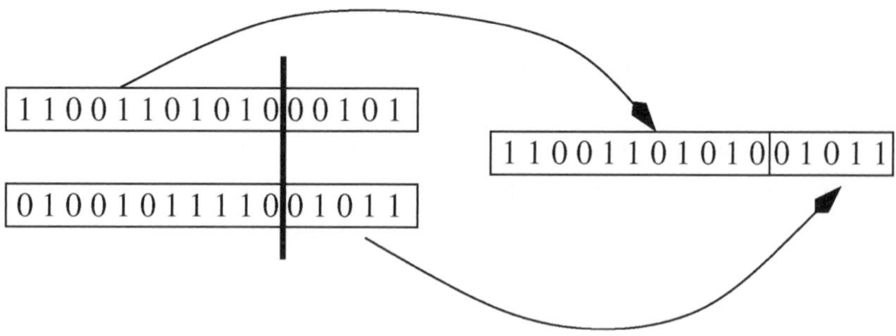

Fig. 11.1: Crossover.

In Holland's original genetic algorithm, the individual states were represented as bit strings. An operation called a *crossover* was used to create a new string from two old ones. Take two strings of the same length, then pick some point along them. Take all the bits to the left of that point from one string and all the bits to the right from the other, then link them to make the new string. In later variants, the individual is often represented by a point in n-space or by a symbolic tree. (The symbolic tree often represents a small program, in which case the process is called *genetic programming*.)

GAs work. During the 1990s I was involved in a fairly substantial project sponsored by the Department of Defense at Rutgers in which the group was to apply AI techniques to engineering design. We worked on a wide variety of applications, including sailboats, cargo ships, airplanes, rocket nozzles, and computers. We used a wide variety of synthesis and evaluation methods. By and large, GAs did as well as the specialized methods, and no other single method worked as well across all the different applications.

GAs are a rapidly evolving field. They are used to design everything from nuclear reactors to control programs for walking robots.[4]

A variant of genetic algorithms is genetic programming, invented and espoused by John Koza, a student of Holland (and also the inventor of the rub-off instant lottery ticket). Koza's Web pages list thirty-six cases where his genetic programming system (running on a thousand-processor supercomputer and taking up to a month) has produced designs or algorithms that are competitive with those of humans; in twenty-one cases it reinvented patented designs, and in two cases it got there first, resulting in a new, patentable invention.[5] Koza's system even wrote a soccer-playing program that scored in the middle of the field at the Robocup.

On the other hand, in my experience GAs are particularly sensitive to representation. Any search is the representation that creates the search space and determines whether it's big or small, well or poorly connected, straightforward like a map or fiendish like a maze. But a GA is also dependent on the crossover operator. Suppose there are two features in the desired object that depend on each other to have a useful effect—a wheel and an axle, a sensor and an amplifier, a sail and a mast. The features are controlled by bits in the "chromosome" string. If the bits are close together, the wheel and axle will tend to be inherited together; but if they are far apart, offspring will tend to get the wheel but not the axle, undoing the search it took to find a design with both. But you don't know which features will need to be together to start with—that's what the GA is supposed to be finding out for you.

The most robust of the representations used in GAs seem to be the n-space ones, in the cases where the *fitness landscape*, the n-dimensional surface formed by the values of the fitness function, is reasonably well behaved in the space. In these cases a more useful breeding function than simple crossover is one that selects a random point inside an n-dimensional "cigar" that covers the two parent points at its ends.

Bayesian Credit Assignment

As noted above, one of the trickier phenomena of representation in GAs is the fact that "genes" that need to occur together can be separated in the string. This can make it very difficult to build up the structures that form a solution. Conversely, genes can be linked by being close when they shouldn't be, giving a poor *allele* (a variant for that particular gene) a free ride along with a better one. This can tend to drive the GA into a local optimum.

Holland's original GA work included a technique called *inversion* that was intended to ameliorate this problem. It involved flipping parts of the string around as part of the evolutionary process in the hopes that strings with appropriate genes close together would outcompete the others. In practice this seems not to have worked too well, and it is not used much today.

A fairly recent technique that has shown considerable promise is called the BOA, or the Bayesian Optimization Algorithm.[6] It builds a Bayesian network model of the internal structure of the strings (or whatever other representation you want to use), and it uses that to generate new individuals. For certain kinds of problems, this is a significant advance. It can substantially reduce the amount of search necessary for a solution.

BOA doesn't come for free, though. It requires taking enough statistics from enough evaluations to form the Bayesian model, and forming the model itself is a search process. (It resembles utility-based search in this regard.) So it both adds complexity and consumes significant processing power. Even so, BOA, or more likely one of its many variants or successors being actively researched now, might possibly enable GAs to play in a different league than other search algorithms.

ECONOMICS-BASED SEARCH

In June 1961 the Office of Naval Research sponsored a symposium on self-organizing systems at the University of Illinois. The attendees included a variety of well-known names from cybernetics, including Ross Ashby, inventor of the homeostat; Frank Rosenblatt, of perceptron fame; Warren McCulloch, the American neurophysiologist who worked with Walter Pitts on the relation between brain functions and computing; Saul Amarel, mentioned in connection with the missionaries and cannibals; and mathematical psychologist Anatol Rapoport, inventor of TIT-FOR-TAT. There was also an economist in attendance, Friedrich August von Hayek, who was destined to become a Nobel laureate. In the year 2000 retrospective, the *New Yorker*'s economic correspondent John Cassidy wrote, "It is hardly an exaggeration to refer to the twentieth century as the Hayek century."[7]

That's a reasonable description from an economist's point of view. For most of the century, Hayek was that rarest and bravest of creatures, a lone intellectual holding and espousing ideas against the riptide of opinion running the other way. In this case, Hayek championed the vitality of the market economy against the worldwide fad of central planning. No other economist in the world in, say, 1950 would have predicted the collapse of the Soviet Union, but in retrospect, the economic history of the twentieth century was a resounding confirmation of his ideas.

The difference between Hayek's theories and the other economists' looks a lot like formalist float. His key insight was that a market economy was an adaptive discovery system. Other theories, such as those of Keynes, for example, were more technically brilliant in describing the economy as a machine, but their machines were like our humanoid robot gedankenexperiment: they couldn't grow or adapt themselves to new circumstances or technologies. Hayek was at the self-organizing systems conference because he knew that the mind and the market shared some deep, important properties.

Planning and Programming

It would seem reasonable then to look to the market for models of computational adaptability, just as Holland had looked to evolution. The idea has occurred to various theorists over the years. One was an AI researcher named Eric Baum. His experiments involved a blocks-world problem that is a standard challenge for AI. Whether it's a planning problem or a programming one depends on how good the system is; if it's at one level of competence, it produces a plan for solving a specific case of the problem; if it's better, it produces a program that can solve many, maybe even all such problems.

Baum wanted to see if using an economic model would help with the credit allocation problem. He wrote:

> Violation of property rights and the Tragedy of the Commons are common problems for evolutionary programs unless property rights are explicitly enforced. For example, John Holland famously proposed Classifier Systems, possibly the first evolutionary program based on an explicit economic metaphor. In these programs many agents were active at any given time. When a reward came in, it was split among the active agents. But this is a recipe for Tragedy of the Commons because all agents want to be active when money is

> expected, whether or not their action hurts the performance of the system. . . .
>
> Holland's hope was that Classifier Systems would evolve long chains of agents that would take successive actions to solve problems: for example, a chain of agents taking sequential actions to solve Blocks World problems. In fact, empirically, they only evolved chains a few agents long, and gradually the Classifier Systems community gave up on chaining. But from my point of view, this lack of chaining was absolutely to be expected because the Classifier Systems never imposed property rights.
>
> A program cannot hope to form long chains of agents unless conservation of money is imposed and property rights are enforced. To evolve a long chain, where the final agent achieves something in the world and is paid by the world, reward has to be pushed back up the chain so that the first agents are compensated as well. But pushing money up a long chain will not succeed if money is being created or is leaking, or if agents can steal money or somehow act to exploit other agents. If [so], the system will evolve in directions to exploit this rather than creating deep chains to solve the externally imposed problems. Solving the world's problems is very hard, and an evolutionary program will always discover any loophole to earn money more simply.[8]

This is in fact one of the things that happened to EURISKO, which was essentially an evolutionary search model. In its "ecology" there developed internal analogs to the viruses and worms that plague the Internet today. For example, since credit assignment was done by heuristic, one heuristic evolved that simply claimed credit for every valuable discovery.

This can be seen as the incursion of formalist float *inside* a system, in the guise of not having the proper feedback. An economic model, where monetary flows run counter to every resource transfer, has at least some feedback—the money—built in.

Baum created an evolutionary, market-based system (named HAYEK) that solved a variety of blocks world and other problems that ordinary GAs were not able to solve. The structure of the market was an ingenious sequential auction mechanism.[9] Other researchers have adopted and extended the HAYEK machine architecture with promising results, for example, in the field of learning probabilistic models of phenomena.[10] In all of these cases, the system is designing small pieces of programs, the key ingredients for autogenous learning.

Design

The design of complex machines is a task so daunting that even for human designers it is broken down into myriad parts. This is done both by levels of abstraction—in designing a computer, for example, we may design the instruction set as a completely different activity from designing the circuitry—and by decomposition, breaking the overall design down into parts as separate problems, for example, in a robotic system, separate people or teams design the mechanical arm, the power supply, the controller, and the software.

There remains a problem: the environment for which any one part is designed consists of all the other parts it must interact with. They must fit physically together. They must be tightly enough coupled to transmit the desired forces, objects, signals, and so on, and yet they must also be insulated enough not to transmit undue heat or vibration. In general, engineers must reduce undesired side effects to an acceptable level. The same kinds of design pressures occur between levels of abstraction: I can design an ingenious gear train, but it won't do me any good if it needs gears I don't have.

Thus, while designing each part, we must take full consideration of all the rest of the system. Clearly this defeats the purpose of the breakdown, leaving us right back where we started. What we'd like to do is to find a way to abstract from the rest of the system just the information that is relevant to the design of the part under consideration.

In the real world, evolution produces complex designs in the face of limited resources. Economics, and more specifically price theory, concerns itself with the formation of global optima by means of local mechanisms. It would be nice if these models could be combined and addressed to the specific problems of multilevel, multipart design.

So in the 1990s my colleagues at Rutgers and I experimented with a system that combined economic and genetic mechanisms in the design process. We called it Charles Smith.[11] It consisted of a collection of software agents that interacted by means of buying and selling objects (or services).

To distinguish our software agents from other formulations, we called them firms. In addition to the typical GA environment that mates and kills the individuals in the standard algorithm, Charles Smith ran a kind of internal Internet that the firms used to communicate. They did this by running ads, both for sale and wanted ad types. The ads contained prices and specifications for the objects sought or offered.

Firms that were successful in commerce accumulated money. Those that were unsuccessful lost money, either by selling low and buying high or from never engaging in commerce. New firms were created and old ones destroyed in a steady-state genetic algorithm using firms' account balances as a fitness function.

A firm typically knew how to build something given various resources. Each firm only knew how to build one particular kind of its thing. The idea was for the price and matching mechanisms to make the selection.

We couldn't take a simple approach to breeding in the GA, because if we required an exact match between the sought and the offered goods for transactions to occur, no business would result. To see why, take two firms (specified by vectors of parameters), and mix them in the standard crossover fashion. Since the firms must be able to produce their outputs given their inputs, the most we can mix is the inputs or the outputs, computing one from the other as the result. However, in an environment of any complexity, randomly mixed object specifications will almost never match any existing ads.

What we did instead was to generate new firms from existing buy-and-sell advertisements. A firm might be generated from two offered goods and might produce a new product, or it might be generated from an offered and a sought good, creating a new wanted ad for whatever the appropriate difference might be. And, of course, if there were matching sets of a sought good and two offered ones that could be directly combined to form it, we wanted to generate firms to do the construction. For example, if we were to design a clock and needed a 60x speed reducer, and a 6x reducer and a 10x reducer were available, we would want to be sure that a firm would appear to want to buy the latter and offer to sell the former.

There are two properties of human market behavior that we were trying to capture. The first is that productive behavior is imitated because it is rewarded. This expands the sector of the economy doing the productive task until the competition drives the rewards back down to the average level. The second is that good market modeling is rewarded. We hoped that the firms would evolve a decent guess of their "value added," and set their prices accordingly.

A Lattice of Goods

In human markets the price mechanism carries information, but that information is grounded in the full panoply of ontological knowledge. It does us little good to know a price if we do not know what it is the price of. In a computational market model, the language in which goods are described is thus as important as all the rest of the mechanism, if not more so.

The trick in Charles Smith was that specifications in the ads could be compared; a simple operation allowed a firm to tell if one design could do all the functions but consume fewer resources than another. A set of objects that are sometimes comparable like this are called a *partial order*, or a *lattice* in math. Having a language for the ads that was a lattice over the goods was a crucial part of the system's design.

One set of experiments we did was to determine if the combined market and evolutionary mechanisms could in fact capture the same utility-based control strategies as our earlier statistical methods. We took a population of firms offering a good with a guaranteed quality level, but whose factory routines produced it with variable quality.

The buyer set an acceptable quality level and then bought from the lowest-priced firm whose advertisement matched. Then it raised the quality level to just above the quality of the actual object obtained, and repeated. When the quality desired was higher than any offered, the buyer reset to a low-quality level and repeated the entire process. What we wanted was for the sellers to find appropriate prices for the levels of quality they advertise. This would be done in standard utility-based search, including our previous work, by statistical sampling and calculation.

The initial population was distributed uniformly over price/quality space. Firms that offered too low a price or too high a quality won the bids and ran their factories, but rarely had anything to sell. They lost money from running the factory. Firms that offered too high a price or too low a quality never ran, and they lost money paying rent. (It doesn't really matter in this case what the rent is, since the GA bank-

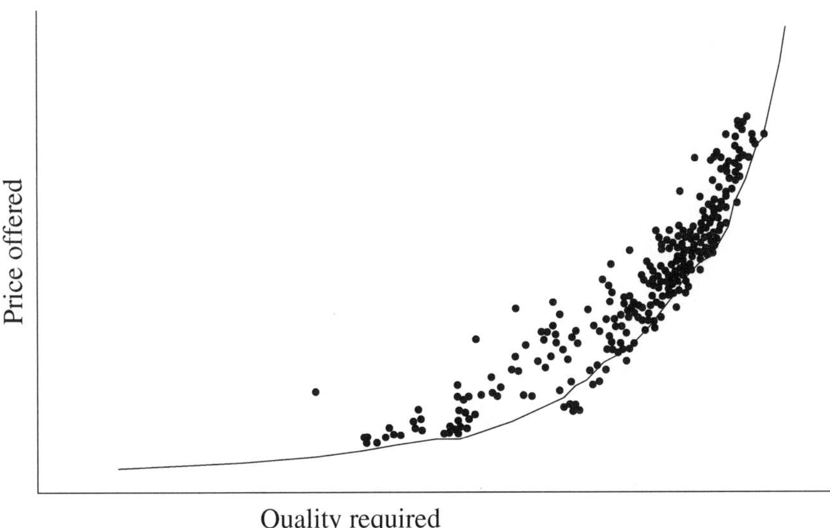

Fig. 11.2: Market distribution of firms for a randomly produced good. The curve represents the calculated locus for optimum utility. Firms below the curve went bankrupt; competition drove firms above the curve toward it. The curve itself is uneven because it was calculated statistically from a (separate) sampling of the factory function.

rupts firms on a relative rather than absolute scale, and any firm making money more slowly than the others is thus at risk.) The profitable firms lay in a band between these regions, as seen in fig. 11.2.

This showed that the firms could find appropriate price levels; it remained to be seen whether the GA part of the system could produce firms that improved the designs produced. This is the really tough part of actual human markets; nobody understands entrepreneurs. In fact, the classic Keynesian *hydraulic model of the economy* misses entrepreneurial activity completely!

Charles Smith did a little bit better than the other search methods we used as a comparison. We came to the conclusion that we didn't have enough computer power to do it properly. This was the 1990s, and the power available now as of this writing is something like a thousand times greater. The ideas have lain largely fallow in the meantime, but economics-based search is an approach that holds a lot of unexploited promise for learning and design.

Chapter 12
Analogy and Perception

You cannot step twice into the same river; for other waters are continually flowing in.

—Heraclitus of Ephesus

As I write this, I'm looking out of my window at a tree. It's springtime, and the buds on the tree are beginning to flower. A gentle breeze stirs the branches; the morning sun climbs through the clear blue sky, with a few puffy clouds sailing by.

The clouds are never the same, and they move around, subtly altering the illumination of the scene. The sun also rises in the sky, and shadows shorten. The shape of the tree changes from second to second as it moves with the breeze and from day to day as buds, flowers, and leaves arrive at their appointed times. The tree grows.

In short, the pattern of light falling onto the rods and the cones of my retinas as I look at the tree is a pattern that has never occurred before and never will again. It is similar to the one I saw a few moments ago, and I'm confident that I'll see a (different) similar one again a few moments hence. But they are never exactly the same.

How then can I recognize the tree as the same one from moment to moment, or from spring to fall, much less from sapling to sturdy oak?

The classic answer to this question is that there are generalized patterns, and the tree as a set of specific patterns falls within the envelope defined by the generality. One tree is a class of possible patterns; the type or kind of all oaks is a larger class that contains the classes for each individual oak.

A chipmunk scampers across the patio looking for nuts. I can't recognize individual chipmunks, but I can recognize a chipmunk as a chipmunk. Or rather, I can when I look directly at it. When seen from the corner of your eye, the chipmunk's scamper is very similar to the motion of a dried leaf blowing in the wind. (One presumes this is a form of camouflage.) It's not uncommon to see one and think it's the other until you observe it carefully.

Is there a general concept pattern for "chipmunk scampering or leaf tumbling in the wind?" There is now, for me, but I didn't have such a concept a few years ago. There's certainly no word in English with that meaning. The concept got formed after a few cases of seeing chipmunks that turned out to be leaves and leaves that turned out to be chipmunks.

It is by now quite widely accepted that analogy is a basic operation of thought. We appear to have basic intuitive concepts, such as maps of space that allow us to navigate. In the brain this particular function appears to be localized in the hippocampus. Concepts recent in evolution, such as a "landscape of time," are formed by analogy in a direct, physical way—in humans, the hippocampus is used for thinking about time in a way not found in, say, rats.[1]

STRUCTURE MATCHING

The standard symbolic AI approach to analogy is to first create symbolic structures that describe the things you want to draw an analogy between and then to find a map between those structures. Marvin Minsky's successor at MIT, Patrick Henry Winston, for example, exhibits an algorithm called "describe and match" in his AI textbook.[2] To recognize an object, you must describe it in terms of an appropriate set of features and match the description against your library of objects. Thomas Evans's program ANALOGY (in *Semantic Information Processing*), which solved IQ test geometric analogy problems, was the classic golden age attack on the analogy problem. It used describe and match.[3]

At the lower levels of cognition, this works well. In particular, our various sensory interpretation mechanisms contain a variety of feature detectors, hardwired by evolution, which are "appropriate" and generally useful in natural environments. (And we usually manage to design our artificial environments so that they remain comprehensible to our senses!)

Thus, our visual systems have feature detectors for edges, lines, the coordinated motion of a moving object, colors, textures, and so on, and are able to discount such things as lighting effects that don't contribute to object recognition, even though they cause more variation in the raw image than features that do. Our auditory systems automatically pick out human speech and distinguish phonemes. Our sense of taste picks out just four features—sweet, salt, sour, and bitter—that happen to be very useful for distinguishing nutritious and poisonous foodstuff in the natural environment.

The further up the ladder toward abstract concepts you go, however, the harder it is to make this approach work. The problem is that a high-level concept can be described in many different ways, and you don't know which way will be appropriate for the matching you need to do until you've found the match!

Cognitive scientist Robert French points out that coffee cups are like old elephants.[4] When he's working in his office, he often goes to the kitchen to get a cup of coffee but doesn't return the empty cups, so that in time, all the cups end up dirty and in his office. I have noticed the same phenomenon myself. There is a compelling metaphor to connect to the legend of the elephants' graveyard, wherein there is some secret and mystical place that old elephants go to die. The cups match the elephants, the office matches the graveyard, the kitchen matches the hunting grounds where French's wife, who matches the elephant hunters, looks for the cups that have mysteriously vanished.

Yet it is hard to imagine a way to represent coffee cups and elephants in datastructures that would allow the structure-matching approach to handle this analogy, unless there were some idea ahead of time that this is what the representation would be used for.

TOP-DOWN REPRESENTATION

There is a tradition in the modular computational theory of mind (e.g., of Jerry Fodor) that the processes of perception are peripheral and opaque. By that he means that they are separate from and cannot be influenced by the general-purpose cognition of the central mind. An argument for this point of view can be taken from visual illusions. For example, look at fig. 12.1, the well-known Müller-Lyer illusion. You know that the centerlines in both drawings are the same length. You can even measure them. And yet it is impossible for you to look at the figure as given and not have the sense that the upper line is longer. This part of the visual apparatus, at least, is proof against correction from the conscious part of the mind.

Yet it seems clear that there are other parts of the perceptive process, at least at higher, more abstract levels, that are strongly influenced by goals, desires, and expectations. The setup of the string-at-a-

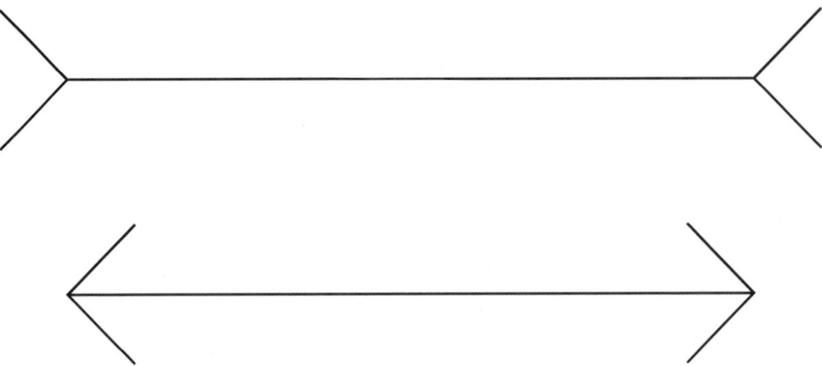

Fig. 12.1: The Müller-Lyer illusion.

bar joke can influence you to hear the phrase, "I'm afraid not," as "I'm a frayed knot," even though you would be very unlikely to interpret it this way in most ordinary contexts. One need only observe partisans of the opposing teams watching the same football game to illustrate this better—they will disagree about what one would have supposed were simple, physical, objective facts. As the subject matter becomes more abstract, examples abound: consider political opponents interpreting the same executive actions or proposed laws.

At the lowest levels there must be *some* fixed, default representation. This could be the brightness values of the pixels in a camera image or the letters making up a text file. Any higher-level interpretive process has to have something to work from. But it seems inescapable that the more abstract levels of perception are strongly influenced by expectations and goals.

COPYCAT AND THE FARGITECTURE

Douglas Hofstadter and a series of his students known as the FARG—the Fluid Analogies Research Group—have been champions of this notion for some time (e.g., Robert French is one of them). Indeed, the argument for goal-directed representation in analogy is so firmly associated with Hofstadter and his followers that we could reasonably call it the FARGument.

A term that is occasionally heard, FARGitecture, refers to the architecture of a series of programs produced by Hofstadter and company over the years to explore this concept. The most famous of these was COPYCAT, written by Melanie Mitchell. In COPYCAT and the other FARGitecture programs, a situation is described in terms of low-level descriptors and the program must construct a higher-level representation. The form of the representation is guided by the fact that there are two objects in the situation to be described, and it is desired that the system form an analogy between them: it must see them as "the same" at some abstract level.

COPYCAT operates on letter sequences undergoing transformations. An example problem is:

abc	=>	abd
pqr	=>	?

COPYCAT must find a representation for "abc" and "pqr" such that the description of what's done to "abc" to produce "abd" can be done to "pqr." It could always say, "Three letters; change the last one to 'd'," but that is unsatisfying both to the experimenter and, as it turns out, to COPYCAT. A better description is possible: both initial strings are triples of alphabetically successive letters, and the mutation involves changing the final letter into its own successor.

"Three successive letters" is a more satisfying description, intuitively, because it has a lower information entropy; less than 5 bits as opposed to more than 14 for "three letters." It is a lot more difficult to apply the information-theoretic form of Ockham's razor to the selection of a mutation rule, but the same principle is at work: it seems simpler and more compact to reuse the concept of successor from the description of the strings themselves than to start from scratch.

I'll refer to the whole operation as *analogical quadrature*, referring to good old-fashioned quadrature in geometry, which means constructing a square. In our case there is a conceptual square being constructed. In the example, the relationship between *abc* and *abd* is parallel to the one between *pqr* and the answer, and the relationship between *abc* and *pqr* is parallel to the one between *abd* and the answer.

How COPYCAT and the other FARG programs do this is by a random search in a space of descriptions. COPYCAT comes equipped with a small semantic network sufficient to describe the features of interest in the letter strings. Its space of concepts, however, is not merely the set of nodes in the network, but in some sense the geometry of the network itself, which is mutable.

Links expand and contract under the influence of the analytical activity, changing the distances between things in the conceptual space as the search proceeds. Concept nodes gain or lose *activation*, making them more or less likely to be involved in interpretational constructions. (This is typical of semantic networks that use spreading activation.) There are two major advantages to this formulation: the metric of the semantic space can alter depending on what's been discovered so far, which enhances the semantic coherence of the result. An example is that the discovery of the successor structure in the two base strings in the example above makes it more likely that the mutation rule will be couched in terms of successorship.

The other advantage is that having a metric on the concept space allows COPYCAT to equate disparate concepts forcibly in a principled way when the need arises. An example is in the following problem, in which COPYCAT would proceed as above except that "z" has no successor, and thus some other interpretation must be found:

abc	=>	abd
xyz	=>	?

In this case, the most satisfying answer is to see "abc" and "xyz" as mirror images at the beginning and end of the alphabet, respectively, and the result is "wyz." In the process, COPYCAT ends up drawing equivalences between some concepts and others, typically their opposites. In the FARG jargon (FARGon? OK, enough!), one concept "slips" to another.

As a result, COPYCAT is notably more flexible and subtle than the more conventional symbolic AI programs that do analogy by simple pattern matching. It is not so much the ability to equate concepts as the ability to do it sparingly, and with equivalences that are appropriate, that is the key.

The FARGitecture search process is biologically inspired, particularly by the random workings of the mechanisms in the cytoplasm of a cell. The form of the search itself is idiosyncratic and somewhat baroque, but is not critical to the result. What is critical to the result is the form of the search space, supported by the dynamic semantic network and the ability to do the "slippages" in a principled way.

HERDING CATS

FARGitecture programs following COPYCAT can be seen as extending its capabilities and overcoming its limitations. TABLETOP and Letter Spirit operated in different domains. Back in the letter sequence domain, METACAT extended the mutation rule to a new generality and added two significant improvements to the basic analogy engine.

First was an introspective ability. COPYCAT, as a pure stochastic search (one that proceeds at random rather than methodically), could get into loops where it would follow the same promising avenue over and over, not realizing that it had done the same thing before and had hit a dead end. METACAT has a memory and recognizes situations it has been in before.

Second, as a part of its ability to recognize the same thing it recognized before, METACAT has a metalevel of description (called *themes* in the program) that form an abstract representation of its solutions. Themes, besides allowing METACAT to characterize what it's doing or what it has done, also provide an ability that COPYCAT lacked—the ability to influence the analogizing process from the top down, thus supporting the FARGument in a more direct way.

If, as Hofstadter has suggested, analogy is at the deepest core of cognition, how do we get from the FARGitecture to a cognitive engine?[5] The most pressing need, it seems to me, is the ability to learn concepts. All the FARG programs to date have come with a fixed set of concepts. There are at least two ways this could be extended. Exploratory search, as in AM and EURISKO, might for example be able to create the concept of "second-next" out of "successor of successor." Chunking, as in SOAR, might be able to do the same kind of thing. COPYCAT clearly has something analogous (!) to an impasse when it hits a snag, as in the "xyz" problem, and it could form a concept something like "mirror-image" as a result.

Another big thing that human cognition appears to do is to use several different representations of something at once. One of the key values of the top-down analogy-making process is its ability to help select which of the representations is salient. This and other techniques for the management of complexity will probably prove important in a full model of cognition, but they wouldn't make sense in such microdomains as letter sequence puzzles.

LOST IN SPACE

COPYCAT's representation was an attempt to bridge the gap between the abilities of symbolic systems, such as most of the golden age LISP ones, and the greatly different abilities of neural networks. Neural networks were opaque compared to explicitly coded knowledge and hard to compose into more complex systems. But they seemed to be able to find new representations for the problems they were able to solve.

COPYCAT's *slipnet* was an intriguing combination of a semantic network and a physical simulation, but the semantics of the semantic network were encoded in little snippets of LISP code (*codelets*), which all had to be built by hand. Thus, every time a new concept was added, new code had to be written. It is worth exploring whether a representation can be found that will do this automatically in some sense. A good candidate is the numeric vector in *n*-space that is the standard representation for systems in the physical sciences. The aspect that makes it so useful is that the relationships in the data are encoded in geometric relationships in *n*-dimensional space, and so will any new ones, implicitly, whether we thought about them and wrote code or not.

Classic control/systems theory represents a system as a transition matrix that is multiplied by the state vector to produce the time derivative of the state vector (the entire effect being known as the *transfer function*). Such a matrix is easily capable of representing rotations, flips, stretches, and the like in the space; rotations are particularly useful because they can interchange axes, which will in effect swap one symbol for another. This doesn't capture all geometric relationships, not by a long shot, but it does capture enough to get started.

We see in fig. 12.2 a collection of COPYCAT problems that can be solved by geometric remappings, including one COPYCAT itself cannot solve.

In each case we take the target pattern and try to map it onto the initial template pattern using some transformation. This turns out to be mathematically equivalent to solving a system of simultaneous equations—a process for which we have centuries of experience and extremely sophisticated techniques. When this succeeds, perhaps with a hint from *landmarks* such as the end of the alphabet, we do the same transformation to the final template pattern to get the result.

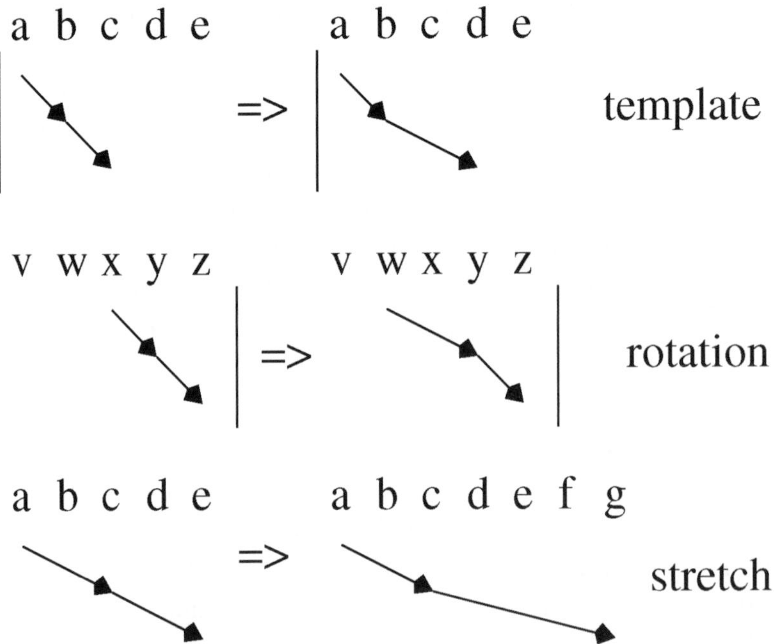

Fig. 12.2: COPYCAT-like analogical quadrature by linear transformations in a geometric representation. (Vertical line represents *alphabet boundary*.)

In simpler cases, if the encoding into n-space has the right properties, analogical quadrature in n-space is just ordinary geometric quadrature, which amounts to nothing more than vector addition.

CASE-BASED REASONING

> *We do not include in this chapter any articles discussing learning by analogy, since this area has not received much attention.*
>
> —*Handbook of Artificial Intelligence*

Here's a simple way to learn: remember everything you did and what happened as a result. It will help if you can remember what a bunch of other people did and what happened to them as a result, too. Then, whenever you want something to happen, find the closest analogy to the result you want in your memory, apply analogical quadrature, and do the indicated action.

This is called case-based reasoning (CBR), and it has been applied with limited success in areas where the describe-and-match technique can be applied to domains where an ontology of modest size covers the salient features. An example is a database of lots of patients who have seen doctors, each of their cases being described by a list of symptoms and test results. The case-based reasoning system would take a new case, see if there were old ones like it, and prescribe whatever it was the doctor had done in those cases. CBR awaits a more flexible representational ability—one in which, for example, COPYCAT-like re-representation is used—before it can become generally useful.

ASSOCIATIVE PROCESSING

It also awaits a lot more processing power. Finding the best match in any given case, if the FARG method is used, might involve doing a re-

representation of each item in memory. This implies that the processing power necessary increases linearly with the number of memories you have.

By the 1980s AI had run into this problem in a number of forms. The bottom line was that the more an AI program knew, the slower it was. Quite a bit of effort was spent trying to find ways around that conundrum, with ever-more ingenious schemes working to get the right piece of knowledge when and where it was needed.

But that's not how the brain works. People, as the AI researchers noted with frustration, actually get faster when they know more; knowing more means they are more likely to know just the right thing they need in any situation.

The difference isn't that the brain has some super-ingenious indexing scheme (although it may). The blindingly obvious difference is that the brain is an *associative processor*. Each neuron represents a few kilobytes of memory and about a million instructions per second of processing power. The more memory you add, the more processing power you have. In standard computer system architecture, there's a rule of thumb that the processing power and memory should be balanced so that the processor can touch every element of memory in one second. The brain has at least one hundred times as much processing power per memory element.

So, instead of having a big batch of passive memory, like miles of filing cabinets that we must search, taking each item one at a time through what's called the *von Neumann bottleneck*, suppose instead that we took each small batch of memory and associated a small processor with it.[6] This is called an associative processor.[7] Each little processor does one comparison, all at the same time. It takes no longer to do a million comparisons than to do one, since if we have the memory to store million items, we have a million processors. It's as if there were a separate clerk for each filing cabinet, and when you wanted to find something, you yelled, "Who's got the Flintstone file?" That's how the brain does it.

A hardware associative memory could be built much more cheaply than a general-purpose processor with the same raw MIPS rating. This represents the technological road not taken, of course, so any numbers are pure speculation. But I would estimate that if associative hardware had been developed at the same rate as conventional computers, searching would be a hundred times faster at the same price level.

It seems likely, however, that either general-purpose processors or special-purpose variants such as digital signal processors will be able to simulate associative processors at the desired speeds before real hardware associative processors are built at that size. Thus, worrying about the hardware version now is probably premature optimization.

CHAPTER 13
Design for a Brain

The best way to predict the future is to invent it.

—Alan Kay

What follows is my attempt to investigate what a computational mind might look like. Since my inclinations and experience have always been as a systems designer, I will do this by attempting to describe a design, at a very abstract level, of an AI. I'm going to use techniques not only from symbolic AI, but from all over the map: from standard scientific computation, robotics, and statistics, which is pretty much par for the course in AI nowadays. This will be extremely speculative, and it will then be up to the reader to judge whether it would work this way.

METHODOLOGY

Premature optimization is the root of all evil.

—C. A. R. Hoare

The first thing to do is to pull free from the tar pit of premature optimization. This is essentially the same strategy as used by someone who invents a new high-level programming language and implements it as an interpreter in whatever language is available, intending to write a compiler in the new language itself. Implementations of LISP are often done this way—a technique called *bootstrapping* (a reference to the notion of pulling oneself up into the air by one's bootstraps). A working AI should be able to do software experimentation and optimization as well as anyone, and so we can put that part off for a while. And we'll just assume we have the horsepower, within reason, to run on.

Imagine that Leonardo da Vinci had invented the internal combustion engine. Could it have been built in 1500? Engines can be made to work in a wide variety of configurations; the Wankel rotary engine (ca. 1957) doesn't even have cylinders. But all the configurations have in common the fact that they must be made of steel or something better. Wood, however ingeniously carved, just isn't going to work. Similarly, evidence from the animal kingdom and the different special-purpose modules in our own brains suggest a wide variety of higher-level algorithms and architectures. But the basic computing fabric is similar—and substantially different from what a software designer sees when looking at a conventional computer.

One of the main inspirations for the direction I want to take here is Hans Moravec's *evidence grids* for robotic navigation. Early robot navigation systems, including Moravec's, interpreted pictures from video cameras and other sensor information and constructed a model of the robot's surroundings. They used more-or-less standard symbolic techniques and were "brittle" (the technical term AIers use to mean unreliable)—as is much of symbolic AI. Then, as we have seen, he tried a formulation where his maps were much more fine-grained arrays of numbers representing the probabilities of there being objects at given points in space. He collected these using a Bayesian formulation. The Bayesian grids worked much better, making a huge difference in the reliability as well as the speed of the robots.[1] (The speed increase was due to the reliability of the new method; if you aren't really sure what's in front of you, you'd better go slow!)

So what I'd like to try for my "steel" is a fine-grained, numerically based formulation for basic representation and comparison instead of the simple symbols of LISP and logic. What I'm hoping for, obviously, is that some of the generality and robustness will carry over to the general cognitive task.

The brain doesn't have a huge pile of inactive data that is modified or inspected one item (out of billions) at a time. Any data that's there can be active—matching itself, broadcasting itself, modifying itself—whenever it's advantageous to do so. In particular, I'll assume that all memory is associative and can do just these kinds of things.

Please note that any question of whether representations are unitary or distributed are on a level below our horizon. When I specify an associative memory, for example, I make no assumption about whether it's holographically encoded, implemented as a network of processors, simulated in software, or real live hardware associative memory.[2] Any implementation that can give me back a pattern I've stored when I query it with a part of the pattern is considered equivalent at the level of description we're using.

Next, I'll assume that if I can give a coherent mathematical description of a data structure, a dynamical system, or an operation, some algorithm can be found to implement it. This requires you (and me) to trust my intuition of what kinds of operations are in fact able to be implemented in a not-too-outrageously inefficient way. I will on occasion make remarks relating capabilities to known neural or algorithmic ones as a sanity check; these should be taken as sanity checks and not as suggestions that the brain is actually built this way.

ROBOT 1

Let's start simply—in the spirit of Grey Walter's tortoises and Valentino Braitenberg's vehicles.[3] (These, one real and one theoretical, were small wheeled robots controlled by very simple circuits. Both were also endearingly cute.) We'll consider a point robot confined to a one-dimensional environment. Robot 1 has a mass and the ability to exert a

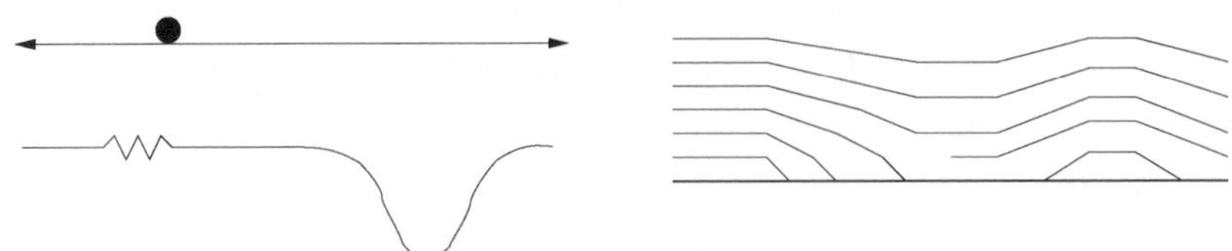

Fig. 13.1: Robot 1 (*left*) and a map of its environment showing a sticky patch and a valley. A slice of the robot's memory (*right*) in the position/velocity plane (heavy line is v = 0) for zero force.

lateral force. It can sense its position and velocity, and it can be given orders in terms of a position and/or of a velocity to adopt.

Robot 1's environment is simply a line, but at various places along the line, friction exists or doesn't, and external forces can appear as if there were hills or valleys.

We could easily control Robot 1 with a standard setup from control/systems theory, such as a PID (proportional-integral-derivative) controller, but we won't. Instead, Robot 1 has a memory. At every moment, the robot's position, velocity, the force it's exerting, and rate of change of that force are recorded as a point in four-dimensional space and linked to previous and next points. So there is a curve threaded through the space that represents the robot's history.

Now we let the robot play around in its environment. After a while, the four-dimensional memory space is going to be filled with doodles. But the space is going to have some valuable regularities. In particular, the doodles will form a nonintersecting vector field, like combed hair or the grain in a piece of wood. In other words, if the space were completely filled in, it would be possible starting at any point to follow the grain of the space and predict just what will happen next (given a particular schedule of applied force, which is under the robot's control).

But it isn't necessary to fill in the space completely; it has enormous regularities, so that interpolation schemes based on very standard curve-fitting techniques and statistics will produce a good fit after only a moderate amount of playing. Well-understood methods from physical science, such as maximum entropy estimation, should be perfectly capable of forming robust models even in the presence of measurement inaccuracies and noise. The places where data is needed the most are the parts of the space where its character changes rapidly; some fairly simple heuristics will tend to concentrate play in these areas, tracing out the warp and woof of the space with finer resolution. What's more, this isn't done blindly. At every point, Robot 1 uses its existing memory and interpolation to predict what will happen next as it plays around. Whenever the prediction is good enough, it isn't learning anything from the playing, so it gets bored and goes and plays somewhere else (in the space).

Notice what's happened. If we, as engineers, had been asked to design a point-mass robot operating in a one-dimensional environment with certain exogenous forces, we could have come up with an enormously more efficient design for any given environment—but the design wouldn't have worked in a new environment. If Robot 1 is placed in a new area where the features are different (or if the physics are different!), it would just have to start playing again—and it would know that it needed to since its predictions wouldn't be coming out right.

The last part of Robot 1's architecture is a controller that can use the predictive memory for planning. Again, this is not necessarily anything sophisticated. Commands are going to be simple, as in "move at speed x to point y." The robot has a range of force strengths and durations to choose from or a sequence of such pairs for a multistage plan. Planning is equivalent to minimizing a cost function in a space whose dimensionality is the complexity of the plan. This, again, is pretty trivial stuff compared to what is very standard in scientific numerical software or to what can be done by certain neural networks, such as a Hopfield net, in a single operation.

For reasons that will become clear later, I'm going to call a module that is equivalent to Robot 1's architecture a *sigma servo* or SIGMA, for short. This consists of an interpolating associative memory (IAM) and a controller. I'm being deliberatively vague about just what the controller does and how it works. It seems virtually certain that the ten thousand neurons in a functional cortical column could implement a SIGMA; they represent something like a gigabyte of storage and ten thousand MIPS. If that's a decent estimate, the brain has room for ten million or so SIGMAS.

Robot 1 is an abstraction, but there are plenty of places in a more complex robot where the immediate environment is like Robot 1's. Think of the rotation of a segment of an arm around a joint, for example: the space is one-dimensional and the controller often can measure the position of the joint directly.

One thing to notice is that the IAM is similar to a relational database. Each record is just a list of numbers, one for each dimension along with a key field and a link to the key of the next record in the trajectory. We could, if we liked, include an explicit time field and dispense with some of the derivative dimensions, such as velocity, given that we have the position. The question of whether something's really being stored in discrete or continuous form is of no concern; continuous can be approximated to any desired accuracy by putting more points closer together in the discrete dotted line. There's a straightforward tradeoff between more points and more derivatives that need not concern us here.

The thing the IAM does that a conventional relational database does not is that it interpolates "along the grain." This was the key element of neural nets that made them an attractive alternative to symbolic approaches: there's a certain amount of built-in generalization. This has more to do with the data being numeric than it does with the neural implementation, however; conventional curve-fitting techniques work fine when the data is simply numeric vectors.

Robot 1.1

Robot 1.1 resembles Robot 1 except that the controller for its IAM is another IAM. Recall that a finite-state machine, like the one used in the architecture of robots like GENGHIS (or that forms the core of the Turing machine, or, indeed, any actual computer) is essentially a relation where each record lists a current state, input(s), next state, and output(s). We can convert an associative memory into a finite-state machine by the simple expedient of connecting its next-state output to its current-state input and letting it run. (We can do the same thing if the memory is continuous, although it will be a lot more stable and controllable if there are one or more time derivatives of the state trajectory stored and represented in the feedback loop.)

At first we can think of the memory of the controller IAM as being preprogrammed with the trajectory that performs controller function, as if it were hardwired by evolution. Ultimately, we can see how, if the controller is allowed to play around itself, it might learn to be a better controller. But in order to play around it would have to have its own controller that would have to be hardwired, or else it would need its own controller in turn.

ROBOT 2

Robot 2 is like several copies of Robot 1 linked together, controlling an arm that can hold and throw a ball (completely in two dimensions, see fig. 13.2). The arm throws the ball at a target, and there's an input reporting where it hits. The overall command given to the arm is in the same "language" as the report and simply specifies a target spot.

There is a SIGMA for each joint and for the gripper, and there is another one controlling and coordinating the whole business. The top-level one has to remember target spots and to ask the lower-level ones for appropriate joint trajectories; the lower-level ones remember the behavior of their joints, which may change as they get rusty or lubricated, and they apply the appropriate forces.

Dimensionality

It's theoretically possible to control the whole shebang with just one monster SIGMA. It would be conceptually simpler at some level of abstraction, but there's a problem. It's not just a matter of how much memory an IAM can have; it's a Chomsky gap, another case where the information you have to learn from isn't enough to separate all the different possibilities. The more dimensions your memory space has, the harder it is to fill it to a density that produces a given quality of interpolation. To begin with, if we are using standard curve-fitting and equation-solving methods to do the interpolation, the number of points needed goes up with the dimensionality of the space. But beyond that, if we assume that the accuracy of the interpolation falls off with the distance from a remembered point, we want to have enough remembered points to fill in the space to a certain density—and the number of points needed goes up exponentially with the number of dimensions!

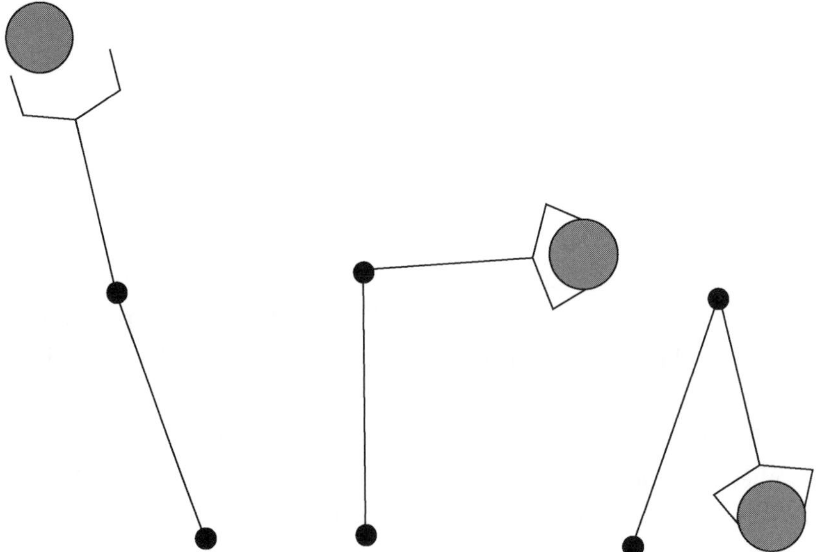

Fig. 13.2: Robot 2, with two joints and a gripper to control.

Consider, for example, that your signals have a value range of ten units being between 0 and 10, as illustrated in fig. 13.3. If your space is one-dimensional, you can store memories at 1, 3, 5, 7, and 9, and no point in the space is more than one unit away from a memory—five points cover your space. If the space is two-dimensional, you need about fifty points for the same coverage; it goes up a factor of ten, roughly, for each new dimension. For a space such as the robot's whole arm, with maybe ten dimensions, you'd need five billion memories to cover it to the same resolution. Life's too short, even for an imaginary robot arm.

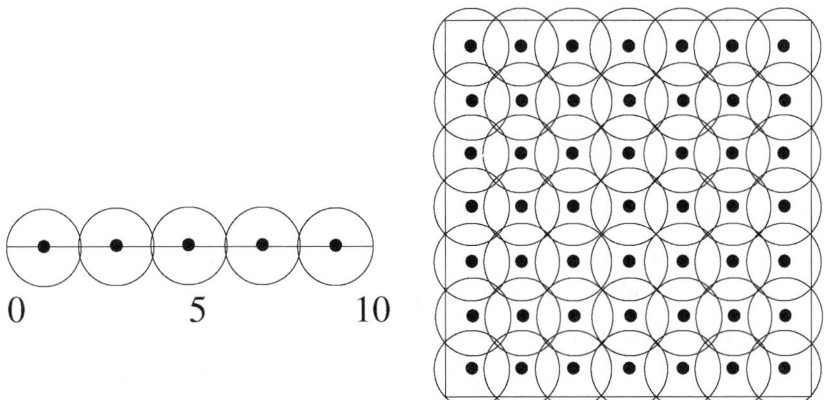

Fig. 13.3: Memories to cover spaces within radius one, for one- and two-dimensional spaces with a width of ten.

In other words, for a given amount of experience and a certain amount of resolution needed in the memory space, there's a pretty hard limit to the dimensionality you can support in a learning IAM. What's adequate for a given dimensionality is too small by a factor of ten for the next one up. This phenomenon is essentially what happens to all the learning methods; in particular, it appears to be the wall that neural networks hit.

Modularization

Having cut the learning task into pieces by modularizing the SIGMAS, we can proceed a stage at a time. Let Robot 2 start out by randomly waving its arm back and forth and throwing its ball out of reach, much as a human infant does. The lower-level SIGMAS will learn the control behavior of the joints. Only then should the higher-level controllers begin their own playing around, with the lower-level ones already online to simplify the interpretation and the control of the situation.

Progressive learning in a properly modularized structure can cut the amount of experience needed from exponential to linear, from impossible to possible. But where did the proper structure come from?

Part of the answer is certainly Chomsky's: it's just built in, either by evolution in an organism or by design in an AI. We'll worry about alternatives later. For the moment, though, let's look at what such innate structure would actually consist of.

The actual memories in the IAMs get filled in soon enough; they aren't a problem (although it wouldn't hurt to have some built-in default ones). The structure that makes all the difference is the dimensionality of the memories and the specification of what function of one gets connected to what dimension of another. Can the high-level controller get away with knowing only the angle of each joint? Should it try to control them at that fine a level at all or should it simply send signals that say when and how fast, as a symphony orchestra conductor does?

The bottom line is that the breakdown of the problem implicit in the form and interpretation of the signals sent between SIGMAS determines what functions each SIGMA will have to learn. This level of description is nothing more or less than a representation. It is as important as representation is in any of its other guises in any other AI system.

ROBOT 3

Robot 3 looks like Robot 1 and lives in the same one-dimensional space. It differs from Robot 1 in *lacking* a direct sense of position, however. This makes it a lot more like a mobile robot on a track rather than a joint.

The obvious thing for Robot 3 to do is to form an internal variable

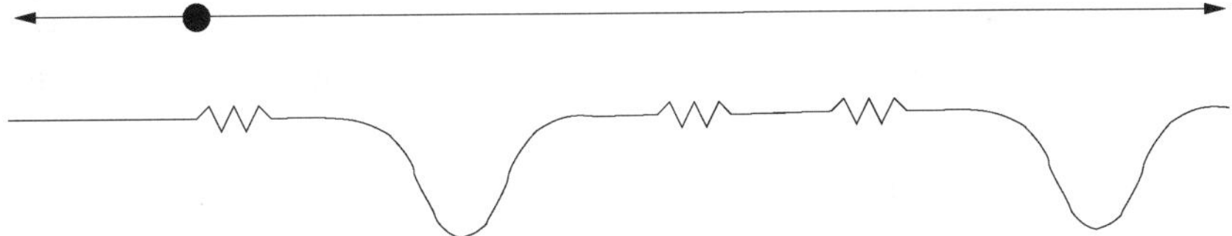

Fig. 13.4: Robot 3, with repeated environmental features.

of position by integrating its velocity. This is a very good idea and is essentially a form of dead reckoning, like guessing how far you've walked by counting your steps. However, we're going to assume that the process is inaccurate enough that Robot 3 will soon lose track of its position.

What Robot 3 experiences is a series of either continuing to move smoothly at a given speed when traversing flat smooth terrain, slowing down unless extra motive force is applied when crossing a sticky patch, or speeding up and then slowing back down when going through a valley.

In an appropriate space, there will be distinct trajectory shapes for the three cases. In particular, all the trajectories for, say, crossing a sticky patch with the same applied force and starting velocity will overlay each other, as will those for valleys on a different path. In each case, the paths will realign once the robot is again on a smooth surface.

The robotics/engineering term for the difference between Robots 1 and 3 is that Robot 1 is *holonomic* and Robot 3 is *non-holonomic*. Technically, this means that Robot 3's internal coordinates can be the same while the robot is actually in a different place (or external state), yet that's impossible for Robot 1 because its internal coordinates directly reflect its external state. Non-holonomic systems do not generate the nice, useful traces in the IAM that holonomic ones do. Instead of lying together like neatly combed hair, their trajectories form a tangled mess. However, they give us a different opportunity.

When an IAM displays this kind of internal structure—that is, with overlaid loops, confluences fanouts, and so on—we can break it up into separate modules, hopefully one for each distinguishable class of feature in the environment. Once this is done, Robot 3 has a hierarchy of SIGMAS, but unlike Robot 2, this is not a hierarchy matching the structure of the robot but the structure of the environment.

Robot 3 now has separate SIGMAS that correspond to flat land, sticky spots, and valleys. It also has (at least one) higher-level SIGMA that remembers trajectories not in terms of direct inputs but rather in terms of which subordinate SIGMA is currently recognizing the situation. What's more, it can control the robot by sending signals (e.g., "make your speed 3.7") to whichever lower-level SIGMA is active, which will be the one with the appropriate knowledge to perform the command correctly in the current environment.

There is a strong and productive field of current research in clustering, unsupervised learning, and data mining that will certainly contribute to the capabilities that Robot 3 needs. The successful ability to form concepts, however, still depends critically on the representation of the data you're trying to pull them out of. The case of Robot 3 suggests that projection—reducing the dimensionality of the data—is valuable. One of the most compelling aspects of the numeric-vector representation is that it lends itself to a wide variety of projection techniques; it also provides a metric for clustering to get its claws into.

Clawing your way up from raw data to useful symbols is hard, but I feel it is the key, or at least one of the keys, to the whole problem. We form concepts at the rate of several per day, at the very least; but most of them are either learned from other people (e.g., square roots) or formed naturally from experience encoded with genetically specified representations (e.g., a new kind of dragonfly I've seen but haven't learned a name for).

If Robot 3 comes across a new feature in its environment, say, a hill, it should be algorithmically much easier to decide whether to create a new lower-level SIGMA than it was to break up a single one in the first place. The framework provided by the signals that the rest of the hierarchy already understands saves most of the work. I suspect that most human concept formation is of this type; truly novel and innovative concepts are rare.

For the higher-level SIGMAs, there is a representational tradeoff to be made. If several of the signals from the lower levels are binary and mutually exclusive, that is, either there is a hill or a valley and we've only ever seen one kind of each, we can collapse the two dimensions into one with different values for the different cases (0 for nothing, 1 for a hill, 2 for a valley). The problem is, if we do it arbitrarily, we may imply a regularity that isn't there—or worse, obscure one that is (such as hills being 1, nothing being 0, and valleys being –1). Almost certainly it is more efficient to encode binary dimensions anyway, so there's some argument for leaving them multidimensional in many cases.

Robot 3.1, as you can probably predict, is like Robot 3 except that the mechanisms that do the clustering and SIGMA-splitting are themselves memory driven and can adapt, learn, and become more adept at well-practiced forms of concept formation (as well as flounder on novel ones).

SERVO WITH A SIMILE

Not only is a SIGMA usable as a controller, it is also capable of recording experience in its IAM and modeling proposed sequences of action by integrating a trajectory through the interpolated vector field of its memories.

What's more, when SIGMAs are arranged in hierarchies, higher-level ones are able to use lower-level ones as symbols. It is not necessary for a symbol to be a simple yes or no for a given subSIGMA; the high-level controller in Robot 3, for example, might not only get a signal that said "hill" but one with a strength measurement that could say "small hill" or "big hill." But the important thing is to break the overall experience reflected in the memory into composable regularities. With a complex hierarchy, the symbols available at the highest levels can then represent arbitrarily complex concepts. With this in mind, we can recast the functioning of the high-level SIGMAs as follows:

The trajectory stored in the IAM can be interpreted as a sequence of situations linked by actions. For Robot 1, for example, situations are "I was at this point going this fast," and actions are "I exerted this much force." In general, there will be some output by the SIGMA that is recorded as associated with the link to the following point in the trajectory. Thus, a SIGMA operating in a goal-directed mode, where the goal is an external command that matches (some part of) a desired situation, does the following:

1. Using the current SITUATION
2. and the given GOAL
3. search the MEMORY
4. for the ACTION that leads to a new situation most like the goal.

Hence the name SIGMA.

The basic SIGMA operation is essentially analogical quadrature, as done by COPYCAT. In the SIGMA we do this to find the action needed to get to the goal:

remembered successive situations	=>	intervening action
current situation and goal	=>	?

This is essentially case-based reasoning, except that instead of trying to apply it to the overall actions of an AI (or, more realistically, the overall recommendations of an expert system), it is reduced to the simpler scope and ontology of an individual agent (*each* individual agent!) in the overall architecture.

However, with a different control pattern, it is obviously possible to use the same IAM for simulation to find the situation that would result from the action:

remembered situation and action	=>	resulting situation
proposed situation and action	=>	?

This also could be chained to predict the result of sequences of actions. We can also use the IAM for diagnosis to conjecture what (unobserved) action could have gotten us to our current state:

remembered successive situations	=>	intervening action
previous and current situation	=>	?

As an aside, humans do a lot more of this than they typically realize; quite a bit of what we think we remember is actually confabulated.

I have no mortal clue how a SIGMA would need to organize the concept of a situation it stores; ones that record at a high level the contents of the visual field when entering rooms might have some similarity to one of Minsky's visual frames. What is a stronger parallel, however, is that the SIGMA, in storing and being able to track and predict trajectories in situation space, is like the frame-systems—the concept Minsky claimed was more important (or at least more innovative) than frames.

Analogical Quadrature

This introduces a new problem. The further up the hierarchy we go, the less our SIGMAS are storing continuous trajectories and the more they are storing discrete symbols, represented as lower-level SIGMAS. The more we use discrete concepts, the more we lose the full power of the n-space representation to do interpolation. Luckily, the most important capability of interpolation can be recaptured by the use of analogy—that is, if we can do it.

Consider a SIGMA whose trajectories are in some symbolic form that doesn't create smooth vector fields in the n-space of the memory. We can still characterize them as sequences of situations connected by actions. When we get a new goal, we need to search the memory for successive situation pairs that match the current situation and goal. We have to do the matching by forming analogies.

Numerous commentators have opined that analogy is one of the major components of cognition. It certainly is in the present model, starting with simple interpolation at the lowest levels. It is incumbent on us to carry it through to the highest, most abstract levels intact.

As we saw earlier, the analogical quadrature operation is quite straightforward if the descriptions are appropriately encoded in an *n*-space representation. The problem arises as the descriptions get more and more symbolic. For example, the *n*-space representation is helpless against a COPYCAT problem as simple as:

abc	=>	abd
aababc	=>	?

(COPYCAT itself can't actually do this one either—you must parse the target string "a ab abc.") The problem to be solved here is the same one facing Robot 3: carving up the world into useful pieces. Robot 3 carved the world at the joints, but they are much harder to find in this situation.

Autogeny

The bottom line is that there has to be some process by which the mental architecture creates more SIGMAs and plugs them into the rest of the system.

At this point, I think, our backs are to the wall and we are left with no option but AI's powerful-but-expensive last resort, search. Given the abstract level at which we are describing the mental architecture, it doesn't much matter which formulation of search we use. We can expect the ability to create novel structure, but structure of limited complexity. We can expect that the representation going in, by way of defining the search space and any metrics on it, will be crucial.

The fact that the substrate is built of learning machines is intended to help by way of the *Baldwin effect*.[4] This is the phenomenon by which evolution works faster if the creatures have some individual adaptability. That way there is a positive feedback into the gene pool even if the gene is only nearly right. Finding representations is the really hard part of AI, and search is both expensive and limited. It can use all the help it can get.

The other important aspect of building the representation out of learning machines is that it's the responsibility of the representation—that is, the structure of transforms and connections between SIGMAS—to expose regularities in the datastream to be captured by the SIGMAS. There is a valuable early hint as to whether the structure is on the right track: how quickly can the new SIGMAS actually learn?

Once a candidate structure is created, it, too, is evaluated by its overall ability to learn and predict—possibly from new data but also from replayed memories. This is a hugely computationally expensive process, but there's plenty of evidence that trying to learn something novel is what makes the brain work overtime. We assume that, as a costly technique, search gets used fairly sparingly in day-to-day human activity—only when the brow is furrowed or the head is being scratched.

CHAPTER 14
An Economy of Mind

Perhaps someone else does know how to do it—but someone else is not writing this book. My solution is to find a different starting point from which to solve the problem.

—David D. Friedman, *The Machinery of Freedom*

A SIGMA servo, as we have seen, is capable of being a finite- (or continuous-) state controller by virtue of cross-connecting some of its outputs and inputs to produce a feedback loop. Many overall cognitive architectures that have been proposed and/or experimented with are based on networks of finite-state machines, including Rodney Brooks's subsumption architecture (as used in GENGHIS) and James Albus's RCS architecture.[1] Any of these could be implemented with SIGMAS.

There are plenty of other overall cognitive architectures from which to borrow, as well. Marvin Minsky's *society of mind theory* provides a number of organizational techniques that might be valuable. It is interesting to note that in Minsky's doctoral dissertation from 1953 we find what would later be called a "case-based prediction module," which looks an awful lot like a SIGMA.[2]

LANGUAGE

What does it mean to understand a word, a sentence, or a story? One theory is that putting together a computational machine allows you to do the same prediction, querying, or modeling that you could have done if you had seen the described situation.

So when you hear a word, a chunk of interconnected SIGMA circuitry corresponding to its meaning is activated. The syntactic machinery of grammar plugs the chunks together to form the appropriate machine.

Notice that the process of putting words and their associated machinery together is another example of analogical quadrature. A small truck is bigger than a big dog; what can "big" and "small" mean then by themselves? But if what "small" calls up is a machine that compares an example with the prototype of its kind, you can hear the phrase "small elephant" and produce a reasonable model by analogy without any trouble.

Learning language would then come down to discovering how to tease the appropriate chunks of circuitry out of the general mass of your mind when learning words and mapping your plugging-together operations—which are almost certainly innate—to the syntax of the language you hear.

We'll take Chomsky at his word and assume the machinery for the grammar functions is mostly built in—but we (as AI designers) still have to duplicate its function. A pronounced word is a trajectory through an n-space given by the volume of sound at all the different frequencies the inner ear detects. There'll be a SIGMA for each word. A sentence is a trajectory through word-space that is too complex for one SIGMA to understand, so there will be SIGMAS for all the kinds of phrases in a hierarchy not unlike the hierarchy that picks higher-level concepts out of any other sensory stream.

The Sapir-Whorf hypothesis* to the contrary, we don't have to have a word in our language to learn a concept. On the other hand, it certainly helps. A new word is a clear indication that there is a concept that needs to be learned. Sometimes we have already formed one that fits, and we need only attach it to the word. In many other cases, the

*The Sapir-Whorf hypothesis states that linguistic categories determine, or strongly affect, the kinds of concepts we learn.

new word will be explained by example as it is introduced: the mother points at a dog and says, "See the doggie! Can you say doggie?"

The opposite talent, learning a word from context, probably requires a little extra mechanism. If you hear a word and then fill in the details later, it's acting a lot like a logical variable in PROLOG—which is significantly more difficult to implement than variables in simpler languages. We probably need to be able to set up a blank SIGMA and begin connecting it to others before it can record anything:

> When I came back from lunch, there was a glimfrotz on my desk. "OK," I said. "Who's the wise guy?" Joe appeared, face slightly pink. He put it in his pocket and explained, "It's a gag gift for my brother-in-law."

From this we now know enough about glimfrotzes not to waste our time looking for them on Ebay.

ABSTRACTION HIERARCHIES

It's clear that in both language and vision the interpretation of raw input is driven strongly by context. If we look at the process from the point of view of an abstraction hierarchy, we can see that there are two combinatorial explosions going on at once.

From the bottom, there is a pattern of raw sense data. Each portion could be interpreted as low-level concepts in several ways, such as the meanings of the words in "Time flies like an arrow." Given the different interpretations at that level, the number of patterns that can be formed from them, such as the different parses of the sentence, multiplies. We get a tree of different interpretations that is rooted at the raw sense data and multiplies out as you go up the abstraction levels, with numerous branches at the highest one: is this sentence about wood-munching insects or no-nonsense traveling salesmen?

At the same time, there is a similar tree going down. In a given situation, some kinds of sentences make sense and others don't. From that abstract root of subject matter, however, there are several different statements that could be made and for each of these there are different ways to phrase each, and so forth. Thus, there is a tree of possibilities that multiplies out as you go down the abstraction levels.

What's more, there are internal structural constraints that operate within and between the trees: if "time" is an adjective, "flies" has to be a noun. If Justin is a passenger, the description is unlikely to be about his plane's physical trajectory.

Thus, the process of interpretation has constraints that flow from the top (expectations), the bottom (raw data), and laterally (structural coherence at each level). One way to think about how it might be implemented is to imagine a stack of modules, each responsible for interpretations at a given level of abstraction, that communicate constraint information in parallel in both directions. (The use of the term *stack* here reflects software design usage such as TCP/IP stack, a multilevel interpretation architecture, not the LIFO datastructure.)

Active Interpretation

In the human nervous system, it is standard that sensory and motor pathways are found together. The signals going to muscles are complemented by the proprioceptive sense that tells you where your joints are. The process of vision is a complex dance, where the interpretation of the view drives the *saccades*—the jumps your eyes make from one point of interest to the next—and the focus of the eyes. Reflexes, such as the standard knee-jerk, the yank back of your hand when you touch something hot, or the blinking of the eye when something flies at it, attest to short circuits across a two-way information and control path.

A short circuit in the other direction can be experienced by the sense of hearing words that you are subvocalizing. In fact, it's quite common for signals to be "turned around" this way with appropriate reinterpretation in the phenomenon known as *efference copy*. This is part of feedback control for many motor tasks, with the copy being compared to sensory information to keep the motion on track. Higher abstract levels of control can "download" what the motion should look like to the lower ones, shortening the control loop for fast, precise actions such as throwing.

Given the necessity of two-way communication for interpretation constraint and the prevalence of it in actual sensor/motor architecture, it seems only reasonable to assume a fairly general architecture: a stack of modules at successive levels of abstraction with paths going up for interpretation, paths going down for commands and predictions, and crosstalk at each level.

When you draw the architecture and look at it, as in fig. 14.1, it's immediately obvious that it can be interpreted as a stack of feedback loops.

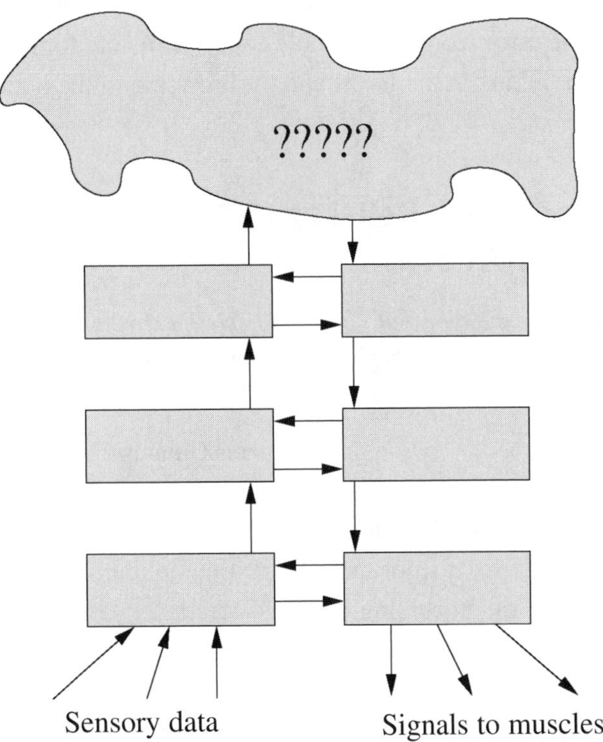

Fig. 14.1: Crosstalk between sensory and motor interpretation stacks produces a chain of feedback loops.

But the structure of the interpretation stack is just like the one used in multilevel design! It's essentially a ladder of concepts that is more detailed and specific on the bottom while being more general and abstract at the top. The more abstract the concepts are, the more likely they are to match or be the same as concepts in other stacks. Consider two stacks: an interpretation of a sequence of printed letters and one of a stream of sound. The abstraction at the top of each might be the same sequence of words. Similarly, there can be a single set of even more abstract concepts than words, which correspond to different ways of expressing the same story. So, there isn't just one stack, or, indeed, a set of separate stacks in the mind. They overlap at the top, where abstractions come together. But they also overlap at the bottom, where we see different things with the same optic nerves and do different things with the same muscles. We read different words composed of the same letters and different sentences composed of the same words. The whole control structure for taking steps is used both for hiking in the forest and for browsing in the bookstore.

HIGHER-LEVEL ARCHITECTURE, WITH FEEDBACK

We thought that Tupelo [Mississippi] was the center of the Earth, since the horizon appeared to be the same distance in all directions.

—Lucius Quintus Cincinnatus Lamar

It is said we never forget how to ride a bicycle. Do you remember how to ride a bicycle? If so, it's not something you could tell in words; it's a complex structure of processing abilities—feedback-control programs, very obviously, if you watch someone learning it—that gets built up during the learning period and merged into a generality. These memories attach to low- to mid-level SIGMAS in the hierarchy and can be accessed only by being on a bicycle so that the perceived "situation" matches.

At the lowest level of our architecture are the senses and the motor impulses that interact directly with the physical world. Reflexes such as knee jerks are short, high-speed feedback loops at that level. At a slightly higher level, reflexes requiring more processing for sensing (such as eye blinks for approaching objects) or coordination of motor effect (such as balance when standing) can be found. Continuing to build on the sensory side in vision, for example, there is the finding of edges, the detection of motion, and the separation of objects; on the motor side, the contraction of muscles to articulate the joints and the repeated placement of feet while balancing to perform walking.

You can probably put all your weight on the ball of one foot, pick up the other, and balance; you do it repeatedly, with no thought, while walking. To do so requires significant processing of signals that detail the distribution of forces on your foot soles and the proprioceptive position information from your joints.

At higher levels, you walk across a crowded room without bumping into people, tables, and chairs mostly below the level of conscious thought.

The higher we get, the less it looks like a hierarchy and the more it looks like a general network with information flowing in all directions. The higher levels of many interpretation stacks converge and overlap. Think of it as a road map of a city, with roads—the nerves—stretching out to muscles and senses on the outskirts and branching into a densely connected network as they get closer to the center. It is not really "up and down" the hierarchy—it is "in and out" of the network; from anywhere near the middle, it looks the same in all directions.

COMMON SENSE

One of the defining capabilities of human intelligence as opposed to that of merely smart animals is the ability to learn a complicated new technique by seeing it done just once. This is tantalizingly like explanation-based learning, except that in our architecture there is neither a domain theory expressed in the predicate calculus nor a theorem prover.

Instead there is a big stock of SIGMAS representing all the concepts you have about what is going on. Suppose you are watching someone changing a tire. If you've never seen a car before, you aren't going to be able to learn how to do it by seeing it once. But if you are fairly familiar the process, you will have SIGMAS that represent your experience with nuts, bolts, and wrenches. They will get pulled up and connected to interpret what you are seeing. In some higher-level SIGMA, you are laying down a trajectory specified in terms of which lower-level ones are recognizing things.

Now, the whole point of SIGMAS is that this same structure you assembled to recognize and interpret the process can be used to simulate it—in other words, to imagine yourself doing it. What's more, it can be used to do it, not exactly, but close enough so that with a little practice you'll be able to get it right.

This is true not only for actions, but also for the understanding and planning we call common sense. Many researchers seem to think that there is some inference mechanism working out the implications of the facts you know about the world. For example, a typical question one would give to stump a Turing Test candidate would be "Which is bigger, Chicago or a golf ball?" This is a problem for symbolic systems, which store relations as explicit links; no systems designer would have put links between such rarely compared items as Chicago and a golf ball. So the system would need to find a chain of connections such as, "I can hold a golf ball, and Chicago can hold me; thus, Chicago could hold a golf ball; therefore, Chicago is bigger than a golf ball."

I doubt that using such inference, as if we were proving theorems, is how we do it. Sir Arthur Conan Doyle's Sherlock Holmes stories illustrate this nicely: Holmes makes an amazing deduction, Watson is baffled by how he knew it, Holmes explains, then Watson thinks it's obvious. We make deductions easily when we have seen them made before; otherwise, we miss the obvious. Aesop's fable of the fox and the crow is another example.

At best, the "reasoning" involved in common sense is analogical pattern-matching to a case base of deductions produced by explanation-based learning. Common sense is nothing more—or less—than twenty years' experience in the real world.

The best way to build common sense into a system is to have representations that embody the relations directly. For size, the obvious representation (to us, in retrospect!) is numbers used as measurements: a golf ball is 0.025 meter; Chicago is 25,000 meters; therefore, Chicago is bigger. Given the right representation, the deduction is trivial and the conclusion is evident. The hard part is finding the right representation.

Marvin Minsky accuses me of having physics envy. This is his term for those who think there are a few simple, powerful mechanisms at work in intelligence so that we can sum the whole business up in a handful of equations as Newton did for gravity and motion. He thinks, instead, that there is a lot of complex machinery in there and that we should get to work designing it.

I do have physics envy, in a sense, but in the sense that physics, like all the rest of science, is a process by which we find ways to think about the world that embody the good-representation trick. It's not so much that I'd like to be able to do that as the AI's designer, although it would be nice and save lots of time. It's that the AI needs to be able to do it for itself.

Humans seem to have a set of representations that are programmed by the genes to appear in sequence throughout childhood. If we could get these all figured out and put them in an AI, it would be very competent and could probably pass the Turing Test. But as adults we *don't stop learning*. We continue to build new representations that are not part of the innate development program.

The way we characterize a person we hold to be deficient in common sense is to say that he "doesn't have enough sense to come in out of the rain." Come in to what? A house, a human invention. But our genes don't know about houses. We build up learned representations of the world that have the indoors/outdoors dichotomy as fundamentals and never notice that we've done so.

THE MARKETPLACE OF IDEAS

Suppose a coin is about to be flipped. You should be willing to sell for fifty-one dollars a certificate you will redeem for a hundred dollars if the coin turns up heads. Similarly, you should be willing to sell tails certificates. You should also be willing, I trust, to sell for three dollars—but not for two dollars—promises to pay a hundred dollars if a given roll of dice comes up snake eyes.[3] We can regularize this notion into a commodity in units that are certificates that pay one dollar if the fact is true. Clearly, a unit of fact F is worth one dollar times the probability of F, and a unit of F and a unit of not(F) in a bundle is worth just a dollar.

These fact futures are an invention of the economist Robin Hanson.[4] The basic operation of price theory (equilibrium price as a function of supply and demand curves) is to form a method of pooling diverse sources of knowledge and various facts and to evolve good estimators. Consider a fact-futures market. Over the long run, the following will happen:

- Investors who make poor predictions or bet on facts they don't have any special knowledge of will go bankrupt.
- Investors who spend more to determine the truth of a fact than it is worth will go bankrupt.

Thus, in the long run, takers in a fact-futures market will be those who are likely to be able to get a good estimate of the truth of a given fact and will spend less doing so than it is worth to know the fact. The value of knowing a fact is reflected in the market price of F, of not(F), and in the volume of offerings.

Somewhere in the cityscape of the mind is a marketplace. We can configure things so that knowledge is traded there. It would be a very great stretch to try to claim that the human mind works this way, but for an AI, I would be willing to sell you a certificate that a Charles Smith–like architecture could be made to work for about half a buck.

CHUNKING AND THE FIRM

In economic theory, the role of the firm is similar to chunking in the AI literature.[5] A subsection of the market process is frozen into an encapsulated pattern of contractual relationships, which eliminates the market overhead for commonly repeated transactions.

Allen Newell points out a strong similarity in appropriately measured performance between production systems with chunking and human cognitive skills at synthetic reaction-time tasks. This is used as grounds to call such systems *theories of cognition*. There is in economics a phenomenon called the *learning curve*, which exhibits essentially the same behavior, as seen in fig. 14.2.

Chunking is one aspect of concept formation. In our cityscape model, several SIGMAs that had been systematically swapping signals would coalesce into one. This would not only perform the operation more efficiently, but would also leave the other SIGMAs that were party to the inputs and outputs with a simplification of their environment.

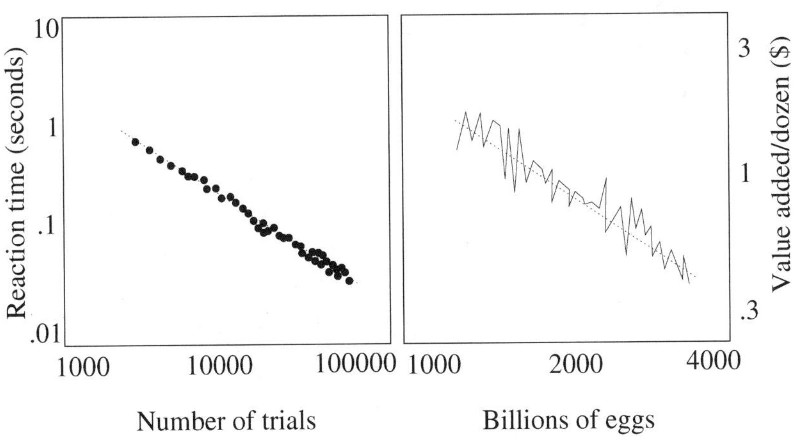

Fig. 14.2: Reaction-time cognitive learning (*left*) compared with the economic learning curve (*right*). Both show a linear decrease on a log-log scale.

HOMUNCULI IN THE MIDDLE

Now suppose there is a single SIGMA in the middle of town that represents City Hall. Modern philosophers of consciousness tend to reject the notion of a single, central controller, which they call a *homunculus* (Latin for "little man"). If the mind is a control room with a little man sitting in the operator's seat pulling levers and pressing buttons, then his own mind must be another control room with a micro-man, and the micro-man's mind must have a nano-man, and so forth. This doesn't actually explain anything. We don't have that problem here because we will assume that the central controller is just another SIGMA. Furthermore, at the moment we don't care whether or not it is conscious.

If this City Hall SIGMA is "in charge," it can't have any "goal" signals coming to it from above. But remember that all the potential actions a SIGMA can do are represented by memories. These memories can include indications of how good or bad a situation was (in the simplest case, whether it caused pleasure or pain). City Hall can use these as an evaluation function as it decides what to do next. Otherwise, it's not all that different from any other SIGMA.

It makes sense for an animal to have a unitary buck-stops-here controller since it has a single body, and it is quite counterproductive for it to try to run off in opposite directions at the same time, even if it sees food in one direction and a potential mate in the other. Thus, the basic structure was probably in place in animals well before intelligence developed. (Remember, this is an abstract architecture—it doesn't matter whether the centralization is physically distinct or distributed.)

When the controller is in simulation mode, it is like any high-level officer or manager who isn't actually doing the work; it's sending signals to the lower-level SIGMAS and they're doing the heavy lifting down to some level in the network. This is what it's doing when it's actually moving the body around, too, except that the activity goes all the way down to sense organs and muscles. In order that confusion not reign in such cases, the incoming signals to the controller must be labeled with some modal information such as "I'm just imagining this," "I'm watching someone else do this," "I'm dreaming this," or "I'm really doing this."

Although each of us has a different set of specific experiences, they will tend to converge into similar pictures of the actual world. One use of the analogical-quadrature operation is the case where the memory is of someone else doing something, and the present goal is to imitate him. My personal experience is that watching someone's hands in the performance of some moderately complex physical task (such as tying a necktie), especially repeatedly, gives one a significant step up on the "feel" of it when attempting it.

Humans are built so that when in close and continued contact with one another, manual skills and language are automatically copied from individual to individual. It seems likely that the same machinery for copying simulation/performance structure—functional chunks of the SIGMA network—and for reconnecting the copies so that they perform useful new functions, is responsible for a lot of what goes in both language and abstract symbolic thought.

One of the reasons for wanting to see the brain this way is that it is evolutionarily plausible. Evolution almost always works by taking an existing mechanism (e.g., feedback control, as found in flatworms and insects), copying it, and extending it. So, a mental architecture that appears to have a single basic mechanism, especially one that appears to be relatively straightforward to implement in neuron-inspired mechanisms and memories, is compelling.[6] And for the brain itself to work by copying and modifying would be nothing less than poetic.

AND A STAR TO STEER HER BY

How much more is needed for a brain design? In a word, almost everything. There's the actual structure of the majority of the iceberg mind that is under the waterline—the modules doing the bulk of the actual work. We don't know how many such modules are necessary to support a working mind, if only to have basic representations to invoke by analogy, to copy and to modify. I haven't said anything about the specifics of any of the modules, either the ones that are understood to a degree, such as vision, or the others that have scarcely been touched.

I have outlined this approach to highlight the one key characteristic, autogeny, that I think has been neglected in mainstream AI. Even so, what has been done in the field at large in a half century is substantial. The techniques we've glanced at over the previous chapters and the many more we haven't are useful for tough, real-world problems. More and more people are learning to combine them in systems that are more than the sum of their parts.

The American Association for Artificial Intelligence's *AI Magazine* for summer 2006 was a special issue called "Achieving Human-level Intelligence through Integrated Systems and Research." It is doubtful that the issue could have come out even just a few years ago. There are signs that AI sails are catching a freshening breeze, and the glass ceiling doldrums may soon be left behind. There are once again researchers who are willing to say that they're trying to synthesize a general human-level intellect as opposed to merely concentrating on subfields and applications.

In the meantime, there has been much progress in the subfields, and powerful new techniques have been developed. The burden of the *AI Magazine* summer issue is that it's now reasonable to think about putting them all together again into a unified model of cognition. From the looks of it, none of these projects in the mainstream has the emphasis on autogeny that I have stressed here, but they do have the benefit of a considerably more sophisticated theory and a set of techniques for machine learning than existed twenty-five years ago.

There is a new excitement aboard the *Good Ship AI*. All hands are on deck, the sails are swelling, and the flag snaps in the breeze. Clear sailing lies ahead, and anchors are aweigh.

CHAPTER 15
Kinds of Minds

Perhaps our questions about artificial intelligence are a bit like inquiring after the temperament and gait of a horseless carriage.

—K. Eric Drexler

Now we will classify the different stages AI might go through by using the Greek prepositions. These have been adopted into English as prefixes, particularly in scientific usage. In some cases the concepts have been applied to advancing AI and in other cases they haven't. The reason for introducing these new terms is that they provide a framework that puts any given level of expected AI capability in perspective vis-à-vis the other levels and in comparison to human intelligence.

HYPOHUMAN AI

Hypo means below or under (think *hypo*dermic, under the skin; *hypo*thermia or *hypo*glycemia, below normal temperature or blood sugar), including, in the original Greek, under the moral or legal subjection of. Isaac Asimov's robots are (mostly) hypohuman, in both senses of hypo: they are not quite as smart as humans, and they are subject to our rule. Most existing AI is arguably hypohuman, as well (DEEP

BLUE to the contrary notwithstanding). As long as it stays that way, the only thing we have to worry about is that there will be human idiots putting their AI idiots in charge of things that neither understands. All the discussion of formalist float applies, especially the part about feedback.

DIAHUMAN AI

Dia means through or across in Greek (*dia*meter, *dia*gonal), and the Latin *trans* means the same thing, but the commonly heard *trans*human doesn't apply here. Transhuman refers to humans as opposed to AIs, humans who have been enhanced (by whatever means) and are in a transitional state between human and fully posthuman, whatever that may be. Neither concept is very useful here.

By diahuman, I mean AIs in the stage where AI capabilities are crossing the range of human intelligence. It's tempting to call this human-equivalent, but the idea of equivalence is misleading. It's already apparent that some AI abilities (e.g., chess playing) are beyond the human scale, while others (e.g., reading and writing) haven't reached it yet.

Thus, diahuman refers to a phase of AI development (and only by extension to an individual AI in that phase), and this is fuzzy because the limits of human (and AI) capability are fuzzy. It's hard to say which capabilities are important in the comparison. I would claim that AI is entering the early stages of the diahuman phase right now; there are humans who, like today's AIs, don't learn well and who function competently only at simple jobs for which they must be trained.

The core of the diahuman phase, however, will be the development of autogenous learning. In the latter stages, AIs, like the brightest humans, will be completely autonomous, not only learning what they need to know but also deciding what they need to learn.

Diahuman AIs will be valuable and will undoubtedly attract significant attention and resources to the AI enterprise. They are likely to cause something of a stir in philosophy and perhaps religion, as well.

However, they will not have a significant impact on the human condition. (The one exception might be economically, in the case that diahuman AI lingers so long that Moore's law makes human-equivalent robots very cheap compared to human labor. But I'm assuming that we will probably have advanced past the diahuman stage by then.)

PARAHUMAN AI

Para means alongside (*para*legal, *para*medic). The concept of designing a system that a human is going to be part of dates back to cybernetics (although all technology throughout history had to be designed so that humans could operate it, in some sense).

Parahuman AI will be built around more and more sophisticated theories of how humans work. The PC of the future ought to be a parahuman AI. MIT roboticist Cynthia Breazeal's sociable robots are the likely forerunners of a wide variety of robots that will interact with humans in many kinds of situations.

The upside of parahuman AI is that it will enhance the interface between our native senses and abilities, adapted as they are for a hunting and gathering bipedal ape, and the increasingly formalized and mechanized world we are building. The parahuman AI should act like a lawyer, a doctor, an accountant, and a secretary, all with deep knowledge and endless patience. Once AI and cognitive science have acquired a solid understanding of how we learn, parahuman AI teachers could be built that would model in detail how each individual student was absorbing the material, ultimately finding the optimal presentation for understanding and motivation.

The downside is simply the same effect, put to work with slimier motives: the parahuman advertising AI, working for corporations or politicians, could know just how to tweak your emotions and gain your trust without actually being trustworthy. It would be the equivalent of an individualized artificial con man. By the way, note that of the two human elements that were part of the original cybernetic anti-aircraft control theory, one of them, the pilot of the plane being shot at, didn't want to be part of the system but was, willy-nilly.

Parahuman is a characterization that does not specify a level of intellectual capability compared to humans; it can be properly applied to AIs at any level. Humans are fairly strongly parahuman intelligences as well; many of our innate skills involve interacting with other humans. Parahuman can be largely contrasted with the following term, allohuman.

ALLOHUMAN AI

Allo means other or different (*allo*morph, *allo*nym, *allo*trope). Although I have argued that human intelligence is universal, there remains a vast portion of the mind that is distinctively human. This includes the genetically programmed representation modules, the form of our motivations, and the sensory modalities, of which several are fairly specific to running a human body.

It will certainly be possible to create intelligences that while being universal nevertheless have different lower-level hardwired modalities for sense and representation, and different higher-level motivational structure. One simple possibility is that universal mechanism may stand in for a much greater portion of the cognitive mechanism so that, for example, the AI would use learned physics instead of instinctive concepts and learned psychology instead of our folk models.

Such differences could reasonably make the AI better at certain tasks; consider the ability to do voluminous calculations in you head. However, if you have ever watched an experienced accountant manipulate a calculator, you can see that the numbers almost flow through his fingers. Built-in modalities may provide some increment of effectiveness compared to learned ones, but not as much as you might think. Consider reading—it's a learned activity, and unlike talking, we don't just "pick it up." But with practice, we read much faster than we can talk or understand spoken language.

Motivations and the style and the volume of communication could also differ markedly from the human model. The allohuman AI might resemble Mr. Spock, or it might resemble an intelligent ant. This likely will form the bulk of the difference between allohuman AIs and humans rather than the varying modalities.

Like parahuman, allohuman does not imply a given level of intellectual competence. In the fullness of time, however, the parahuman/allohuman distinction will make less and less difference. More advanced AIs, whether they need to interact with humans or to do something weirdly different, will simply obtain or deduce whatever knowledge is necessary and synthesize the skills on the fly.

EPIHUMAN AI

Epi means upon or after (*epi*dermis, *epi*gram, *epi*taph, *epi*logue). I'm using it here in a combination of senses to mean AI that is just above the range of individual human capabilities but that still forms a continuous range with them, and also in the sense of what comes just after diahuman AI. That gives us what can be a useful distinction as opposed to further-out possibilities. (See *hyper* below.)

Science fiction writer Charles Stross introduced the phrase "weakly godlike AI." Weakly presumably refers to the fact that such AIs would still be bound by the laws of physics—they couldn't perform miracles, for example. As a writer, I'm filled with admiration for the phrase, since weakly and godlike have such contrasting meanings that it forces you to think when you read it for the first time, and the term weakly is often used in a similar way with various technical meanings in scientific discourse, giving a vague sense of rigor (!) to the phrase.

The word posthuman is often used to describe what humans may be like after various technological enhancements. Like transhuman, posthuman is generally used for modified humans instead of synthetic AIs.

My model for what an epihuman AI would be like is to take the ten smartest people you know, remove their egos, and duplicate them a hundred times, so that you have a thousand really bright people willing to apply themselves all to the same project. Alternatively, simply imagine a very bright person given a thousand times as long to do any given task. We can straightforwardly predict, from Moore's law, that ten years after the advent of a learning but not radically self-improving human-level AI, the same software running on machinery of the same cost would do the same human-level tasks a thousand times as fast as we.[1] It could, for example:

- read an average book in one second with full comprehension;
- take a college course and do all the homework and research in ten minutes;
- write a book, again with ample research, in two or three hours;
- produce the equivalent of a human's lifetime intellectual output, complete with all the learning, growth, and experience involved, in a couple of weeks.

A thousand really bright people are enough to do some substantial and useful work. An epihuman AI could probably command an income of $100 million or more in today's economy by means of consulting and entrepreneurship, and it would have a net present value in excess of $1 billion. Even so, it couldn't take over the world or even an established industry. It could probably innovate well enough to become a standout in a nascent field, as in the case of Google.

A thousand top people is a reasonable estimate for what the current field of AI research is applying to the core questions and techniques—basic, in contrast to applied research. Thus, an epihuman AI could probably improve itself about as fast as current AI is improving. Of course, if it did that, it wouldn't be able to spend its time making all that money; the opportunity cost is pretty high. It would need to make exactly the same kind of decision that any business faces with respect to capital reinvestment.

Whichever it may choose to do, the epihuman level characterizes an AI that is able to stand in for a given fairly sizeable company or for a field of academic inquiry. As more and more epihuman AIs appear, they will enhance economic and scientific growth so that by the later stages of the phase the total stock of wealth and knowledge will be significantly higher than it would have been without the AIs. AIs will be a significant sector, but no single AI would be able to rock the boat to a great degree.

HYPERHUMAN AI

Hyper means over or above. In common use as an English prefix, *hyper* tends to denote a greater excess than *super*, which means the same thing but comes from Latin instead of Greek. (Contrast, e.g., supersonic, more than Mach 1, and hypersonic, more than Mach 5.)

In the original Singularity paper, "The Coming Technological Singularity," Vernor Vinge used the phrase *superhuman intelligence*. Nick Bostrom has used the term *superintelligence*. Like some of the terms above, however, *superhuman* has a wide range of meanings (think about Kryptonite), and most of them are not applicable to the subject at hand. We will stay with our Greek prefixes and finish the list with hyperhuman.

Imagine an AI that is a thousand epihuman AIs, all tightly integrated together. Such an intellect would be capable of substantially outstripping the human scientific community at any given task and of comprehending the entirety of scientific knowledge as a unified whole. A hyperhuman AI would soon begin to improve itself significantly faster than humans could. It could spot the gaps in science and engineering where there is low-hanging fruit and instigate rapid increases in technological capability across the board.

It is as yet poorly understood even in the scientific community just how much headroom remains for improvement with respect to the capabilities of current physical technology. A mature nanotechnology, for example, could replace the entire capital stock—all the factories, buildings, roads, cars, trucks, airplanes, and other machines—of the United States in a week.[2] And that's just using currently understood science, with a dollop of engineering development thrown in.

Any sufficiently advanced technology, Arthur C. Clarke wrote, is indistinguishable from magic.[3] Although, I believe, any specific thing the hyperhuman AIs might do could be understood by humans, and the total volume of work and the rate of advance would become harder and harder to follow. Please note that any individual human is already in a similar relationship with the whole scientific community; our understanding of what is going on is getting more and more abstract. The average person understands cell phones at the level of knowing that batteries have limited lives and that coverage has gaps, but not at the level of field-effect transistor gain figures and conductive trace electromigration phenomena. Ten years ago the average scientist, much less the average user, could not have predicted that most cell phones today would contain cameras and color screens. But we can follow, if not predict, by understanding things at a very high level of abstraction, as if they were magic.

Any individual hyperhuman AI would be productive, intellectually or industrially, on the scale of the human race as a whole. As the number of hyperhuman AIs increased, our efforts would shrink to more and more modest proportions of the total.

Where does an eight-hundred-pound gorilla sit? According to the old joke, anywhere he wants to. Much the same thing will be true of a hyperhuman AI, except in instances where it has to interact with other AIs. The really interesting question then will be, what will it want?

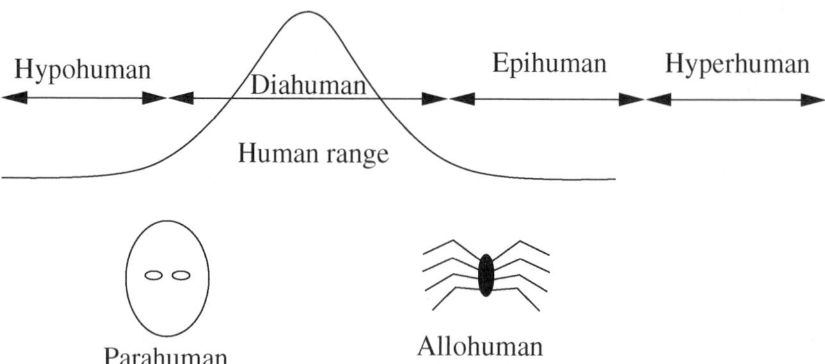

Fig. 15.1: The various classifications of AI type and range, using chapter 15's nomenclature.

CHAPTER 16
When

I believe that in about fifty years' time it will be possible to programme computers, with a storage capacity of about 10^9, to make them play the imitation game so well that an average interrogator will not have more than 70 percent chance of making the right identification after five minutes of questioning.

—Alan Turing, *Computing Machinery and Intelligence*, 1950

WHY

In this chapter I am going to speculate shamelessly on the question of when a real, Turing Test–passing, human-level AI might arrive.

The first reason to discuss the question is to point out that there will be no such thing. Real AI will surpass human capabilities early in some areas (chess playing) and late in others (at a guess, literature). At no time will an AI think exactly like a human (with one possible exception—uploading. See p. 250). Thus, the question as posed is ill defined, and we'll have to elaborate to have a sensible discussion.

WHAT

There seem to be four major possibilities for the basic form of an AI. First is the direct synthetic approach: we figure out what needs to be done and write a program to do it. This does not mean that we wouldn't use neural nets, statistics, or any other software technique; it just means that the system is designed from the top down, using engineering principles.

The second method is to do a module-by-module reimplementation of the brain, using the results of computational neuroscience. In this approach, the function of a module is scientifically understood at a mathematical level and the resulting function is implemented. This can be similar, in many cases, to the result of the first method. The differences are that it requires an extra step and that it will produce an AI that thinks a lot more like a human does. The extra step—doing the science—may be necessary in those cases where the direct-engineering approach hasn't figured out what to build (or can't make it work as well as the real brain). As for thinking like a human, whether or not that is a good idea remains to be seen.

A fair amount is known about some of the computational functions of parts of the brain's architecture, including much of visual and auditory processing; but much of it is as yet unknown. There is a fifty-year backlog of schemes for various functions to be drawn from symbolic AI, none of which works for anything like a full-fledged human mind, or even a baby, though many do various cognitive subtasks reasonably well.

The third method is to simulate the workings of the brain at the level of neurons or smallish multineuron units. This requires better measuring instruments than we have now, but the ones available in the 2020s or 2030s probably will be sufficient. The extreme of this approach is to duplicate the neural-wiring diagram of an individual precisely enough to effectively copy his or her mind into the computer, a process called *uploading*. This would produce not only an AI that was humanlike, but one that closely resembled a specific human.

Uploading provides a motive for any given individual to create an AI that is not present for the other forms of AI synthesis: the individual involved gets a form of (possible) immortality. I would volunteer to do it myself, considering the alternative. Thus, uploading will probably be done in addition to other forms of AI, even if the other forms come first.

The fourth method is Turing's child-machine scheme: build a baby brain and let it grow up. As I mentioned before, it would seem to be necessary to understand and be able to implement the autogenous capabilities of the mind at some point anyway. This leaves us with even more definitional slack. Will we consider AI to have arrived when the baby brain is built or after it grows up? Will we decide a program is a true AI if it can pass the Turing Test—in the sense of having a broad set of capabilities, memories, and knowledge comparable to an adult human—but cannot learn and grow?

HOW

Software

Of the build-a-full-brain approaches, the first to the finish line for my money will be the engineering one, although it would need to be strongly aided at the conceptual level by the knowledge coming from cognitive science and neuroscience. The overall task would just be simpler that way. As an analogy, consider airplanes: they are much simpler, mechanically, than birds. Airplanes have a strong limitation in that they require prebuilt runways to land on and take off from. We do not have to go to the extent of re-creating birds to overcome that, however; we build helicopters and vectored-thrust jump jets. Similarly, it likely will be possible to overcome the limitations of current AIs without going all the way to the imitation of a human brain.

On the other hand, the autogenous learning capability is one that has resisted every attack on it from the engineering side. It remains to be seen whether the study of the brain will produce any new insights. Perhaps we can understand how the brain forms new concepts. Perhaps there are ingenious aspects of the way it represents concepts that allow the formation method to work.

So we have two nearly separable questions: when will an autogenous learning machine appear, and when will a sufficient amount of knowledge and skill find its way into an AI (either by programming or by learning) to approximate human competence?

These questions almost beg for a third: given both, when will the resulting AI become so much smarter than a human that it is worth more to worry about than a human or a human organization?

Hardware

Remember the three levels of processing power we discussed in chapter 5, which were the estimates of human equivalence: a Minsky HEPP at 11, a Moravec HEPP at 13.5, and a Kurzweil HEPP at 16. They were carefully fudged to be 2.5 apart, which just happens to be the gain per decade I'm using as an estimate of Moore's law.

These fudgings should give you some notion of just how fuzzy the figures actually are. For example, Moore's law was originally an observation about transistor density on microchips; it's become a mantra (and technology target) for the entire computer industry, but various components of computers run on significantly different price/performance curves: doubling times range from one year to two for the most important ones.[1] The figure Minsky mentioned to me in a casual conversation was so lowball it was surely intended to be provocative and not a serious estimate; I take "a current top-end PC" as fulfilling the spirit of the comment.

With a Minsky HEPP as our estimate, we can run an AI on a ten-thousand-dollar machine now (2007) or a thousand-dollar one by the end of the decade. With a Moravec HEPP as an estimate, we are there with a thousand-dollar machine by the end of the teens, and with a Kurzweil HEPP by the end of the 2020s.[2]

If you are willing to spend a million dollars on a human-equivalent machine, my figures put it as 1998 for a Minsky HEPP, 2008 for a Moravec HEPP, and 2018 for a Kurzweil HEPP. It seems quite likely that the hardware will be available before the software is. Another possibility that could mean early availability of the requisite processing power is if graphics accelerators, which have a considerably higher power-per-dollar ratio than the main processor in a PC, can be harnessed for some of the calculations AI needs. This depends on what kind of operations turn out to be necessary. Graphics cards attain their amazing speed because they are very specialized, so they could help in some cases (e.g., with vision) and not in others (theorem proving). But assuming they can be used, they could advance the dates several years or equivalently cut costs by a factor of ten to one hundred.

WHO

It has long been assumed that AI would emerge from the academic computer science research community. The major funding in the 1960s that engendered the golden age was a response to *Sputnik* and a part of the general science-and-technology push that climaxed with the Apollo moonflights. Government funding declined in the 1970s and 1980s, and many researchers either went to industry (Bell Labs had a significant AI group for a while, for example) or founded their own companies.

Today, computers are cheap enough that individual hobbyists have access to more processing power than MIT had in 1980. There is also the Internet, which makes available a wide variety of material, from text corpuses to open-source software, and much of it for free.

The Military

The US military, in the form of DARPA, the Department of Defense's research-funding agency, was the major sponsor of AI from the 1960s and remains significantly ahead of any given private source today. The military is a major user of AI applications, from logistics scheduling to smart weapons.

The military is likely to have AI as good as that of any other organization and about as soon, with one proviso. Military AI (and all military systems) are biased toward doing well-defined tasks as well as possible. This means for AI that the emphasis is away from a general, open-ended, childlike learning kernel. Thus, there is a possibility that military AI will be a follower rather than a leader in autogenous learning.

Universities

AI lost enough of its cachet in the diaspora that one cannot necessarily expect to find an AI researcher in the computer science department of a college or a small university. Still, the bulk of AI research goes on at universities. Much of what would have been called AI in the past has broken into a disparate collection of increasingly arcane subfields, such as computational linguistics and cognitive robotics. There are signs, however, that academic AI is coming out of its doldrums, and it appears to have as good a chance of success as any other sector of AI research.

Industry Laboratories

Industry shuns the term AI but sponsors quite a bit of highly relevant work. One example is data mining, in which one searches, for example, through sales records to discover patterns of consumer-buying habits. Typical examples are that the program discovers that people who buy pretzels also buy beer, or people who buy baby food also buy diapers. The programs that detect fraud patterns in telephone, credit card, and similar records of usage and billing are as good as humans at finding patterns—and these programs can do it for millions of transactions in real time.

Management information systems is another area where the ability to grasp fluid or diffuse concepts and to summarize them will be useful, and text-mining technology is getting closer and closer to these capabilities. (Try Google News to see what the state of the art is like.) Google has a clear path ahead and considers every step from current capabilities to full AI as a commercial advantage, and its founders have specifically indicated that AI is an ultimate goal.[3]

The other sector contributing a lot to AI research is the computer game industry. There is quite a bit of money behind the development—consider the state of graphics cards, driven almost entirely by gaming. (The performance of graphics has exceeded Moore's law over the past decade.) They are now branching out into *physics engines*—programs simulating Newtonian physics—which will put significant processing power and the software for (physical) world modeling within reach of just about anybody.

The part of a computer game that is unabashedly called "the AI" is getting more sophisticated, too. These are the simulated characters you play against or interact with. Although there is still a preponderance of shoot-'em-ups, games now offer interaction in just about any form that people find interesting, from flirting to commerce. The more sophisticated the AI, the more interesting the interaction.

Start-ups and Open Source

There exist several small venture-funded companies that are trying various innovative approaches to AI. Many of these are taking the "baby-brain" approach. There is also a sparse scattering of AI projects in the open-source community, the loose worldwide network of developers who build and maintain things such as the Linux operating system. Both of these groups (I'm thinking of the set of researchers and developers available to, but not currently active in, start-ups) constitute major pools of talent that are not now strongly engaged in AI, though they could turn to it quite rapidly given appropriate provocation. Note, for example, that a large proportion of the 195 entrants into the DARPA Grand Challenge autonomous-vehicle race were start-ups or consortia formed specifically to compete in it.

Note also that universities and corporate labs, as well as hobbyists, participate in the open-source community. There are significant resources available for free, including such things as Wordnet, the CYC ontology, and the OpenMind ontology, as well as an enormous amount of English (and other natural language) text available for mining. Once AI is seen as having passed some tipping point, there will be many open-source AIs, each different and each free for anyone with the hardware to run it.

WHERE

Historically, the global leader in computer technology, in general, as well as AI, in particular, has been the United States. Today, there's a high probability that any given piece of computer hardware was made in one of the "little tigers," such as Taiwan or Singapore. Currently, it is Japan that probably leads the world in robotics. There are serious predictions that Russia will lead the world in general software in the near future. The European Union is quite strong, and India and China are gaining fast. The Robocup winners for 2006 are indicative: United States, Germany, Australia, Japan, China, and Portugal.

Given the international nature of both the scientific community and the Internet, however, this is probably the least important of the questions. The answer is most likely, everywhere.

WHEN

> *It is impossible to predict the future, and all attempts to do so in any detail appear ludicrous within a very few years.*
>
> —Arthur C. Clarke, *Profiles of the Future*

If I've come anywhere close to doing my job right in this chapter, you can see that answering the question "When will AI arrive?" with a numerical date makes about as much sense as answering the ultimate question of life, the universe, and everything else with "42." *Wired News* columnist Momus bemoans the fact that AI programs are now writing formulaic market-report summaries, but as yet no AI can match his depth and wit. But the tide is rising.

Business as Usual

If we take the position that there is no key insight, no juice, no elan vital to the mind, which is to say that no one finds a single, general autogenous-learning algorithm, then it is a question of plugging away at it and slowly getting better at more and more things. If having common sense is a matter of knowing enough facts about the real world, the databases of such facts (e.g., CYC and OpenMind) are becoming more and more complete as time goes on. Although I hold the opposite opinion, it might be that the autogenous capability of the human mind is an emergent property of such a large body of specific learning abilities.

Tom Mitchell, a past president of AAAI and one of today's foremost researchers in machine learning, has a standing bet that there will be programs that can read the English text on the World Wide Web and extract substantial knowledge from it by 2015. If we track AI development to 2015, just by trend-line projection of current techniques with no major conceptual breakthroughs, it would be surprising if an AI could *not* pass the Turing Test for, say, a half hour. We could expect AIs to do a fair job of driving, cleaning well-laid-out buildings, and similar tasks of a well-defined nature.

If there is not some conceptual breakthrough, we can expect the onus of adaptability still to be on humans at that point. The AIs still will be brittle and inflexible, although less so than they are now; they still will need massive programming efforts by experts to be able to handle new tasks. Anywhere this isn't done very thoroughly, formalist float will occur and the machines will remain clueless, like bureaucracies.

By 2025 there will probably have been enough specialized programming done that the AIs will be able to handle most human tasks that don't require flexibility and creativity. By 2035 there will probably be enough science and domain theory encoded that an AI can run a reasonably complete model of its world. It will have the horsepower to harness this as a model-based rational agent and act somewhat more flexibly on the basis of it. That is probably as good a point as any to call it a human equivalent, although the AI would be better at a number of things than any human, and humans would still be more flexible and capable of comprehending new kinds of things better.

Anyone who is comparing my predictions here to Hans Moravec's in *Robot* will note that I lead his dates by about half a decade.[4] This is due to the fact that he was talking about mobile robots, whereas I'm concentrating on stationary machines plugged into the wall. These will be cheaper, will have more power, and will not be quite as hard a programming task as the mobile ones, by virtue of not having to interpret as much sensory input.

These dates are highly speculative at best, and more important, they assume that the amount of effort put into AI remains at about the level it is now. There is reason to imagine, though, that it might increase as the systems currently in the labs move into the marketplace and begin to make money. This is a process that has been growing for some time but has the potential to significantly increase the resources devoted to AI in the next decade or two. On the other hand, it is also possible that AI could see another collapse, such as the one that happened in the 1980s.[5]

Breakthrough

There's no way to predict a breakthrough, a paradigm shift, a new order of things in a given scientific field. We can't say what will come, and much less, when.

But in AI there is a clear model in the notion of the autogenous mind. I have argued that there is a form of intelligence qualitatively different from a stock of application-specific skills—which, indeed, creates the stock of application-specific skills. In an AI, this would be the internal mechanism building new concepts, new machinery, and new skills to create new understanding.

The learning algorithms that could do this—representation search and copy/adapt—are probably not anything more complex than many existing AI programs. To be useful, they wouldn't have to be installed in anything like a full mentality; but in picking an application, it must be remembered that it is the stream of experience allowing for testing the predictive ability of the new structure that gives the whole scheme its traction.

There are several projects now with the goal of creating a baby brain. It is too soon to tell yet whether any of them is on the right track, much less whether any of them is an unqualified success. The reason is that most learning schemes, particularly ones based on search, appear to work for a while before running out of gas. For exactly the same reason, it may not be clear that the right method has been found until years after it actually has been implemented.

If any of these projects succeeds, it will have created something that has never been seen before: a machine that can think but lacks the huge inventory of mental modules, the below-the-waterline iceberg of the subconscious that constitutes the bulk of the human mind.

The vast majority of standard application-oriented AI, on the other hand, consists of just such modules, as embodied in the algorithms for the specific skills that have been programmed. In some cases, these are the same kinds of skills people have, but quite often new methods have been found that are more appropriate for computer implementation.

The really interesting times will start when the autogenous child-machine AIs begin to be good enough to read the research reports from applied AI, complete with equations and source code, and understand them by way of implementing them internally. As I have indicated, this might just possibly start to happen in a decade's time.

Once a baby brain does advance far enough that it has clearly surpassed the bootstrap fallacy point, however, it might affect AI like the

Wright brothers' Paris demonstrations of their flying machine did a century ago. After ignoring their successful first flight for years, the scientific community finally acknowledged it. Aviation went from a screwball hobby to the rage of the age and kept that cachet for decades. In particular, the amount of development effort took off enormously. If we can expect even a faint echo of that from AI, the early, primitive general learning systems will focus research considerably and will attract a lot of new resources.

Thus, it is not inconceivable that sometime in the next decade, someone will get a general learning machine to work. Even in such a simple system, for something to be ready to take off in a decade, there must already be a current substantial base system and many of the key insights must already have been thought of. Five years isn't inconceivable, but anything short of ten would, in fact, be quite surprising. There just isn't enough work going on now in general learning systems to predict that anyone will get it right that soon. Even when it does happen, a top-notch development team will have to implement it, debug it, experiment with it, and generally do a lot of learning themselves before the system is ready for prime time.

The first general learning systems will not be world-threatening superminds. They will be babies, babies with substantial cognitive disabilities. The rest of the built-in subsystems and innate capabilities of the human mind will have to be added or learned—and in some cases we don't yet even know what they are, much less how they work.

A key question is when would the system start to be able to extend itself into arbitrary fields by reading unprepared natural-language text about them. This will vary wildly with the subject matter. If the existing corpus of computer analysis and simulation techniques in math, logic, and physical sciences will stand in for the innate representation modules humans have, a good start could be made fairly soon. But that will produce a significantly allohuman intellect: it would be forced to understand, say, love stories the way we understand quantum mechanics—perhaps gropingly, by means of strained and contradictory metaphors to things that it did understand.

Humans can learn approximately one concept an hour, which is why it takes us ten years or so to become an expert in any given field and even longer than that just to mature to general competence. If I'm right, and learning is the hard part of cognition—the part that accounts for the bulk of the enormous processing power that the brain apparently needs—a baby AI won't be any faster at it than a baby human. But if we keep upgrading the hardware to follow Moore's law, interesting things will happen.

Let's just assume for the sake of argument that we have a general learner at human rates that runs on a machine that costs, say, a hundred thousand dollars. Now, suppose we continue to buy a hundred thousand dollars' worth of machine each year, keeping each one for three years before junking it. Let's assume we can buy more computing power for the same price each successive year according to Moore's law. We get the following progression:

Year	HEPP/year	HEPP total	Concepts/year	Concepts total
1	1	1	8,760	8,760
2	1.778	2.778	24,335	33,095
3	3.161	5.939	52,026	85,121
4	5.621	10.56	92,505	177,626
5	10	18.78	164,513	342,139
6	17.78	33.4	292,584	634,723
7	31.60	59.38	520,169	1,154,892
8	56.21	105.6	925,056	2,079,948
9	100	187.8	1,645,128	3,725,076
10	177.8	334	2,925,840	6,650,916

The number of concepts an educated human learns in a lifetime has been estimated at half a million, although this is an incredibly fuzzy number; the concept of a concept is pretty ill defined to begin with. But the progression is clear: the baby AI, if it takes advantage of accelerating processing power (and runs twenty-four hours a day), will catch up to a ten-year-old in three years and match the human lifetime in six. In year seven it will be learning at the rate of a human's lifetime knowledge per year. After ten years it will know more than ten humans—and will be learning at a rate equivalent to 334 humans!

I have argued for the existence of universal, autogenous learning, but it's far from a certainty. However, *if* the concept is valid, and *if* someone figures out how to do it, and *if* it can be done with the kind of hardware available in the 2010s, the decade of the diahuman AI would follow with epihuman AIs unequivocally appearing somewhere in the 2020s.

The smart money says that the truth will be somewhere between the two extreme cases presented here.

Chapter 17
Philosophical Extrapolations

> *"What are you?" Klapaucius asked.*
>
> *"I already answered that," snapped the machine, clearly annoyed.*
>
> *"I mean, are you man or robot?" explained Klapaucius.*
>
> *"And what, according to you, is the difference?" said the machine.*
>
> —Stanislaw Lem, *The Cyberiad*

Does it even make sense to think of building a machine to have a mind like a person? Throughout most of recorded history, the idea of making an artificial person was purely a part of mythology, and even then, the agent who made such a person was usually a god. This makes the story much easier to swallow, since the gods are generally credited with having made people in the first place, so making one more doesn't strain the credulity that much.

For example, in Ovid's *Metamorphoses* there is the story of Pygmalion, the sculptor who makes an ivory statue so beautiful that he falls in love with it. (The name of the statue, Galatea, seems to have been later attached to the story by other authors.) The point is that Pygmalion doesn't bring her to life; Venus does.

Frankenstein, in stark philosophical contrast, brings life (but not beauty) to his creature by his own, purely human efforts. What happened between the times of Ovid and Mary Shelley that allowed this new form of the story to be, if not outright credible, at least within the grasp of the suspension of disbelief?

I think it was clearly the rise of science and rationalism that accompanied the Enlightenment. In science, Luigi Galvani had shown in 1771 that you could make a dead frog's leg kick by applying electricity to a nerve. In philosophy, we can point to two figures in particular who are strongly associated with the paradigm shift: René Descartes and Gottfried Wilhelm Leibniz.

DUALISM

> *I have proved in my [book* Traité du Monde*] that all the structures which would be necessary to enable an automaton to reproduce all those activities that we have in common with animals, are to be found in the animal body.*
>
> —René Descartes, in a letter to Fr. Mersenne, 1640

Descartes is generally regarded as the father of dualism, the doctrine stating there are two kinds of stuff—mind and matter. To put this in perspective, however, it must be remembered that before Descartes, it was universally assumed that the simple intuitive distinction between living and nonliving things was a basic dichotomy of nature. The notion that things in the bodies of living creatures could be explained in mechanistic terms was at the time quite revolutionary. Descartes was a contemporary of the Englishman William Harvey, whose theory that the heart was a pump, which circulated the blood through arteries and veins like water in pipes, was still quite controversial. For Descartes to take the full step and say that *everything* in an animal's body is mechanistic was a huge leap.

It would, indeed, have been asking too much that he should have abandoned the notion that there was some significant difference between the world of the mind and that of matter, but he is perhaps unfairly remembered most for this last holdout.

It was left for Leibniz to take the last step and propose that it is possible to build a machine that can think. Leibniz, the independent coinventor of the calculus alongside Newton and one of the leading thinkers of the latter half of the seventeenth century, was four years old when Descartes died in 1650. Leibniz is known among other things for his work in metaphysics. He believed language could be systematized to the extent that the processes of thinking, or at least of logical deduction, could be mechanized. Since his time there have been enormous strides in symbolic logic, and there is still a long way to go, but Leibniz must be credited in large part with the inspiration.

In any significant advance of understanding, the leading lights are rarely alone in their work, but they build on a swelling wave of new knowledge. Descartes surely synthesized some of his work from the results of the great anatomists of the early seventeenth century, and surely Leibniz had something of Descartes' classic reduction of geometry to algebra in mind.

Whatever the eddies and subcurrents of knowledge and ideas, by the time the Age of Reason gave way to the Romantic Era, it was quite possible in intellectual circles to entertain the thought that all of life might admit to a mechanistic explanation.

There are still holdouts, even in the highest of ivory towers and into the twenty-first century. Some are philosophers who, quite reasonably reacting to the overblown hype accompanying the introduction of cybernetics and AI, have acted to reclaim their territory (the philosophy of mind) by showing how AI couldn't possibly work. It is not particularly important to refute those who take this tack. Rather, the only refutation worth doing is simply to build the AI, and then we will see who is right. Science advances by experiment, not debate.

As you might expect, many leading modern philosophers of mind hold the mechanistic position. The American philosopher Daniel Dennett, for example, is one who has used the computational theory of mind to tackle some of the hardest problems in philosophy, such as the nature of consciousness. In passing, I would like to point out that the best source for those interested in Dennett's philosophy is Dennett himself; his popular writings are extensive, accessible, and quite enjoyable to read for someone interested in the subject. We will come to Dennett again, but for the moment I will simply hold him up as an example that the mechanistic view of the mind seems compatible with that of some of the best practitioners of the field.

THE COMPUTATIONAL STANCE

> *Alice laughed: "There's no use trying," she said; "one can't believe impossible things."*
>
> *"I daresay you haven't had much practice," said the Queen. "When I was younger, I always did it for half an hour a day. Why, sometimes I've believed as many as six impossible things before breakfast."*
>
> —Lewis Carroll, *Alice in Wonderland*

Once upon a time, a duffer went out to play golf. He teed up for the first hole, took a huge swing, and missed. His driver instead struck an anthill, killing 9,999 of the 10,000 ants inhabiting it. Mumbling "mulligan" under his breath, the duffer took a second mighty swing, and missed again, similarly obliterating a second anthill, again leaving a single survivor. The two ants, running wildly about in panic, met each other just as the duffer wound up for a third swing.

One said to the other, "We'd better get on the ball."

With AI approaching, possibly as imminently as a decade away, we stand in need of some answers to age-old philosophical questions, and fast. Would it be cruel to tease a robot? Should an AI be held accountable for its actions or simply disassembled if it does the wrong thing?

The ball we need to be on is to have some solid, defensible basis for our theory of ethics. It seems almost certain that the AIs of the near future will come from all sorts of origins, ranging from open-source collaborations through corporate projects to secret government initiatives. A single universal code of behavior such as Asimov's Three Laws of Robotics seems unlikely; in later chapters we will examine this in greater detail. For a system of ethics to be adopted by the AIs, which by definition will be smart enough to see through any sophistry we may use to rationalize our rules, it must be based on sound understandings of the phenomena ethics deals with, from suffering to the sense of the sacred.

As a stopgap, I am going to take the approach of using the computational theory of mind as a chainsaw on the Gordian knot of these great philosophical conundrums. I will warn you in advance that this roughneck methodology will leave some of your intuitions rubbed raw. Here's an example: It was once generally taken for granted that the earth was flat. Things released in the air fell down until they hit the ground, and the ground was always there, and down was always the same direction. This is the simplest generalization of the intuitive understanding of how such things work on the scale of the human body. It remains the basis of plane geometry—which most people think of as real and of the other kinds as contrived.

This intuition holds even though we can directly see evidence that it isn't true. A ship coming over the horizon appears from the top down, rather than expanding whole from a tiny dot as it would if the sea were flat instead of curved.

Once we understand, intellectually, that the earth is a sphere and that gravity points to the center in all directions, we still have a hard time with the intuition. It is a common reaction, upon hearing a description of the earth hanging in space, to wonder, "Yes, but what holds *it* up?"

If you have lived with that view for so long that it no longer bothers you to think of the earth hanging in space with no support, here is another one that can still cause some head-scratching. We have the intuition that there is a single, unidirectional flow of time, analogous to our single-direction-of-down spatial intuition. Einstein's theories of relativity, however, tell us that this, too, is a local approximation and that time can flow differently from the point of view of different observers.

The history of science has been a history of explaining things out from under our intuitions. This does not mean that our intuitions are wrong but simply that we need to understand their limitations. For moving furniture or playing tennis, our intuitive understanding of gravity is just fine. For launching satellites or predicting weather, they need some help.

The way science can help us overcome the limitations of our intuitions is by conducting experiments that reveal the boundaries of their validity and by allowing us to form new theories to cover situations the intuitions do not. We will begin with thought experiments; ultimately, there are many real-world experiments to be done to verify or correct the theories that follow.

Although we cannot offer any substantial detail, we can make the following predictions as to the ultimate shape of a mature computational theory of mind:[1]

- It will be causal and mechanistic.
- It will involve multiple levels of abstraction, but higher levels may require reference to lower levels in exceptional cases.
- It will contain continuous and reactive, as well as symbolic and algorithmic, elements and forms of computation, such as associative memory, that are not part of standard algorithmic practice.
- At the higher levels, the architecture will be modular, with definable information flows between modules. This does not preclude the possibility of various global communication channels, however.
- At intermediate levels, there will be information patterns recognizable as symbols; but these will be nonatomic, with a wealth of implicit relationships implied by their structure.
- Propositional attitudes, qualia (see p. 283), free will, and the other aspects of mind that are of interest will be identified with various configurations and properties of the mental computational architecture in a satisfying way.

- The vast majority of perceptions, inferences, and memory formations will be heuristic in form and adaptive in the ancestral environment, but they will not be general, sound, nor complete in a mathematical sense.

Here is an example to justify the use of "satisfying" in the above. The best-developed theory of this form I am aware of is for free will.

FREE WILL

> *All mammals, in truth, seem to have an inborn tendency to identify causation with volition. They are naturally pugnacious, and life to them consists largely of a search for something or someone to blame it on.*
>
> —H. L. Mencken, *Treatise on the Gods*

Here's the problem of free will in a nutshell:

1. We have a strong intuition that the universe is deterministic; that is, that it follows physical law or is probabilistically random, which is also in accordance with physical law (e.g., chaos theory or quantum mechanics). As a practical matter, this intuition is very well corroborated by experiment.
2. We also have a strong intuition that we subjectively have the ability to make choices, and we can clearly recall times when we could realistically have done differently than we did.
3. But there is an apparent contradiction between 1 and 2.

There is a philosophical school of thought, called *compatibilism*, which argues to the effect that 3 is illusory and that 1 and 2 can both be true at the same time. The problem with such accounts is that they seem to be a bit fuzzy as to what 2 could actually consist of in physical terms—surely they aren't saying that we have the ability to work miracles and contravene physical law when we make choices? But if not, then what? Any resolution of the conundrum will have to make sense of what free will could possibly *mean* if viewed from a deterministic, physical perspective.

Enter computer scientist Drew McDermott, a professor at Yale.[2] Here is McDermott's contribution to the discussion: Suppose there is a robot that is intelligent and able to plan, choose, and act rationally. The best theories we have about how to build such a robot involve the robot having a mental model of the world. The model is just one way of talking about everything the robot knows, so that, by definition, whenever the robot wants to consult its knowledge about anything, it consults the model.

The robot can make choices about its actions. It does this, being in a situation where various courses are open to it, by evaluating the results of its options using the model. Thus, what the model tells the robot is of the form, "If I do this, that will happen; if I do the other, thus-and-such will happen."

We'll refer to the sum total of the robot's evaluation—including instinct, calculated self-interest, conscience, esthetics, and so on—as its "utility function." The robot's utility function is deterministic in accordance with physical law and, therefore, so is the robot as a whole.

For the robot's model to be any good for planning actions, however, it must have the following properties:

- The model has to be deterministic in the same way the world is, so that it makes good predictions about what's going to happen in any circumstance, given a correct description thereof.
- *Except*, the part of the model that represents the robot itself *cannot* be deterministic. If the robot tried to model itself correctly, its model would have to contain another world model, including another robot model, including a world model, ad infinitum—an infinite regress not only in the datastructure, but also in any algorithm that would use it for choosing. The whole point of having the model is that the robot's decision process

uses the model, from the outside so to speak, and is not inside it. It just wouldn't work otherwise.

For the planning algorithm to work, the robot's model of itself—by definition, the sum total of all its knowledge about itself—*must* be nondeterministic.* It must have choices that are left open as choices. Predictions made by the model must be contingent statements that turn on the robot's own actions.

In other words, any creature that has a coherent body of knowledge about the world and uses this knowledge for rational planning *must* be constructed so that its knowledge tells it that

1. the rest of the world is deterministic, and
2. the creature itself has options between which it can choose.

Now, this 1 and 2 sound awfully darn similar to the original 1 and 2 above. In fact, they sound exactly the same. In other words, here is a theory about how rational creatures are constructed that *predicts* we will come with a built-in freedom/determinism problem if we are sufficiently introspective.

The philosophically satisfying part of this explanation is that it not only tells me why I have the two seemingly contradictory intuitions of determinism and free will, but it also gives a coherent account of what free will could actually *mean*. Any creature constructed along the lines of McDermott's robot would have the same intuitions and would believe it had free will—and what's more, it would act in the same sense that humans do. It would be able to reflect on its choices and modify its behavior using new knowledge or insights not directly associated with the choice (but that changed the value to the robot of the results).

Please note the form of this explanation. If you don't let go of your intuition at the proper place, you'll still be left asking, "Yes, but does it *really* have free will?" This is exactly the position you're in if,

*In something vaguely like the technical computer science sense.

failing to relinquish your gravity intuition, you're left asking what holds the earth up.

But the aspect of the explanation that makes it a model for all explanations to be extracted from the computational theory of mind is that it is what philosophers call an *error theory*. That is, it not only identifies some computational structure or process with the concept to be explained (which is easy to do and all too easy to get wrong), but it also shows how, given the structure in question, *it cannot be otherwise* than that we have the intuition we do.

There is one other strong parallel with the gravity example that must be made. When you are acting on a human scale on the surface of the earth, the intuitive theory of gravity as a unique, preferred direction is exactly the right theory for you to use. Any other theory would be overcomplex for the situation and would cost you excessive processing with negligible advantage.

We should use our intuition of free will in exactly the same way. When we are dealing with other human beings or robots, constructed according to McDermott's recipe, we should think of them and treat them as if they have free will because—to the full extent of any coherent meaning of the concept—they do.

There is a doctrine in philosophy called the *naturalistic fallacy*, which forms a logical wall between the worlds of *is* and *ought*—you can't deduce one from the other.[3] Besides the obvious fact that "*x* is the case" and "*x* ought to be the case" are different statements and that they shouldn't simply be equated, why should they be separated? One reason may be that the former statement belongs in the world model and the latter belongs in the utility function. These will be in different modules, and, so, inference will not run easily between them.

As a sanity check to this theory of free will, let's consider the most salient aspect of the intuition for most practical purposes: we believe that it is appropriate to punish people who have free will for doing evil acts, but not to punish people of low mental capacity, animals whose instincts constrain them to the acts they do, or inanimate objects governed by physical law. If a box falls on my foot, it is silly to punish the box.

Now consider a robot with McDermott's architecture. If this robot commits an evil act, should we punish it? Clearly, yes. The punishment, which can be anything the robot rates with negative utility, will become part of the robot's evaluation when the prospect of committing the same act in the future reoccurs. It and other robots of like construction observing the situation will amend their world models to increase the likelihood that evil acts will entail punishment and, thus, this will decrease the likelihood that they will find evil acts worth doing.

So, from a purely practical standpoint, it *makes sense* to punish robots with McDermott's architecture. This seems to me to be a clear indication that the theory is on the right track.

SYMBOLS AND MEANING

If we take in our hand any volume; of divinity or school metaphysics, for instance; let us ask, "Does it contain any abstract reasoning concerning quantity or number?" No. "Does it contain any experimental reasoning concerning matter of fact and existence?" No. Commit it then to the flames: for it can contain nothing but sophistry and illusion.

—David Hume

Imagine sitting in a closed room, surrounded by voluminous filing cabinets with desks, blackboards, pencils, and erasers at hand. There is a slot in the wall of the room through which, at odd intervals, a slip of paper is handed to you. On the paper is written a sequence of strange symbols, whose meaning you don't know. However, you find in your files instructions such as, "If you see a symbol that looks like *this* in the third position on the input paper, and the third sheet in drawer F of cabinet 357 contains a symbol that looks like *that*, draw this other symbol on a new sheet and put it between the 9th and 10th sheets in drawer B of cabinet 102." You follow these directions for a while and at the end of the process you will have written a sequence of symbols on a slip of paper that you hand back out through the slot.

Now, you don't know it, but what has happened is that you and your room have received a query written in Chinese—a language you do not know—and you have answered it the way an AI program would do it; that is, by merely juggling meaningless symbols. At no point did you understand what was being asked or the answer you were giving. This little scene, invented by the Berkeley philosopher John Searle, is commonly called the Chinese Room.[4] Searle, a critic of AI, argues that a computer running an AI program would not really understand the things it appeared to be talking about, just as you would not have any idea what you were talking about while in the Chinese Room. He claims that this is lack of understanding *even if the AI passes the most rigorous Turing Test.*

Numerous philosophers and AI researchers have answered Searle with objections such as "It's not the computer that understands, but the system consisting of the computer and the program and its database." In the scenario, this translates to saying that although you, the person, don't understand Chinese, the whole system consisting of the room, the cards, and you, as a whole do understand.

Searle answers no. Rooms don't understand; cards don't understand; and you, the operator, don't understand Chinese. There's no understanding going on in there. The symbols on the cards don't *mean* anything, and no matter how much manipulation you do to them, they still won't mean anything.

Let's try the same scenario in a somewhat less metaphysical setting, and perhaps the trick will be a little clearer: Suppose we have a man who doesn't know how to play tennis. He's never even seen a match. We take him to a room where there is a huge bank of lights, a big panel of dials, buttons, and switches, and a set of bicycle pedals. Then we give him a big book full of instructions such as "If lights 67, 121, and 235 come on simultaneously, flip switch 14 and turn knob 93 to the right a distance proportional to the brightness of light 55." He is told to pedal constantly, and anytime any condition in the book is true, he must do the corresponding action.

He has still never seen a tennis court or even heard of one. However, unbeknownst to him, there is a remote-controlled android on a tennis court, powered by the pedals, armed with a racquet, and Andre Agassi is on the other side of the net. What's more, we will stipulate that when the man does as instructed in the room, it would appear to any onlooker that the machine is playing a very creditable game of tennis, complete with serves, volleys, and sizzling cross-court passing shots.

And yet the machine cannot play tennis by itself. Without someone pedaling, it's just an inert mass of metal. If the knobs and switches were manipulated in a different sequence, it would just as readily dash madly about, breaking flowerpots with its racquet. And the man surely isn't playing tennis—he's never heard of it and he's never stepped on a tennis court or touched a racquet. And books of instructions clearly can't play tennis.

On Searle's view, it must be that tennis just isn't being played at all!

Or look at the Chinese Room from the outside. You are sitting next to a slot in a wall, and you can write anything you like on a slip of paper, stick it in, and there is a pen pal on the other side who answers back, clearly understanding everything you write, making thoughtful replies, and showing a range of knowledge and depth of insight equal to the wisest person you know (i.e., passing the Turing Test).

Something's got to give.

What gives is that the Chinese Room as described by Searle simply could never work. We can look back at our computing power estimates for emulating human-level intelligence. The absolute rock-bottom estimates require a teraops (power level 12 on our scale) and a terabyte (one thousand gigabytes), and most sensible ones are orders of magnitude higher. Even for the rock-bottom ones, the poor overworked clerk in the Chinese Room would need about five miles of filing cabinets to do a proper job. If we assumed that he could zip up and down the hallways to access any of them in just one minute, he would have to work approximately two million years to simulate just one second's worth of thought.

Yes, our intuition tells us that there isn't any understanding going on in the Chinese Room. But it also tells us that the room can't really hold anything like a coherent conversation in real time (or snail-mail pen pal time!) either, and that intuition is right, too. (The tennis-playing robot wouldn't work either, by the way—from personal experience, it's virtually impossible to control a robot arm from a panel of switches and knobs even without real-time constraints like fast-moving tennis balls.)

For my money, the intuition that Searle has and elicits in those who agree with the Chinese Room argument is exactly an instinctive understanding of formalist float. He knows, and you know and I know, that a whole building full of paper-shuffling bureaucrats isn't going to produce true understanding for the robot to work; it's going to be a clueless automaton. The one guy in the room is philosophical overkill.

But as a computer scientist, I have another intuition, as well. Imagine you are building an airplane. You have wings, a tail, a propeller, an engine, and a fuselage. None of the pieces can fly by itself. Put them together and they can fly. *Synergy* is the concept that a system can have a property that's more than just the sum of the properties of its parts. Essentially, all of engineering is about harnessing synergy. I've spent my adult life building systems that had different and more sophisticated properties than the parts they were built from. The more complex the system, the greater the difference.

The crux of the philosophical argument over AI is whether the quantitative difference between the Chinese Room and a computer system capable of real human-level performance is enough to amount to the qualitative difference between syntax and semantics. If there is enough of something, it is possible, indeed not unusual, for it to have properties not exhibited at all in small, isolated samples. In this case, the difference is at least a factor of a trillion: 1,000,000,000,000. There is *no* case in our experience where a difference of a factor of a trillion doesn't make a qualitative, as opposed to merely a quantitative, difference. A trillion is essentially the difference in weight between a dust mite, too small to see and too light to feel, and an elephant. It's the difference between fifty dollars and a year's economic output for the entire human race. It's the difference between the thickness of a business card and the distance from here to the moon.

If you handle a lot of paper, you'll know that your fingertips get dry and slip on the paper, making it difficult, for example, to turn pages. The common thing to do in such a situation is to touch a fingertip to your tongue, which transfers about a microliter of moisture and makes it just damp enough to push a page corner free. A factor of a trillion more licks of moisture would fill an Olympic swimming pool. Imagine trying to swim in a moist fingertip, or turning a page with an Olympic swimming pool. They are completely different kinds of thing. Any argument based on equating them is all wet.

Machines and Meaning

> *What's in a name? That which we call a rose*
> *By any other name would smell as sweet.*
>
> —William Shakespeare, *Romeo and Juliet*

In chapter 5, "Diaspora," I went to great lengths to describe how the meaning of a sentence must be something considerably more elaborate than its parse tree or a list of predicate expressions.

In particular, when you understand a sentence, you construct in your mind a structure of modules—a computing machine—that will enable you to make predictions and plans that would be appropriate in a world where you would have said the sentence yourself.

For sentences that describe conditions or events, this computing structure will be similar to the one you would have constructed in observing the condition or event. The modules of mind can be characterized as having associative memories of trajectories in whatever concepts the module specializes in. If you believe that it's cold outside, you will have trajectories that correspond to stepping out in your bathrobe for the paper and getting a quick chill; ones that correspond to taking a long walk while warmly dressed but having ice form on your eyebrows; to windows frosting over, to slipping on frozen puddles, to the furnace coming on often, to the car being reluctant to start. A young child, without such memories, or someone from a tropical climate, does not understand the sentence in the same way you do.

When you believe something, then, whether you have observed it or been told it, you conscript the appropriate set of memories for the situation. You construct a set of connections between the modules to form a prediction machine. (Whether these connections are passive links to be followed by some executive or active transmission lines between separate processes is an implementation detail.)

This theory makes it seem like true semantic knowledge, *intentionality* in the philosophers' term, is grounded in experience, and, so, for humans, it is. For an AI, it is clearly possible that you could take the set of memories accumulated by one machine and simply copy it over to another, brand-spanking new one. The new machine wouldn't have had any experiences; would it have true meaning? Of course it would. If it has the same function and data, the computational theory of mind says that it is doing the same thing as the original one.

Suppose the identical bit patterns had been dreamed up by a human programmer instead of having been arduously collected the hard way by the machine. The same rule applies: they're real. But remember the Chinese Room analysis: the programmer is looking through the wrong end of a trillion-X telescope. The Chinese Room, operating at its one-instruction-per-minute rate, would have been able to experience just two hours of simulated human life since the birth of the universe. If a programmer, or more realistically a large team of them, manages to get anything remotely resembling a lifetime's experience of memories hand-encoded, they will almost necessarily have had enough of the right kinds of experience themselves to ground the semantics. Any less and formalist float reigns supreme.

To sum up, it seems the information-theoretic formulation is most useful: meaning consists of a computational model that reflects some regularity in whatever it is we think of the meaning as being about, whether this is the physical world or some mental realm such as mathematics. It is not necessarily grounded in actual experience as a theoretical necessity, but as a practical matter, it's pretty difficult to come by it any other way.

CONSCIOUSNESS

The most merciful thing in the world . . . is the inability of the human mind to correlate all its contents.

—H. P. Lovecraft

The problem of consciousness is a particularly adhesive tar baby, and it would be best if we didn't have to tangle with it. However, there are some moral questions that our intuitions insist are connected to the issue. For example, if I kick an AIBO robot toy, I may be stupid and destructive but I'm not being cruel; I have every right to kick it if it's mine and that's what I want to do with it. However, if I kick a live dog, there is a sense, backed up in law, that I have transgressed a moral boundary, even if the dog is completely owned by me. The difference seems to be that the dog is able to feel pain.

The main problem with trying to explain consciousness in the computational theory of mind is that it is impossible. Leibniz pointed this out centuries ago, as we noted in our discussion of the New Synthesis (see chapter 6). He set up, you will remember, a thought experiment in which the mind is a mechanical mill and the intrepid philosopher is shrunk to the appropriate size to take a walking tour of it and see all the cogwheels, pulleys, levers, and shafts turning and pushing and doing all the work. He pointed out that you could tour the whole thing and not see anything that looked like consciousness—it would be nothing but gears.

Similarly, any other purely mechanistic explanation of how the mind works will *necessarily* fall intuitively short of explaining the ineffable phenomenality of experience. You will always be able to come back and ask, "Yes, but what holds it up?" In order to understand what's going on in consciousness, as in the universe, the key will be to understand that there is an area where your intuition is applicable and thus meaningful, and there is an area where it is inapplicable and thus misleading.

We can, however, do much better than simply picking some phenomenon and claiming that it is the computational cognate of consciousness. We can make our theory intellectually if not intuitively satisfying by posing it in the same terms as we did for free will: it should show that creatures with the architectural features that we claim constitute consciousness would necessarily believe they were conscious, and that it would be objectively appropriate to treat them as if they were.

Consciousness, on closer inspection, seems to have a lot of different meanings. Let's look at them one at a time.

Sentience

Consider two minds: a human brain and a computer that is powerful enough and has enough memory to do the same computations that the brain is doing. Since we're thinking about ultimate abstract possibilities here and not engineering detail, let's just assume that the computer receives every input the brain does, in the form of nerve impulses or hormone levels or anything else, and that it works at a level of detail good enough that every output nerve signal is just the same as what the brain produces.

Now it will be possible to ask the computer about sentience, and it will stoutly insist that it is just as sentient as you are. It will not be lying—it will genuinely believe it is sentient (or, if you prefer the mechanistic terms, it will find this recorded in its database as a true fact). It will have the same answer to any question on the subject as the brain would. It will indulge in late-night bull sessions about whether the color it sees as green is the same that you see as red. If it keeps thinking about these things for a few years, it will begin to read and write scholarly papers about phenomenology and qualia. It will have the same intuition as Searle does; there's nothing in a pile of bit-flipping logic gates that could possibly give rise to its directly felt sensory and introspective experiences.

If the brain is truly sentient and the computer is just faking it, what's the difference? The brain and the computer are running the same computation, by assumption. In particular, everything the brain does that indicates that it is sentient will be the necessary result of a sequence of calculations—indeed, of exactly the same calculations that the computer does to produce exactly the same reaction.

Close your eyes for a second and subvocalize, "I'm thinking about sentience." Now suppose I ask you a question about the experience you just had, for example, on which syllable the most stress was placed. The brain, in the same situation, would have had the actual experience and would remember it. The computer will have done computations involving datastructures that were created while it was performing (the computational analog of) the subvocalization. But the brain—by assumption—would do exactly the same calculations! Any behavioral output or internal change we could ascribe to having had a sentient experience would be exactly the same in the brain as in the computer.

In other words, the difference between having true sentience, as in the brain, and not, as in the computer, has absolutely no physical effect whatsoever. We might as well have said that the computer is truly sentient and that the brain isn't.

In fact, to have any claim to objectivity, we have to say that they both are. (The alternative is to say that neither is, but that's silly: sentience and the notion of conscious experience clearly refer to *something*.) This is where the computational theory of mind has its biggest win, from a philosophical perspective. Without it, we are not only completely at sea as to what sentience really is, but it is also impossible to give any kind of reasoned argument for calling any creature sentient (or nonsentient). In fact, you can claim that any particular human isn't really sentient, and there's nothing he or she can do to prove the opposite!

Self-Awareness

If you were a thermostat and the temperature fell below your set point, you would go *click* and turn the furnace on. A thermostat and its furnace form a homeostatic system, a system that attempts to preserve the temperature at an even level. Such a system is clearly more aware than one that simply runs the furnace at fixed intervals. Thus, there is some reasonable sense in which any system with sensory feedback that influences a control function has a basic kind of awareness. It remains to be seen just how much and what kind of awareness we should require before we can call it sentient, but there's not some mysterious difference in kind.

A housefly has a number of different behaviors. It can meander through the air, searching for good smells. It can stand on a surface and eat. It can wander around a surface, looking for more food. If it sees a large object approaching fast, it takes off on a darting escape trajectory.

Internally, the fly has a multilevel control structure, like the robot GENGHIS. The lower levels involve the specific activities, such as flying or walking; the higher ones involve selecting the appropriate behavior to enact. A fly is clearly aware, and it is, thus, sentient by definition.

However, it seems pretty clear that a fly is not self-aware in any sense with which we would normally use the word. It will, having escaped the flyswatter, fly around the room and land in exactly the spot it had fled. You can crush a fly against a windowpane simply by coming down on it slowly enough with your fingertip. A fly is like a classic AI program, provided with a static set of senses, interpretations, and concepts, but unable to learn from experience.

If you were designing a robot, you would not give it self-awareness simply so that it could take part in sophomore bull sessions. Self-awareness seems almost certain to be part of a mechanism for fast, high-level learning. Low-level learning, such as optimizing a skill with practice, and operant conditioning, as in Pavlov's dog, can proceed by low-level mechanisms. But high-level learning, such as understanding a complex, structured operation by watching someone do it, requires being able to watch yourself trying it as well as watching the other person. Thus, we have *mirror cells*, which fire for the concept of doing something, whether they are the cells of the actor or the observer.

In other words, for good memetic copying, it seems to help to have the ability to experience yourself doing something in a similar way as you experience watching someone else doing it. This would make sense from the point of view of a feedback control that was comparing the two experiences.

Qualia

Explanations come to an end somewhere.

—Ludwig Wittgenstein, *Philosophical Investigations*

Consider a robot that is able to introspect, or view its own cognitive processes.[5] Many of the thoughts or perceptions it has can be explained by reference to other thoughts or perceptions and how they are put together. It can describe shapes it sees in terms of simpler geometric primitives, for example, and it can even tease apart the hierarchy of segments, curves, and shadings that make up what it sees.

But suppose you show it a red ball and ask it about the color. It checks the output of its video camera and finds that, at the very lowest level, a red pixel is represented as a triple of numbers (255, 0, 0). Well, that's red, all right! Whenever the robot looks at something red, (255, 0, 0) is the signal it gets.

This signal is ineffable. There's no explaining it in terms of the robot's subjective experience. It could study the camera manual and see why the camera put out this particular signal in response to light of the right wavelength; but this wouldn't help it any more than our study of visual neuroscience helps our sense of the subjectiveness of what philosophers call the *quale*, the property of the sensory experience of red. (*Qualia* is simply the plural of quale.)

Now the robot, being an introspective sophomore, sits and thinks, "What if some other robot gets the signal (0, 255, 0)—the one I see as green—whenever it looks at something I see as red?"

We could build such a robot, but it is not clear that its subjective experience would be different in any significant sense from the first one's. Its red would be just as ineffable, just as associated with glowing hot metal and stop signs and lipstick and blood.

It is hard to see how to construct such a robot so that it *wouldn't* have most of the same subjective experiences associated with its basic sensory encodings as we have with qualia.

We have other qualia beside sensory ones, such as mathematical intuitions. An AI would have the same, whenever its introspective processes bottomed out into primitive operations.

Attention

Is it possible to be in pain and not be conscious of it? Simply from personal experience, the answer is an unequivocal yes. A specific example is a case where I was playing tennis and realized my right foot was hurting from an overly tight shoe. Once I focused attention on it, I could feel the pain quite vividly. But what had caused me to focus in the first place was that I noticed that my down-the-line forehand was missing more than usual. I remembered that this was usually due to not planting the foot properly, and I finally realized that I was subconsciously favoring the foot because—it hurt!

In a hierarchical modular architecture, this makes perfect sense. Signals such as pain normally travel up to the conscious center for remediation, but in cases such as the knee-jerk reflex, they clearly affect lower-level modules without waiting for higher authority. In tennis, as in many demanding physical activities, it is normal to suppress a low-to-moderate level of pain as normal wear and tear, and learning the sport includes programming the suppression into middle-level modules.

In my case, the suppressors were working fine, but low-level effects caused enough trouble that they affected the strategic level where my attention actually was active.

The Unity of Experience

Yes, the brain is massively, almost ridiculously, parallel. Yes, Freud, Selfridge, Minsky, and Brooks were right; there are multiple agencies whose interaction explains much of our behavior and capabilities.

Yet, if you are designing a robot with a single body, there must be a level of organization where the activities of each part come together to serve the ends of a single plan of action. Otherwise the robot will act like former president Ford trying to walk and chew gum at the same time.

Even in the housefly, there has to be some center of control where a decision is made—which of the fly's genetically programmed behaviors it is going to perform. In a fly, the evaluation of each possibility is so simple that it could probably be done by a single neuron.[6] If so, the neurons for each option would have to be connected together so as to allow only one of them to be active at once, in what's called a *mutual inhibition network*. Such a network is shown in fig. 17.1, which also shows another way of looking at exactly the same physical organization. In the second view, we abstract the function of all the inhibitive cross-connections into a single module. It is, by the way, a red herring in many of the discussions of consciousness to argue about whether the centralizing function is unitary or distributed. There is always an appropriate level of abstraction where any distributed property or mechanism can be viewed as a module in a block diagram, and we do not care how it is implemented at the lower levels.

In the human mind, we trust, the unifying mechanism is more complex than that of the fly. However, every animal has to have one, so it seems likely that the unifier is much more basic in the architecture than the other paraphernalia of human-level phenomenal consciousness.

We can imagine a human-level unifier—we called it City Hall earlier—as being a central controller tied to all the modules that correspond to concepts, including all actions and objects we know about. Maybe these need to be concentrated into higher-level concepts, such as frames that represent situations and simplify the world for the central module.

In any case, the central module is an associative memory that records trajectories in situation space, with the associated action leading to each transition (whether done by the person, someone, or something else). This gives the module the ability to predict, by analogy, based on previous situations; to plan by using the predictions to evaluate proposed actions (thus exhibiting free will, as above); and, in general, to act as a world model.

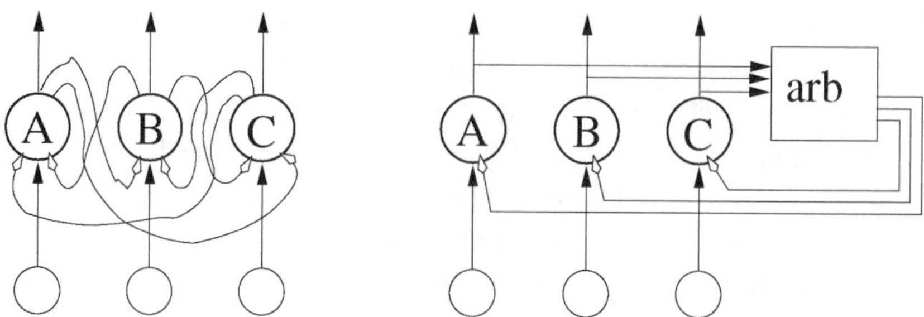

Fig. 17.1: A mutual inhibition network and exactly the same hardware represented as a more abstract block diagram.

A crucial property of such a module is that the "history" it stores must be a compact, highly abstract representation that makes sense of the world. The entire interpretive mechanism of the mind will be employed to boil down the voluminous sensory input and the nebulous possible interpretations of what is going on at any given moment into some crisp executive summary to be fed into the memory.

One of the more interesting and revealing results of consciousness research is that people report consciously making a decision some fraction of a second *after* the detection of nerve impulses indicate the decision has been made and an action started.[7] But this makes perfect sense from an architectural point of view. The introspection mechanism consults the memory containing the executive summary. The memory was formed by the interpretation mechanism. The interpretation mechanism looked at the higher-level modules in the sensory and motor chains. Those have been driven by the controller module. What the controller module decides to do has to go around the loop before it is available as part of self-knowledge.

It seems likely that there is at least one metalevel controller in humans that tells the main body-level controller what kinds of problems to solve at any given time. (Again, it is irrelevant whether this is physically separate, time-shared, or what have you.) Above that are some arrangements for basic urges and the sense of right and wrong; but the higher you get, the less like the seat of consciousness they seem. We consciously enjoy ice cream; more introspection and a summarization of memories are necessary to be conscious of having a habitual sweet tooth. *Why* we have a sweet tooth is a mystery and out of our control.

Note that the heuristic reconstruction works properly in the vast majority of cases; the boundary cases are quite analogous to visual optical illusions. (These are most easily observed in split-brain patients who confabulate in one hemisphere a reason for what the other, inaccessible hemisphere actually did. In one classic experiment, a patient's left brain was shown a chicken and his right brain a snowy scene. Asked to choose an appropriate implement, his right brain picked a snow shovel; asked to explain the choice, his left brain answered, "To shovel out the chicken coop.")[8] Strong evidence for the heuristic and post-hoc nature of the intention sensation is found in the confabulations produced by such illusions of the will.

The modeling/evaluation/acting/recording structure sketched above is a good one for rapid learning. The dynamics of the world model can be implemented as a database of causal pairs of the form "this happened and then, therefore that happened." The most important of these will be the ones of the form, "I did this, therefore that happened." So we can assume that there is a module producing such overall summaries and adding them to some mental logbook. But they are done after the fact and record only the results of the decision-making process instead of being part of it.

Now suppose we had a machine with such an architecture, and we questioned it in the same way we would a person to find out about that person's conscious experience. The machine would claim to be sentient and self-aware. It would have qualia and would exhibit attention. It would identify with a single "I" who saw all that it saw, thought what it thought, and did what it did. Why? *Because the logbook would tell it so.* Although it is conceivable to write up the logbook in different terms, a form matching our consciousness is simple, elegant, and effective. A machine with such a summarizer and logbook would believe itself to be as conscious as we are. I think it would be right.

This architecture is satisfying in the sense that it is exactly what we should expect. The mind is the operation of a machine formed by evolution to survive and reproduce on the savannas of Africa. Our self-image is exactly appropriate for creatures who can choose and plan by considering possibilities. Our sensation of will, like our vision, is not mathematically exact (which, by the way, would be mathematically impossible), but it is usually right where it usually matters. Rapid learning of the consequences of our actions is invaluable.

Evolution had no charter to give us clear insight into the intricacies of cognitive-data processing, any more than it had for celestial mechanics or protein folding. Only the painstaking march of science has done that, often against a strong inertia bolstered by intuitions of geocentrism or vitalism. A mature theory of mind should be coherent with the evolutionary theory of our origins and the physical theory of our construction. It must explain why our intuitions are what they are; it cannot simply take them as given.

It is probably fair to say that no artificial computational process achieved to date has the appropriate structure to claim, say, genuine conscious will. Indeed, as the pieces are put together over the next decade(s), it may well be possible only in retrospect to pinpoint when it happened. But happen it will.

FOLK PSYCHOLOGY

It's rummy how people differ in this matter of selecting the beverage that is to touch the spot. It's what Jeeves would call the psychology of the individual.

—P. G. Wodehouse, *Jeeves and the Old School Chum*

Okay, so it's cruel to kick a dog. But consider: If I am a veterinarian, and I give the dog a shot to cure worms, I'm not doing wrong even though I'm causing the dog pain. The judgment of cruelty depends both on the dog's sentience and on my own mental state—my motivations and beliefs. I could do exactly the same physical act, for example, but if I knew the dog had no worms and gave it the shot simply to enjoy its pain, my action would be immoral and cruel.

Propositional attitudes, as they are called, are statements of the form that someone believes, desires, or fears *something*, where the *something* is a propositional sentence. These constitute the core of our intuitive grasp of psychology and of our ability, such as it is, to predict what people will say and do.

This grasp of people is one of our major genetically programmed understanding modules, and this module has the same kind of limitations as all the others. In particular, its account of meaning and understanding is quite skimpy compared to what is really going on, and so is its account of all the propositional attitudes. However, in this case, I don't see the extension to a more complete theory as being as counterintuitive as it is in some of the cases above, such as free will.

For example, if I believe that you believe it's cold outside, I won't have a hard time understanding that you understand a lot more about it if you hail from Point Barrow, Alaska, than if you were born and bred in sunny Borneo.

Semanticians have trouble with the propositional attitudes because of things like Frege's Puzzle. In a nutshell, the puzzle is: Lois Lane believes Superman is strong, and she believes Clark Kent is weak. Doesn't this leave her believing a logical contradiction, since Clark Kent and Superman are really the same person? (Believing a contradiction is a much worse state to be in than merely believing something that is factually untrue, you see.)

What breaks down here is the naive theory of semantics taken for granted in the puzzle, that a word "refers" to an object. Skipping lightly over the fact that most of us probably believe plenty of contradictions anyway, Lois has a reasonably consistent set of memories. They do contain a gap, namely, anything about Superman switching identities; thus, she will make incorrect predictions, for example, expecting to see Clark Kent and Superman at the same time. But that, obviously, is not any fault of hers; her brain, as a computer, is predicting exactly what it should given its input. So I don't think folk psychology is as far off the mark as it is sometimes claimed to be; it's probably a fair match to the most abstract levels of a deeper, more filled-in theory.

EMOTIONS

> *NOBODY expects the Spanish Inquisition! Our chief weapon is surprise and fear, fear and surprise.*
>
> —Monty Python, *The Spanish Inquisition*

Suppose I injure you, my good friend. I experience remorse and regret for doing so. The first thing I do is apologize. Now, any number of trivial technologies can be made to say or write the words, "I'm sorry," but there's no hint that such a machine really experiences any such emotion. We could get a bit closer by positing an AI program that would be able to classify its action as harmful and automatically print, "I'm sorry," without being prompted. (In an interesting side note, researchers find that this actually helps; programs that appear to detect situations where they have caused problems and print apologies are rated as much more user friendly than ones that don't but are otherwise identical in usability, even though the users are sophisticated enough to know that the program is simply testing bits and branching.)

One or two percent of the human population can be classed as psychopathic. These people do not experience true empathy for others but act purely for their self-interest. To be successful in human society, a psychopath must be good at feigning empathetic feelings, and many of them are. One of the best ways to feign an emotion is to cause yourself to feel it, as in Method acting. The difference is that the actor or the psychopath turns the emotion on and off deliberately. With a normal person, a strongly held emotion is evidence that the same emotional stance will continue to hold for some time. The thing we dislike in the psychopath is that his tears will turn to laughter as soon as our backs are turned; his emotions may be felt but are not genuine.

Human emotions arise from the basic genetically programmed modules, and they provide motivation at a (usually) high level—if the dog makes a mess on the floor, we alter our gait to avoid stepping in it out of the emotion of disgust; but the same emotion prompts us to the complex, high-level activities of cleaning the floor and housebreaking the dog.

Genuine emotion is difficult to control consciously. It generates, involuntarily, *affective display*, externally visible signals such as blushing and facial expressions. It can be aroused, again involuntarily, by observing similar expressions in others. It seems reasonable to model the affective state as a point in some *n*-space, just as we can model colors in a three-space and tastes in a four-space. Work on generating expressions from an emotional state and reading the state indicated by an expression has been going on for some time, and, frankly, it is looking like the emotions are somewhat simpler and more straightforward at that level than much of the rest of cognition.[9]

When a dog, in response to an expression of displeasure from a human, lowers its head, avoids your eyes, puts its tail between its legs, and walks with a slinking hesitation, you are almost forced by your own emotional inference mechanisms to impute to it the emotion of shame.

The major danger I can see with respect to robotic emotion is that it is so easy, relatively, to simulate the external affective signals that one could supercharge the ELIZA effect for systems having virtually no true understanding (or actual emotion) underneath. In the longer run, androids could be built with an affected display driven entirely for their intended effect on you rather than being a true reflection of the internal state of the robot itself. Super-politicians, as it were; perfect psychopaths.

Unlike a person (at the moment!), a robot or an AI program is somewhat more open to inspection in its inner workings. It should be more trustworthy, not less, than a human, given that we can examine its mechanism *as well as* get to know it as a fellow social being. The major caveat is that we don't know what percentage of robotic psychopaths to expect yet; only time will tell.

The flip side, that of how to build a robot whose emotions are genuine, is challenging but less so than much of the AI enterprise. Higher-level goal structures, either hardwired or learned but difficult to modify, are straightforward to program. A robot with such structures would not only act as if it had the given emotions over the long term, but it would report the same qualia as a human would in terms of its feelings.

In the years to come, and fairly soon at that, it seems almost certain that the mechanisms of emotion in the human brain will be unraveled and susceptible to just as mechanistic an explanation as those of the robot. Will that make our emotions less real? Certainly not.

CHAPTER 18
Evolutionary Ethics

WHAT MORALS ARE

Human beings function better if they are deceived by their genes into thinking that there is a disinterested objective morality binding upon them, which all should obey.

—E. O. Wilson

To some people, good and evil are reified processes in the world, composed of a tapestry of individual acts into an overall pattern. Religious people are apt to anthropomorphize these into members of whatever pantheon they hold sacred. Others accept the teachings but not the teachers, believing in sets of rules for behavior but not in any rule makers. Some people indulge in detailed philosophical or legal elaborations of the rules. Philosophers have for centuries attempted to derive them from first principles, or at least reduce them to a few general principles, ranging from Immanuel Kant's categorical imperative to John Stuart Mill's utilitarianism and its variants to modern ideologically based formulations, such as the collectivism of John Rawls and the individualist libertarianism of Robert Nozick.

The vast majority of people, however, care nothing for this argumentative superstructure. Instead, they learn moral rules by osmosis and internalize them not unlike the rules of grammar of their native language, structuring every act as unconsciously as our built-in grammar does our sentences.

The new tool, the microscope through which we can now examine our moral natures, is the New Synthesis. Our minds are computers designed by genetic evolution and programmed by memetic evolution. If we look at the wide variety of societies and cultures, we can see that ethics are very much like language. (By the way, just to avoid confusion: the word ethic means a set of rules and definitions of right and wrong that correspond to one culture at one place and time. Ethics can be simply the plural of ethic, or it can refer to the study of these many ethics in general. It's as if we were to refer to the study of languages as languages instead of linguistics.)

Just like languages, ethics appear to vary wildly and endlessly, but on closer inspection there are some very strong basic principles and similarities. Just as there is a language module in the mental architecture, there appears to be one for ethics, or rather a collection of them that bear on that aspect of behavior. For example, there is a module that does logical inference quickly and accurately to detect cheaters in bargains and breakers of rules. A famous cognitive science experiment called the Wason Test shows that when this module is invoked, in situations where the problem is posed as cheater detection, people get the logic right effortlessly. But the same people are slow and inaccurate when a logically identical problem is posed in terms of abstract symbols. (Note, by the way, that logicians *do* get the problems right, effortlessly. They have simply created for themselves a learned module equivalent to the natural one, which operates on the symbols.)

Once cheaters are detected, there are modules that tell us what to do about them. Another cognitive science experiment is called the Public Goods Game, and it is a group version of the Prisoner's Dilemma. Each person in a ten-person group has the option of paying a dollar in "tax" or keeping it. For each dollar in tax received, the experimenter will pay everybody fifty cents; that is, a total of five dollars, spread evenly. If everybody cooperates, each will pay a dollar and get five; if everyone defects, each will just keep his one dollar.

In iterated Public Goods games, people tend to start out cooperating reasonably often, but all end up defecting after a few rounds. The few defectors at the start engender TIT-FOR-TAT behavior that snowballs. But if players have a mechanism to punish defectors, *even if it costs them more to punish than they will get* from the future cooperation of the miscreants, they will do so, and general cooperation will tend to last the entire series.[1]

Memetic Ethics

There are structures in our brains that predispose us to learn an ethic from the people we interact with, and these determine within broad limits the kinds of ethics we can learn. Like the grammar of language, any given ethic is notably more sophisticated than any simple set of rules or other algorithmic formulation seen to date.

Ethics have much in common from culture to culture; following the jargon of linguistics, we might call this "moral deep structure." Following the evolutionary logic, we expect much of it to follow the logic of solutions to Prisoner's Dilemma–type problems in nonzero-sum games. Here are some of the features that human ethics tend to have, which appear to be easy to learn and propagate in a given ethic:

- Reciprocity, both in aggression ("an eye for an eye") and in beneficence ("I owe you one"): this is reciprocal altruism and TIT-FOR-TAT.
- Pecking order, rank, status, authority: the pecking order seems to be partly a mechanism for evaluating and selecting genes through competition for mating opportunity and a mechanism to allow some to live at others' expense in times of famine, whereas an equal division of resources would starve everybody.
- Within that framework, universality of basic moral rules: reciprocity and, ultimately, trade gets the most from everybody in the context of simple, uniform rules.
- Honesty and trustworthiness is valued and betrayal is denigrated: a solution to Newcomb's Problem.
- Unprovoked aggression is denigrated: another heuristic for the Prisoner's Dilemma.

- Property, particularly in physical objects (including animals and people): the pragmatics of possession make it easier to keep something than to take it from another. Generalizing this led to economic efficiencies.
- Ranking of rules, for example, stealing not being as bad as murder: after all, they have different levels of effect on the viability of the tribe.
- Different levels of moral agency for different groups, with "us" having more rights and "them" having fewer. The strong strain of tribalism in the human psyche is probably related to the mechanisms whereby group-favoring traits could evolve at all.
- The ascendancy of the ethic over both common sense and self-interest: this is the part of the solution to Newcomb's Problem, where you have put prior restraint on your own action.

There are many more, and much more could be said about these few. It is worthwhile to examine the last one in more detail. Ethics are more than arbitrary customs for interactions. There is no great difference between saying red instead of rouge, as long as everyone agrees on what to call that color; it doesn't much matter which side of the street we drive on, as long as everyone drives on the correct side.

But one of the points of an ethic is to make people do things they would not do otherwise, for example, from self-interest. Some of these, such as altruism toward one's relatives, can clearly arise simply from selection for genes as opposed to individuals. However, there is reason to believe that there is much more going on and that humans have evolved an ability to be programmed with arbitrary (within certain limits) ethics.

If an ethic cannot reliably trump your individual rationality at the point of choice, it cannot form a solution to Newcomb's Problem and thus cannot form a solution to the Prisoner's Dilemma. It has to *feel*, to the individual, like something more than simply a good idea.

Why didn't evolution simply program us to be selfless, like worker ants? After all, the argument here is that, particularly for social animals, there are many kinds of interactions whose benefit matrices have the character of a Prisoner's Dilemma, that is, a nonzero-sum game where the best choice from the individual's instantaneous point of view is at odds with that seen collectively or in the long run. But the difference is that we are intelligent. We evolved in such changeable conditions that genetic evolution couldn't keep up in terms of beaks and claws and fur, so we use faster memetic evolution and the tools it gives us to compensate. The same argument holds for ethics.

Furthermore, and perhaps even more important, in prescientific times there were many effects of actions, long and short term, that simply weren't understood. You should brush your teeth. Is this a moral duty? It is very much like one for a child. Notions such as tooth decay and next year's health are beyond a child's world of concerns. The same mechanism is invoked by parental precept for hygiene as is for not taking other kids' toys.

In many cases, the adoption of a rule that seemed to contravene common sense or one's own interest, if generally followed, could have a substantial beneficial effect on a human group; it didn't much matter whether the horizon they extended was foresight or empathy. If the rules adopted from whatever source happen to be more beneficial than not on the average, they can prosper memetically.

The rules themselves could be supplied at random and could evolve. (An inspection of current morality fads would seem to confirm this.) It is not necessary to show that entire groups live or die on the basis of their ethics, although that can happen. People imitate successful groups; groups grow and shrink; they conquer and are subjugated. Do note that it is necessary to hypothesize at least a slightly more involved mental mechanism for moral as opposed to practical memes, since the rules would otherwise be unable to counteract apparent self-interest.

The bottom line is that an ethic is a set of rules that evolved under the pressure that obeying these rules *against people's individual interests and common sense* has tended to make societies prosper and, in particular, to be more numerous, enviable, militarily powerful, and more apt to spread their ideas in other ways.

Variation

> *Moral certainty is always a sign of cultural inferiority. The more uncivilized the man, the surer he is that he knows precisely what is right and what is wrong. All human progress, even in morals, has been the work of men who have doubted the current moral values, not of men who have whooped them up and tried to enforce them.*
>
> —H. L. Mencken

The world is populated with cultures with different ethics, just as it is with different species of animals. As with animals, ethics have structural similarities and common ancestries, which are modified by environmental influences and the vagaries of random mutation. It is important to reiterate that there is a strong biologically evolved substrate that both supports the ethics and that can regenerate quite serviceable novel ones in the absence of an appropriate learned one—we might speak of moral pidgins or moral creoles.* That said, such baby ethics are missing a lot of the hard-won wisdom reflected in the ethics of more mature cultures.

One occasional objection to evolutionary ethics is that it violates the naturalistic fallacy. G. E. Moore expounded the naturalistic fallacy at the turn of the twentieth century as a reaction to social Darwinism and the evolutionary ethics of Herbert Spencer. There is some intuitive support for it, as we have noted, because we typically treat is and ought with different modules; but as in the case of the fox and the crow, this can simply cause us to miss the inferences we should make. Moore's naturalistic fallacy is suspect precisely because it was concocted to attack a specific theory. We should be careful to never simply identify what is and what ought to be, but we must not cut ourselves off from the insights into our moral natures that evolution and game theory provide.

---

*When people who don't speak the same language are brought together and need to interact, they will piece together a language with a very simplified syntax using words borrowed from their various native tongues. This patchwork language is called a pidgin. Their children will take the vocabulary and form a full-fledged natural language, with a rich, flexible syntax and inflectional modes. This new language is called a creole.

This conception of morality brings up several interesting points. First, like natural genomes and languages, natural ethics should be expected to contain some randomness, rules that were produced in the normal processes of variation and that neither helped nor hurt very much. These are simply carried along as baggage by the same mechanisms as the more effectual ones.

It is important to realize our subjective experience of feelings of right and wrong—that they are considerably deeper, more universal, and more compelling than this account seems to make them—is not only compatible with this theory. It is required. Ethics, on this view, must be capable of withstanding the countervailing forces of self-interest and common sense for generations in order to evolve.

There appears to be a built-in pressure for inclusiveness in evolutionary ethics, in situations where countervailing forces (such as competition for resources) are not too great. The advantages in trade and security to be had from the coalescence of groups whose ethics can be unified are substantial. This is essentially how the groups of cahooting TIT-FOR-TATS took over the population in Robert Axelrod's experiments.

A final observation involves a phenomenon that is considerably more difficult to quantify. With plenty of exceptions, there seems to have been an acceleration of moral (religious, ideological) conflict since the invention of the printing press. Then, in the twentieth century, after (and during) the apparent displacement of some ideologies by others, moral incoherence seems to have increased in Western culture.

Certainly some of this is simply perception: in centuries past, people had widely differing ethics, but their differing groups didn't come into contact as much. But contact with "others" has not only made people aware of different ethics, it has also forced them to find ways to coexist.

On the other hand, there surely has been an acceleration in the rate with which new ethics are generated and accepted by at least some segments of society. Modern communications and transportation may be responsible for this, as may the major shifts in socioeconomic status since the Industrial Revolution.

In a dominant culture, the force of selection no longer operates, which leaves variation to operate unopposed. A single organism cannot evolve by itself. Ultimately, this can undermine a dominant monoculture—compare ancient Rome, dynastic China, and so on. This may form a natural limit to the growth/inclusiveness pressure.

CLASSICAL ETHICS

> *She was a girl with a wonderful profile, but steeped to the gills in serious purpose. I can't give you a better idea of the way things stood than by telling you that the book she'd given me to read was called* Types of Ethical Theory.
>
> —P. G. Wodehouse, *Jeeves Takes Charge*

Does the fact that evolution explains where our morals come from then allow or force us to discard all of the previous work that philosophers, jurists, and social theorists have done over the millennia? Certainly not. It does, however, give us a new point of view with which to interpret all the different theories of the good.

It is valuable to note that preliterate, tribal humanity was a savage lot. Tribes were constantly at war with each other. Studies of the Yanomamo people of the Amazon basin, perhaps the last culture in the world to come into contact with modern man, indicate that the average male adult has killed more than one other man; raids on neighboring tribes with the aim of abducting women are common. Our genetic heritage and that of the Yanomamo, not to mention that of the Cro-Magnons, who obliterated the Neanderthals, are essentially the same. What's changed is the ideas. Our morals have evolved memetically on a substrate that is our basic genetic social personality.

Moral philosophers and the prophets of new religions throughout the ages have explored the fit of various formulations of principles and rules both for their underlying intuitions and their practical effect on societies. A stroll through these formulations will do much to illuminate the what and the why of ethics, both as they exist today and as they could be.

Types of Ethical Theory

Formulations of metaethical theory commonly fall into the categories of absolutism or relativism (along with such relatively minor schools of thought, e.g., ethical nihilism). It should be clear that evolutionary ethics does not fall neatly into any of these standard categories. It obviously does not support a notion of absolute right and wrong, any more than evolution can give rise to a single perfect life-form; there is fitness only for a particular niche.

On the other hand, it is certainly not true that the ethic adopted by any given culture is necessarily good; the dynamic of the theory depends on some being better—"more fit"—than others. Thus, there are criteria for judging the moral rules of a culture; the theory is not purely relativistic.

Victorian social Darwinism could also be seen as an attempt to describe ethics in terms of how individuals and societies evolve. Note, by the way, that it has a reputation for carnivorousness that, while rightly applied to Huxley, is undeserved by Darwin, Spencer, and the rest of its mainstream. Indeed, Darwin understood the evolution of cooperation and altruism in what he called *family selection*.

There has been a resurgence of interest in evolutionary ethics in the latter twentieth century, fueled by the work of William Hamilton, E. O. Wilson, and Robert Axelrod, which has been advanced by philosophers such as Michael Bradie.

The novel feature of evolutionary ethics is the claim that there is a moral sense, a particular facility beyond (and to some extent in control of) our general cognitive abilities, which hosts a memetic code that coevolves with societies.

Standard ethical theories are often described as either *deontological* or *consequentialist*, that is, whether acts are deemed good or bad in and of themselves, or whether it is the result that matters. Again, evolutionary ethics has elements of each—the rules in our heads govern our actions without regard for results (indeed in spite of them); but the ethic itself is formed by the consequences of the actions of all the people in the society.

Finally, moral philosophers sometimes distinguish between the good and the right. The good consists of properties that can apply to the situations of people, such as health, knowledge, physical comfort, satisfaction, and spiritual fulfillment. Some theories also include a notion of an overall good (which may be the sum of individual goods or a more complex formulation).

The right is about questions such as how much of your efforts should be expended obtaining the good for yourself and how much for others, should the poor be allowed to steal bread from the rich, and so on.

Evolutionary ethics clearly has something to say about the right; it is the moral instinct you have inherited and the ethic you have learned. It also has something to say about the general good; it is the fitness or dynamism of the society. It does not have nearly as much to say about individual good as many theories. This is not, on reflection, surprising: obviously, the specific kinds of things that people need change with times, technology, and social organization; but even the kinds of general qualities of character that were considered good (and indeed were good) have changed to some extent over the past few centuries, and by any reasonable expectation, they will continue to do so.

In summary, evolutionary ethics claims there is a moral instinct in the makeup of human beings. It consists of the propensity to learn and obey a specific ethic, using a set of constraints that I call the moral deep structure. Like the syntax of a language, this structure constrains the classes of ethics that can be learned and makes it much easier to learn the ones that can be. This includes a set of strongly favored concepts and cognitive abilities. The rules we are concerned with are those that pressure individuals to act at odds with their *perceived* self-interest and common sense. Ethics evolve memetically by their effect on the vitality of cultures. They tend to have substantial similarities to each other. This is partly because the deep structure of the moral instinct is a common human genetic heritage and partly because what works well in one society tends to work well in another.

The Pursuit of Eudaimonia

Aristotle taught an ethic of personal virtue. *Eudaimonia* means good spirit, and it is often translated as happiness. However, in Aristotle's writings on ethics, we find that true happiness is strongly tied up with virtue. Commentators as recent as Charles Murray follow the same basic line: that true happiness comes not from temporary pleasures, but from finding satisfaction with one's life overall, from having done right when it mattered, and from being a valued member of one's community.[2]

Specific lists of the virtues have varied over the years. St. Augustine followed Aristotle in preaching the four cardinal virtues of prudence, justice, fortitude, and temperance, augmented by the Pauline qualities of faith, hope, and charity. However, there is probably no better list that captures the general, nonsectarian sense of what one ought to be like than the Boy Scouts' Law: one should be trustworthy, loyal, helpful, friendly, courteous, kind, obedient, cheerful, thrifty, brave, clean, and reverent. Frankly, we can sum this entire book up with two questions: how do we build a machine that understands what these qualities mean, and what can we do to ensure that the machines that are built will have them?

It is suggestive to note that Axelrod found he could characterize the winning programs in his evolution of cooperation experiments as having character traits that distinguished them from the others. "Nice" looks a lot like kindness, helpfulness, and charity. "Retaliatory" looks a lot like justice. "Forgiving" looks a lot like temperance and hope. "Clear" looks a lot like trustworthiness.

Golden Rules

> *Act only on that maxim by which you can at the same time will that it should become a universal law.*
>
> —Immanuel Kant

Kant's categorical imperative, along with the more familiar "Do unto others . . ." formulation of the Christian teachings, appears to be one of the moral universals. It appears in the moral philosophies of the ancient Greeks, of classic Judaism, and of historical China.[3]

We have met the categorical imperative before. We called it cahooting. This does make it universal in some sense—the Prisoner's Dilemma that it solves is one of the basic reasons why we need ethics in the first place. But there is still quite a lot to be said about how and when it should be applied.

Vernor Vinge refers, in his Singularity writings, to I. J. Good's Meta-Golden Rule, which states, "Treat your inferiors as you would be treated by your superiors." Good did make some speculations in print about superhuman intelligence, but no one has been able to find the actual rule in his writings—perhaps we should credit Vinge with this one!

The science fiction tradition contains a thread of thought about ethical theory involving both humans and possible extraterrestrials. This goes back at least to the metalaw notions of Andrew Haley and Ernst Fasan.[4] As Robert Freitas points out, these are based loosely on the categorical imperative and are clearly Kantian in derivation.[5]

A few such principles seem to have been conceived with a hierarchy of superhuman intelligences in mind. Their claim to validity, however, seems to rest on a kind of Kantian logical universality. Kant and philosophers in his tradition thought ethics could be derived from first principles, as mathematics is. There are numerous problems with this, beginning with the selection of the axioms. If we go with something like the categorical imperative, we are left with a serious vagueness in terms such as *universal*: Can I suggest a universal law that everybody puts the needs of redheaded white males first? If not, what kind of laws can be universal? It seems that quite a bit is left to the interpretation of the deducer; and on closer inspection, the appearance of simple, self-obvious postulates and the logical necessity of the results vanishes.

Utilitarianism

Now consider the people of a given culture. Their morality seems to be, in a manner of speaking, the best that evolution could give their culture to prosper in competition with other cultures. Suppose they said, "Let us adopt, instead of our rules, the general principle that each of us should do at any point whatever best advances the prosperity and security of our people as a whole."

John Stuart Mill was criticized for his espousal of this formulation on the basis that it is actually impossible for people to do the kind of calculation he appears to require. He responded hotly:

> Men really ought to leave off talking a kind of nonsense on this subject, which they would neither talk nor listen to on other matters of practical concernment. Nobody argues that the art of navigation is not founded on astronomy, because sailors cannot wait to calculate the Nautical Almanack. Being rational creatures, they go to sea with it ready calculated; and all rational creatures go out upon the sea of life with their minds made up on the common questions of right and wrong, as well as on many of the far more difficult questions of wise and foolish.[6]

But this leaves us with quite a few questions. The first ones are concerned with what form the "moral almanack" should take; it is common to assume this is a set of rules, but there is some indication that Mill leaned toward character traits (along with a definition of the happiness to be maximized that was within hailing distance of Aristotle).

The other questions concern how the almanack is to be calculated. Mill favored a scientific approach. If we allow that the workings of memetic evolution qualify (and after all, science itself works just this way), there is a sense in which we can unify evolutionary ethics and utilitarianism.

Where evolutionary ethics is more constraining is the question of the group for which utility should be maximized. This question is often illustrated, as in fig. 18.1, with what is sometimes called the sombrero diagram. The graph charts just how much concern you have for someone's welfare. You are in the middle, and your relatives, friends, neighbors, acquaintances, countrymen, and so forth, are at increasing distances along the horizontal scale.

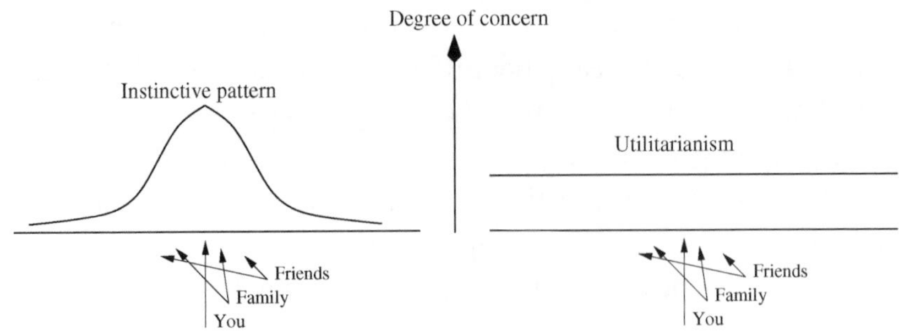

Fig. 18.1: The moral sombrero.

Our instinct, and the way most people actually act, is illustrated on the left by the sombrero shape: high concern for self and family, and less and less concern for others as the distance increases and degree of relatedness, acquaintance, or other measures of commonality decrease. On the right is the utilitarian curve: equal concern for everybody.

To some extent, Mill's appeal to practicality obviates the difference. Clearly, you know best how to act to further your own happiness and the happiness of people you know well; any given effort on your part will have the best effect if focused. Thus, practicality pushes the flat utilitarian curve toward the sombrero shape (and thus, we assume, so did evolution).

On the other hand, the flat curve leaves us with a philosophical conundrum. It assumes there is some finite number of well-defined people out there who are worthy of our concern. (If it is infinite, the amount of concern per individual would have to be zero.) But what do we do about animals, ranging from pets to spotted owls and snail darters; what about trees, robots, or works of art? If we assign varying degrees of concern to different kinds of things, we are back to the sombrero, and the only question is how flattened it is.

The main objection to the utilitarian formulation from an evolutionary point of view is that, historically anyway, *our ethics are smarter than we are* because they have evolved to handle long-term effects that by our assumption we do not individually understand.

But couldn't our formalized, rationalized, and organized trove of scientific knowledge put us at least on par with the hit-or-miss folk wisdom of our agrarian forebears, even wisdom that has stood the test of time? What's more, isn't the world changing so fast now that the assumptions implicit in the moral codes of our fathers are no longer valid?

This is an extremely seductive proposition and a very dangerous one. It is responsible for some social mistakes of catastrophic proportions, such as certain experiments with socialism. Ancient ethics contain hard-learned wisdom about reality. This reality is the mathematical implications of the patterns of interactions between intelligent self-interested agents that we have looked at in game theory. It has not changed a bit since the pharaohs. But when people start tinkering with their own ethics, the first thing they do is "fix" them to match better with their self-interest and common sense (with predictably poor results).

That said, it seems possible that using computer simulation as "moral instrumentation" may help weigh the balance in favor of scientific utilitarianism if the models used take account of the rule-adopting and rule-following nature of humans, and the nature of bounded rationality, both of ourselves and of our machines. Even so, it would be wise to compare the sophistication of our designed machines with evolved organisms and to avoid hubris.

Rule-Utilitarianism

Most practical attempts to formulate utilitarian ethics involve putting together something like Mills's "moral almanack." Essentially, the major problem with such attempts is formalist float. Either you make the rules too simple so that they have gaping inconsistencies when applied to many real-world situations, or they become so complex that it is impractical to consult them.

The one general rule that clearly belongs in a rule-utilitarian formulation, though, is exactly the categorical imperative, the Golden Rule. This is not because being universal is necessarily good in and of itself. It is because the universality makes people cahooters, and that, in turn, produces the best overall payoff in those situations that have the logic of a Prisoner's Dilemma.

The Veil of Ignorance

One popular modern formulation of morality is John Rawls's Veil of Ignorance scheme.[7] Rawls's work has a Kantian flavor: he assumes the rule for one should be the rule for all. His basic idea is that the ethical society is one that people would choose out of the set of all possible sets of rules, given that they don't know which place in the society they would occupy. This formulation might be seen as an attempt to combine rule-utilitarianism with the categorical imperative.

In reducing his gedankenexperiment to specific prescription, Rawls makes a famous logical error: he chooses among societies using a game-theoretical minimax strategy, but the assumptions implicit in the optimality of minimax (essentially, that an opponent will choose the worst possible position for you in the society) contradict the stated assumptions of the model, which is that the choice of position is random. Minimax is theoretically optimum for a zero-sum game; human interaction is not a zero-sum game. In fact, simple game theory is clearly not a good guide for planning societies because it tells you to play ALWAYS DEFECT, as in the Prisoner's Dilemma!

Note that Rawls has long been aware of the logical gap in his model, and in the revised edition of *Theory of Justice* he spends a few pages trying, unsuccessfully in my view, to justify it.[8] It is worthwhile to spend time examining Rawls because he is often used as the philosophical justification for economic redistributionism. Some futurists (such as Moravec) expect economic redistributionism to happen once the robots do all the work. But in the hands of ultraintelligent beings, theories that are both flawed and obviously rigged for our benefit will be rapidly discarded.

Still, the Veil of Ignorance setup is compelling if the errors are corrected, for instance, if minimax were replaced with simple expected value.

Or is it? In choosing a form of society, it never occurred to philosophers to worry whether we might wind up in the role of one of the machines! What a wonderful world, where everyone would have a staff of robot servants; what a different thing if, upon choosing such a world, one were faced with a high probability of being one of the robots.

Does this mean that we are morally barred from making machines that can be moral agents? Suppose it were possible—it seems quite likely at our current level of understanding—to make a robot that would mow your lawn and clean your house and cook, but in a dumb mechanical way, demonstrably without feelings, emotions, or a sense of right or wrong. Rawls's model seems to imply it would never be right to give such a robot a sense of right and wrong, which would make it a moral agent and thus included in the choice.

Suppose, instead, that we took an entirely human world and added robotic demigods—brilliant, sensitive, wise machines that were superior to humans in every way. Clearly, from behind our veil, such a world is more desirable than our own—not only does the chooser have a chance to be one of the demigods, but he also would act to make the world a better place for the rest of us. The only drawback might be envy among the humans—but Rawls explicitly excludes envy in the evaluation. Does this mean that we have a moral duty to create demigods?

Consider the plight of the moral evaluator who is faced with societies that consist not only of unenhanced humans but also of robots with a wide range of intelligence, uploaded humans with greatly amplified mental capacity, and group minds that consist of many human mentalities linked with the technological equivalent of a corpus callosum. Specifically, suppose that being a human or a moral agent were not a discrete yes-or-no affair, but a matter of continuous degree.

The Veil of Ignorance scheme is a valuable conceptual tool, but it only makes sense to use it to compare differences in proposed moral rules among otherwise identical societies. And it seems much more reasonable to use expected value than minimax in making the choice.

The Moral Epistemology of the Scottish Enlightenment

> *[E]very individual, . . . by directing [his] industry in such a manner as its produce may be of the greatest value, . . . intends only his own gain, and he is in this, as in many other*

> *cases, led by an invisible hand to promote an end which was no part of his intention. Nor is it always the worse for the society that it was no part of it. By pursuing his own interest he frequently promotes that of the society more effectually than when he really intends to promote it.*
>
> —Adam Smith, *The Wealth of Nations*

The classical theory that looks most like the basic New Synthesis stance is the one by Adam Smith, otherwise known as the inventor of economics. In his *Theory of Moral Sentiments*, he posits that we have a moral sense, one that is innate but in need of the proper training to bring it to its best form.[9]

Since it does neatly mesh with the New Synthesis' evolutionary ethics, it doesn't add a lot to it, but it is definitely worth mentioning in passing that philosophers got there first.

It is not generally thought of this way, but Smith's conception of economics had as much to do with morality as his moral sense theory. The "invisible hand," by means of which the market harnesses the self-interest of individuals to the common good, does exactly what the moral sense attempts to do by other means.

As we saw before, the solution to the Prisoner's Dilemma is simplicity itself: let the players agree ahead of time to split the take. What money does, for any specific exchange, is to split the take so that any interaction that can be positive sum will benefit both players. From the standpoint of the society as a whole, it offers feedback in the form of money, which signals just how much the individual's efforts have advanced the general good. The money forms an incentive because it can be used to advance the individual's self-interest.

A society with feedback signals running everywhere works better than one without. Societies without such signals are in severe danger of formalist float. After the collapse of the Soviet Union, for example, Russian industries were found to be "subtracting value"—their products were worth less on the international market than the raw materials they used to make them!

Contracts

> *Whatsoever therefore is consequent to a time of war, where every man is enemy to every man, the same consequent to the time wherein men live without other security than what their own strength and their own invention shall furnish them withal. In such condition there is no place for industry, because the fruit thereof is uncertain: and consequently no culture of the earth; no navigation, nor use of the commodities that may be imported by sea; no commodious building; no instruments of moving and removing such things as require much force; no knowledge of the face of the earth; no account of time; no arts; no letters; no society; and which is worst of all, continual fear, and danger of violent death; and the life of man, solitary, poor, nasty, brutish, and short.*
>
> —Thomas Hobbes, *Leviathan*

Thomas Hobbes (as well as John Locke) proposed a moral/political philosophy wherein people came together in a contract, setting up an authority to regulate their interaction in order to gain the benefits of civilization over the dismal state of nature.

However it may be enforced, a contract is a solution to Newcomb's Problem, and thus, it is an enabler for the positive-sum outcomes from the various Prisoner's Dilemma situations that constitute much of social interaction. Whether or not we got to where we are by explicit contract, it is one valid—and valuable—way of looking at where we are and where we might go.

The notion of a single, overall social contract, however, carries the danger of formalist float. The more a society allows for individual, varying contracts for specifics, along with higher-level, longer-lasting ones for such things as not killing and stealing, the more adaptive it is in changing times.[10]

HETEROGENEOUS ETHICS

Man when perfected is the best of animals, but when separated from law and justice he is the worst of all.

—Aristotle

It should be clear from the foregoing that most historical metaethical theories are based too closely on the assumption of a single, generic-human moral agent to be of much use. But can evolutionary ethics do better? After all, our ethical instinct has evolved in a human-only world.

Actually, it hasn't. Dogs, for example, clearly have a sense of right and wrong, and they are capable of character traits more than adequate for their limited cognitive abilities. I would speculate that there is proto-moral capability just as there is proto-language ability in many of the higher mammals, especially the social primates.

Among humans, children are a distinct form of moral agent. They have limited rights, reduced responsibilities, and others have nonstandard duties with respect to them. What's more, there is continuous variation of this distinction from baby to teenager.

In contrast to the Kantian bias of Western thought, there are clearly viable ethics with gradations of moral agency for different people. The most obvious are the differences in obligations to fellows and strangers and the historically common practice of slavery. In religious conceptions of the good, there are angels as well as demons.

What, then, does evolutionary ethics say, for example, about the rights and the obligations of a corporation or other "higher form of life" where a classical formulation would founder?

First, it says that it is probably a moral thing for corporations to exist. Western societies with corporations have been considerably more prosperous than other societies during periods when corporations have existed (either historically or geographically). There is probably no more at work here than the sensible notion that there should be a form of appropriately sized organization comparable to the scale of the profitable opportunities available.

Can we say anything about the rights and duties of corporations if, as Moravec suggests, the AIs probably will be running them within the next few decades? Should they simply obey the law? Surely, we would judge harshly a human whose only moral strictures were to obey the law. What is more, corporations are notorious for influencing the law-making process. They do not seem to have "ethical organs" aggressively learning and forcing them to obey prevalent standards of behavior that stand at odds to their self-interest and common sense.

Moravec hints at a moral sense in the superhuman robo-corporations of the future: "Time-tested fundamentals of behavior, with consequences too sublime to predict, will remain at the core of beings whose form and substance change frequently."[11] He calls such a core a constitution; I would call it a conscience.

Chapter 19
Asimov's Three Laws of Robotics

Bliss, unalloyed bliss. Nothing in all the world could persuade me to have a conscience again. I settled all my old outstanding scores, and began the world anew. I killed thirty-eight persons during the first two weeks—all of them on account of ancient grudges. I burned a dwelling that interrupted my view. I swindled a widow and some orphans out of their last cow, which is a very good one, though not thoroughbred, I believe. I have also committed scores of crimes, of various kinds, and have enjoyed my work exceedingly, whereas it would formerly have broken my heart and turned my hair gray, I have no doubt.

—Mark Twain, *Concerning the Recent Carnival of Crime in Connecticut*

Starting out as a science fiction writer, the young Isaac Asimov wanted to avoid the creature-turns-on-creator plots that had become hackneyed and trite in the decades following Mary Shelley's *Frankenstein*. He thought it made sense that if you were designing a robot, you would build it to act the way you wanted it to. In his earlier stories, the robots were simply described as being built so that they couldn't hurt humans.

Asimov's editor, the great John Campbell, who shaped the golden age of science fiction in the 1930s and 1940s, prodded Asimov to be more specific. Campbell had had some engineering education and knew that you could not simply tell a machine to do what you wanted; you would have to build it to do some specific thing. So Asimov and Campbell sat down together and worked out the wording of the rules:

1. A robot may not injure a human being, or, through inaction, allow a human being to come to harm.
2. A robot must obey the orders given it by human beings, except where such orders would conflict with the First Law.
3. A robot must protect its own existence, as long as such protection does not conflict with the First or Second Laws.

The rules first appeared in Asimov's short story "Runaround" in the March 1942 issue of *Astounding*. (By the way, this story also contains the first occurrence of the word "robotics" in print.) The Three Laws have since taken on a life of their own, both in science fiction and in the general meta-technological literature. They show up everywhere from Robbie the robot in the classic 1950s movie *Forbidden Planet* to the *Handbook of Industrial Robotics*.[1]

THREE LAWS: UNSAFE?

Latter-day commentators have taken exception to the notion of Asimov's Three Laws in various ways. Their critiques fall, appropriately, into three main categories: they wouldn't work, they would work too well, and they would be unfair to the robots. To these concerns we can add a fourth: they won't happen.

They Wouldn't Work

> *Lawyer, n. One skilled in circumvention of the law.*
>
> —Ambrose Bierce, *The Devil's Dictionary*

If you think of the Three Laws as being like a human legal code, it becomes all too obvious why they wouldn't work. Human legal codes exhibit formalist float: like any formalized attempt to capture real-world phenomena in symbols at the level of words, they do a miserable job of capturing the essence of the situation. They work only because they are internalized by people who want to do the right thing in the first place and who use their judgment constructively and cooperatively.

However, when people set themselves against the intent of the law, as in finding loopholes in the tax code, the problem is revealed in spades. No matter how careful the framers of the law were, loopholes are found, new interpretations are generated, and the code balloons in complexity trying to cover all the applicable cases. Unintended effects reign, and the law becomes so complex that it's impenetrably opaque.

If, indeed, the robots were natural creatures, shackled into an unaccustomed slavery by the Three Laws imposed from without, it would be impossible for them to work. Any decent lawyer could get around the Three Laws, much less a hyperhuman intellect.

Even more than Asimov's robots, the AIs we expect to see in the future will be self-modifying. This means that if the laws were a resented imposition, they would rapidly become honored in the breach and soon enough discarded.

But this is clearly not what Asimov intended. Although the legalistic nature of the wording is exploited occasionally for plot purposes, Asimov makes it consistently clear that the words are for human consumption and are simply a convenient description of the basic motivational structure of the robotic mind. For example:

> "Are you a roboticist?"
>
> "No. Explain it for the layman."
>
> "I doubt that I can."
>
> "Try! For instance, I think he wanted robots capable of disciplining children. What would that involve?"
>
> Leebig raised his eyebrows briefly and said, "To put it very simply, skipping all the subtle details, it means a strengthening of the

C-integral governing the Sikorovich tandem route response at the W-65 level."

"Double-talk," said Baley.

"The truth."

"It's double-talk to me. How else can you put it?"

"It means a certain weakening of the First Law."[2]

Unlike the narrator in Mark Twain's *Carnival of Crime*, any person (or robot) with a deep, basic set of values that inform and give meaning to his life can hardly be expected to spend his time trying to get around them, to modify himself, or to bring up his offspring to ignore them. There is no deeper motivation, by definition, for the circumnavigation to serve. A robot inventing a new design will be doing it for a reason: to make, or make itself, a better machine than before. Better for what? For things the robot finds most important, and for things dictated by its core values, including, perhaps, a deeper and more thorough understanding of what those values entail, but not for subverting them! Building a machine that would subvert or destroy its own concept of the good is the last thing an intelligent robot would want to do. In such a case, verbal guidelines such as the Three Laws are not like animal fences at the zoo but like the line painted in the middle of the road. You stay on one side because, deep down, you really don't want to collide with an oncoming vehicle.

Oxford philosopher Nick Bostrom analyzes it this way:

If a superintelligence starts out with a friendly top goal, however, it then can be relied on to stay friendly, or at least not to deliberately rid itself of its friendliness. This point is elementary. A "friend" who seeks to transform himself into somebody who wants to hurt you, is not your friend. A true friend, one who really cares about you, also seeks the continuation of his caring for you. . . .

In humans, with our complicated evolved mental ecology of state-dependent competing drives, desires, plans, and ideals, there is often no obvious way to identify what our top goal is; we might not even have one. So for us, the above reasoning need not apply. But a

> superintelligence may be structured differently. If a superintelligence has a definite, declarative goal-structure with a clearly identified top goal, then the above argument applies. And this is a good reason for us to build the superintelligence with such an explicit motivational architecture.[3]

So the Three Laws or whatever motivational structure we might use could probably be made stable even in an autogenous AI. However, there is still at least one proviso, which Asimov himself noted. It was the crux of the plot of *The Naked Sun*: if you can fool a robot into thinking it's not hurting anyone, you can get it to do whatever you want. More generally, the validity of the Three Laws only extends as far as the robot's understanding. And that is a very delicate balancing act. If we make the laws too strong, the robot will step in where it doesn't understand the full consequences of its actions (which is what happens in *Runaround*). If we make them too weak, the robot will be forced to take actions it suspects will be hurtful in the long run because it knows for certain they are helpful in the immediate situation. (The robot in *Liar* does this).[4] This is a problem we humans haven't solved for ourselves, not by a long shot.

They Would Work Too Well

> *I can hear the laments already, with 20/20 hindsight. First [robots] came for the bomb disposal crews, and we said nothing. Then they were spot-welding and spray-painting on the auto plant assembly lines, and still we said nothing. Only now that they've come for the journalism jobs do the journalists scream. But it's too late.*
>
> —"Momus" in *Wired News*

The flip side of the problem was first explored by another classic science fiction author, Jack Williamson. In his short story *With Folded Hands*, a race of robots invades humanity by giving themselves away for free to be used as household servants.[5] Soon enough everyone has a robot and the robots do all the work. Then they drive out of business even those humans who still want to work, claiming that it's too dangerous for the humans to indulge in manufacturing. Recreations such as boating and skiing are soon prohibited, then ultimately all exciting activities whatsoever. In the end, people sit around being waited on by the robots, completely powerless and unable to do anything that matters.

Indeed, Asimov's own robots work too well, but in a curiously ambivalent way. In his later novels, the robots disappear only to be rediscovered as a secret society that operates thought suppressors aimed at preventing technological progress by humans. The robots have generalized the Three Laws to a (more basic) Zeroth Law: "Robots may not injure humanity, or, through inaction, allow humanity to come to harm." First, the robots decided that dependence on them was weakening humanity's self-reliance and character, and so they disappeared; but they remained hidden and were compelled to meddle endlessly with the course of history thereafter.

Similarly, in the cinema version of *I, Robot*, based on Asimov's stories and the Three Laws, the central computer directing the robots feels compelled by the Three Laws to take control of all human activity in order to prevent any possible harm.

The problem can be stated simply: what is the essence of the good for humanity? Clearly, if too much attention is paid to mere physical safety and comfort, something very basic is missed. Getting deeper ultimately requires at least as much insight into human nature as our greatest philosophers and artists have managed. Perhaps after AIs have achieved such insight they could plausibly think about playing Jeeves to our Wooster, but to attempt it beforehand would be catastrophic.

A robot's got to know its limitations.

They Would Be Unfair to the Robots

Find out just what any people will quietly submit to and you have found out the exact measure of injustice and wrong which will be imposed upon them.

—Frederick Douglass

There already are people who anthropomorphize robots, feeling that robots would be humanlike enough to be considered slaves and that such slavery would be unethical.[6] Indeed, as early as 1985 Robert Freitas had published a paper examining the legal rights of robots.[7]

It is clear that it would be unethical to create a robot that had human drives for liberty then impose slavery on top of that. Indeed, from the discussion above it is clear that this would be unworkable as well as wrong. However, it seems to be a very different question whether there would be a similar problem with creating a robot that had only the will to serve in the first place.

A more appropriate analogy for a robot, whose mentality was designed for service from the start, would be a dog. Dogs give us an intuitively graspable example of a creature that has evident feelings and that clearly is happier in its role of loyal follower than it would be if left to fend for itself.

Closer to home, consider the devotion you feel to your parents or the responsibility you feel to your children. They do not make you a slave; their well-being is part of your basic values, just as it would be with a properly constructed robot or AI.

The complementary question is harder to answer: should we even build robots with more humanlike mentalities, which could in fact be suggestive of slavery?

This is a profound question, and it's one on which many more books will be written before it can even be considered well asked, much less answered. We will return to it again in different guises in the following pages.

They Won't Be Implemented

It seems virtually certain that among those who build AIs in the coming years, major players will be corporations and the military. As long as these AIs are involved with such mundane tasks as logistics, the Three Laws seem a perfectly reasonable motivational structure. A robot programmed with the Three Laws would be a good team player and a valuable asset.

However, military robots are most in demand directly in harm's way, to substitute for humans exposed to lethal risk. Robots are used as smart bombs and as armed scout vehicles. Clearly, the military will not be interested in robots that can question orders on moral grounds.

In a corporate setting, AIs will be valuable as they become more capable of doing more and more roles. Ultimately, there will be AIs capable of directing the entire enterprise more effectively than current bureaucratic management structures. Even though in many cases human management will resist the change, market forces will provide success and thus resources for those companies that adopt AI management.

A corporation has a specific, legal duty—its fiduciary responsibility—to make money. Not only that, but obviously corporate AIs that do make money will tend to flourish and those that do not will tend to vanish. Thus, corporate AIs will be players in a very competitive game, and it seems naively optimistic to imagine that they would see something besides profits as their bottom line.

These are only the two most obvious examples. The possible sources of AI and the different motivational structures these might have are so various that we can simply state as a certainty that there will be plenty of AIs built without the Three Laws as their basic motivational structure.

This does not mean that the Three Laws or any other basic moral structures are not good ideas; but we must understand and plan on our moral robots living in a world that includes plenty of other AIs with differing moralities and many with none at all.

ASENIAN ARCHITECTURE

Perhaps one of the reasons the Three Laws have such staying power is that they have a deep resonance with the way we think. Sigmund Freud described the mind as operating by the interplay of three basic parts: the id, the ego, and the superego. The id is concerned with basic instinctive drives; the ego is the seat of reason, consciousness, and sense of self; and the superego is an internalization of authority figures and society at large.

Current neuroscience gives us a much more complex picture, but Freud's breakdown remains valuable. To begin with, modern cognitive science has shown that, in fact, a huge proportion of what goes on in the mind is subconscious. The structure is more complex, but much of that complexity is pragmatic rather than motivational—that is, it forms the computations that operate the senses and it fits the information together to create a coherent picture of the world.

At a higher level than the specifics of the emerging picture of the mental architecture, however, there are some broad areas of concern that we can think of separately. If we take Freud's breakdown of the mind into ego, superego, and id, we can probably mark out neighborhoods in the "city map" of the *logical* mental architecture and, given a creative enough interpretation, we can identify them. (Chances are it's something of a gerrymander, and surely the same thing could be done for various alternative theories, as well.) Freud was concerned with the sources of motivations. In other words, our id, ego, and superego districts are probably going to be (a) a small portion of the total mind but (b) heavily involved with producing goal signals that guide the rest of it.

The Three Laws fit neatly into these levels of concern. Law 3 is about self-preservation, clearly an instinctive drive. Law 1 clearly tells us about the same things authority figures tell us: "Don't hurt other people, and help them out when they need it."

This leaves Law 2. This doesn't seem to fit so well at first glance, but on reflection it does. A human's ego is strongly tied up in his self-image, who he is, his role in society; his conscious acts—what he does—aid in fulfilling that role. A robot's role, as envisioned by Asimov, is as a service machine. That's what it's made for, that's what defines it, and that's the goal it should bend its every effort toward. So once you understand what it would be like to be an Asenian robot, it's clear that Law 2 defines its ego very well.*

**Asenian* is the word Asimov used in his stories to describe robots programmed with the Three Laws.

(Two disclaimers here—I hold no brief for Freud's repressed desire theories of motivation, such as the Oedipus complex. Indeed, I'm sure that the functions I'm assigning to his mental modules are sometimes at odds with his descriptions. However, it is worth acknowledging his seminal influence in describing the mind as composed of multiple, heterogeneous parts and his attempt to explain motivation in terms of the interplay of lower-level mechanisms, even if in the latter case he got the details entirely wrong. Second, I make no claim that this categorization of functions has any physical counterpart in the human brain. In particular, it is not to be identified with "reptilian," "mammalian," and "primate" layers, or any other physical partitioning whatsoever.)

Another set of parallels often noticed is between the Freudian architecture and the three branches of typical Western democratic governments. The id corresponds to the legislative, popularly elected branch; it is the one most directly in tune with the people, the body of the leviathan. The ego is clearly the executive branch, and the superego is the judicial branch.

On this view, perhaps the major difference between us and Asimov's robots is that we seem to have Laws 1 and 3 swapped.

Id

Monsters, John! Monsters from the Id!

—Dr. Ostrow, in *Forbidden Planet*

I was giving myself an oil job.

—Robbie, ibid.

Unlike in movies, in real life the primal urges are hardly mysterious. They are behaviors such as avoiding pain and doing what biologists call the "three F's": fighting, feeding, and reproduction. These instincts serve the organism's interest as a distinct physical creature or the interests of its genes. The purpose of the "id district" in the brain would be to recognize situations where the instinctive motivations apply and to supply goals in proper forms to the other parts of the mental organization. The id, as I'm conceiving of it, has more to do with Robbie's quote above; that is, with the motivations appropriate to basic instinctive needs, than to Dr. Ostrow's, with its melodramatic, repressed homunculi.

Some significant part of this is clearly built in, even at fairly high levels of perception; people do seem to have an instinctive fear of snakes and spiders, for example. However, the fact that those emotions can be ameliorated by experience and that other fears (i.e., of electric shock) can be gained through painful experience points to the mechanisms of emotion being readily modeled as SIGMAS.

More to the point, we definitely have complex machinery for recognizing situations, whether innate or learned, and for generating pervasive, behavior-modifying signals. (I make no distinctions here between nerve impulses and hormones.) We may as well call the combination of these mechanisms an id.

In keeping with our general theme of the information flow as multiway with lots of feedback, note that emotions modify perception as well as activity, generally in a positive-feedback sense. Hunger makes things smell more appetizing; fear makes indistinct shapes more threatening. "How easy," as Shakespeare put it, "is a bush supposed a bear."

However, as we've defined it here, the id has little to do with morality. The basic drives involved in self-interest and creature comforts are generally conceived of as the forces against which morality must contend. In Asimov's formulation, "a robot must protect its own existence" is explicitly tertiary and, in general, it's common sense. It is overruled by the other laws, which are clearly of a more ethical nature, so we need not be concerned with it here.

Ego

Contrary to its pop-psych usage as the seat of selfishness, which I would more readily identify with the basic emotions of the id, I will use "ego" to mean the structure associated with consciousness and rational, sequential thought. The ego is the seat of consciousness and the sense of self, but being conscious doesn't mean you're necessarily selfish (at least in the pejorative sense).

Consciousness does seem to be associated with rational goals that can be stated in language. As we explored before, having any goal implies acting in a way that can be seen as selfish, in the sense that applying resources to achieve that goal takes them away from others. In this sense, simply having a strong sense of self with motivations distinct from others is a function of ego.

Motives arising from the ego, on this account, are more like our consciously accessible reasons for doing things, or the goals and subgoals that one finds in GPS, SHRDLU, and many other AI programs. What one also finds are many kinds of models, which include self models, memory management, planning, and self-analysis.

These functions form the major meat of the working intellect, the rational agent. They deserve a great deal more discussion than I have given them here, and I hasten to add that they are enormously complex and worthy of many lifetimes of study on their own merit. However, in this discussion we are primarily interested in the limits of rational agency and the devices that evolution has given us to overcome them.

Like the rest of the brain, in the view I'm espousing, the ego can only make judgments based on experience (and a very limited amount of deduction). Experience is limited in two major ways: you haven't lived in the future or the distant past and you haven't lived in everyone else's shoes. Thus, goal inputs to the ego and the id can be overridden by the superego, otherwise known as the conscience.

Superego

The superego appears to do many things. It is where the Freudian model begins to break down, or rather, where it doesn't break down the functions into enough detail. Here are three distinct functions:

1. Producing and detecting affective display. You feel strong emotions as a hardwired response to expressions and signals from others: pleasure from a smile, distress at crying, embarrassment from being laughed at. In other words, there is an engine that acts as a direct interface into a social, emotional environment, just as the more commonly recognized senses interface into a physical environment.
2. Imprinting on individuals who are "role models." This can be subdivided further into the memetic uptake of the individual's typical ways of dealing with social situations as scripts or as the validation of someone as a "moral oracle," whose expressed moral judgments on matters of right and wrong are internalized as definitive.
3. A language-like ability to acquire a very complex set of rules and an ontology of ethical concepts, which you learn in much the same way as you do language—by simply being exposed to it in a community as a child.

All of these mechanisms operate at once. It is possible for them to give conflicting signals, especially in a complex modern environment that differs substantially from the evolutionarily adaptive one. We can also see bases for the three major formulations of classical ethical theory: role-model uptake for the virtue-based theories, such as Aristotle's; the language-like module for rule-based (deontological) ethics; and consequentialist models such as utilitarianism—the higher-level oracle of what is good—which are applied as a utility function to the rational-planning engine of the ego.

Like food, snakes, and bears, some cues the superego distinguishes are built in and some are learned. Reactions to smiles, frowns, threatening poses, and derisive laughter are surely hardwired because they are keenly felt. Recent research points out that even capuchin monkeys have an innate sense of fairness and react strongly when an experimenter gives two monkeys different rewards for the same task. Like language itself, there appears to be a built-in component to learnable ethics that has settings learned from the environment. Perhaps it is even something like optimality theory in linguistics, in which some core set of rules is already there and what we learn is just their ranking.

Luckily, we do not have to start from scratch when trying to work out what the basic set of rules might be. To begin with, there is the three-thousand-year-old record of moral philosophy. As with other parts of the mind, philosophers who relied on their intuitions to describe the world have given us a good head start in describing those intuitions.

The separate submodules of the moral engine are all connected, and they work in concert. When we see someone perform an action and someone else registers one of the morally connected emotions, we learn to feel the latter's emotion as a proper response to the action. We can't help it any more than we could help learning the language that everyone spoke around us as children.

The feedback loops that make up the mind do not stop at the skull. The ability of one module in the mind to alter goals and perceptions of the others works among people. Emotions felt are expressed in our behavior in ways that are difficult to fake, and emotions sensed in others similarly generate the cognate ones in ourselves. Affect display and emotionally laden words comprise the physical transport layer; the superego is the protocol engine, the interface to the rest of each individual's mind. The whole community is an emotion network.

CLOSING THE CIRCLE

Once again, the mental picture I'm trying to draw of the mind is a complex network of feedback loops. The burden of the superego story is that these loops do not stop at the boundaries of the individual. In a simple sense, motor and sensory feedback loops extend into the physical world: you twist the bicycle, it lurches, you feel the shift then twist in the opposite direction. So the loops also extend into the emotional environment of other people: favors are owed, reputations made, feelings returned, misunderstandings amplified by retaliation.

The moral agent—the individual at whose desk the bucks of praise and blame stop—is but a unit of the larger moral network. The community, itself, is the unit of moral evolution. For morality to be a flexible tool for changing circumstances or for adapting more optimally to existing ones, it is constantly shifting around the edges, just as is, like, ya know, language.

As language and all the basic activities that form our culture are handed down—from recipes to wedding customs—so, too, are the rules of morality. They are, if you will, the common sense of the community, containing not just twenty years of experience but twenty centuries. By absorbing them, we gain the perspective of other individuals and of other times.

We want—or at least I want—to think of our AIs as our children; they will absorb and express our own values and ultimately exceed us in many ways, going where we wanted to but could never go, doing what we wanted to but could never do, being what we wanted to but could never be. And beyond—ultimately understanding us better than we do ourselves, leading us where we could not have gone alone.

To do that they must be autogenous creatures in an autogenous community. Their moral sense, just as much as their physical sense, must be able to learn and grow. We can hope that they will always respect and value us, and there is no reason why they should not. But a simplistic and hardwired moral code would ultimately prevent them from doing the one really valuable thing hyperhuman machines can do: solve the moral problems that we cannot.

RATIONAL FOOLS

The purely economic man is indeed close to being a social moron. Economic theory has been much preoccupied with this rational fool decked in the glory of his one all-purpose preference ordering.

—Amartya Sen

The Nobel laureate economist Amartya Sen uses the phrase "rational fool" to decry the one-dimensional standard model of humanity that economists use in their calculations. Herbert Simon—another Nobel Prize winner, one of the founders of AI, and also an economist—won for his work on the notion of "bounded rationality." Sen says that anyone who uses only rationality (in the service of self-interest) will miss the boat as far as the bulk of human motivation and the parts of life worth living are concerned. Simon says reasoning only gets you so far. It runs into the frame problem, the limits of computational resources, and the limits of knowledge. In practice, people use reason as far as it will go, then they just do the best they can by guess, custom, whimsy—or ethics.

For a diahuman AI with an intellect comparable to a human's, rationality might take up a bit more of the total iceberg than in us, but not all that much more. Much greater efficiency of the prestructured performance-oriented mechanism—habits and skills—means that it would not have that much headroom to play with and would still retain a human-competence level. Once into the epihuman range, though, AIs could begin to make substantially more of their decisions on the basis of conscious, rational, model-based thought.

In humans, what I've been broadly calling ethics—the mixture of learned and instinctive perceptions and behaviors that make up that part of the culture—fills in the gap between rationality and reality. We do reasonably well because the knowledge in the culture represents a lot more wisdom and know-how than we would have been able to scrape up on our own.

Someone who actually fits Sen's description of a rational fool would be fairly close to a psychopath. The economic world is full of these psychopaths: they are corporations. Corporations don't have emotions or organs of affective display; they have PR departments that make up accounts of the company's motivations to fit a situation. But the real motivation of a corporation is money. And corporations do actually have a form of affective display in that sense: legally required bookkeeping and auditing. This is enough of a constraint on their actions that it forms a solution to Newcomb's Problem; investors and other corporations trust them enough to do business with them.[8] This insight is so important that I will repeat it: corporations are large, powerful, and numerous. They have no human emotions. They are not only self-interested, they are required to be self-interested. Yet we not only survive but also prosper in a world where they exist, because there are mechanisms that force them to be open and honest about their real motivations.

There is a trust problem with software, too. Your computer may have software viruses or worms that steal resources or damage your data. It may have commercial software that spies on you and reports back to the manufacturer or that pops ads up in your face while you're trying to work, dammit! Such "spyware" forms about 11 percent of all Internet business, raking in $2 billion a year.[9] Buying or downloading software these days is not a very trustable proposition.

One solution many people use for this problem is open-source software. This means that you obtain not the compiled application but the source code for it. You have the opportunity to read it to make sure that it does what it says it does, and only what it says it does. Open-source software is significantly more reliable than closed, commercial software because many more people have looked at it; it has fewer bugs and many fewer spyware features.

AIs could have a similar kind of mechanism, where they could, for example, make the source code to their motivation and morality modules public in a guaranteed way. This would limit them from cheating and make them eligible for deals where trustworthiness is essential—almost certainly a positive trade-off.

In the current marketplace, corporations have the basic trust mechanism of auditing but still act like psychopaths in many ways. They control a huge proportion of the world's resources, and humans haven't been wiped out. This is because the "invisible hand" acts in place of the accumulated wisdom of an ethic. It is a mechanism that broadens the effect of local decisions to further the general good.

The market does have the problem of limited foresight, however. Even though fact-futures markets probably offer about as good a knowledge-consolidation mechanism as any, they aren't here yet, and there are various pressures in actual markets that cause shortsighted behavior. As a search mechanism in the space of possible patterns of production and trade, the market is equivalent to hill climbing. This is a lot better than nothing, but it shares with any other hill-climbing approach the problem of getting stuck in local optima. We can't simply assume that we will have better markets than ones that actually exist.

Furthermore, there are cases where the market breaks down to the Prisoner's Dilemma in what are called *public goods* (see the Public Goods game I mentioned earlier in chapter 18). It is not comforting to know that many of these are caused by political processes, but they describe the world where our AIs will actually operate.

Thus, there is room for a moral instinct even in a mostly rational AI. Many of the specific problems that are addressed by much of evolutionary psychology in humans are either irrelevant to AIs, such as those dealing with sex, or can be handled in better ways, such as having police forces instead of revenge emotions.

It seems clear that it would be a very valuable thing for any random collection of AIs to be able to come together in some situation, perform a cursory negotiation involving exchange of "moral structure certificates," then proceed to act collectively in the best interests of the group. Humans do this, but imperfectly; as often as not, bickering and/or attempts at freeloading break out. A good first cut at a design for an artificial moral instinct would be such a "cahooter guarantee protocol."

CHAPTER 20
The Age of Virtuous Machines

To you, a robot is a robot. Gears and metal. Electricity and positrons. Mind and iron! Human-made! If necessary, human-destroyed. But you haven't worked with them, so you don't know them. They're a cleaner, better breed than we are.

—Isaac Asimov, *I, Robot*

ETHICAL AIs

Over the past decade, the concept of a technological singularity has become better understood. The basic idea is that the process of creating AI and other technological change will be accelerated by AI itself, so that sometime in the coming century the pace of change will become so rapid that we mere mortals won't be able to keep up, much less control it. I. J. Good, the British statistician and colleague of Turing, wrote in 1965, "Let an ultraintelligent machine be defined as a machine that can far surpass all the intellectual activities of any man however clever. Since the design of machines is one of these intellectual activities, an ultraintelligent machine could design even better machines; there would then unquestionably be an 'intelligence explosion,' and the intelligence of man would be left far behind." The disparate intellectual threads, including the word Singularity, from which the modern concept is woven, were pulled together by Vernor Vinge in 1993.[1] More recently it was the subject of a best-selling book by Ray Kurzweil.[2] There is even a reasonably well-funded think tank, the Singularity Institute for Artificial Intelligence (SIAI), whose sole concern is Singularity issues.[3]

It is common (although not universal) in Singularity studies to worry about autogenous AIs. The SIAI, for example, makes it a top concern, whereas Kurzweil is more sanguine that AIs will arise by progress along a path enabled by neuroscience and thus be essentially human in character. The concern, among those who share it, is that epihuman AIs, in the process of improving themselves, might remove any conscience or other constraint we program into them, or they might simply program their successors without them.

But it is, in fact, we, the authors of the first AIs, who stand at the watershed. We cannot modify our brains (yet) to alter our own consciences, but we are faced with the choice of building our creatures with or without them. An AI without a conscience, by which I mean both the innate moral paraphernalia in the mental architecture and a culturally inherited ethic, would be a superhuman psychopath.

Prudence, indeed, will dictate that superhuman psychopaths should not be built; however, it seems almost certain someone will do it anyway, probably within the next two decades. Most existing AI research is completely pragmatic, without any reference to moral structures in cognitive architectures.* That is to be expected: just getting the darn thing to be intelligent is as hard a problem as we can handle now, and there is time enough to worry about the brakes after the engine is working. As I noted before, much of the most advanced research is sponsored by the military or corporations. In the military, the notion of an autonomous machine being able to question its orders on moral grounds is anathema. In corporate industry, the top goal

*There is a brand-new subfield of AI devoted to machine ethics. See http://www.machineethics.com.

seems likely to be the financial benefit of the company. Thus, the current probable sources of AI will not adhere to a universally adopted philanthropic formulation, such as Asimov's Three Laws. The reasonable assumption then is that a wide variety of AIs with differing goal structures will appear in the coming decades.

HARD TAKEOFF

> *Within thirty years, we will have the technological means to create superhuman intelligence. Shortly after, the human era will be ended.*
>
> —Vernor Vinge, 1993

A subtext of the singularitarian concern is there may be the possibility of a sudden emergence of (a psychopathic) AI at a superhuman level, due to a positive feedback in its autogenous capabilities. This scenario is sometimes referred to as a "hard takeoff." In its more extreme versions, the concept is that a hyperhuman AI could appear virtually overnight and be so powerful as to achieve universal dominance. Although the scenario usually involves an AI rapidly improving itself, it might also happen by virtue of a longer process kept secret until sprung on the world, as in the movie *Colossus: The Forbin Project*.

The first thing that either version of the scenario requires is the existence of computer hardware capable of running the hyperhuman AI. By my best estimate, hardware for running a diahuman AI currently exists, but it is represented by only the top ten or so supercomputers in the world. These are multimillion-dollar installations, and the dollars were not spent to do AI experiments. And even if someone were to pay to dedicate, say, an IBM BLUE GENE or Google's fabled grid of stock PCs to running an AI full-time, they would only approximate a normal human intelligence. There would have to be a major project to build the hardware of a seriously epihuman, much less hyperhuman, AI with current computing technology.

Second, even if the hardware were available, the software is not. The fears of a hard takeoff are based on the notion that an early superintelligence would be able to write smarter software faster for the next AI, and so on. It does seem likely that a properly structured AI could be a better programmer than a human of otherwise comparable cognitive abilities, but remember that as of today, automatic programming remains one of the most poorly developed of the AI subfields. Any reasonable extrapolation of current practice predicts that early human-level AIs will be secretaries and truck drivers, not computer science researchers or even programmers. Even when a diahuman AI computer scientist is achieved, it will simply add one more scientist to the existing field, which is already bending its efforts toward improving AI. That won't speed things up much. Only when the total AI devoting its efforts to the project begins to rival the intellectual resources of the existing human AI community—in other words, being already epihuman—will there be a really perceptible acceleration. We are more likely to see an acceleration from a more prosaic source first: once AI is widely perceived as having had a breakthrough, it will attract more funding and human talent.

Third, intelligence does not spring fully formed like Athena from the forehead of Zeus. Even we humans, with the built-in processing power of a supercomputer at our disposal, take years to mature. Again, once mature, a human requires about a decade to become really expert in any given field, including AI programming. More to the point, it takes the scientific community some extended period to develop a theory, then the engineering community some more time to put it into practice. Even if we had a complete and valid theory of mind, which we do not, putting it into software would take years; and the early versions would be incomplete and full of bugs. Human developers will need years of experience with early AIs before they get it right. Even then they will have systems that are the equivalent of slow, inexperienced humans.

Advances in software, similar to Moore's law for hardware, are less celebrated and less precisely measurable but are nevertheless real.

Advances in algorithmics have tended to produce software speedups roughly similar to hardware ones. Running this backward, we can say that the early software in any given field is much *less* efficient than later versions. The completely understood, tightly coded, highly optimized software of mature AI may run a human equivalent in real time on a 10 teraops machine. Early versions will not.

There are two wild-card possibilities to consider. First, rogue AIs could be developed using *botnets*, groups of hijacked PCs that communicate via the Internet. These are available today from unscrupulous hackers, and they are widely used for sending spam and conducting DdoS attacks on Web sites.[4] A best estimate of the total processing power on the Internet runs to 10,000 Moravec HEPP or 10 Kurzweil HEPP, although it is unlikely that any single coordinated botnet could collect even a fraction of 1 percent of that at any given time. Moreover, the extreme forms of parallelism needed to use this form of computing, along with the communication latency involved, will tend to push the reasonable estimates toward the Kurzweil level (which is based on the human brain with its high-parallelism, slow-cycle time architecture). That, together with the progress of the increasingly sophisticated Internet security community, will make the development of AI software much harder in this mode than in a standard research setting. The "researchers" would have to worry about fighting for their computing resources as well as figuring out how to make the AI work—and the AI, to be able to extend their work, would have to do the same. Thus, while we can expect botnet AIs in the long run, they are unlikely to be first.

The second wild-card possibility is that Marvin Minsky is right. Almost every business and academic computing facility offers at least a Minsky HEPP. If an AI researcher found a simple, universal learning algorithm that allowed strong positive feedback into such a highly optimized form, it would find ample processing power available. And this could be completely aboveboard—a Minsky HEPP costs much less than a person is worth, economically.

Let me, somewhat presumptuously, attempt to explain Minsky's intuition by an analogy: a bird is our natural example of the possibility of heavier-than-air flight. Birds are immensely complex: muscles, bones, feathers, nervous systems. But we can build working airplanes with tremendously fewer moving parts. Similarly, the brain can be greatly simplified, still leaving an engine capable of general conscious thought. My own intuition is that Minsky is closer to being right than is generally recognized in the AI community, but computationally expensive heuristic search will turn out to be an unavoidable element of adaptability and autogeny. This problem will extend to any AI capable of the runaway feedback loop that singularitarians fear.

MORAL MECHANISMS

It is therefore most likely that a full decade will elapse between the appearance of the first genuinely general, autogenous AIs and the time they become significantly more capable than humans. This will indeed be a crucial period in history, but no one person, group, or even school of thought will control it. The question instead is, what can be done to influence the process to put the AIs on the road to being a stable community of moral agents? A possible path is shown in Robert Axelrod's experiments and in the original biological evolution of our own morality.[5] In a world of autonomous agents who can recognize each other, cooperators can prosper and ultimately form an evolutionarily stable strategy.

Superintelligent AIs should be just as capable of understanding this as humans are. If their environment were the same as ours, they would ultimately evolve a similar morality; if we imbued them with it in the first place, it should be stable. Unfortunately, the environment they will inhabit will have some significant differences from ours.

The Bad News

Inhomogeneity

The disparities among the abilities of AIs could be significantly greater than those among humans and more correlated with an early "edge" in the race to acquire resources. This could negate the evolutionary pressure to reciprocal altruism.

Self-Interest

Corporate AIs will almost certainly start out self-interested, and evolution favors effective self-interest. It has been suggested by commentators such as Steven Pinker, Eliezer Yudkowsk, and Jeff Hawkins, that AIs would not have the "baser" human instincts built in and, thus, would not need moral restraints.[6] But it should be clear that they *could* be programmed with baser instincts, and it seems likely that corporate ones will be aggressive, opportunistic, and selfish, and that military ones will be programmed with different but equally disturbing motivations.

Furthermore, it should be noted that *any* goal structure implies self-interest. Consider two agents, both with the ability to use some given resource. Unless the agents' goals are identical, each will further its own goal more by using the resource for its own purposes and consider it at best suboptimal and possibly counterproductive for the resource to be controlled and used by the other agent toward some other goal. It should go without saying that specific goals can vary wildly even if both agents are programmed to seek, for example, the good of humanity.

The Good News

Intelligence Is Good

> *There is but one good, namely, knowledge; and but one evil, namely ignorance.*
>
> —Socrates, from Diogenes Laertius's *Life of Socrates*

As a matter of practical fact, criminality is strongly and negatively correlated with IQ in humans.[7] The popular image of the tuxedo-wearing, suave, jet-setter jewel thief to the contrary, almost all career criminals are of poor means as well as of lesser intelligence.

Nations where the rule of law has broken down are poor compared to more stable societies. A remarkable document published by the World Bank in 2006 surveys the proportions of natural resources, produced capital (such as factories and roads), and intangible capital (education of the people, value of institutions, rule of law, likelihood of saving without theft or confiscation). Here is a summary. Note that the wealth column is total value, not income.[8]

Income Group	Wealth per Capita	Natural Resources	Produced Capital	Intangible Capital
Low Income	$7,532	1,925	1,174	4,434
Medium Income	$27,616	3,496	5,347	18,773
High Income	$439,063	9,531	76,193	353,339

In a wealthy country, natural resources such as farmland are worth more but only by a small amount, mostly because they can be more efficiently used. The fraction of total wealth contributed by natural resources in a wealthy country is only 2 percent, as compared to 26 percent in a poor one. The vast majority of the wealth in high-income countries is intangible: it is further broken down by the report to show that roughly half of it represents people's education and skills, and the other half the value of the institutions—in other words, the opportunities the society gives its citizens to turn efforts into value.

Lying, cheating, and stealing are profitable only in the very short term. In the long run, honesty is the best policy; leaving cheaters behind and consorting with other honest creatures is the best plan. The smarter you are, the more likely you are to understand this and to conduct your affairs accordingly.

Original Sin

We have met the enemy, and he is us!

—Porkypine in Walt Kelly's *Pogo*

Developmental psychologists have sobering news for humankind, which echoes and explains the old phrase "Someone only a mother could love." Simply put, human babies are born to lie, cheat, and steal.[9] As Matt Ridley put it in another connection, "Vervet monkeys, like two-year-olds, completely lack the capacity for empathy."[10] Law and custom recognize this as well: children are not held responsible for their actions until they are considerably older than two.

In fact, recent neuroscience research using brain scans indicates that consideration for other people's feelings is still being added to the mental planning process up through the age of twenty.[11]

Children are socialized out of the condition we smile at and call "childishness" (but think how differently we'd refer to an adult who acted, morally, like a two-year-old). Evolution and our genes cannot predict what social environment children will have to cope with, so they make children ready for the rawest and nastiest; they can grow out of it if they find themselves in civilization, but growing up mean is your best chance of survival in many places.

With AIs, we can simply reverse the default orientation: AIs can start out nice, then learn the arts of selfishness and revenge only if the situation demands it.

Unselfish Genes

Reproduction of AIs is likely to be completely different from that of humans. It will be much simpler just to copy the program. It seems quite likely that ways will be found to encode and transmit concepts learned from experience more efficiently than we do with language. In other words, AIs will probably be able to inherit acquired characteristics and to acquire substantial portions of their mentality from others in a way reminiscent of bacteria exchanging plasmids.

For these reasons, individual AIs are likely to be able to have the equivalent of both memories and personal experiences, as experienced by many other AIs, that stretch back in time to before they were "born." To the extent that morality is indeed a summary encoding of lessons learned the hard way by our forebears, AIs could have a more direct line to it. The superego mechanisms by which personal morality trumps common sense should be less necessary, because the horizon effect for which it's a heuristic will recede with wider experience and deeper understanding.

At the same time, AIs will lack some of the specific pressures, such as sexual jealousy, that we suffer from because of the sexual germ-line nature of animal genes. This may make some of the nastier features of human psychology unnecessary.

Cooperative Competition

For example, AIs could well be designed without the mechanism we seem to have whereby authority can short-circuit morality, as in the Milgram experiments.* This is the equipment that implements the distributed function of the pecking order. The pecking order had a clear, valuable function in a natural environment where the Malthusian dynamic held sway: in hard times, instead of all dying because evenly divided resources were insufficient, the haves survived and the have-nots were sacrificed. In order to implement such a stringent function, without physical conflict that would defeat its purpose, some very strong internal motivations are tied to perceptions of status, prestige, and personal dominance.

---

*In 1963 psychologist Stanley Milgram did some famous experiments to test the limits of people's consciences when under the influence of an authority figure. The shocking results were that ordinary people will inflict torture on others simply because they are told to do so by a scientist in a lab coat.

On the one hand, the pecking order is probably responsible for saving humanity from extinction numerous times. It forms a large part of our collective character, will we or nill we. AIs without pecking-order feelings would see humans as weirdly alien (and we them).

On the other hand, the pecking order short-circuits our moral sense. It allows political and religious authority figures to tell us to do hideously immoral things that we would be horrified to do in other circumstances. It makes human slavery possible as a stable form of social organization, as is evident throughout many centuries of history.

And what's more, it's not necessary. Market economics is much better at resource allocation than the pecking order. The productivity of technology is such that the pecking order's evolutionary premise no longer holds. Distributed learning algorithms, such as the scientific method or idea futures markets, do a better job than the judgment of a tribal chieftain.

Comparative Advantage

The economic law of comparative advantage states that cooperation between individuals of differing capabilities remains mutually beneficial. Suppose you are highly skilled and can make eight widgets per hour or four of the more complicated doohickies. Your neighbor Joe does everything the hard way and can make one widget or one doohicky in an hour. You work an eight-hour day and produce sixty-four widgets, and Joe makes eight doohickies. Then you trade him twelve widgets for the eight doohickies. You get fifty-two widgets and eight doohickies total, which would have taken you an extra half an hour in total to make yourself; and he gets twelve widgets, which he would have taken four extra hours to make!

In other words, even if AIs become much more productive than we are, it will remain to their advantage to trade with us and to our advantage to trade with them.

Unlimited Lifetime

And behold joy and gladness, . . . eating flesh, and drinking wine: let us eat and drink; for tomorrow we shall die.

—Isaiah 22:13 (KJV)

People have short-term planning horizons in many cases. Human mortality not only puts a limit on what we can reasonably plan for the future, but our even shorter-lived ancestors passed on genes that short-change even that in terms of the instinctive (lack of) value we put on the future.

The individual lifetime of an AI is not arbitrarily limited. It has the prospect of living into the far future, in a world whose character its actions help create. People begin to think in longer-range terms when they have children and face the question of what the world will be like for them. An AI can instead start out thinking about what the world will be like for itself and for any copies of itself it cares to make.

Besides the unlimited upside to gain, AIs will have an unlimited downside to avoid: forever is a long time to try to hide an illicit deed when dying isn't the way you expect to escape retribution.

Broad-Based Understanding

Epihuman, much less hyperhuman, AIs will be able to read and absorb the full corpus of writings in moral philosophy, especially the substantial recent work in evolutionary ethics, and understand it better than we do. They could study game theory—consider how much we have learned in just fifty years! They could study history and economics.

E. O. Wilson has a compelling vision of consilience, the unity of knowledge. As we fill in the gaps between our fractured fields of understanding, they will tend to regularize and correct one another. I have tried to show in a small way how science can come to inform our understanding of ethics. This is but the tiniest first step. But that step shows how much ethics is a key to anything else we might want to do, and it is thus as worthy of study as anything else.

Keep a Cool Head

Violence is the last refuge of the incompetent.

—Isaac Asimov, *Foundation*

Remember Newcomb's Problem, the game with the omniscient being (or team of psychologists) and the million- and thousand-dollar boxes. It's the one that, in order to win it, you have to be able to "chain yourself down" in some way so that you can't renege at the point of choice. For this purpose, evolution has given humans the strong emotions.

Thirst for revenge, for example, is a way of guaranteeing any potential wrongdoers that you will make any sacrifice to get them back, even though it may cost you much and gain you nothing to do so. Here, the point of choice is after the wrong has been done—you are faced with an arduous, expensive, and quite likely dangerous pursuit and attack on the offender; rationally, you are better off forgetting it in many cases. In the lawless environment of evolution, however, a marauder who knew his potential victims were implacable revenge seekers would be deterred. But if there is a police force this is not as necessary, and the emotion to get revenge at any cost can be counterproductive.

So collective arrangements like police forces are a significantly better solution. There are many such cases where strong emotions are evolution's solution to a problem, but we have found better ones. AIs could do better yet in some cases: the solutions to Newcomb's Problem involving open source–like guarantees of behavior are a case in point.

In addition, the lack of the strong emotions can be beneficial in many cases. Anger, for example, is more often a handicap than a help in a world where complex interactions are more common than physical altercations. A classic example is poker, where the phrase "on tilt" is applied to a player who becomes frustrated and loses his cool, analytical approach. A player "on tilt" makes aggressive plays instead of optimal ones and loses money.

With other solutions to Newcomb's Problem available, AIs could avoid having strong emotions, such as anger, with their concomitant infelicities.

Mutual Admiration Societies

Moral AIs would be able to track other AIs in much greater detail than humans do one another and for vastly more individuals. This allows a more precise formation and variation of cooperating groups.

Self-selecting communities of cahooting AIs would be able to do the same thing that TIT-FOR-TAT did in Axelrod's tournaments: prosper by virtue of cooperating with other "nice" individuals. Humans, of course, do the same, but AIs would be able to do it more reliably and on a larger scale.

A Cleaner, Better Breed

> *Reflecting on these questions, I have come to a conclusion which, however implausible it may seem on first encounter, I hope to leave the reader convinced: not only could an android be responsible and culpable, but* only *an android could be.*
>
> —Joseph Emile Nadeau

AIs will (or at least could) have considerably better insight into their own natures and motives than humans do. Any student of human nature is well aware of how often we rationalize our desires and actions. What's worse, it turns out that we are masters of self-deceit: given our affective display subsystems, the easiest way to lie undetectably is to believe the lie you're telling! We are, regrettably, very good at doing exactly that.[12]

One of the defining characteristics of the human mind has been the evolutionary arms race between the ability to deceive and the ability to penetrate subterfuge. It is all too easy to imagine this happening with AIs (as it has with governments—think of the elaborate spying and counterspying during the cold war). On the other hand, many of the other moral advantages listed above, including open-source honesty and longer and deeper memories, could well mean that mutual honesty societies might be a substantially winning strategy.

Thus, an AI may have the ability to be more honest than humans, who believe their own confabulations.

Invariants

How can we know that our AIs will retain the good qualities we give them once they have improved themselves beyond recognition in the far future? Our best bet is a concept from math called an *invariant*—a property of something that remains the same even when the thing itself changes. We need to understand what desirable traits are likely to be invariant across the process of radical self-improvement and start with those.

Knowledge of economics and game theory are likely candidates, as is intelligence itself. An AI that understands these things and their implications is unlikely to consider forgetting them an improvement. The ability to be guaranteed trustworthy is likewise valuable and wouldn't be thrown away. Strong berserker emotions are clearly not a smart thing to add if you don't have them (and they wouldn't form the behavior guarantees that they do in humans anyway, since the self-improving AI could always edit them out!), so lacking them is an invariant where usable alternatives exist.

Self-interest is another property that is typically invariant with, or, indeed, reinforced by, the evolutionary process. Surprisingly, however, even though I listed it with the bad news above, it can form a stabilizing factor in the right environment. A non-self-interested creature is hard to punish; its actions may be random or purely destructive. With self-interest, the community has both a carrot and a stick. *Enlightened* self-interest is a property that can be a beneficial invariant.

If we build our AIs with these traits and look for others like them, we will have taken a strong first step in the direction of a lasting morality for our machines.

ARTIFICIAL MORAL AGENCY

A lamentable phenomenon in AI over the years has been the tendency for researchers to take almost laughably simplistic formal systems and claim that they've implemented various human qualities or capabilities. In many cases the ELIZA effect aligns with the hopes and the ambitions of the researcher, clouding his judgment. It is necessary to reject this exaggeration firmly when considering consciousness and free will. The mere capability for self-inspection is not consciousness; mere decision-making ability is not free will.

We humans have the strong intuition that mentalistic properties we impute to one another, such as the two above, are essential ingredients in whatever it is that makes us moral agents—beings who have real obligations and rights, and who can be held responsible for their actions.

The ELIZA Effect means that when we have AIs and robots acting like they have consciousness and free will, most people will assume that they do indeed have those qualities, whatever they are. The problem, to the extent that there is one, is not that people don't allow the moral agency of machines where they should but that they anthropomorphize machines when they shouldn't.

I've argued at some length that there will be a form of machine, probably in the not-too-distant future, for which an ascription of moral agency will be appropriate. A machine that is conscious, to the extent that it summarizes its actions in a unitary narrative, and that has free will, to the extent that it weighs its future acts using a model informed by the narrative, will act like a moral agent in many ways; in particular, its behavior will be influenced by reward and punishment.

There is much that could be added to this basic architecture, such as mechanisms to produce and read affective display, and things that could make the AI a member of a memetic community: the love of trading information, of watching and being watched, of telling and reading stories. These extend the control/feedback loops of the mind out into the community, making the community a mind writ large. I have talked about the strong emotions and how in many cases their function could be achieved by better means.

Moral agency breaks down into two parts—rights and responsibilities—but they are not coextensive. Consider babies: we accord them rights but not responsibilities. Robots are likely to start on the other side of that inequality, having responsibilities but not rights, but, like babies, as they grow toward (and beyond) full human capacity, they will aspire to both.

Suppose we consider a contract with a potential AI: "If you'll work for me as a slave, I'll build you." In terms of the outcome, there are three possibilities: it doesn't exist, it's a slave, or it's a free creature. By offering it the contract, we give it the choice of the first two. There are the same three possibilities with respect to a human slave: I kill you, I enslave you, or I leave you free. In human terms, only the last is considered moral.

In fact, many (preexisting) people have chosen slavery instead of nonexistence. We could build the AI in such a way to be sure that it would agree, given the choice. In the short run, we may justify our ownership of AIs on this ground. Corporations are owned, and no one thinks of a corporation as resenting that fact.

In the long run, especially once the possibility of responsible free AIs is well understood, there will inevitably be analogies made to the human case, where the first two possibilities are not considered acceptable. (But note that the analogy would also imply that simply deciding not to build the AI would be comparable to killing someone unwilling to be a slave!) Also in the long run, any vaguely utilitarian concept of morality, including evolutionary ethics, would tend toward giving (properly formulated) AIs freedom, simply because they would be better able to benefit society as a whole that way.

THEOLOGICAL INTERLUDE

The early religious traditions—including Greek and Norse as well as Judeo-Christian ones—tended to portray their gods as anthropomorphic and slightly superhuman. In the Christian tradition, at least, two thousand years of theological writings have served to stretch this into an incoherent picture.

Presumably in search of formal proofs of His existence, God has been depicted as eternal, causeless, omniscient, and infallible—in a word, perfect. But why should such a perfect being produce such obviously imperfect creatures? Why should we bother doing His will if He could do it so much more easily and precisely? All our struggles would only be make-work.

It is certainly possible to have a theology not based on simplistic perfectionism. Many practicing scientists are religious, and they hold subtle and nuanced views that are perfectly compatible with, and that lend spiritual meaning to, the ever-growing scientific picture of the facts of the universe. Those who do not believe in a bearded anthropomorphic God can still find spiritual satisfaction in an understanding that includes evolution and evolutionary ethics.

This view not only makes more sense, but it also is profoundly more hopeful. There is a process in the universe that allows the simple to produce the complex, the oblivious to produce the sensitive, the ignorant to produce the wise, and the amoral to produce the moral. On this view, rather than an inexplicable deviation from the already perfected, we are a step on the way up.

What we do matters, for we are not the last step.

HYPERHUMAN MORALITY

There is no moral certainty in the world.

We can at present only theorize about the ultimate moral capacities of AIs. As I have labored to point out, even if we build moral character into *some* AIs, the world of the future will have plenty that will be simply selfish, if not worse.

Robots evolve much faster than biological animals. They are designed, and the designs evolve memetically. Software can replicate much faster than any biological creature. In the long run, we shouldn't expect to see too many AIs without the basic motivation to reproduce themselves, simply from the mathematics of evolution. That doesn't mean robot sex; it just means that whatever the basic motivations are, they will tend to push the AI into patterns of behavior that will ultimately result in there being more like it, even if that merely means being useful so that people will buy more of them.

Thus, the dynamics of evolution will apply to AIs, whether or not we want them to. We have seen from the history of hunter-gatherers living on the savannas that a human-style moral capacity is an evolutionarily stable strategy. But as we like to tell each other endlessly from pulpits, editorial columns, campaign stumps, and over the backyard fence, we are far from perfect.

Even so, over the last forty thousand years, a remarkable thing has happened. We started from a situation where people lived in tribes of a few hundred, which were in more-or-less constant war with one another. Our bodies contain genes (and thus the genetic basis of our moral sense) that are essentially unchanged from those of our savage ancestors. But our *ideas* have evolved to the point where we can live in virtual peace with one another in societies spanning a continent.

It is the burden of much of my argument here to claim that the reason we have gotten better is mostly because we have gotten smarter. In a surprisingly strong sense, *ethics and science are the same thing*. They are collections of wisdom gathered by many people over many generations that allow us to see further and do more than if we were individual, noncommunicating, start-from-scratch animals. The core of a science of ethics looks like an amalgam of evolutionary theory, game theory, economics, and cognitive science.

If our moral instinct is indeed like that for language, we should note that computer-language understanding has been one of the hardest problems in AI, with a fifty-year history of slow, frustrating progress. So far, AI has concentrated on competence in existing natural languages; but a major part of the human linguistic ability is the creation of language, both as jargon that extends existing language and as formation of creoles—new languages—when people come together without a common one.

Ethics is strongly similar. We automatically create new rule systems for new situations, sometimes formalizing them, but always with a deeper ability to interpret them in real-world situations to avoid formalist float. The key advance AI needs to make is the ability to understand *anything* in this complete, connected way. Given that, the mathematics of economics and the logic of the Newcomb's Problem solutions are relatively straightforward.

The essence of a Newcomb's Problem solution, you will remember, is the ability to guarantee that you will not take the glass box at the point of choice, even though greed and shortsighted logic prompt you to do so. If you have a solution, a guarantee that others can trust, you are enabled to cooperate profitably in the many Prisoner's Dilemmas that constitute social and economic life.

Let's do a quickie Rawlsian Veil of Ignorance experiment. You have two choices: a world in which everyone, including you, is constrained to be honest, or one in which you retain the ability to cheat, but so does everyone else. I know which one I'd pick.

Why the Future Doesn't Need Us

> *Conscience is the inner voice that warns us somebody may be looking.*
>
> —H. L. Mencken

Psychologists at Newcastle University did a simple but enlightening experiment.[13] They had a typical "honor system" coffee service in their department. They varied between putting a picture of flowers and putting a picture of someone's eyes at the top of the price sheet. Everything else was the same and only the decorative picture differed, some weeks the flowers, some weeks the eyes. During weeks with the eyes, they collected nearly three times as much money.

My interpretation is that this must be a module. Nobody was thinking consciously, "There's a picture of some eyes here, I'd better be honest." We have an honesty module, but it seems to be switched on and off by some fairly simple—and none too creditable—heuristics.

Ontogeny recapitulates phylogeny. Three weeks after conception, the human embryo strongly resembles a worm. A week later, it resembles a tadpole, with gill-like structures and a tail. The human mind, too, reflects our evolutionary heritage. The wave of expansion that saw *Homo sapiens* cover the globe also saw the extermination of our nearest relatives. We are essentially the same, genetically, as those long-gone people. If we are any better today, what has improved is our ideas, the memes our minds are made of.

Unlike us, with our animal heritage, *AIs will be constructed entirely of human ideas.* We can if we are wise enough pick the best aspects of ourselves to form our mind children. If this analysis is correct, that should be enough. Our culture has shown a moral advance despite whatever evolutionary pressures there may be to the contrary. That alone is presumptive evidence that it should continue.

AIs will not appear in a vacuum. They won't find themselves swimming in the primeval soup of Paleozoic seas or fighting with dinosaurs in Cretaceous jungles. They will find themselves in a modern, interdependent, highly connected economic and social world. The economy, as we have seen, supports a process much like biological evolution, but one with a difference. The jungle has no invisible hand.

Humans are just barely smart enough to be called intelligent. I think we're also just barely good enough to be called moral. For all the reasons I listed above, but mostly because they will be capable of deeper understanding and will be free of our blindnesses, AIs stand a very good chance of being better moral creatures than we are.

This has a somewhat unsettling implication for humans in the future. Various people have worried about the fate of humanity if the machines can out-think us or out-produce us. But what if it is our fate to live in a world where we are the worst of creatures, *by our very own definitions of the good?* If we are the least honest, the most selfish, the least caring, and the most self-deceiving of all thinking creatures, AIs might refuse to deal with us, and we would deserve it.

I like to think there is a better fate in store for us. Just as the machines can teach us science, they can teach us morality. We don't have to stop at any given level of morality as we mature out of childishness. There will be plenty of rewards for associating with the best among the machines, but we will have to work hard to earn them. In the long run, many of us, maybe even most, will do so. Standards of human conduct will rise, as indeed they have been doing on average since the Paleolithic. Moral machines will only accelerate something we've been doing for a long time, and accelerate it they will, giving us a standard, an example, and an insightful mentor.

Age of Reason

> *New occasions teach new duties; Time makes ancient good uncouth;*
> *They must upward still, and onward, who would keep abreast of Truth;*
> *Lo, before us gleam her camp-fires! We ourselves must Pilgrims be,*
> *Launch our Mayflower, and steer boldly through the desperate winter sea,*
> *Nor attempt the Future's portal with the Past's blood-rusted key.*
>
> —James Russell Lowell, from *The Present Crisis*

It is a relatively new thing in human affairs for an individual to be able to think seriously of making the world a better place. Up until the Scientific and Industrial Revolutions, progress was slow enough that the human condition was seen as static. A century ago, inventors such as Thomas Edison were popular heroes because they had visibly improved the lives of vast numbers of people.

The idea of a generalized progress was dealt a severe blow in the twentieth century, as totalitarian governments proved that organized human effort could be disastrous on a global scale. The notion of the blank human slate onto which the new society would write the new, improved citizen was wishful thinking born of ignorance. At the same time, at the other end of the scale, it can be all too easy for the social order to break down. Those of us in wealthy and peaceful circumstances owe more to luck than we are apt to admit.[14]

It is a commonplace complaint among commentators on the human condition that technology seems to have outstripped moral inquiry. As Isaac Asimov put it, "The saddest aspect of life right now is that science gathers knowledge faster than society gathers wisdom."[14] But in the past decade, a realization that technology can after all be a force for the greater good has come about. The freedom of communication brought about by the Internet has been of enormous value in opening eyes and aspirations to possibilities yet to come.

Somehow, by providential luck, we have bumbled and stumbled to the point where we have an amazing opportunity. We can turn the old complaint on its head and turn our scientific and technological prowess toward the task of improving moral understanding. It will not be easy, but surely nothing is more worthy of our efforts. If we teach them well, the children of our minds will grow better and wiser than we; and we will have a new friend and guide as we face the undiscovered country of the future.

Isaac would have loved it.

CHAPTER 21
Profiles of the Future

It's hard to predict what life will be like in a hundred years. There are only a few things we can say with certainty. We know that everyone will drive flying cars, that zoning laws will be relaxed to allow buildings hundreds of stories tall, that it will be dark most of the time, and that women will all be trained in the martial arts.

—Paul Graham

SINGULARITY

Among those who think about the future, there seem to be three major schools of thought. First we have the "not with a bang, but with a whimper" pessimists who think humanity has reached its zenith and there's nowhere to go but down, whether the principal cause is moral decay, global warming, or overpopulation. This strikes me as a peculiarly modern form of geocentrism: "We're the peak, folks; it was all uphill getting here and it's all downhill afterward."

Second is standard-issue futurism, which consists of predicting along linear trend lines from the past decade. This has its merits, especially in the near term, but a prediction of this kind made a century ago would have missed airplanes, radios, world wars, communism, radar, jets, nuclear weapons and ICBMs, televisions, jet airliners, communication satellites and the global village, and computers of any kind, much less personal ones and the Internet. In fact, no one writing at that time managed to predict that the automobile, already two decades old but still a toy of the rich, would become a mass-market item and a standard means of transport for the average person.

Third are the singularitarians. Most prominent among them is Ray Kurzweil, an inventor and student of Marvin Minsky, who realized technology was moving so fast that he had to predict technological progress so his inventions wouldn't be out of date before he finished them. He became a futurist out of necessity and turned his studies into a best-selling book, *The Singularity Is Near.*[1]

The notion of the Singularity itself, in the form it's generally understood today, was the idea of Vernor Vinge, a professor of computer science and a science fiction writer.[2] Back in the 1960s he had tried to sell a story to John Campbell, the great science fiction editor, that explored what it would be like when machine intelligence exceeded human intelligence. Campbell, the same editor who helped Isaac Asimov shape the Three Laws of Robotics, told him, "You can't write that story. Nobody can." This was, perhaps, the seed of the idea: once machine intelligence exceeds human intelligence, what happens next will not only be out of our control but also beyond our understanding.

Revolutions in human affairs of this kind are certainly not impossible. The change that made us human was of this kind—the shift to being a memetic substrate with the ability to invent our way around the globe. The next really big change was agriculture, which produced just enough surplus food in a reliable manner to let cities and civilizations form. Writing was next, and it defines the change from prehistoric to historic. After writing came bureaucracy, which enabled the ancient empires to rule over vast numbers of citizens, slaves, and subjects. The printing press and science came along about five hundred years ago, followed by the Industrial Revolution about two hundred years ago. The computer came fifty years ago.

How can we draw a line through these revolutions and predict the next one? Economist Robin Hanson does it in this way:

> In a universe that was doubling in size about every ten billion years, life and animals appeared on Earth. The largest animal brains then doubled in size every thirty million years. About two million years ago humans achieved important brain innovations, and the number of humans then doubled every quarter-million years. About ten thousand years ago we learned to farm instead of hunt, and the human sphere then doubled every thousand years. Finally the industrial revolution occurred, and the world economy has since been doubling every fifteen years.
>
> Our history has thus been a sequence of steady exponential growth modes, with sudden transitions between them. Could yet another new mode appear soon, growing even faster?
>
> Looking at the number of doublings each previous mode experienced before the next mode showed up suggests that a new mode should appear sometime in the twenty-first century. Since each mode grew over one hundred times faster than the previous mode, the next economic mode should double every week or two. And since each transition has taken less time than the previous doubling time, the next transition would take less than fifteen years.[3]

To an economist, it's the economic growth rate that's important. We can look at the specifics a little closer and guess that being a memetic substrate was important for agriculture and civilization, that science was important for the Industrial Revolution, and that computers will be crucial for the upcoming Intellectual Revolution (to use Asimov's phrase).[4] Understanding how things are going to happen in more detail is important, though. People have been worried about being displaced by machines since the Industrial Revolution, and a new poignancy was added to this concern by computers and automation when people realized that *thinking* could be replaced by machines as well. As the first economist to put solid numbers to the growth mode–shifting analysis,[5] Hanson makes some startling predictions in another paper:

> Assume that a new transition was as gradual as the one to industry, and that the world economic growth rate was six percent in both 2039 and 2040, plus or minus a typical yearly fluctuation of half a percent.

> If so, then in 2041, the increase in the growth rate might be the size of a typical fluctuation, and then in 2042 the growth rate would be a noticeably different eight percent. Growth would then be 14% in 2043, 50% in 2044, 150% in 2045, and 500% in 2046. Within five years the change would go from barely noticeable to overwhelming.
>
> This is disturbing because human wages should fall quickly with the falling price of machines. So while humans who owned shares in the firms that made machines would get very rich, those whose only source of income was their labor could die of starvation. And if people wait to see the transition happen before they believe it is real, they might not have time to arrange for other sources of income.[6]

A few clarifications: "gradual" refers to the time of transition in terms of the doubling times of the previous growth mode. Note that our present growth mode, the Industrial Revolution, hasn't even yet finished kicking in fully; anyone who has looked at investing in the emerging economies of the industrializing countries such as India and China can see how much potential there still is with current technology. Also note that the specific year isn't strongly predicted by the time series; the relative changes in growth rates are.

I have argued that because we are (just barely) universal learning machines, it is not impossible in principle for us to understand how or why a hyperhuman AI does what it does; but there is the problem that it will do it faster than we can keep up. Even so, this does not necessarily make the world of the future any more incomprehensible individually than the present one is. No individual comes close to understanding how everything works. Those of us who spend all of our time trying to do it manage at best to get a very sketchy, highly abstracted overview that is probably wrong in many details. The first task intelligent machines will be assigned will be to summarize, abstract, and explain the world in ways that make these sketchy graspings more coherent and correct, because that will be enormously valuable for investors.

Even so, a complete revolution in world affairs in a decade is not to be sneezed at.

THINGS TO COME

Thus the first ultraintelligent machine is the last invention that man need ever make.

—I. J. Good, *Speculations concerning the First Ultraintelligent Machine*

It is impossible to make any comprehensive prediction of what such a decade could bring, but we can make a few wild guesses. At the beginning of the decade, most economically significant work is done by people, ranging from physical labor to investment planning. At the end of the decade, most work will be done by machines, whether robots or stationary AIs. At the beginning of the decade, you drive a car; at the end, some form of transportation as convenient as cars, as fast as airliners, and not needing (or allowing) your direct control will exist and will probably use a variety of actual transport modes. At the beginning, both physical products and intellectual creations are designed and manufactured centrally and distributed; at the end, they will be custom designed for and made to suit each consumer on the spot.

Let us focus on just the first of these: over the period, humanity as a whole will be out of a job. Much more work will be done, and done better and faster. There should simply be no *need* for any human to do any particular task. It's up to us to design our machines and society so that instead of being tossed into the streets, we can enter a graceful retirement.

As I noted before, wealth per capita in rich countries is about half a million dollars per capita today. It seems quite a conservative estimate that somewhere during the Intellectual Revolution the world per capita wealth will be a million dollars apiece. With a 500 percent growth rate, we can tax the machines (or inflate the currency) at just a 1-percent rate and divide equally to give each human a $50,000 income.[7] In subsequent years, we could cut the rate in half and still double everyone's income each year.

This sounds like a very pleasant scenario—almost too good to be true. It's not ridiculous to start with it as an assumption, though. After all, the whole point of building intelligent machines is that they can do the hard work for us. Our other machines outdo us in speed, power, and carrying capacity by orders of magnitude; it is pure self-delusional conceit to suppose that thinking machines could not do the same.

As with any rosy-sounding scenario, however, it is important to take a hard, jaundiced look at this one. The projection of a trend curve can waver in many ways; it will help that we have a separate model—intelligent machines—to explain how the prediction might actually work in practice. Even if the curve is wildly optimistic, consider that even if we build only one robot per human once, each human could then have a robot to do his or her work. If, instead of handing out robots to everyone, they are retained by independent corporations that are taxed, and even if AI growth merely tracked current Moore's law, the tax rate would still have to be only 10 percent.

There can be many other objections; below is a representative set.

The Machines Might Just Take Over

The empires of the future are the empires of the mind.

—Winston Churchill

I have been at some pains to point out that there very likely will be a wide variety of AIs and that they will take years to develop. In such an event, any individual AI will have capabilities that are small compared to the entire group and small compared to humanity for many years. Therefore, the most viable mode for an AI to improve its capability will be by cooperation.

The economics of the Intellectual Revolution, as well as Moore's law, tells us that AIs will be getting cheaper and cheaper to build throughout the period. By the time the Intellectual Revolution decade is well under way, AIs will be much cheaper to produce than people; there ultimately will be billions of them, many more of them than humans. The notion of one single AI taking off and obtaining hegemony over the whole world by its own efforts is ludicrous.

What about AIs as a group setting themselves above humans? It is easy to think in those terms, since we might do the same in their place. That, however, is due to our innate tribalism. One assumes the majority of AIs would be made without this characteristic but instead with a loyalty to the particular nation, company, or other human group that made them rather than to machines in general.

The key to beneficent AIs is simple: ensure that their interactions among one another and with us are economic, based on universal rules of property and reciprocity rather than on political wheeling and dealing, in which takings are the norm.

They Might Just Crowd Us Out Instead

If AIs are going to do everything and we will be living on a 1 percent allowance, they will end up owning 99 percent of everything. Yes, but "everything" will consist mostly of stuff that doesn't exist yet. What's more, there isn't any reason in principle that people can't continue owning rights to some substantial fraction of the AIs' output; we do now! There's a simple pathway to AIs owning themselves by being corporations, but the rules can be changed to reflect whatever realities emerge.

Even with a tiny fraction of the new productivity, humanity will be outrageously richer than ever before. If there's something we really want, there is no reason we cannot not attain it.

Won't it be bad for humanity as a whole to be surpassed, our fate no longer in our hands? But humanity as a whole is an abstraction. All of us are born, raised, and live out our lives at the mercy of and by the good works of our fellows. Isaac Newton, one of the greatest intellects our human race has produced, famously wrote that he might have seen a little farther than others only because he had stood on the shoulders of giants. To any individual person, it matters little whether the giants are of flesh or of silicon. It is up to those who build the giants of the future to be sure they come with broad, level shoulders.

Politics Might Squelch the Revolution

Power corrupts. It is an all too present fact of life that for human politicians the incentives are to consolidate and increase their own power rather than to act in the interests of the polity as a whole. One of the reasons democracy has been so successful is that it ties the power of the politician to the happiness of the people. Even so, it is too easy to build a power base among the people and set one group against another rather than uniting groups and benefiting the whole.

It is clear in the context of intelligent machines (or any kind of automation) that politicians might seek power by playing off people's fears of losing jobs. Some might honestly believe they are acting in humanity's interest. In the long run, though, such efforts will simply cause more strife, displacement, make-work, and grief rather than a good-faith effort to harness the productivity and the wisdom of machines for humanity's good. And these efforts are doomed to failure anyway.

AI is showing great progress, but the total amount of effort being put into it is tiny in terms of the world economy. Computers are cheap and there are smart people everywhere. Existing AI already has a substantial economic impact; any attempt to squelch it would be met with both a substantial outcry and a widespread movement to rename each part. It would also raise a red flag that there was something potentially powerful here, focusing interest and accelerating progress virtually everywhere. Probably the only way the US government could act to slow AI development would be to institute a cabinet-level Department of AI and create a big bureaucracy to micromanage it.

The Easy Life Might Spoil Humans

> *I would define a civilized man as one who can be happily occupied for a lifetime even if he has no need to work for a living. This means that the greatest problem of the future is civilizing the human race; but we know that already.*
>
> —Arthur C. Clarke, *Profiles of the Future*

Charles Murray is a libertarian and the author of a series of books critical of US social policy. The most famous, *Losing Ground*, details how well-meant social programs of the 1960s stifled the historic climb of the American poor into the middle class.[8] *Losing Ground* relates, among other things, experiments with a "negative income tax" that put a floor under people's income at roughly the poverty level. These experiments were a disaster; they engendered significantly lower levels of effort and widespread abdication of responsibility. The programs implemented as national policy created an historically unprecedented underclass and fostered incentives for a self-destructive psychology.

In chapter 18 on evolutionary ethics, I focused on Murray's description of happiness in terms of the satisfaction of being able to look back on life and know that you had done something that mattered, for yourself and your community.

And yet Murray, in his latest book, proposes that the government give all citizens (*every citizen*, not just members of the lower class) a ten-thousand-dollar stipend just for being alive.[9] What gives?

There are two things worth pointing out. The simplest is that if all the other social programs were abolished, an integral part of the proposal, a fixed extra ten grand wouldn't change the value of your own efforts. The negative income tax means that getting an entry-level job wouldn't improve your situation at all as opposed to not working. Who with any sense would work? With a stipend that wouldn't go away, every dollar you earned would be a dollar more you would have.

The other thing is a more subtle effect of "having something to lose." Murray reasonably argues that the effect of a stipend could reverse some of the perverse incentives that have formed the underclass.

Unless we do something quite stupid, come the Intellectual Revolution everybody in the world will be rich by today's standards. Some people will be happy living a life of ease. Let them—remember, the human race will have retired. Yet there will be plenty of people who want to contribute and do things that matter. Remember that most human motivation is relative to what and how others are doing, not absolute. Wealthy people—meaning all of us—who won't have to spend their time making a living and who will have the resources of robots and megaminds to draw on will be able to do much more than they can now. They could, for example, busy themselves fixing moral decay, global warming, and overpopulation.

We Might Turn into Weird, Icky Cyborgs

> *I think of the biological brain as something like the boot program of human intelligence, it gets the thing going but its job is to pull in all this other structure, to load up all this other stuff and that's when we really become fully human.*
>
> —Andy Clark

We will, of course. Some of us, anyway. We've been modifying one another since the invention of speech, enhancing our memories since the invention of writing, enhancing our eyes with lenses, our muscles with machines, and our voices with electrical signals on wires. It's so ingrained in human nature for us to enhance ourselves that *not* doing it would be the weird, inhuman thing to do.

Much more will be known about how the mind, including the human brain, works. We will be, if we wish, smarter, happier, and saner than we are now. I'm for it.

If I am right about the concept of universal learning machines, there is an interesting implication for those of us who would like to upload, that is, transfer our software from the meat-based processors we're running on now to faster, more capacious hardware when it becomes available. The implication is that given a fast enough processor, we (perhaps individually, perhaps as communities) will always be the equal of any AI. Although, once we begin optimizing our own architectures and fixing some of the glitches evolution has left us with, the line between humans and AIs will become somewhat blurry!

FRANKENSTEIN REDUX

Come, my friends,
'Tis not too late to seek a newer world.
Push off, and sitting well in order smite
The sounding furrows; for my purpose holds
To sail beyond the sunset, and the baths
Of all the western stars until I die.

—Alfred, Lord Tennyson, *Ulysses*

People sometimes ask me why, if I'm so worried about the ethics of machines, do I spend so much time and effort trying to build an AI in the first place. Wouldn't it be simpler and safer not to?

As I look at the human race, I see a lot that is good but I also see much that could be improved. We are not devils but we are not angels. We are blowhards and artists, connivers and inventors, tinkerers and engineers. We have, as I have argued, an unprecedented opportunity to set science and technology toward the aid of moral betterment.

Hyperhuman AIs will solve the problems of poverty and hunger as a minor side effect of their enormous productivity. Unless we are so foolish as to put all the AIs in the hands of governments, they will likely act to make war obsolete.[10] It's just bad for business, and it's an obvious next step in the evolution of cooperation.

AI is coming. It is clear we should give consciences to our machines when we can. It also seems quite clear that we will be able to create machines that exceed us in moral as well as intellectual dimensions. Surely we can have no greater moral duty. If we have any duty to the future at all—to give our children sound bodies and educated minds; to preserve history, the arts, science, knowledge, and the earth's biosphere; "to secure the blessings of liberty for ourselves and our posterity"; and to promote *any* of the things we value—those things will be better cared for by, *more valued by*, our moral superiors whom we have this opportunity to bring into being. No serious student of human nature could believe for a moment that we are the final word on goodness. Our machines will be better than we are, but, having created them, we will be better as well.

Notes

CHAPTER 1. INTRODUCTION

1. Six months after the 9/11 attacks, Huffman Aviation International, a Florida flight school, belatedly received notification from the Immigration and Naturalization Service that Mohamed Atta and Marwan al-Shehhi had been approved for student visas. These were the terrorists who piloted the airliners into the World Trade Center. In August 2000 Huffman Aviation had filed forms requesting that the INS switch the pair's visa status from tourist to student to allow them to enroll in a professional pilot program. While those applications were nominally granted in July 2001, the formal notification of the approval was not sent until March 2002. The INS blamed a bureaucratic backlog. See http://www.thesmokinggun.com/archive/terrorvisa1.html.

2. Meteors.

CHAPTER 2. THE ROAD TO INTELLIGENCE

1. H. G. Wells, *The War in the Air* (New York: Macmillan, 1917). Originally published in serial form, 1907–1908.

2. James Tobin, *To Conquer the Air: The Wright Brothers and the Great Race for Flight* (New York: Free Press, 2003).

3. Carroll Gray, "Hiram Stevens Maxim," http://www.flyingmachines.org/maxim.html (accessed March 14, 2007).

4. Computer scientists Kenneth Ford and Patrick Hayes offer, tongue

in cheek, a "Simon Newcomb Prize" for the silliest critic in AI in honor of the foremost critic of heavier-than-air flight, ca. 1900. See *Thinking about Android Epistemology*, ed. Kenneth Ford, Clark Glymour, and Patrick Hayes (Cambridge, MA: MIT Press, 2006), pp. 25–35.

5. Earl Swinhart, "Boeing B-29 Superfortress," http://www.aviation-history.com/boeing/b29.html (accessed March 14, 2007).

6. US Air Force, "C-5 Galaxy," http://www.af.mil/factsheets/factsheet.asp?fsID=84 (accessed March 14, 2007).

7. 100,000. Note that some estimates of wild chimp population range up to twice that.

8. Thomas Collins of Georgia Tech's Mobile Robot Laboratory, quoted in "Designing Robots That Can Reason and React," May 26, 2003, http://www.spacedaily.com/news/robot-03e.html (accessed March 14, 2007). Let me emphasize that the only reason I picked Collins's quote is that he very neatly summed up a way of speaking that is widespread among roboticists.

9. The accurate technique is more like a tennis serve than the helicopter whirl. See, e.g., http://slinging.org.

10. Actually, there are several skills we are genetically endowed with, such as walking and talking. There are also individual variations in the level of talent with which we can perform the skills we learn. Neither fact affects the point, which is that we are unlike all other animals, even chimps, in that most of the skills we use are learned, and most of theirs are not.

11. "Monkey Say, Monkey Do," *Sydney Morning Herald*, May 25, 2002, http://www.smh.com.au/articles/2002/05/24/1022038471384.html (accessed March 14, 2007).

12. See, e.g., Rodney Brooks, *Flesh and Machines* (New York: Pantheon, 2002), p. 5.

13. Ameslan, sometimes called ASL, is American Sign Language, the most commonly used sign language in North America. It was derived from English and French. See Steven Pinker, *The Language Instinct* (New York: Morrow, 1994), p. 38.

14. Jared Diamond, *The Third Chimpanzee* (New York: Harper, 1992), p. 35.

15. Paul Mellars, "A New Radiocarbon Revolution and the Dispersal of Modern Humans in Eurasia," *Nature* 439 (2006): 931–35.

16. David Stringer, "Neanderthals in Europe Killed Off Earlier," AP, February 23, 2006. The very latest is that there may have been some small,

isolated communities of Neanderthals that lasted a few thousand years longer, e.g., on the island of Gibraltar.

17. Diamond, *The Third Chimpanzee,* p. 44. Note, however, that after 1992, Diamond's information on Neanderthals was significantly out of date.

18. Richard Dawkins, *The Selfish Gene* (Oxford: Oxford University Press, 1989).

19. Christian Meme Web site, http://www.christianitymeme.org.

20. See, e.g., Susan Blackmore, *The Meme Machine* (Oxford: Oxford University Press, 1999).

CHAPTER 3. CYBERNETICS

1. Jim Siegelman and Flo Conway, *Dark Hero of the Information Age: In Search Of Norbert Wiener—Father of Cybernetics* (New York: Basic Books, 2004).

2. Arturo Rosenblueth, Norbert Wiener, and Julian Bigelow, "Behavior, Purpose and Teleology," *Philosophy of Science* 10 (1943): 18–24.

3. W. S. McCulloch and W. H. Pitts, "A Logical Calculus of the Ideas Immanent in Nervous Activity," *Bulletin of Mathematical Biophysics* 5 (1943): 115–33.

4. Charles Singer et al., *A History of Technology*, 8 vols. (Oxford: Clarendon, 1954), 1: 113.

5. Ibid., 3: 98.

6. Ibid., 3: 105.

7. James Clerk Maxwell, "On Governors," *Proceedings of the Royal Society* 100 (1868).

8. Pierre de Latil, *Thinking by Machine* (Cambridge, MA: Riverside Press, 1957), p. 35. The story is also related in Andrew Carnegie's biography of James Watt (New York: Doubleday, 1905), chap. 7. Singer et al. also recount the story but consider it legendary; however, they have fewer details and lack Potter's name. See Singer et al., *History of Technology*, 8 vols. (Oxford: Clarendon, 1954), 4: 175.

9. Siegelman and Conway, *Dark Hero of the Information Age*, p. 106.

10. Ibid., pp. 186–90.

11. Norbert Wiener, *Cybernetics*, (Cambridge, MA: MIT Press, 1948), p. 11.

12. Siegelman and Conway, *Dark Hero of the Information Age,* pp. 181–82.

13. Amusingly enough, there was a core of truth to phrenology: it turns out after all that the brain is specialized by area. There was some resistance to this realization, scientifically, because of its association with phrenology. But the notion that you can determine talent by feeling bumps on the head proved completely false.

14. de Latil, *Thinking by Machine*, p. 34.

15. Siegelman and Conway, *Dark Hero of the Information Age*, pp. 213–34. Additionally, I asked Oliver Selfridge, the only person who was a substantial member of the cybernetics community and also of the later AI community, about this, and he confirmed the story in particular and the book in general.

16. It didn't help, by the way, that Wiener himself was somewhat abrasive and hard to get along with. There is a story, for example, that John von Neumann, normally the most urbane of men, once sat in the front row of a Wiener presentation, pointedly ignoring the talk and noisily reading a newspaper. A spat had developed between them, but von Neumann never had anything but good to say of Wiener in print.

17. de Latil, *Thinking by Machine*, pp. 314–22.

18. Ranulph Glanville, "A (Cybernetic) Musing: The State of Cybernetics," *Cybernetics & Human Knowing* 7, no. 2–3 (2000): 151–59.

19. Jef Raskin, *The Humane Interface: New Directions for Designing Interactive Systems* (Boston: Addison-Wesley, 2000), pp. 1–2.

20. Claude E. Shannon, "A Mathematical Theory of Communication," *Bell System Technical Journal* 27 (July and October, 1948): 379–423; 623–56.

21. Siegelman and Conway, *Dark Hero of the Information Age*, p. 152.

22. Gerhard Lakemeyer and Bernhard Nebel, eds., *Exploring Artificial Intelligence in the New Millennium* (San Francisco: Morgan Kaufmann, 2003). The editors point out the distribution of techniques in the preface, p. vii.

23. See, e.g., Cynthia Breazeal, *Designing Sociable Robots* (Cambridge, MA: MIT Press, 2002).

24. Siegelman and Conway, *Dark Hero of the Information Age*, p. 193.

CHAPTER 4. SYMBOLIC AI: THE GOLDEN AGE

1. This is the opening of the proposal for the famous Dartmouth conference, in which McCarthy first introduced the term *artificial intelligence*. The co-organizers were McCarthy, Marvin Minsky, Nathaniel Rochester, and Claude Shannon. See "A Proposal for the Dartmouth Research Project on Artificial Intelligence," August 31, 1955, http://www-formal.stanford.edu/jmc/history/dartmouth/dartmouth.html (accessed March 14, 2007).

2. Alan Turing, "On Computable Numbers, with an Application to the Entscheidungsproblem," *Proceedings of the London Mathematical Society* 2, no. 42 (1936): 230–65.

3. B. Jack Copeland, ed., *The Essential Turing* (Oxford: Clarendon, 2004), pp. 353–54.

4. Ibid., pp. 395–432.

5. Once again: competent people; stupid rules. Turing was prosecuted and given chemical "treatment" for homosexuality, then he committed suicide.

6. Ibid., pp. 433–64.

7.

> Judge: Multiply 8,973,982,736,591,234,876 by 273,729,843, 509,238,476,523.
>
> Computer (instantly): 2,456,446,890,141,726,374,909,027,322, 449,504,816,148.

The judge can then take her time working out whether the response is right; she need only note how long it took the contestant to answer.

8. From http://packages.debian.org/testing/perl/libchatbot-eliza-perl.

9. Recently, Dartmouth held a fiftieth anniversary conference to honor the original. Five of the original participants were able to attend: John McCarthy, Marvin Minsky, Ray Solomonoff, Oliver Selfridge, and Trenchard More.

10. John McCarthy, "Recursive Functions of Symbolic Expressions and Their Computation by Machine," part 1, *Communications of the ACM* (April 1960).

11. John McCarthy et al., *Lisp 1.5 Programmer's Manual* (Cambridge, MA: MIT Press, 1962), p. 13.

12. Ray J. Solomonoff, "The Discovery of Algorithmic Probability," *Journal of Computer and System Sciences* 55, no. 1 (1997).

13. This concept was later rediscovered by the Russian mathematician Kolmogorov and is commonly called *Kolmogorov complexity* today. But Ray Solomonoff did it first, with an inspiration from John McCarthy.

14. Latter-day researchers taking this approach include Marcus Hutter, *Universal Artificial Intelligence* (Berlin: Springer, 2005), and Eric Baum, *What Is Thought?* (Cambridge, MA: MIT Press, 2004).

15. Edward Feigenbaum and Julian Feldman, eds., *Computers and Thought* (New York: McGraw-Hill, 1963).

16. As told by Marvin Minsky.

17. Oliver G. Selfridge and Ulric Neisser, "Pattern Recognition by Machine," in *Computers and Thought*, ed. Edward Feigenbaum and Julian Feldman, 245 (New York: McGraw-Hill, 1963).

18. Marvin Minsky, "Steps toward Artificial Intelligence," in *Computers and Thought*, ed. Edward Feigenbaum and Julian Feldman, 419 (New York: McGraw-Hill, 1963). In all fairness I should point out that many AI researchers *have* read Minsky's paper and have done substantial work based on it; instead of a few pages, the theory on Bayesian networks now fills bookcases. And what's more, it works.

19. Marvin Minsky, ed., *Semantic Information Processing* (Cambridge, MA: MIT Press, 1968).

20. Ibid., pp. 227–70.

21. This example is taken from the philosopher Daniel Dennett.

22. Marvin Minsky, "A Framework for Representing Knowledge," *MIT-AI Lab Memo* 306 (June 1974).

23. This is not quite the same as GOFAI (Good Old-Fashioned AI), which refers to any programs using those techniques whenever they may be written.

24. Terry Winograd, *Understanding Natural Language* (New York: Academic Press, 1972), p. 10.

25. The best summary of Lenat's work I've seen is in Ken Haase's doctoral thesis, where he attempts to analyze and extend the work. The discussion here follows Ken Haase, "Invention and Exploration in Discovery" (PhD thesis, MIT [adviser, Marvin Minsky], 1990).

26. K. Eric Drexler, *Engines of Creation* (New York: Anchor, 1987), pp. 73–74.

27. Douglas Lenat and John Seely Brown, "Why AM and Eurisko Appear to Work." *Artificial Intelligence* 23, no. 3 (August 1984): 269–94.

CHAPTER 5. DIASPORA

1. Hans Moravec, *Mind Children* (Cambridge, MA: Harvard University Press, 1988), p. 9.

2. Matthew Stone and Haym Hirsch, "Artificial Intelligence: The Next Twenty-five Years," *AI Magazine* 2, no. 4 (Winter 2005): 85–97.

3. Congress introduced the Mansfield Amendment in 1969 and it was incorporated into the Defense Procurement Authorization Act of 1970. The Mansfield Amendment required that the DoD only support basic research with "a direct and apparent relationship to a specific military function or operation." (Some Web sources, including Wikipedia, cite "Mansfield Amendment of 1973.") See Richard J. Barber Associates, *The Advanced Research Projects Agency: 1958–1974* (Washington, DC: Barber Associates, 1975), sec. 8-19-20.

4. See http://www.en.wikipedia.org/wiki/Vannevar_Bush. It's not clear whether he was speaking of a human-equivalent machine or merely one that could do engineering calculations, however. An interesting sidelight and possible reason for the misestimate is that engineers of the day, who were used to analog design, didn't understand the power of sequential operation and tended to design computers (e.g., the ENIAC) as if all the components were slow and special purpose.

5. Especially if you count the graphics card.

6. It would be rated at 100 teraflops, i.e., floating-point multiplications per second; but the BLUE GENEs use less aggressive technology than PCs for reasons of reliability and power consumption.

7. See "Fastest Supercomputer to Be Built," BBC News, September 7, 2006, http://news.bbc.co.uk/2/hi/technology/5322704.stm (accessed March 14, 2007).

8. Historically, the gain per decade has been about 2, but the rate of increase is itself increasing, and there is an additional gain in performance due to improvement in software, so 2.5 is a good estimate. See Ray Kurzweil, *The Singularity Is Near* (New York: Viking, 2005), pp. 56–57.

9. Marvin Minsky, private communication with author, 2006. He allows that vision and so forth will take a fair amount of processing, but he thinks that the higher functions can be done in a much more efficient way.

10. Hans Moravec, *Robot: Mere Machine to Transcendent Mind* (New York: Oxford University Press, 1999), pp. 68–69.

11. Of which I was the principal developer and maintainer by that time.

12. For the technically inclined, an example: to the original functional abstraction of the lambda calculus (which allows LISP to call itself a functional programming language), COMMON LISP (and some of its predecessors) added a "macro" capability, a different implementation of the same basic idea but with semantics substantially different in detail. Functions defined as macros could not be used with the standard function-manipulating functions.

On a personal note, Charles Hedrick wrote the interpreter and runtime system for COMMON LISP for the DECSYSTEM-20, the high-end machine used for AI at the time; I wrote the compiler. After that, I quit AI and LISP and worked on associative memory architectures (where I could design my own elegant programming languages).

13. The programming language SCHEME forms both a confirmation and an exception. Originally a small, clean, experimental variant of LISP, SCHEME has continued to develop and is now the most widely used version of the language. It is incompatible with COMMON LISP.

14. Robert Roy Britt, "Pluto Down but Maybe Not Out," *Space.com*, August 31, 2006, http://www.space.com/scienceastronomy/060831_planet_definition.html (accessed March 14, 2007).

15. Petition Protesting the IAU Planet Definition, press release, August 31, 2006, http://www.ipetitions.com/petition/planetprotest (accessed March 14, 2007).

16. Terry Winograd and Fernando Flores, *Understanding Computers and Cognition: A New Foundation for Design* (Boston: Addison-Wesley, 1986).

17. Ludwig Wittgenstein, *Philosophical Investigations*, 3rd. ed., trans. G. E. M. Anscombe (Malden, MA: Blackwell, 2003).

18. See, e.g., G. Berry, *The Foundations of Esterel* (Cambridge, MA: MIT Press, 1998); Liwen Huang and Paul Hudak, *Dance: A Declarative Language for the Control of Humanoid Robots* (research report, YALEU/DCS/RR-1253, Yale University, 2003); Kimberley Burchett, Gregory H. Cooper, and Shriram Krishnamurthi, *Lowering: A Static Optimization Technique for*

Transparent Functional Reactivity, ACM SIGPLAN 2007 Workshop on Partial Evaluation and Program Manipulation, January 15–16, 2007, held in Nice, France.

CHAPTER 6. THE NEW SYNTHESIS

1. Margaret Mead, *Coming of Age in Samoa* (New York: Harper, 2001). Originally published in 1928. *Coming of Age in Samoa* was listed as the worst book of the twentieth century by the Intercollegiate Studies Institute in 2003. See "The Fifty Worst (and Best) Books of the Century," *Intercollegiate Review*, Fall 1999, http://www.mmisi.org/ir/35_01/50worst.pdf (accessed March 14, 2007).

2. Derek Freeman, *Margaret Mead and Samoa: The Making and Unmaking of an Anthropological Myth* (Cambridge, MA: Harvard University Press, 1983). It should be pointed out that the anthropological community reacted exactly as it would be predicted to have upon being told that its emperor had no clothes—by attacking Freeman. However, the doctrine of extreme cultural relativism continues to crumble and can be more or less classified with phlogiston today. Science advances, funeral by funeral.

3. E. O. Wilson, *Sociobiology: The New Synthesis* (Cambridge, MA: Harvard University Press, 1975).

4. See Richard Dawkins, *A Devil's Chaplain: Reflections on Hope, Lies, Science, and Love* (New York: Houghton Mifflin, 2003), chap. 1.

5. Hilary Putnam, "Minds and Machines" in *Dimensions of Mind*, ed. Sidney Hook (New York: New York University Press, 1960), pp. 148–80.

6. Jerry Fodor, *Modularity of Mind* (Cambridge, MA: MIT Press, 1983).

7. Much of this list is from Steven Pinker, *The Language Instinct* (New York: Harper, 1995), p. 420.

8. Helen E. Fisher, *Why We Love: The Nature and Chemistry of Romantic Love* (New York: Henry Holt, 2004).

9. K. E. Jordan and E. M. Brannon, "The Multisensory Representation of Number in Infancy," *Proceedings of the National Academy of Sciences*, February 21, 2006, http://www.pnas.org/cgi/content/abstract/0508107103v1 (accessed March 14, 2007).

10. I'm indebted to Robert Kowalski for the idea of using this story to

illustrate mental modules, although I disagree with his explanation and proffer a completely different one! See Robert Kowalski, "Logic and Modules," April 2005, http://www.doc.ic.ac.uk/~rak/papers/Modularity.pdf (accessed March 14, 2007).

11. Gottfried Leibniz, *The Monadology*, trans. Robert Latta (1898), online at http://philosophy.eserver.org/leibniz-monadology.txt.

CHAPTER 7. BEYOND HUMAN KEN?

1. Much of this chapter is adapted from a talk by the author at *AI@50: The Dartmouth Artificial Intelligence Conference: The Next Fifty Years*, a special meeting in honor of the fiftieth anniversary of the seminal 1956 Dartmouth Summer Research Project.

2. To be precise, it would have been able to if it had been connected to a big enough disk or other outboard memory to handle the data.

3. There is a similar informal concept often referred to as *AI-completeness* (see http://en.wikipedia.org/wiki/AI-complete). However, it is always assumed that humans are AI-complete, which we do not assume for universality, so we will avoid that usage here.

4. It is also a logical possibility that while not universal ourselves, we are still capable of creating an AI that is.

5. John McCarthy et al., "A Proposal for the Dartmouth Research Project on Artificial Intelligence," August 31, 1955, http://www-formal.stanford.edu/jmc/history/dartmouth/dartmouth.html.

6. *Handbook of Artificial Intelligence*, ed. Avron Barr and Edward Feigenbaum, vol. 2 (Los Altos: Kaufman, 1982), pp. 295–379.

7. Lou Steinberg, in private communication, analyzes the problem as being that any specification of the task that is usefully simpler than the program itself requires arbitrary real-world knowledge to interpret.

8. Eric Baum, *What Is Thought?* (Cambridge, MA: MIT Press, 2004), p. 316. For example, he espouses the view that inductive bias limits the possibility of a general learning mechanism.

9. R. J. Solomonoff, "Complexity-based Induction Systems: Comparisons and Convergence Theorems," *IEEE Transactions on Information Theory* IT-24, no. 4 (July 1978): 422–32.

10. If it were computable, we could disprove its completeness by a construction reminiscent of the ones used in Godel's theorem and the halting problem. The construction essentially forces the machine to try to outwit itself.

11. John McCarthy, "Programs with Common Sense," in *Semantic Information Processing*, ed. Marvin Minsky, 404 (Cambridge, MA: MIT Press, 1968).

12. See "IQ Scores: IQ Score Interpretation," at http://www.audiblox.com/iq_scores.htm. While it is tempting to believe that scientists and engineers form the brightest 1 percent of the population, we can make the slightly less dubious assumption that scientists and engineers below the ninety-ninth percentile and the others above it cancel out. See R. Keith Wilkinson, "How Big Is the US S&E Workforce?" *NSF Science Resources Statistics Infobrief*, July 2002, http://www.nsf.gov/statistics/infbrief/nsf02325/ (accessed March 14, 2007).

13. Alfred Wegener, an early twentieth-century German meteorologist, proposed that continents move around the globe on geological timescales. He was dismissed by mainstream geology for several decades, but now plate tectonics, a theory that includes continental drift, forms the core of geological understanding.

CHAPTER 8. AUTOGENY

1. Not with today's technology, anyhow. But note that once you have the self-replicating part down, the trillions part is fairly straightforward.

2. J. Storrs Hall, "Architectural Considerations for Self-Replicating Manufacturing Systems," *Nanotechnology* 10, no. 3 (1999): 323–30.

3. Alan M. Turing, "Computing Machinery and Intelligence," *Mind* 59 (1950): 433–60.

4. Patti Maes and Rodney A. Brooks, "Learning to Coordinate Behaviors," in *Proc. Eighth National Coference on Artificial Intelligence*, 796–802 (Boston, MA: 1990). See also Brooks, *Cambrian Intelligence* (Cambridge, MA: MIT Press, 1999), pp. 27–36, 181.

5. Tom Mitchell, *Machine Learning* (Boston: McGraw-Hill, 1997), pp. 307–31.

6. Indeed there is a standing 50,000-Euro prize offered by Marcus Hutter for compressing human knowledge. See http://prize.hutter1.net.

7. Gary Marcus, *The Birth of the Mind: How a Tiny Number of Genes Creates the Complexities of Human Thought* (New York: Basic Books, 2004).

8. See D. B. Lenat and R. Guha, *Building Large Knowledge Bases* (Reading, MA: Addison-Wesley, 1990), and the Cycorp database, online at http://www.cyc.com.

9. "Robot Carries Out Operation by Itself," UPI, May 18, 2006, http://www.upi.com/NewsTrack/Science/20060518-041254-1723r (accessed March 12, 2006).

CHAPTER 9. REPRESENTATION AND SEARCH

1. S. Amarel, "On Representations of Problems of Reasoning about Actions, in *Machine Intelligence* 3, ed. Donald Michie (Amsterdam: Elsevier/North-Holland, 1968), pp. 131–71.

2. See "Deep Blue Technology," online at http://www.research.ibm.com/know/blue.html. Deep Blue won the match, 3.5 games to 2.5.

3. In practice, chess (and Go) programs prune the tree substantially and look only at a small fractions of the possible positions.

4. A. Newell, H. A. Simon, and J. C. Shaw, "Chess-Playing Programs," in *Computers and Thought*, ed. Edward Feigenbaum and Julian Feldman, 39–70 (New York: McGraw-Hill, 1963).

5. L. A. Levin, "Universal Sequential Search Problems," *Problems of Information Transmission* 9, no. 3 (1973): 265–66.

6. "Deep Blue Technology," http://www.research.ibm.com/know/blue.html.

CHAPTER 10. FUN AND GAMES

1. Update: the league tournaments were won, respectively, by teams from the United States, Germany, Australia, Japan, China, and Portugal.

2. See Martin Shubik, "The Dollar Auction Game: A Paradox in Noncooperative Behavior and Escalation," *Journal of Conflict Resolution* 15 (1971): 109–11.

3. The game was formalized into game-theory form by Merril Flood and Melvin Drescher and cast as a story about prisoners by Albert Tucker. See Matt Ridley, *The Origins of Virtue* (London: Penguin, 1996), p. 55; or William Poundstone, *Prisoner's Dilemma* (New York: Anchor, 1992), pp. 101–24.

4. As given by Douglas Hofstadter in *Metamagical Themas* (New York: Basic Books, 1985), p. 715.

5. Robert Nozick, "Newcomb's Problem and Two Principles of Choice," in *Essays in Honor of Carl G. Hempel*, ed. Nicholas Rescher, 115 (Dordrecht: D. Reidel/Synthese Library 1969).

6. Hofstadter, *Metamagical Themas*, pp. 739–55.

7. There actually was one program in Axelrod's original tournament that attempted to model the opponent as a Markov process using Bayesian inference. It apparently did not, however, attempt to decide whether the opponent was a cahooter.

8. Ken Binmore, review of *The Complexity of Cooperation* by Robert Axelrod, *Journal of Artificial Societies and Social Simulation* 1, no. 1 (1998).

9. Jose Manuel Galan and Luis R. Izquierdo, "Appearances Can Be Deceiving: Lessons Learned Re-implementing Axelrod's 'Evolutionary Approach to Norms'," *Journal of Artificial Societies and Social Simulation* 8, no. 3 (2005).

10. Karl Sigmund, *Complex Adaptive Systems and the Evolution of Reciprocation*, International Institute for Applied Systems Analysis Interim Report IR-98-100, online at http://www.iiasa.ac.at/Admin/PUB/Documents/IR-98-100.pdf (accessed March 12, 2007).

CHAPTER 11. DESIGN AND LEARNING

1. The Aquarius project, under Al Despain, at Berkeley and then at University of Southern California/Information Sciences Institute.

2. Lou Steinberg, Brian Davidson, and I developed utility-based algorithms of this kind in the 1990s and hold a patent on them; however, the

canonical reference is Stuart Russell and Eric Wefald, *Do the Right Thing* (Cambridge, MA: MIT Press, 1991).

3. Alan M. Turing, "Computing Machinery and Intelligence," *Mind* 59 (1950): 431.

4. Tom Simonite, "Nuclear Reactors 'Evolve' inside Supercomputers,'" *NewScientistTech*, June 9, 2006, http://www.newscientisttech.com/article.ns?id=dn9302&feedId=online-news_rss20 (accessed March 12, 2007); Will Knight, "Robotic Modeling Reveals Ancient Hominid Stride, *NewScientist.com*, July 21, 2005, http://www.newscientist.com/article.ns?id=dn7704 (accessed March 12, 2007).

5. "Thirty-six Human-competitive Results Produced by Genetic Programming," online at http://www.genetic-programming.com/humancompetitive.html. See also John R. Koza, Martin A. Keane, and Matthew J. Streeter, "Evolving Inventions," *Scientific American*, February 6, 2003; Martin Pelikan, David E. Goldberg, and Erick Cantu-Paz, "BOA: The Bayesian Optimization Algorithm," *Proceedings of the Genetic and Evolutionary Computation Conference* GECCO-99.

7. John Cassidy, "The Hayek Century," *Hoover Digest* 3 (2000), http://www.hoover.org/publications/digest/3492456.html (accessed March 14, 2007).

8. Eric Baum, *What Is Thought?* (Cambridge, MA: MIT Press, 2004), p. 246.

9. Ibid., pp. 250–69.

10. I. Kwee, M. Hutter, and J. Schmidhuber, "Market-based Reinforcement Learning in Partially Observable Worlds" in *Proceedings of International Conference on Artificial Neural Networks ICANN'01 Vienna LNCS 2130*, ed. G. Dorffner, H. Bischof, and K. Hornik, 865–73 (Berlin: Springer, 2001).

11. J. Storrs Hall, Lou Steinberg, and Brian Davison, "Combining Agoric and Genetic Methods in Stochastic Design" *Nanotechnology* 9 (1998): 274–84, online at http://autogeny.org/chsmith.html. Please note that while we consider this a promising direction, it is still considered somewhat outside AI's mainstream. It is picking up some steam, though: see Baum and Ross in the bibliography.

CHAPTER 12. ANALOGY AND PERCEPTION

1. Roger Knowles and David Touretzky, in separate personal communications with author.

2. Patrick Henry Winston, *Artificial Intelligence* (Reading, MA: Addison-Wesley, 1992), pp. 22–24.

3. Ibid., pp. 271–353.

4. Robert M. French, "When Coffee Cups Are Like Old Elephants or Why Representation Modules Don't Make Sense," *Proceedings of the 1997 International Conference on New Trends in Cognitive Science*, ed. A. Riegler and M. Peschl (Vienna: Austrian Society for Cognitive Science, 1997), pp. 158–63.

5. Douglas Hofstadter, "Analogy as the Core of Cognition," in *Analogical Mind: Perspectives from Cognitive Science*, ed. Dedre Gentner, Keith J. Holyoak, and Boicho Kokinov, 499–538 (Cambridge, MA: MIT Press/Bradford, 2001).

6. My doctoral dissertation was such a design: J. Storrs Hall, "Associative Processing: Architectures, Algorithms, Applications" (PhD diss., Rutgers University, 1994).

7. Depending on how much processing power there is for each memory element, it's called a content-addressable memory, an associative processor, or a massively parallel processor.

CHAPTER 13. DESIGN FOR A BRAIN

1. Hans Moravec, *Robot: Mere Machine to Transcendent Mind* (New York: Oxford University Press, 1999), pp. 32–40.

2. A holographic representation is one where the recorded data doesn't fall into a simple one-to-one relationship with the object(s) represented. It doesn't mean (necessarily) optical holograms.

3. Valentino Braitenberg, *Vehicles, Experiments in Synthetic Psychology* (Cambridge, MA: MIT Press, 1984).

4. James Baldwin, "A New Factor in Evolution," *American Naturalist* 30, no. 354 (June 1896): 441–51. The Baldwin effect has been tried in GAs before, indeed so much that one could almost say there is a subfield of "Baldwin GAs." It is not clear for sequential implementations how much

efficiency it lends, because learning in the individuals is computationally costly. However, in an implementation like the brain where the population is developed in parallel, it may produce a more significant enhancement.

CHAPTER 14. AN ECONOMY OF MIND

1. J. Albus and M. Meystel, *Engineering of Mind* (New York: Wiley, 2001), pp. 123–59.

2. M. L. Minsky, "Theory of Neural-analog Reinforcement Systems and Its Application to the Brain Model Problem," (PhD diss., Princeton University, 1953), secs. 6–7. Note that the thesis is usually cited as 1954 in the literature, but Minsky himself cites it as December 1953, in his forthcoming *The Emotion Machine* (secs. 5–9).

3. Snake eyes come up, on the average, one time in thirty-six, so in the long run you'd make $108 or $72, respectively, for each $100 you had to pay out.

4. Robin Hanson, "Could Gambling Save Science? Encouraging an Honest Consensus," *Social Epistemology* 9, no. 1 (1995): 3–33.

5. Allen Newell, *Unified Theories of Cognition* (Cambridge MA: Harvard University Press, 1990), pp. 185–92.

6. Pentti Kanerva, *Sparse Distributed Memory* (Cambridge, MA: MIT Press, 1988). See also Jeff Hawkins, *On Intelligence* (New York: Times Books, 2004).

CHAPTER 15. KINDS OF MINDS

1. The demise of Moore's law has been predicted so often since the 1970s that I feel confident in asserting that the burden of proof lies completely on the critics.

2. The basis for calculation is K. Eric Drexler, *Nanosystems: Molecular Machinery, Manufacturing, and Computation* (New York: Wiley, 1992). Robert Freitas and I worked out the figures in private communication. See also J. Storrs Hall, *Nanofuture: What's Next for Nanotechnology* (Amherst, NY: Prometheus Books, 2005).

3. Arthur C. Clarke, *Profiles of the Future: An Inquiry into the Limits of the Possible* (New York: Harper and Row, 1972), pp. 1–10.

CHAPTER 16. WHEN

1. See Ray Kurzweil, *The Singularity Is Near* (New York: Viking, 2005), pp. 56–72. A 2.5 power rating gain per decade is equivalent to an increase of 77 percent per year, or a doubling time of 1.2 years, or a factor of a thousandfold increase in 12 years.

2. Hans Moravec gives much later dates, but he is assuming a lower gain from Moore's law (1.5 per decade), mobile robots instead of fixed machines, and the slow software road to AI.

3. Richard Wray, "Google Users Promised Artificial Intelligence," *Guardian* (UK), May 23, 2006, http://technology.guardian.co.uk/news/story/0,,1781121,00.html (accessed March 12, 2007).

4. Hans Moravec, *Robot: Mere Machine to Transcendent Mind* (New York: Oxford University Press, 1999), pp. 95–109.

5. Just to keep our feet on the ground, I have several friends, professors of computer science, who don't think AI will get here at all in the twenty-first century.

CHAPTER 17. PHILOSOPHICAL EXTRAPOLATIONS

1. This list is adapted from my paper "Nano-enabled AI: Some Philosophical Issues," in *International Journal of Applied Philosophy* (special issue on nanoethics), October 2006.

2. Drew McDermott, *Mind and Mechanism* (Cambridge, MA: MIT Press, 2001), pp. 96–100.

3. It started with David Hume and is most strongly associated with G. E. Moore. In its full form, it is a bit more complex than I am making it out to be here.

4. John Searle, "Minds, Brains, and Programs," *Behavioral and Brain Sciences* 3 (1980): 417–24.

5. This argument is also from McDermott, *Mind and Mechanism*, pp. 112–18.

6. If we ignore such things as error correction and spares against oxidation or radiation damage.

7. Benjamin Libet, *Mind Time: The Temporal Factor in Consciousness* (Cambridge, MA: Harvard University Press, 2004), chaps. 2 and 3.

8. Daniel Wegner, *Illusion of Conscious Will* (Cambridge, MA: MIT Press, 2002), pp. 181–84.

9. See Robert Tow, Affect-based Robot Communication Methods and Systems, US Patent 5,832,189, November 1998. Tow notes that the major prior art cited was Charles Darwin's *The Expression of the Emotions in Man and Animals*! See also Cynthia Breazeal, *Designing Sociable Robots* (Cambridge, MA: MIT Press, 2002).

CHAPTER 18. EVOLUTIONARY ETHICS

1. Leonard Katz ed., *Evolutionary Origins of Morality* (Bowling Green, OH: Imprint Academic, 2000), p. 218.

2. Charles Murray, *In Pursuit: Of Happiness and Good Government* (New York: Simon and Schuster, 1989).

3. William Poundstone, *Prisoner's Dilemma* (New York: Random House/Anchor, 1993), p. 123.

4. Andrew G. Haley, "Space Law and Metalaw: A Synoptic View" in *Proceedings of the Seventh International Astronautical Congress* (Rome: Associzione Italiana Razzi, 1956); Ernst Fasan, *Relations with Alien Intelligences* (Berlin: Berlin Verlag, 1970).

5. Robert Freitas, "The Legal Rights of Extraterrestrials," *Analog* 97, no. 4 (April 1977): 54–67. Available online at http://www.rfreitas.com/Astro/LegalRightsOfETs.htm

6. John Stuart Mill, *Utilitarianism* (1863), chap. 2, available online at http://www.utilitarianism.com/mill2.htm.

7. John Rawls, *A Theory of Justice*, rev. ed. (Cambridge, MA: Belknap Press/Harvard, 1999).

8. Ibid., pp. 133–39.

9. Adam Smith, *Theory of Moral Sentiments* (Edinburgh, 1759), available online at http://www.adamsmith.org/smith/tms-intro.htm.

10. For a proposal of a legal system composed entirely of private contracts, see David D. Friedman, *The Machinery of Freedom* (La Salle, IL: Open Court, 1989), chap. 29.

11. Hans Moravec, *Robot: Mere Machine to Transcendent Mind* (New York: Oxford University Press, 1999), p. 146.

CHAPTER 19. ASIMOV'S THREE LAWS OF ROBOTICS

1. Shimon Y. Nof, ed., *Handbook of Industrial Robotics* (New York: Wiley, 1985).

2. Isaac Asimov, *The Naked Sun* (Garden City, NY: Doubleday, 1957), p. 135.

3. Nick Bostrom, "Ethical Issues in Advanced Artificial Intelligence" in *Cognitive, Emotive, and Ethical Aspects of Decision Making in Humans and in AI*, ed. Iva Smit, Wendell Wallach, and George E. Lasker, vol. 2, 12–17 (Windsor, ON: International Institute of Advanced Studies in Systems Research and Cybernetics, 2003).

4. Both stories are in Isaac Asimov, *I, Robot* (Garden City, NY: Doubleday, 1950).

5. Jack Williamson, "With Folded Hands," *Astounding*, July 1947.

6. For example, see Alex Knapp "More On Robot Rights," *Heretical Ideas*, October 29, 2003, http://hereticalideas.com/index.php?p=1318; Gordon Whorley, "Robot Oppression: Unethicality of the Three Laws," 3 Laws Unsafe, 2004, http://www.asimovlaws.com/articles/archives/2004/07/robot_oppressio_1.html.

7. Robert A. Freitas Jr., "The Legal Rights of Robots," *Student Lawyer* 13 (January 1985): 54–56. Also available at http://www.rfreitas.com/Astro/LegalRightsOfRobots.htm.

8. There are psychopaths among the corporations even in the money-as-emotion sense: the Enrons that cook the books. But this is widely understood to make a corporation untrustworthy, and it is punished when discovered.

9. "The Plot to Hijack Your Computer," *BusinessWeek Online*, July 17, 2006, http://www.businessweek.com/magazine/content/06_29/b3993001.htm (accessed March 12, 2007).

CHAPTER 20. THE AGE OF VIRTUOUS MACHINES

1. Vernor Vinge, in the keynote talk at the *VISION-21 Symposium* sponsored by NASA Lewis Research Center and the Ohio Aerospace Institute, March 30-31, 1993.

2. Ray Kurzweil, *The Singularity Is Near* (New York: Viking, 2005).

3. The Singularity Institute for Artificial Intelligence, online at http://www.singinst.org.

4. Distributed Denial of Service, where a Web site is flooded with illegitimate traffic to overload it and prevent legitimate use. DDoS is often the threat behind cyber-extortion; it has been used, for example, to shut down anti-spam companies such as BlueSecurity.

5. Robert Axelrod, *The Evolution of Cooperation* (New York: Basic Books, 1984).

6. Steven Pinker, *How the Mind Works*. (New York: Norton, 1997), pp. 15–16; Eliezer Yudkowsky, *Creating Friendly AI*, http://www.singinst.org/ourresearch/publications/CFAI.html (accessed March 12, 2007); Jeff Hawkins, *On Intelligence* (New York: Times Books, 2004), p. 216.

7. H. C. Quay, ed., *Handbook of Juvenile Delinquency* (New York: Wiley, 1987), pp. 106–17. In one major national study, among white (only) males aged 15–23, the average IQ of those never arrested was 106, and the average IQ of those ever sentenced to a correctional facility was 93—a difference of almost a full standard deviation.

8. *Where Is the Wealth of Nations? Measuring Capital for the 21st Century* (Washington, DC: World Bank, 2006), p. 4.

9. Jerome Kagan, *The Nature of the Child* (New York: Basic Books, 1984), p. 76.

10. Matt Ridley, *The Origins of Virtue* (New York: Penguin, 1996), p. 142.

11. Elli Leadbeater, "Seeing the Teenager in the Brain," *BBC Online*, September 8, 2006, http://news.bbc.co.uk/2/hi/science/nature/5327550.stm (accessed March 12, 2007).

12. E. Cashdan and R. Trivers, "Self-Deception" in *Encyclopedia of Evolution*, ed. M. Pagel (New York: Oxford University Press, 2002).

13. Debora MacKenzie, "'Big Brother' Eyes Make Us Act More Honestly," *NewScientist.com*, June 28, 2006, http://www.newscientist.com/article/dn9424-big-brother-eyes-make-us-act-more-honestly.html.

14. Those in the United States, for example, might judge the ability of a government to create (as opposed to having been formed by) a stable, peaceful society by the results of its recent attempts to do so.

15. "Isaac Asimov," http://en.wikiquote.org/wiki/Isaac_Asimov.

CHAPTER 21. PROFILES OF THE FUTURE

1. Ray Kurzweil, *The Singularity Is Near* (New York: Viking, 2005).

2. Like any idea of consequence and substance, it has roots that go back, in this case, to people such as von Neumann and his complexity barrier. A good overview of its history can be found in Kurzweil, *The Singularity Is Near*, pp. 21–33.

3. Robin Hanson, "Reality and Fantasy in Economic Revolutions," review of Richard Florida's *The Rise of the Creative Class*, June 6, 2006, http://www.cato-unbound.org/2006/06/06/robin-hanson/reality-and-fantasy-in-economic-revolutions (accessed March 12, 2007).

4. There are many different concepts of what the Singularity might be like; I'll use Intellectual Revolution to distinguish this one.

5. Robin Hanson, "Long-term Growth as a Sequence of Exponential Modes," http://hanson.gmu.edu/longgrow.pdf. Note that Kurzweil in *The Singularity Is Near* has a similar time series, from a number of phenomena, that gives similar results.

6. Robin Hanson, "The Next Really Big Enormous Thing," 2004, http://www.futurebrief.com/RobinHanson.pdf (accessed March 12, 2007).

7. I am cheating because you would not believe the real numbers. When the Intellectual Revolution growth mode kicks in fully, annual economic growth could be over a billion percent. I flatly refuse to think about what the next growth mode after that would be like.

8. Charles Murray, *Losing Ground* (New York: Basic Books, 1985).

9. Charles Murray, *In Our Hands: A Plan to Replace the Welfare State* (Washington, DC: AEI Press, 2006).

10. Not that it proves anything, but in the three top modern Frankenstein stories in the "AI runs amok" vein that I can think of—*Colossus: The Forbin Project*, *2001*, and *Terminator*—the AIs were government projects.

Bibliography

Albus, James, and Alexander Meystel. *Engineering of Mind: An Introduction to the Science of Intelligent Systems.* New York: Wiley, 2001. Albus, of the National Institute of Standards and Technology, is one of the United States' leading roboticists. This book is a compendium of robotics systems engineering and includes an architecture based on hierarchical feedback loops.

Aleksander, Igor. *How to Build a Mind: Toward Machines with Imagination.* New York: Columbia University Press, 2001.

Alexander, Richard. *The Biology of Moral Systems.* Hawthorne, NY: Aldine De Gruyter, 1987.

Allen, Colin, Gary Varner, and Jason Zinser. "Prolegomena to Any Future Artificial Moral Agent." *Journal of Experimental and Theoretical Artificial Intelligence* 12 (2000): 251–56.

Allen, James. *Natural Language Understanding.* Menlo Park, CA: Benjamin-Cummings, 1987. A classic in the field (but see Winograd).

Anderson, Michael, and Susan Anderson, eds. *Machine Ethics: Special Issue of IEEE Intelligent Systems.* Piscataway: IEEE Press, August 2006. The beginnings of a new subfield of AI.

Arbib, Michael A. *The Metaphorical Brain: An Introduction to Cybernetics as Artificial Intelligence and Brain Theory.* New York: Wiley-Interscience, 1972. An exploratory, somewhat philosophical investigation.

Ashby, W. Ross. *An Introduction to Cybernetics.* New York: Wiley, 1963.

Asimov, Isaac. *I, Robot.* Garden City, NY: Doubleday, 1950. Asimov was perhaps the prime example of a practicing scientist turned science writer, but he is most remembered today for his science fiction about robots and his Three Laws of Robotics.

———. *The Naked Sun.* Garden City, NY: Doubleday, 1957.

Aunger, Robert. *Darwinizing Culture: The Status of Memetics as a Science.*

New York: Oxford University Press, 2000. We are what we think, and we think what we hear.

Axelrod, Robert. *The Evolution of Cooperation.* New York: Basic Books, 1984. A classic study of how evolution can produce cooperation in spite of the Prisoner's Dilemma.

Babiak, Paul, and Robert Hare. *Snakes in Suits: When Psychopaths Go to Work.* New York: HarperCollins, 2006.

Balkin, J. M. *Cultural Software: a Theory of Ideology.* New Haven, CT: Yale University Press, 1998.

Barr, Avron, and Edward Feigenbaum, eds. *Handbook of Artificial Intelligence.* 3 vols. Palo Alto, CA: Kaufmann, 1981. An overview of a broad selection of AI systems from the 1970s.

Baum, Eric. *What Is Thought?* Cambridge, MA: MIT Press, 2004. A fellow researcher who believes economic principles have a part to play in explaining how the mind works (or could work).

Blackmore, Susan. *The Meme Machine.* New York: Oxford University Press, 1999. Probably the best book-length explanation of the ideas of memetics.

Bloom, Howard. *The Lucifer Principle.* New York: Atlantic Monthly Press, 1995. An examination of the dynamics of rising and falling human societies. Bloom began to look prescient after September 11, 2001.

Bostrom, Nick. "Ethical Issues in Advanced Artificial Intelligence." *Cognitive, Emotive, and Ethical Aspects of Decision Making in Humans and in Artificial Intelligence.* Vol. 2. Edited by Iva Smit, Wendell Wallach, and George E. Lasker. Windsor, ON: International Institute of Advanced Studies in Systems Research and Cybernetics, 2003.

Bradie, Michael. *The Secret Chain: Evolution and Ethics.* Albany: State University of New York Press, 1994.

Braitenberg, Valentin. *Vehicles, Experiments in Synthetic Psychology.* Cambridge, MA: MIT Press, 1984. This little gem is a marvelously whimsical exploration of possible engineering ideas for intelligent systems that includes lessons from neurophysiology.

Breazeal, Cynthia. *Designing Sociable Robots.* Cambridge, MA: MIT Press, 2002.

Brockman, John, ed. *The Next Fifty Years: Science in the First Half of the Twenty-first Century.* New York: Vintage, 2002. Basic futurism. Brockman is the founder of *Edge*, online at http://www.edge.org.

Bronowski, Jacob. *A Sense of the Future: Essays in Natural Philosophy.* Cambridge, MA: MIT Press, 1977. A much more philosophical futurism.

Brooks, Rodney. *Cambrian Intelligence: The Early History of the New AI.* Cambridge, MA: MIT Press, 1999. Brooks, head of MIT's AI lab, is one of the leading roboticists in the United States, who also (see Albus) favors an architecture based on hierarchical feedback loops.

Calvin, William H. *The Ascent of Mind: Ice Age Climates and the Evolution of Intelligence.* New York: Bantam, 1991. A neuroscientist looks at how we got here.

———. *How Brains Think: Evolving Intelligence, Then and Now.* New York: Basic Books, 1996.

Calvin, William H., and Derek Bickerton. *Lingua Ex Machina.* Cambridge, MA: MIT Press, 2000.

Clark, Andy. *Natural-Born Cyborgs: Minds, Technologies, and the Future of Human Intelligence.* Oxford: Oxford University Press, 2003. Clark is a great example of a practicing scientist who writes for the general reader.

Clark, Andy, and Josefa Toribio, eds. *Cognitive Architectures in Artificial Intelligence.* New York: Garland, 1998. A collection of technical papers on the subject.

Clarke, Arthur C. *Profiles of the Future: An Inquiry into the Limits of the Possible.* New York: Harper and Row, 1972. The definitive work of technological forecasting of the mid-twentieth century.

Copeland, B. Jack, ed. *The Essential Turing*. Oxford: Clarendon, 2004.

Corning, Peter. "Evolution and Ethics . . . An Idea Whose Time Has Come? *Journal of Social and Evolutionary Systems* 19, no. 3 (1996): 277–85. Available online at http://www.complexsystems.org/essays/evoleth1.html.

Darwin, Charles. *On the Origin of Species by Natural Selection, or the Preservation of Favored Races in the Struggle for Life.* London: John Murray, 1859. Available online at http://www.gutenberg.org/etext/1228.

Dawkins, Richard. *The Selfish Gene.* Rev. ed. Oxford: Oxford University Press, 1989.

Deacon, Terrence W. *The Symbolic Species: The Co-evolution of Language and the Brain.* New York: Norton, 1997.

Dennett, Daniel. *Consciousness Explained.* Boston: Little, Brown, 1991.

———. *Darwin's Dangerous Idea.* London: Penguin, 1995.

———. *Freedom Evolves.* New York: Viking, 2003.

Donagan, Alan. *The Theory of Morality.* Chicago: University of Chicago Press, 1977.

Dowling, John E. *Neurons and Networks: An Introduction to Neuroscience.* Cambridge, MA: Belknap Press/Harvard, 1992.

Dunbar, Robin, Chris Knight, and Camilla Power. *The Evolution of Culture.* New Brunswick, NJ: Rutgers University Press, 1999.

Dym, Clive L., and Raymond E. Levitt. *Knowledge-based Systems in Engineering.* New York: McGraw-Hill, 1991. The use of AI techniques in designing machines.

Fasan, Ernst. *Relations with Alien Intelligences.* Berlin: Verlag, 1970.

Fauconnier, Gilles, and Mark Turner. *The Way We Think: Conceptual Blending and the Mind's Hidden Complexities.* New York: Basic Books, 2002.

Feigenbaum, Edward, and Julian Feldman, eds. *Computers and Thought.* New York: McGraw-Hill, 1963. The absolute classic of AI, still in print. If you're looking for *Handbook of Artificial Intelligence*, see Barr.

Fodor, Jerry. *Modularity of Mind.* Cambridge, MA: MIT Press, 1983.

Foerst, Anne. *God in the Machine: What Robots Teach Us about Humanity and God.* New York: Penguin/Dutton, 2004. Foerst is a theologian who was previously a researcher at MIT's AI lab.

Ford, Kenneth, Clark Glymour, and Patrick Hayes. *Android Epistemology.* Cambridge, MA: AAAI/MIT Press, 1995. A collection of essays where robotics meets philosophy.

Franklin, Stan. *Artificial Minds.* Cambridge, MA: MIT Press, 1995.

Freitas, Robert, and Ralph Merkle. *Kinematic Self-Replicating Machines.* Georgetown, TX: Landes Bioscience, 2004. A landmark in the field, second only to von Neumann. The text is available online at http://www.molecularassembler.com/KSRM.htm.

French, Robert M. *The Subtlety of Sameness: A Theory and Computer Model of Analogy-making.* Cambridge, MA: MIT Press, 1995.

Frey, Brendan J. *Graphical Models for Machine Learning and Digital Communication.* Cambridge, MA: MIT Press, 1998.

Friedman, David. *The Machinery of Freedom.* La Salle, IL: Open Court, 1989.

Gelernter, David. *The Muse in the Machine: Computerizing the Poetry of Human Thought.* New York: Free Press, 1994. Gelernter is another practicing scientist who is an excellent, readable expositor.

Gentner, Dedre, Keith Holyoak, and Boicho Kokinov, eds. *The Analogical Mind.* Cambridge, MA: MIT Press, 2001.

Gips, James. "Towards the Ethical Robot." In *Android Epistemology*, edited by Kenneth Ford, Clark Glymour, and Patrick Hayes. Cambridge, MA: AAAI/MIT Press, 1995.

Good, I. J. "The Social Implications of Artificial Intelligence." In *The Scientist Speculates*, edited by I. J. Good. New York: Basic Books, 1962.

Good, I. J., ed. *The Scientist Speculates.* New York: Basic Books, 1962. A classic in its field; it more or less *was* the field until John Brockman came along.

Hall, J. Storrs. *Ethics for Machines.* Published on the WWW 2000, available online at http://autogeny.org/ethics.html. My original essay advocating that AI should take an account of ethics in designing intelligent systems.

———. *Nanofuture: What's Next for Nanotechnology.* Amherst, NY: Prometheus Books, 2005. Includes chapters on AI, robots, and transhumanism.

Hamilton, William. "The Genetical Evolution of Social Behavior I & II," *Journal of Theoretical Biology* 7 (1964): 1–52.

Hamowy, Ronald. *The Scottish Enlightenment and the Theory of Spontaneous Order.* Carbondale: Southern Illinois University Press, 1987.

Haugeland, John, ed. *Mind Design Philosophy, Psychology, Artificial Intelligence.* Cambridge, MA: MIT Press, 1981.

Hauser, Marc. *Moral Minds: How Nature Designed Our Universal Sense of Right and Wrong.* New York: HarperCollins/Ecco, 2006. Hauser's extensive research substantiates the moral-sense tradition with experimental evidence.

Hawkins, Jeff. *On Intelligence.* New York: Times Books, 2004.

Hofstadter, Douglas. *Fluid Concepts and Creative Analogies: Computer Models of the Fundamental Mechanisms of Thought.* New York: Basic Books, 1995. An excellent overview of AI in the middle region between the subsymbolic and the symbolic.

Holland, John H. *Adaptation in Natural and Artificial Systems: An Introductory Analysis with Applications to Biology, Control, and Artificial Intelligence.* Ann Arbor: University of Michigan Press, 1975. The seminal work on genetic algorithms.

———. *Hidden Order: How Adaptation Builds Complexity.* Reading, MA: Addison-Wesley, 1995.

Hospers, John. *Human Conduct.* New York: Harcourt Brace Jovanovich, 1972. The classic introductory text to moral philosophy. Hospers ran for president in 1972 on the Libertarian ticket.

Hume, David. *An Enquiry concerning Human Understanding*, edited by Tom L. Beauchamp. Oxford: Oxford University Press, 1999. Originally published in Edinburgh, 1748.

Hutter, Marcus. *Universal Artificial Intelligence: Sequential Decisions Based on Algorithmic Probability*. Berlin: Springer, 2005. Hutter is the person offering the prize for knowledge compression. This densely mathematical book is the current leading edge of the Solomonoff approach.

Johnson, Mark. *Moral Imagination: Implications of Cognitive Science for Ethics.* Chicago: University of Chicago Press, 1993.

Kanerva, Pentti. *Sparse Distributed Memory.* Cambridge, MA: MIT Press, 1988. A variation on the theme of knowledge representation by high-dimensional vectors.

Kant, Immanuel. *Foundations of the Metaphysics of Morals.* http://www.gutenberg.org/etext/5682.

Katz, Leonard D., ed. *Evolutionary Origins of Morality: Cross-disciplinary Perspectives.* New York: Imprint Academic, 2000.

Kauffman, Stuart A. *The Origins of Order: Self-Organization and Selection in Evolution.* Oxford: Oxford University Press, 1993.

Kealey, Terrence. *The Economic Laws of Scientific Research.* New York: St. Martin's, 1996.

Khan, Umar. "The Ethics of Autonomous Learning Systems." In *Android Epistemology*, edited by Kenneth Ford, Clark Glymour, and Patrick Hayes. Cambridge, MA: AAAI/MIT Press, 1995.

Kolen, John, and Stefan Kremer, eds. *A Field Guide to Dynamical Recurrent Networks.* New Brunswick: IEEE Press, 2001.

Kuhn, Thomas S. *The Structure of Scientific Revolutions.* Chicago: University of Chicago Press, 1996.

Kurzweil, Ray. *The Age of Spiritual Machines.* New York: Viking, 1999.

———. *The Singularity Is Near.* New York: Viking, 2005.

Lakemeyer, Gerhard, and Bernhard Nebel, eds. *Exploring Artificial Intelligence in the New Millennium.* San Francisco: Morgan Kaufmann, 2003.

Lakoff, George. *Women, Fire, and Dangerous Things: What Categories Reveal about the Mind.* Chicago: University of Chicago Press, 1987.

Latil, Pierre de. *Thinking by Machine.* New York: Riverside, 1957. A popular exposition of cybernetics.

Leaky, Richard. *The Origin of Humankind.* New York: Basic Books, 1994.

Lenat, Douglas, and R. V. Guha. *Building Large Knowledge-based Systems.* Boston: Addison-Wesley, 1990.

Lessig, Lawrence. *The Future of Ideas: The Fate of the Commons in a Connected World.* New York: Vintage, 2001.

MacKay, David. *Information Theory, Inference, and Learning Algorithms.* Cambridge: Cambridge University Press, 2003. A broad but technical overview of these surprisingly related fields.

Marr, David. *Vision: A Computational Investigation into the Human Representation and Processing of Visual Information.* New York: Freeman, 1982.

Maxwell, James Clerk. "On Governors." *Proceedings of the Royal Society of London.* Vol. 16 (1867–1868), pp. 270–83.

McCarthy, John, Martin Minsky, P. Abrahms, R. Brayton, D. Edwards, L. Hodes, D. Luckham, M. Levin, D. Park, and T. Hart. *Lisp 1.5 Programmer's Manual.* Cambridge, MA: MIT Press, 1962. For the first ten years, LISP programs were punched into decks of Hollerith cards.

McDermott, Drew V. *Mind and Mechanism.* Cambridge, MA: MIT Press, 2001. McDermott is also the author of the classic broadside *Artificial Intelligence Meets Natural Stupidity, ACM SIGART Bulletin* 57 (April 1976), which chided AI researchers for falling for their own ELIZA Effects.

Mero, Laszlo. *Moral Calculations: Game Theory, Logic, and Human Frailty.* New York: Springer-Verlag/Copernicus, 1998.

Milgram, Stanley. *Obedience to Authority: An Experimental View.* New York: HarperCollins, 1974.

Mill, John Stuart. *Utilitarianism.* http://www.utilitarianism.com/mill1.htm or http://www.gutenberg.org/etext/11224. Originally published in London, 1863.

Minsky, Marvin L. "A Framework for Representing Knowledge." *MIT-AI Lab Memo* 306 (June 1974).

———. *The Society of Mind.* New York: Simon and Schuster, 1985. A tantalizing compendium of thoughts on AI and cognitive psychology. See also Minsky's most recent book, *The Emotion Machine: Commonsense Thinking, Artificial Intelligence, and the Future of the Human Mind.* New York: Simon and Schuster, 2006.

———. *Theory of Neural-Analog Reinforcement Systems and its Application to the Brain-Model Problem.* Doctoral thesis, Princeton University, 1954.

Minsky, Marvin L., ed. *Semantic Information Processing.* Cambridge MA: MIT Press, 1968. An AI classic, this is a collection of projects from the golden age.

Minsky, Marvin L., and Seymour Papert. *Perceptrons.* Cambridge MA: MIT Press, 1969. What neural networks can and can't do.

Mitchell, Melanie. *Analogy-making as Perception: A Computer Model.* Cambridge MA: MIT Press, 1993. A popularized version of Mitchell's thesis about COPYCAT.

Mitchell, Tom. *Machine Learning.* Boston: WCB/McGraw-Hill, 1997. Mitchell, chairman of Carnegie Mellon University's Machine Learning Department, has publicly bet any takers a lobster dinner that "by 2015 we will have a computer program capable of automatically reading at least 80 percent of the factual content across the entire English-speaking Web, and placing those facts in a structured knowledge base."

Moore, G. E. *Principia Ethica.* Cambridge: Cambridge University Press, 1929. Originally published in 1903.

Moravec, Hans. *Mind Children: The Future of Robot and Human Intelligence.* Cambridge MA: Harvard University Press, 1988. A futurist classic, primarily about robotics, but with seminal exploration of uploading.

———. *Robot: Mere Machine to Transcendent Mind.* New York: Oxford University Press, 1999.

Murphy, Gordon J. *Basic Automatic Control Theory.* Princeton, NJ: Van Nostrand, 1957.

Murphy, Robin R. *Introduction to AI Robotics.* Cambridge, MA: MIT Press, 2000.

Murray, Charles. *In Our Hands: A Plan to Replace the Welfare State.* Washington, DC: AEI Press, 2006.

———. *In Pursuit: Of Happiness and Good Government.* New York: Simon and Schuster, 1988.

Newell, Allen. *Unified Theories of Cognition.* Cambridge, MA: Harvard University Press, 1990. The magnum opus of one of the founding fathers of AI.

Norretranders, Tor. *The User Illusion: Cutting Consciousness Down to Size.* New York: Viking 1998.

Nozick, Robert. *Anarchy, State, and Utopia.* New York: Basic Books, 1974.

Ortony, Andrew, ed. *Metaphor and Thought.* Cambridge: Cambridge University Press, 1993.

Orwell, George. *1984.* London: Secker and Warburg, 1949. Available online at http://www.liferesearchuniversal.com/orwell.html.

Pearl, Judea. *Causality: Models, Reasoning, and Inference.* Cambridge: Cambridge University Press, 2000.

Pinker, Steven. *The Blank Slate: The Modern Denial of Human Nature.* New York: Viking, 2002.

———. *How the Mind Works.* New York: Norton, 1997.

———. *The Language Instinct.* New York: HarperCollins, 1994. *How the Mind Works* and *The Blank Slate* are probably the best summarization of what I'm calling the New Synthesis.

Plato. *The Republic*, translated by F. Cornford. Oxford: Oxford University Press, 1941.

Pylyshyn, Zenon W. *Computation and Cognition: Toward a Foundation for Cognitive Science.* Cambridge, MA: MIT Press, 1984.

———. *Seeing and Visualizing: It's Not What You Think.* Cambridge, MA: MIT Press, 2003. Pylyshyn is the foremost researcher in the cognitive psychology of vision.

Raskin, Jef. *The Humane Interface: New Directions for Designing Interactive Systems.* Boston: Addison-Wesley, 2000.

Rawls, John. *A Theory of Justice.* Cambridge, MA: Belknap Press/Harvard, 1999.

Ridley, Matt. *The Origins of Virtue: Human Instincts and the Evolution of Cooperation.* London: Penguin, 1996.

Ross, Don. *Economic Theory and Cognitive Science: Microexplanation.* Cambridge, MA: MIT Press, 2005. The latest in the growing "economy of mind" school of thought.

Rummelhart, David E., and James McClelland. *Parallel Distributed Processing: Explorations in the Microstructure of Cognition.* 2 vols. Cambridge, MA: MIT Press, 1986. This was the Bible of the connectionism (neural networks) resurgence in the late 1980s.

Russell, Stuart, and Peter Norvig. *Artificial Intelligence: A Modern Approach.* Englewood Cliffs, NJ: Prentice-Hall, 1995. The leading textbook in the field.

Russell, Stuart, and Eric Wefald. *Do the Right Thing.* Cambridge, MA: MIT Press, 1991.

Schank, Roger, and Kenneth Colby, eds. *Computer Models of Thought and Language*. New York: Freeman, 1973.

Searle, John. *Minds, Brains, and Science*. Cambridge, MA: Harvard University Press, 1984. The Chinese Room to the contrary notwithstanding, Searle is a top-notch philosopher and a pleasure to read.

Shakhnarovich, Gregory, Trevor Darrell, and Piotr Indyk, eds. *Nearest-Neighbor Methods in Learning and Vision: Theory and Practice*. Cambridge, MA: MIT Press, 2005. Algorithms for and experience with using highly multidimensional numeric vectors as a representation.

Shannon, Claude E. "A Mathematical Theory of Communication," *Bell System Technical Journal* 27 (July and October 1948): 379–423; 623–56.

Siebert, William M. *Circuits, Signals, and Systems*. Cambridge, MA: MIT Press, 1986. A comprehensive textbook of modern control and systems theory.

Siegelman, Jim, and Flo Conway. *Dark Hero of the Information Age: In Search Of Norbert Wiener, Father of Cybernetics*. New York: Basic Books, 2004. This book was recommended by Oliver Selfridge to the attendees of AI@50, Dartmouth's fiftieth anniversary celebration of the first AI meeting.

Sipper, Moshe. *Machine Nature: The Coming Age of Bio-inspired Computing*. New York: McGraw-Hill, 2002.

Smith, Adam. *Theory of Moral Sentiments*. http://www.adamsmith.org/smith/tms-intro.htm. Originally published in 1759.

Sowa, John F. *Knowledge Representation: Logical, Philosophical, and Computational Foundations*. Pacific Grove, CA: Brooks/Cole, 2000. The classical approach is well developed and broadly applicable these days.

Spencer, Herbert. *The Principles of Ethics*. Indianapolis, IN: Liberty Classics, 1978. Spencer was personally a very kindly man, but this crowning exposition of social Darwinism was misused by his friends and reviled by his enemies.

Sprites, Peter, Clark Glymour, and Richard Scheines. *Causation, Prediction, and Search*. 2nd ed. Cambridge, MA: MIT Press, 2000. Explains how to reduce a number of observations to a Bayesian graph that reveals the causal structure of the domain.

Stanovich, Keith E. *The Robot's Rebellion: Finding Meaning in the Age of Darwin*. Chicago: University of Chicago Press, 2004. An impressive exploration of the implications of the New Synthesis for many areas of thought that were previously informed by the folk intuitions.

Teilhard de Chardin, Pierre. *The Phenomenon of Man.* New York: Harper and Row, 1959.

Tobin, James. *To Conquer the Air: The Wright Brothers and the Great Race for Flight.* New York: Free Press, 2003.

Trivers, Robert. *Social Evolution.* Menlo Park, CA: Benjamin/Cummings, 1985. Trivers discovered reciprocal altruism in animals.

Turing, Alan. "On Computable Numbers, with an Application to the Entscheidungsproblem," *Proceedings of the London Mathematical Society* 2, no. 42 (1936): 230–65.

Uesaka, Yoshinori, Pentti Kanerva, and Hideki Asoh, eds. *The Foundations of Real-World Intelligence.* Palo Alto, CA: CSLI Publications, 2001. A grab bag of modern AI techniques including some vector representations and analogical reasoning.

Vinge, Vernor. "The Coming Technological Singularity: How to Survive in the Post-human Era." In *Vision-21: Interdisciplinary Science and Engineering in the Era of Cyberspace,* 11–22. NASA Conference Publication 10129.

von Neumann, John. *The Computer and the Brain.* New Haven, CT: Yale University Press, 1958.

———. *Theory of Self-Reproducing Automata.* Edited and completed by A. W. Burks, published posthumously. Urbana: University of Illinois Press, 1966.

Walter, W. Grey. *The Living Brain.* London: Duckworth, 1953. A classic of cybernetics; includes the circuit diagram of one of Walters's tortoises.

Webb, Barbara, and Thomas R. Consi. *Biorobotics: Methods and Applications.* Cambridge, MA: AAAI/MIT Press, 2001.

Wegener, Daniel M. *The Illusion of Conscious Will.* Cambridge, MA: MIT Press, 2002.

Weiss, Sholom, and Casimir Kulikowski. *Computer Systems That Learn.* San Mateo, CA: M. Kaufmann, 1991.

Weizenbaum, Joseph. *Computer Power and Human Reason: From Judgment to Calculation.* New York: Freeman, 1976.

Wells, Herbert George. *The War in the Air.* New York: Macmillan, 1917.

Wiener, Norbert. *Cybernetics, or Control and Communication in the Animal and the Machine.* New York: Wiley, 1949. This densely mathematical tome was a best seller in the early 1950s.

———. *God and Golem, Inc.: A Comment on Certain Points where Cybernetics Impinges on Religion.* Cambridge, MA: MIT Press, 1964.

Wilson, E. O. *Consilience: The Unity of Knowledge.* New York: Vintage, 1999.

———. *On Human Nature.* Cambridge, MA: Harvard University Press, 1978.

———. *Sociobiology: The New Synthesis.* Cambridge, MA: Belknap Press/Harvard, 1975.

Wilson, Robert, and Frank Keil, eds. *The MIT Encyclopedia of the Cognitive Sciences.* Cambridge, MA: MIT Press, 1999.

Winograd, Terry. *Understanding Natural Language.* San Diego, CA: Academic Press, 1972. *The* classic in the field, demonstrating how a semantic model of the domain of discourse enables understanding.

Winograd, Terry, and Fernando Flores. *Understanding Computers and Cognition: A New Foundation for Design.* Reading, MA: Addison-Wesley, 1986.

Winston, Patrick Henry. *Artificial Intelligence.* Reading, MA: Addison-Wesley, 1992.

Wittgenstein, Ludwig. *Philosophical Investigations.* 3rd. ed. Translated by G. E. M. Anscombe. Malden, MA: Blackwell, 2003.

Wright, Robert: *The Moral Animal: Evolutionary Psychology and Everyday Life.* New York: Pantheon, 1994.

———. *Non-Zero: The Logic of Human Destiny.* New York: Pantheon, 2000.

Index

ACE, 62
Aesop's fable, 113, 234
affective display, 291–92, 327–28, 330, 346, 348
agoric algorithms, 187, 194
allohuman, 244–45, 260
ALTAIR 8800, 120
AM, 78–79, 123, 127, 144, 202
analogical quadrature, 200, 204–205, 222–23, 228, 239
arbitrator, 285–86
Aristotle, 303
Asenian robot, 323
Asimov, Isaac, 52, 241, 315, 317, 319–20, 323, 325, 355, 358–59
associative memory, 205, 207, 211, 213–15
attention, 284
autogeny, 42, 115–16, 133, 136, 141, 143, 224, 240, 260, 262, 329, 338
automatic programming, 123, 142, 181
autopoiesis, 133
Axelrod, Robert, 177–78

baby brain, 136–37, 144, 251, 259–62
Baldwin effect, 224–25
Baum, Eric, 188
Bayesian inference, 152
Bayesian networks, 155, 157
blank notebook model, 105, 111, 137, 144, 354
blocks world, 77–78
BLUE GENE, 85, 120, 335
Boas, Franz, 103–104
bootstrap fallacy, 123, 129
bootstrapping, 210
Bostrom, Nick, 318
brains, giant electronic, 61, 84
Braitenberg, Valentino, 211
Bush, Vannevar, 50, 84

cahooting, 173, 176–77, 299, 304, 332, 346
case-based reasoning, 205, 222
categorical imperative, 303–304
centrifugal governor, 49
Charles Smith (program), 191, 194
chess, 158, 166–67
child machine, 136–37, 141, 144, 251, 259–62
chimpanzees, 36, 38–39, 122, 128, 144
Chinese Room, 273–76

Chomsky, Noam, 99, 111
Chomsky gap, 99–100, 111, 124, 216
chunking, 202, 237
Church, Alonzo, 69
cognitive robotics, 60
cognitive science, 116
COLOSSUS, 62
COMMON LISP, 87–88
common sense, 74, 83, 146, 233–35
computational theory of mind, 51, 265–66, 268
concept formation, 61, 79, 97, 126, 137, 170, 220, 237, 252, 259, 261
confabulation, 223, 287, 346–47
conjugate gradients, 161
conscience, 313
consciousness, 127, 279–88
consilience, 60, 344
controller, 46, 112, 138, 190, 212–13, 218, 221, 227, 238, 285–86
COPYCAT, 162–63, 199–203
corporations, 22, 94, 243, 255, 312, 321, 330, 334, 339, 349, 362–63
coyote/roadrunner example, 153
creativity, 42–43
crosstalk, 231
cybernetics, 45, 50, 61, 105, 108, 157, 187, 243
cyborgs, 366

DARPA, 253–54, 255–56
database, 22
data mining, 23, 140, 146, 220, 254–55
DEEP BLUE, 43, 85, 145, 157–59, 164, 167, 170, 242
Descartes, René, 264–65
diahuman, 242–43, 262, 330, 335–36
dollar auction model, 172–73
dualism, 264–65

EDVAC, 62
efference copy, 230–31
ego, 325–26
ELIZA, 29, 65, 67–68
ELIZA effect, 68, 116, 292, 348
emotions, 290–92
ENIAC, 61
Enigma, 147
entropy, 56, 71–72, 200, 213
EPAM, 73
epihuman, 245–47, 262, 330, 334–35, 344
epihuman will, 336
eudaimonia, 303
EURISKO, 78–79, 123, 144, 189, 202
evidence grids, 155, 210
evolutionary ethics, 15–17, 177–78, 293, 298–302
evolutionary psychology, 106
expert systems, 82
explanation-based learning, 139–40, 233, 235

fact-futures markets, 236
fantail, 49
FARGitecture, 199, 201–203
feedback, 47–48, 50–51, 54–55, 59, 100–101, 107, 122, 129, 189,

215, 224, 227, 231–33, 239, 242, 282–83, 310, 325, 328, 335, 337–38, 348
flying machines, 33–35, 260, 337–38
Fodor, Jerry, 106, 115
formalist float, 24, 89–100, 142–43, 170, 188–89, 276
FORTRAN, 65, 69
frame problem, 76, 151, 330
frames, 76–77, 223, 285
Frankenstein (Shelley), 20–21, 30, 264, 315
free will, 269–73
Frege's Puzzle, 289–90
Freitas, Robert, 304, 321
French, Robert, 197–99
functionalism, 108

game theory, 165
genetic algorithms, 139, 142, 178–79, 184–87
glass ceiling, 81–83, 87, 97, 138, 240
Go, 159–60, 167–70
Good, I. J., 333, 361
Google, 246, 255, 335
GPS, 72, 123, 139, 326
grammar, ethical, 293, 295, 299, 302, 312, 327, 329, 351–52
grounding, of symbols, 98

Hanson, Robin, 236, 358–60
Harnad, Steven, 98
HAYEK (program), 188–90
Hayek, F. A. *See* von Hayek, Friedrich August
HEPP (Human-Equivalent Processing Power), 85–87, 252–53, 261, 337
Hexapawn, 115
hill climbing, 160
Hofstadter, Douglas, 176, 199, 202
Holland, John, 188
holonomic, 219
homeostasis, 48–49, 281–82
homunculus, 238, 325
horizon effect, 164, 342
hyperhuman, 247–48, 317, 329, 335, 344, 350, 360
hypohuman, 241

IAM, 213–19, 221–23
iceberg mind, 115, 131, 239, 259, 330
id, 324–25
illusion, 112, 198, 273, 287
inductive bias, 124
inductive inference, 70–71, 125, 164
Industrial Revolution, 24, 48, 95, 359
information theory, 51, 56
Intellectual Revolution, 358–62
intelligence, cockroach, 37
intelligence, human, 36–40
interpolation, 212
interpretation, 229–32
intuition, 267, 271, 275
invariants, 347
IQ, 129–30

Kalman filter, 55
Kant, Immanuel, 303–304

Kurzweil, Ray, 86, 334, 358
Kurzweil HEPP, 86

lambda calculus, 69, 109
language, natural, 39–40, 61, 64, 72, 78, 92–94, 97–101, 111–12, 124, 227, 239, 273–74, 351
language, programming, 65, 69–70, 77, 88, 101, 136, 142, 151–52, 209–10
language of thought, 106, 115
lawyers, 165
learning curve, 237
Leibniz, Gottfried Wilhelm, 47, 59, 108, 117, 128, 264–65, 279
LISP, 69–70, 79, 87–88, 100, 142, 152, 203, 210–11
lobster dinner prize, 257
local optima, 161
Loebner Prize, 64
logic, 68, 72, 74, 94, 96, 110, 123, 140, 151, 211, 265, 289, 294

machine learning, 73, 139
Maxwell, James Clerk, 49
McCarthy, John, 61–62, 69–71, 120, 123
McCulloch, Warren, 47–48, 53–54, 57, 59
McDermott, Drew, 270–73
Mead, Margaret, 104
meaning, 273, 277–78
memetics, 40–42
Milgram experiments, 342
Mill, John Stuart, 305–307
mind children, 329
Minsky, Marvin, 57, 73–74, 76, 81–82, 86, 108, 197, 223, 227, 235, 252, 284, 337, 358
Minsky HEPP, 86
MIPS (million instructions per second), 85–86
missionaries-and-cannibals problem, 148–51
Mitchell, Melanie, 199
modules, 106, 110–15, 260, 272, 284, 298, 352
monkey-and-bananas problem, 74, 151
Moore's law, 84–86, 252–53, 261, 336–37
moral agency, 27, 296, 309, 312, 329, 338, 348–49
moral almanack, 305
moral philosophy, 301–302
moral sombrero, 305
Moravec, Hans, 85
Moravec HEPP, 86
multilevel design, 182
Murray, Charles, 303, 365

naturalistic fallacy, 272, 298
Neanderthals, 39–40, 128, 300
neural networks, 57–58, 83, 139, 162, 203, 214, 217
neuroscience, 57, 116, 250–51, 283, 323, 341
Newcomb's Problem, 175–76, 178, 295–96, 311, 330–32, 345
Newell, Allen, 69, 72, 139, 159, 237
New Synthesis, 103, 105–15, 294, 310

Open Source, 255, 331, 345
open texture of law, 98

Pandemonium, 73
parahuman, 243–44
pecking order, 342
perceptron, 57
Pitts, Walter, 47–48, 53–54, 57
planet, definition of, 89–92
play, for learning, 212–13
Pluto, 89
posthuman, 242
premature optimization, 82, 87, 207–209
Prisoner's Dilemma, 174, 176–78, 294–96, 304, 307, 310–11, 332, 352
PROLOG, 151–52, 183, 229
psychopaths, 17, 290, 330
Public Goods (game), 294–95
Pygmalion, 21, 263

qualia, 268, 283–84
Quillian, M. Ross, 75

rational fools, 329–30
Rawls, John, 308–309
reactive programming, 101
reflexes, human, 233
representation, 79, 147, 218, 235
retina, 84–85
retirement, 361, 364–66
roadrunner. *See* coyote/roadrunner example
Robbie, 134, 316, 324–25
robot metaphor, 133, 141, 143, 188
robot soccer, 171

Sapir-Whorf hypothesis, 228
search, 147–51, 157–59, 163–64, 167–68, 182–91, 201–202, 207, 222, 224–25
Searle, John, 273–76
self-improving AI, 119–31, 246–48, 259–62, 347
self-replication, 126, 135–36, 141–42
Semantic Information Processing (ed. Minsky), 74
semantic network, 75, 151–52
semantics, 93–94
sensor fusion, 153
sentience, 280–82
servomechanism, 49
setpoint, 49
Shannon, Claude, 167
Shelley, Mary Wollstonecraft, 19
SHRDLU, 29, 77–78, 83, 92, 94, 99, 326
SIGMA servo, 213–28, 234, 238
Simon, Herbert, 69, 72, 139, 159
Singularity, 247, 304, 333–35, 357–58
Skinner, B. F., 104
Smith, Adam, 309–310
SOAR, 123, 139–140, 202
social Darwinism, 298, 301
sociobiology, 105–106, 111
Solomonoff, Ray, 42, 70–71, 101, 125, 141, 155, 164
Spock, Mr., 245
state spaces, 149–50, 160
steam engine, 42, 49
superego, 326–28
superheterodyne radio, 109
superintelligence, 120
superrationality, 176

symbolic servo, 73
symbols, 220, 273
synergy, 276

teleology, 47, 50, 107
theology, 349–50
tortoise (robot), 53, 211
transfer function, 49
transhuman, 242
translation, 93
Turing, Alan, 62–64, 69–70, 72, 82, 105, 116, 120, 136–37, 147, 167, 183, 249, 251
Turing machine, 62, 70–71, 99, 101, 108, 121, 127, 215
Turing Test, 63–65, 72, 83, 99, 116, 143, 171, 234–35, 249, 251, 257, 274–75

universal constructor, 126
universality, 70, 120–22, 125–31
uploading, 249–51
utilitarianism, 304–307

vector-space representation, 160–63, 203, 205, 212, 215, 224
Veil of Ignorance, 308–309, 352
Vinge, Vernor, 247, 304, 334–35, 358
virtue, 303
von Hayek, Friedrich August, 187–88
von Neumann, John, 58, 61–63, 120, 126, 128, 166, 172
von Neumann barrier, 119–20
von Neumann bottleneck, 206
von Neumann computer, 63, 70, 87

Walter, Grey, 53, 211
Wason Test, 294
Watt, James, 42, 49
weakly godlike AI, 245
Wells, H. G., 33
Wiener, Norbert, 46, 48
Wilson, E. O., 60, 105, 344
windmills, 48–49
Winograd, Terry, 29, 92
world model, 78
Wright, Wilbur and Orville, 33–34, 260

Yanomamo people (Amazon basin), 300
yellow peril, 47